KATYŃ

KATYŃ

Stalin's Massacre and the Seeds of Polish Resurrection

ALLEN PAUL

NAVAL INSTITUTE PRESS

Annapolis, Maryland

Naval Institute Press
118 Maryland Avenue
Annapolis, MD 21402-5035

Originally published in 1991 by Charles Scribner's Sons
Naval Institute Press paperback edition 1996

Library of Congress Cataloging-in-Publication Data
Paul, Allen (M. Allen), 1939–
    Katyń:the untold story of Stalin's Polish massacre / Allen Paul.
        p.   cm.
    Includes bibliographical references and index.
    ISBN 1-55750-670-1
    1. Katyń Forest Massacre, 1940.   I. Title.
D804.S65P38   1991
940.54'05'094762—dc20   91—4773

10 9 8 7 6 5 4 3 2 1   03 02 01 00 99 98 97 96

Printed in the United States of America on acid-free paper ∞

to Jacek Jędruch

whose life exemplified the tenacity
and courage of the expatriate Poles

Contents

Preface

<<<<<<<<<<

But for an accident of nature, Soviet president Mikhail S. Gorbachev might never have publicly acknowledged, as he did on April 13, 1990, his nation's guilt in the Katyń Forest massacre. On that same day forty-seven years earlier, Germany announced its discovery of thousands of Polish officers who had been shot and buried in a scenic glade overlooking the Dnieper (or Dnepr) River near Smolensk. Fate alone accounted for the finding of these bodies. Weeks earlier a wolf, digging in a mound, had uncovered human bones a short distance from the headquarters of the Wehrmacht's 537th Signal Regiment.* By pure happenstance the Germans had stumbled onto one of the great propaganda opportunities of the war, and they exploited it skillfully to divide the Allies at a pivotal point in the conflict. From that moment, prospects for an independent postwar Poland were set on the road to oblivion, and Katyń, like an evil star, glowed over the injustice that befell that luckless land.

Gorbachev's revelation was remarkable in many respects. For nearly

---

*There is some ambiguity about the sequence of events that led to the discovery of the graves in Katyń Forest. Colonel Friedrich Ahrens testified at Nuremberg and to the U.S. Congress that a wolf dug open the graves at the end of January or in early February 1943. Ahrens confirmed that the hole dug by the wolf was discovered at this time by Russian laborers working for the Wehrmacht, but that he was not advised of the discovery until approximately four to six weeks later. An unnamed Russian witness who escaped to the West provided a different, though not necessarily conflicting, version. He claimed that in the spring of 1942 Poles engaged by the Germans in collecting scrap military equipment near the forest were taken by local peasants to the graves and marked them with a cross. In January 1943 the witness read an article about the Polish army-in-exile's search for its missing officers. He connected this story with what had happened the previous spring and reported the matter to the local German field police. He said that an exploratory dig was undertaken in late February and that a body was found. It is possible that the grave was lightly covered and that the body from this same grave was uncovered by the wolf. The author believes Colonel Ahrens's account to be the more authoritative.

half a century, the Soviets had steadfastly maintained their innocence and taken extraordinary measures to defend it. Stalin himself told the Poles in 1941 that their men must have escaped to Manchuria. That fifteen thousand men from three widely separated camps west of the Volga could make their way undetected across Siberia—this, of course, was preposterous, and the Poles knew it. But what could they do? The Hitler-Stalin partnership, which cost them their country, had suddenly become a bloodbath; swallowing their pride, the Poles had just made an uneasy agreement with Stalin to organize an army in Russia to fight Hitler. Over the next months, they anxiously searched for their missing men, but faced Soviet dissembling at every turn. Then came the German discovery and the truthful accusation that the Bolsheviks had murdered the men shortly after their capture during the Nazi-Soviet invasion of 1939. Overnight the Soviets' feigning of ignorance in the plight of their own prisoners was replaced by a specific explanation: The Poles, they said, had been engaged in construction work and "fell into the hands of German-Fascist hangmen" when Soviet troops withdrew from the Smolensk area in the summer of 1941. Even so, the bodies of men from only one of the three camps—less than a third of the total—had been found. Where were the others? On this question the Soviets remained silent for nearly half a century.

Nor were the Soviets alone in suppressing evidence of their guilt. Churchill and Roosevelt aided Stalin greatly in this regard. Both were aware of convincing circumstantial evidence of Soviet guilt. Both knew that the controversy had been twisted by Stalin into an excuse for breaking off diplomatic relations with the government of Poland. Both knew that massive deportations had been carried out in eastern Poland in an effort to Sovietize the region. Both knew Stalin was grooming a puppet regime to replace the legitimate government. But both men feared, especially in 1943, that Stalin might sign a separate peace with Hitler. They knew also that their first war aim—the crushing of the German Reich—would be a much more difficult task without Soviet manpower and economic resources. That Big Three unity should be compromised for any reason thus became unthinkable to both leaders. If preserving unity meant turning a blind eye to Katyń's mountain of evidence against the Soviets, then so be it.

Such expediency, no matter how justified by the ends to be achieved, carried a price. On May 24, 1943—less than six weeks after the Germans announced their discovery of the graves—Sir Owen O'Malley, the British ambassador to the London-based Polish government-in-exile, wrote in a confidential memorandum for the British War Cabinet:

> We have in fact perforce used the good name of England like the murderers used the little conifers to cover up a massacre. . . . May it not be that we now stand in danger of bemusing not only others but ourselves; of falling . . . under St. Paul's curse on those who can see cruelty "and burn not"? . . . It may be that the answer lies, for the moment, only in something to be done inside our own hearts and minds where we are masters. . . . If the facts about the Katyn massacre turn out to be as most of us incline to think, shall we vindicate the spirit of these brave unlucky men and justify the living to the dead.

Here, then, we have the contours of a large and complex crime. It provides a wide field of vision for the tragedy of Poland and for a great moral dilemma that confronted the Allies over the last half of the war. Yet these motifs are only part of the story. Equally if not more fascinating are the details and drama of the human lives swept up in this calamity: how the victims met their fates; why and how they were liquidated; the exceptional professional qualities of those murdered; the brutal hardship faced by so many of their families; and, ultimately, a half century of individual struggles for justice in what truly may be called a crime against a nation and humanity.

This book is an attempt to present the crime in a complete context. To do that, the murders must be examined as part of a massive effort to Sovietize Poland. The executions at Katyń came to symbolize that effort in all its horrible consequences, for two reasons. First, the Katyń murders were the most dramatic and clear-cut example of the brutal methods Stalin used to eliminate Poland's educated class; among these methods was the deportation of vast numbers of men, women, and children who perished from starvation, forced labor, and neglect. Second, Stalin cleverly manipulated the circumstances in which the Katyń murders were finally discovered in 1943 to deal the legitimate government of Poland a lethal blow. The Polish government never recovered from the wound he inflicted and the pain of it has been etched deeply in the collective memory of the Polish people. Katyń thus became a complex symbol of Polish suffering at the hands of Stalin. Existing work on the subject does not, in my view, approach the crime in this manner.

I should warn the reader that my undertaking began on unfamiliar terrain, where quicksand abounds. To skirt the most obvious potential pitfalls, I have relied heavily throughout my research on the records of a select committee of the United States Congress, which in 1951 and 1952 conducted the most comprehensive investigation of the crime ever undertaken. The published records of this committee provide a wealth of information—much of it gathered from primary sources— about the crime. I have also examined other records of this committee, records opened to the public for the first time in 1989. These documents shed further light on efforts by the U.S. government between 1943 and 1945 to suppress evidence of Soviet guilt. In the course of my research I have examined important collections of material on Katyń (the word here and elsewhere represents the crime in its totality) at the Piłsudski Institute in New York, the Sikorski Institute and the Public Records Office in London, and the Museum of History and Photography in Kraków. Along the way I have met and interviewed many people in the United States and abroad who have firsthand knowledge of the crime and the setting in which it occurred. Among these were three survivors of the liquidations, and the special investigator who led the 1951–1952 congressional inquiry. They have provided invaluable information and insight on many aspects of the story.

Inevitably, perhaps, such an undertaking becomes a personal odyssey that leaves lasting impressions. In front of the Katyń memorial in Warsaw's military cemetery on All Souls' Day in 1989, I saw a steady stream of parents explaining, in hushed tones, to their children the meaning of the large granite cross before them. At its base, a sea of candles bore silent witness to the tenacious memory of the Poles. On the platform at Warsaw Central Station, I marveled at the families of victims clamoring to board the first caravan by train to the graves in Katyń Forest. Ironically, like the victims, they also would be transported by a Soviet train. In the apartment of a former ballerina, now an activist in a group called Katyń Families, I attended the first meeting of an independent committee of Polish historians investigating the crime. The effects of decades of censorship were immediately apparent: They had never seen many important source materials that had long been available in the West. One of my most lasting impressions is of a woman whose father was killed at Katyń, whose mother and grandmother were deported to Siberia, and who herself was narrowly rescued from Poland at the end of the war. When I said that this seemed too much for one family, she replied, unemotionally, "As a Pole, I do not feel that my story is exceptional."

My interest in Katyń began in 1986, when I heard the crime discussed as a barrier to reform in Eastern Europe and the Soviet Union.

At the time I was studying at the Center for European Studies in Bologna, Italy, a part of Johns Hopkins University's School of Advanced International Studies. Katyń was described (correctly, as it now turns out) as an unacknowledged crime of Stalinism and a distortion of history that the Soviets must one day confess in order to normalize their relations with the Poles. Its status as one of World War II's last important unsolved mysteries intrigued me, but almost a year passed before I wandered into the Library of Congress to investigate further. There, on a lazy, rainy Sunday afternoon, I found the published records—all 2,362 pages—of the Select Committee to Investigate the Katyń Forest Massacre.

Thumbing through the letters, memorabilia, and photographs of the murdered men, I was spellbound. Photographs of husbands', sons', and fathers' bullet-pierced skulls appeared beside the last familial words these men had written and received—"Dear Joseph: There is again happiness in our hearts and at home because your third letter has arrived. . . . I enclose a Christmas wafer.* Irena"; "Irena, darling, you need not worry about me at all. The worst has already passed. . . . Joseph"; "Dearest Daddy: . . . There is nobody now to read a bedtime story to Wiesio, so he reads it himself, but he prefers to look at the atlas. I suffer often from a sore throat. Otherwise we are all well. . . . Oleńka."

In the months that followed I began a careful study of these records. In retrospect I believe my attraction to them was deepened by a tragedy in my own family. In the spring of 1987, pericarditis, a disease rarely fatal today, suddenly claimed the life of a younger brother at age thirty-nine. In this event I was confronted by one of life's deepest mysteries: a senseless and untimely death. So, too, were the deaths at Katyń: The men were struck down at random in the prime of their lives. This caused me to wonder how their families had dealt with misfortunes more terrible by far than my own. From there I gravitated toward a decision to seek out the victims' kin and learn as much as I could from them. No other facet of my research has been so rewarding.

Among the families, both in the United States and in Poland, I found many people who were willing to share painful memories that revealed the full scope of this tragedy. Not only were fifteen thousand of Poland's "best and brightest" liquidated, mass deportations

---

*An unconsecrated communion wafer shared by Polish families at the traditional Christmas Eve dinner.

involving 1.5 million or more Poles were undertaken as part of the same policy to eviscerate the country. Many of the families of the murdered men were among those deported. These policies were part of a continuum of persecution that confronted Poland's middle class and professional elite, first under the period of joint Nazi-Soviet domination, then under Hitler's heel alone, and finally under Stalin's coercive rule.

The narrative that follows describes how the persecution affected the lives of three families: the Hoffmans and Pawulskis, both of Lwów (now Lvov), and the Czarneks of Kraków. The liquidations claimed the husband in each family: in order an attorney, a regular army officer, and a physician. Each of these men perished at the peak of his professional career. One of the families, the Czarneks, suffered the daily repressions of life under the German General Government. The Hoffman family experienced wrenching separation: The mother was deported to Siberia and her infant daughter remained in Poland. The Pawulskis were taken from Poland to the edge of China, back to and across the Caspian Sea, on through the Middle East, down the length of Africa, then to England, and finally America. For more than two years of this journey, their survival was daily in doubt.

These accounts are important because they suggest not only the scope of the tragedy but also why the Poles, in their own way, triumphed in the end. History had prepared them well, in three previous partitions, for occupation and oppression by foreign powers. It had shown them that they could survive as a stateless nation—that they could preserve their identity in the face of cruel and relentless oppression. Through all the horrors under Hitler and Stalin, they held fast to this belief. Nor did they waver when the new postwar order imposed yet another form of totalitarian rule. The murders at Katyń were never forgotten because these deaths had come to symbolize the threat to eradicate Poland and her people. In the end, that tenacity was vindicated in the rebirth of an independent Poland.

Soviet acknowledgment of the crime was also a bittersweet measure of the Poles' triumph. It meant, at long last, that the Soviets had begun to embrace values learned centuries earlier by the Poles and never relinquished—principal among them the worth and dignity of every human being. It signaled, perhaps, the fading of an ancient rivalry and the first steps toward a new era of peace and harmony. That prospect the Poles had indeed earned.

Trapped as they were at the seismic center of a worldwide convulsion, millions of Poles were forced to pay the totalitarians with their lives and their freedom. But fate did not curse them completely. For in the end, they did, indeed, triumph through courage, dignity, and an abiding belief in themselves.

Acknowledgments

<<<<<<<<<<<<<

I am indebted to several persons for their help with this book. The support of my editor Edward T. Chase at Scribners has been particularly important. From the outset we shared the view that the subject should be developed in a broad context. His advice on structure and his critical judgment in general have been indispensable. Editor Erika Goldman of Scribners also provided excellent advice in many areas, and Jolanta Benal was a superb copy editor.

Without Leona Schecter, my agent, the book would not have come to Scribners' attention. I am especially grateful to her for her skill in bringing us together and for her many helpful suggestions about the book's content. Her husband, Jerrold, a former *Time* bureau chief in Moscow, assisted me with important contacts in the Soviet Union. Victor Gold, a good friend for many years, offered invaluable help and encouragement in the early stages of my research and writing. Joanna Banach, Albert Chrost, Natalie Debarbaro, and Wojciech Stasiak ably translated a number of materials.

Others have saved me from errors of fact and flawed interpretations. Anthony Sheehan, a good friend and specialist on Eastern Europe, has been especially helpful in this regard. Among the families I was writing about were two experts in Polish history, Jacek Jędruch and Iwo Pogonowski, who took a special interest in my work. I am deeply grateful for their suggestions about sources, for materials they translated, and for their help and encouragement in many other areas. No doubt the book still contains points that each of these historians will disagree with. Its remaining shortcomings are my responsibility.

In developing the book's personal narratives, I spent many hours talking to Ewa Hoffman Jędruch, Magdalena Czarnek Pogonowska, Maria Pawulska Rasiej, and Paweł Zaleski. Even when venturing into still-painful matters, each of them favored my questions with patience, good humor, and a remarkable recall of important and interesting detail. Now that I am finished, I feel that the book is as much theirs as mine.

A word of tribute to my family most definitely is in order. My sister, Mary Rayfield Paul, patiently tracked down invaluable research materials on many occasions. I drew heavily on the knowledge and experience of my mother, Elaine Mayo Paul, who is a professional historian. Her well-reasoned challenges caused me to rethink and sharpen a number of interpretations. She made many other contributions, for which I am deeply grateful.

Finally, the contribution of my wife, Betsy, is immeasurable. In addition to her own work, she spent many hours in libraries in London, New York, and Washington looking for material. Her ideas and questions served to deepen my thinking about the subject. Without her encouragement, I would never have attempted to write the book; and without her constant support and companionship, I could never have finished it.

I am indebted to Ron Chambers, Director of the Naval Institute Press, for making this paperback edition of the book possible. The Institute's Managing Editor, Mary Lou Kenney, was especially helpful with revisions and additions, and Linda Cullen, Paperback Editor, made many useful suggestions.

Note on Sources

<<<<<<<<<<

For half a century no issue in Polish-Soviet relations has been more sensitive than the Katyń Forest massacre. Until Solidarity's rise in the late seventies, "Katyń" was officially a nonword, an absolute taboo, in Poland. Even families of victims shunned association with it, knowing that careers could be harmed, if not destroyed, by its mere mention in public.

Katyń was excised almost completely from the media. In February 1977, a Polish censor defected to Sweden with seven hundred pages of censors' classified documents. They included instructions to ensure that Polish media followed the *Great Soviet Encyclopedia*'s brief version of Katyń, attributing guilt to the Nazis. These documents also warned censors that the names of Katyń victims must not be published. The defecting censor later said, "That was the limit of what I could take." Among the dead was his own grandfather.

In April 1987 the Communist parties of Poland and the Soviet Union agreed to a joint study of several sensitive issues that caused deep animosity between the countries. Solidarity called it the Campaign to Eliminate Blank Spots because a full explanation had long been lacking for most of the matters to be examined. The Katyń Forest massacre and the mass deportation of Poles from lands seized by the Soviets in 1939—separate aspects of the same policy to eliminate the Polish elite—were not on the list. Authorities on both sides still considered these events too sensitive to address. Two years later, with democratic reforms about to sweep Eastern Europe, a spokesman for the Communist government of Poland was forced to admit that "everything indicates that the crime was committed by the Stalinist NKVD [secret police]." Then, on April 13, 1990, Gorbachev admitted Soviet responsibility for Katyń, but said little else about the matter. The Soviets would not provide a complete explanation; important aspects of the crime were left unclarified.

Excisions, blank spots, and misrepresentations are a problem in every official account of the crime except one. The Polish government-in-exile diligently sought and reported all the facts it could discover—and it is noteworthy that these efforts contributed to that government's own destruction. In the crime's immediate aftermath, the Soviet Union provided several grotesque and twisted versions of what happened. Nazi Germany embellished the facts to exacerbate tensions between the Allies. Great Britain and the United States actively suppressed evidence to prevent Western opinion from turning against the Soviets—both during the war and at Nuremberg, where a botched Soviet indictment of the Nazis for the Katyń murders was quietly dropped. Even the "neutral" investigation of Katyń undertaken by the U.S. Congress in 1951 and 1952 was tainted by the desire to use Katyń as anticommunist propaganda during the Korean War. To one degree or another, ulterior motives have made the truth secondary in all these official sources, leaving the record not so much blank as blurred. These accounts can be drawn on only selectively to clarify Katyń's meaning and importance.

The most important remaining sources are individuals with a direct personal knowledge of Soviet efforts to eradicate the Polish elite. Even here inherent limits confront us: The trail has grown cold; memory often plays tricks; and reliable records are difficult to find. Still, such recollections provide indispensable insight. To those who lost husbands, sons, and fathers in the massacre and to those who were deported, the Soviet policy was not an abstraction; it is a central event of their lives. Only they can put the scope and barbarity of what happened in true perspective. Any motive they may have had to embellish their accounts so as to prove Soviet guilt has now been removed. Their accounts thus become more valuable than ever, particularly in view of continuing Soviet reticence on the subject.

For these reasons I have favored personal recollections in the narrative that follows. It draws heavily on many hours of discussion with people who were directly affected by the policies to eradicate the Polish elite and the country as they knew it. I believe that their revelations help explain why Katyń became such a powerful symbol to the Poles. But hear them out for yourself and come to your own judgment about these mysterious murders and their aftermath.

Finally, it is important to remember that these individual voices tell a story that could not be suppressed, no matter how strong the taboo, how deep the excisions, how subtle the ulterior motives. The durability of this story was predicted by Polish ambassador Stanisław Kot as far back as November 1, 1941, when he approached the Soviets with yet another inquiry about his country's missing soldiers. "People are not like steam," Kot fumed. "They cannot evaporate." In this case, truth, like matter, was indestructible.

KATYŃ

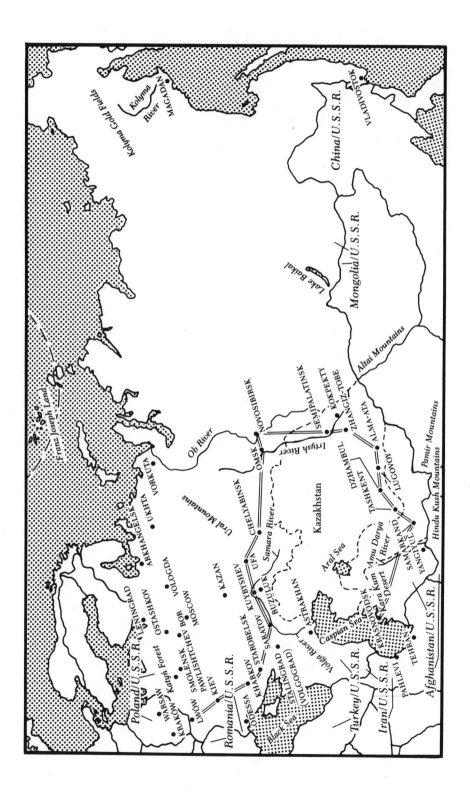

CHAPTER 1

The Interlude

<<<<<<<<<<<

In a sense it was the last train to Zakopane. Certainly it would be remembered that way: a relaxed holiday journey in the last interlude before the war.

At the *główna*, or main, station in Kraków, on the morning of August 1, 1939, the Poles came aboard in a hubbub of excitement, jostling luggage, bikes, cooking utensils, and hiking gear for a month-long visit in the countryside. Many knew one another. The adults chatted amiably about the perfect summer weather and made political small talk about recent diplomatic successes of the government in Warsaw. Most shunned talk of war. The subject was too dreary, the threat too remote—almost taboo for a holiday excursion. Settling back, the passengers relaxed as their caravan pulled away from the platform, drifting from under the canopy into a glaring sun. From the station the train rambled slowly to the outskirts of the ancient walled city beside the Vistula River, then gathered speed as it began a winding journey south into the foothills. Frequent stops were planned for vacationers leaving the train to stay in scenic villages that dotted the highlands. But most of the passengers would stay on board for the full seventy-five-mile, five-hour trip to Zakopane, which nestles in a narrow valley of the central Carpathian Mountains, or Tatry, as the Poles call them.

Zakopane beckoned with stunning beauty. A branch of the Dunajec River, called the White Dunajec, ran swiftly along a valley floor flanked by sheer rock stretching upward four thousand feet or more. Nestled among these peaks were high mountain lakes well within hiking range. Hot springs delighted bathers and added a magical effect. Their vapors swirled into a mist at the top of Mount Giewont, the valley's most familiar landmark. Capped with a large steel cross, the mountain resembled a reclining knight. The mist around it was said to be the smoke from the warrior's pipe. Adding to nature's endowment, the 1930s brought a modern ski lift, international ski competitions, boom-

1

ing commercial development, and more visitors from Poland and abroad. At Zakopane a new Poland put on its best face.

The Poland of 1939 was a vulnerable land. Many of the well-to-do Zakopane-bound passengers still bore painful memories of a dismembered and destitute homeland that held only the promise of independence at the end of World War I. Like Lenin, the legendary Marshal Józef Piłsudski had found power in the streets and used it well to reestablish a Poland that had been partitioned for more than a century by three rapacious neighbors—Austria, Prussia, and Russia. In the vacuum caused by the collapse of these empires, the Poles had redefined much of their borderland at gunpoint. In by far the most important confrontation, Piłsudski had defeated the Soviet Union in 1920 and established Polish hegemony in a no-man's-land between the two countries that contained an ethnic admixture of cultures, religions, languages, and political aspirations. The door to Western Europe had been slammed shut for the Bolsheviks with this victory. To the Bolshevik-loathing, history-conscious Poles, it ranked with King Jan III Sobieski's 1683 rout of the Ottoman Turks at the gates of Vienna as a contribution to western civilization.

Piłsudski was a new Sobieski, towering like a demigod over the new Poland. His military success led to the establishment of the Second Republic of Poland as a constitutional democracy in 1921. Choosing to remain in the background, Piłsudski watched in dismay as a succession of governments groped ineffectively with the economic, social, and political difficulties of the new nation. Taking matters into his own hands, he staged a successful coup in 1926, installing his own men and limiting parliamentary power. Piłsudski remained the éminence grise, but by the time of his death in 1935, an authoritarian government had been firmly established in Warsaw. That year the nation's constitution had been revised to make Poland's president responsible only "to God and history." By then it was also clear that only one institution in Poland, the army, could bridge class, ethnic, religious, and regional differences to define any semblance of national unity.

Piłsudski left behind an oligarchy in which his devoted protégé, Colonel Józef Beck, orchestrated Poland's foreign policy on a high wire stretched taut by German expansionist aims and by deep distrust of the Soviet Union. On January 5, 1939, Adolf Hitler told Beck at Obersalzberg that the free city of Danzig (now Gdańsk) should be returned to the Reich and that Germany wanted the right-of-way for a superhighway and double-track railroad across the Polish Corridor (Polish Pomerania) to East Prussia. Beck politely refused, knowing that his countrymen would be shocked and compromised by such a concession.

It became increasingly clear as the new year unfolded that the occupation of Austria and the Sudetenland in 1938 had merely whetted Hitler's voracious appetite. Bohemia and Moravia were occupied in mid-March. Troops also were sent to "protect" Slovakia. Suddenly German troops rimmed Poland from three directions—along its border with East Prussia and Pomerania in the north, along the Slovak border in the southwest, and in the Reich itself to the west. Devising a sound defense in this 1,750-mile horseshoe was virtually impossible. But the Poles, unlike their neighbors to the south, left no doubt that they would resist German aggression with force.

Polish obduracy did not restrain Hitler. It inflamed him. As 1939 unfolded, he stepped up his demands for Danzig and access to East Prussia across Polish Pomerania, adding to the sense of urgency by ordering German troop movements along the frontier. But Beck and his government would not budge; as Hitler turned up the pressure, they stubbornly refused to negotiate. Faced with Polish intransigence, Hitler's irritation quickly turned into a boiling rage.

On the surface the Polish position did not seem foolhardy. Slowly the British and French leaders were coming to the view that appeasement would not work. When Hitler's demands on Danzig and the Corridor surfaced so quickly after the swallowing of Czechoslovakia, the British and French concluded that the line must be drawn at Poland. At the end of March 1939, the British offered a surprising plan to bring Hitler to his senses. The British prime minister, Neville Chamberlain, proposed a guarantee of Polish independence. Beck accepted without a moment's hesitation, and on March 31 Chamberlain told Parliament that His Majesty's government would lend Poland "all support in their power" in the face of German aggression. In a reflection on the weakness of Britain's cross-Channel partner, Chamberlain noted almost as a postscript that the French "have authorized me to make it plain that they stand in the same position. . . ." But the British prime minister had chosen his words with great care. He was erecting a diplomatic deterrent. Even so, for Beck and the Poles it seemed to achieve one of Piłsudski's most ardently sought goals: a British commitment to safeguard the Polish republic.

A week later, on April 6, Beck convinced Chamberlain to go one step further by signing a mutual-assistance pact with Poland. The public commitment in this bilateral agreement went further than the vague guarantee of March 31. The agreement provided for reciprocal support and permitted the Poles to use their own discretion in deciding what constituted a threat to their independence. Beck returned to Poland to a hero's welcome.

On May 5, a confident Beck told the Sejm (parliament) that Poland wanted peace, but she did not want peace at any price. At the conclusion of his speech, he said: "There is only one thing in the life of men, nations and states which is without price, and that is honor." His reference to honor struck a deep chord in the Polish character, a quality that often, unfortunately, made the Poles seem like reckless romantics. Both Beck and the Polish people believed that they had faced down the Führer, that no sane man would attack in the face of the new guarantees.

To the Poles heading south for Zakopane, as to most of their countrymen, it seemed that Beck's diplomacy had put Hitler in a suicidal position if he attacked. Germany had ninety-eight divisions of uneven quality. France alone could put the equivalent of one hundred and ten divisions in the field. The Poles had thirty divisions and twelve cavalry brigades. The British had only a few divisions of ground troops, but added a preponderance of sea power. The bombing capability of the British and French air forces roughly offset that of the Germans. If the Wehrmacht attacked Poland, the French air force was expected to attack Germany immediately and the French army was supposed to begin an offensive on the fifteenth day. The British air force was to strike back at Germany immediately, while the British army began a buildup on the Continent. Conventional wisdom held that, under these circumstances, if the Polish army could withstand the Wehrmacht for a few weeks, the Germans would be trapped in the same kind of two-front conflict that bled them white in World War I.

Like most of their countrymen, the Zakopane-bound passengers assumed that Hitler was boxed in. They assumed that he would behave logically. They assumed that he would respect the guarantees. And their assumptions made the war clouds—already amassed into thunderheads—invisible. The passengers were unfazed by Hitler's incredible hunches, his uncanny instincts. It never occurred to them that Hitler might understand the Allies better than Beck did, that keen judgment and instinct told Hitler that the West would not mount an offensive to save Poland. This meant the tables were turned. If all its assumptions were wrong, the entire Polish strategy collapsed in a heap. If the guarantees were worthless, of course there would be no front in the west. Which made it suicide for the Poles—not the Germans—to fight. And how long could the Poles possibly last? Whether they held out for a few weeks or more, what difference would it make? With no one coming to their aid, the Wehrmacht eventually would destroy them. None of these were thoughts for a holiday excursion. Yet there was one more faulty assumption: In all the focus on the West, everyone also assumed that Poland's eastern frontier was secure. But such was not the case. At the very moment the vacationers meandered toward Zakopane, secret signals were flashing: The Germans and the Soviets, ideological archenemies, were verging toward a shocking rapprochement. Under the cover of trade talks, the first hints of a possible nonaggression treaty between these two giants were surfacing. Once such a document was signed, the Poles—not the Germans—would face a two-front war and devastation beyond description.

But for the caravan winding south through the ripening grain fields and the ancient sub-Carpathian villages, war worries seemed far away. Passengers laughed about trivialities and discussed interesting tidbits of news such as the German failure to show up for the latest Air Challenge, a European competition for light planes. The Poles had won the event for three consecutive years. There was much chuckling on the train that the Germans were too embarrassed to show up for the 1939 competition. In this happy frame of mind the vacationers fanned out across the highlands with little inkling of the disasters that lay ahead.

Magda Pogonowska remembered well the atmosphere of the last interlude. We were hiking along a wooded trail near her home in Blacksburg, Virginia, in July 1989 when she told me, "All through the summer people were asking would there be a war or not. Almost everybody had decided that there would be no such thing. No one seemed to believe it would happen." The Polish government had been firm with Hitler, it was backed by strong allies, and, according to Magda, "We thought eventually we would win if it came to fight."

She had come to the United States in 1957 as the wife of Iwo Pogonowski, a Polish expatriate who had been captured by the Germans in their 1939 invasion and spent the war in Gestapo prisons and the concentration camp at Oranienburg-Sachsenhausen. He survived the famous death march of Brandenburg. Like many Poles of his generation, Iwo had been cut off from his native land as the communists consolidated their hold on the country between 1944 and 1947. His birthplace, Lwów, had been annexed by the Soviet Union, and his relatives there were facing persecution. By 1947 he had given up hope of returning. In the mid-fifties he finished his education at the University of Tennessee and became a member of its faculty. He obtained U.S. citizenship and later began work as an engineer, building oil-drilling platforms in the Gulf of Mexico and in many other parts of the world. Magda had come to the United States as a physician, and within three years had established herself in Houston as a specialist and lecturer in radiology. In 1972 the couple moved to Blacksburg, where Magda had her own practice in diagnostic radiology. Iwo continued to design drilling platforms and began writing and lecturing on Polish issues. He also designed and built a spacious hilltop home with a commanding view of the Blue Ridge Mountains. But despite their comfortable life in America, neither had ever become reconciled to the disappearance of the Poland they had known growing up. A half century earlier that world had seemed secure to Magda Czarnek as she and her family rode the train toward Zakopane for vacation.

Dr. Zbigniew Czarnek and his family left the train at Skawa, a village of a hundred houses near the end of the foothills before the steep climb into the valley of Zakopane began. At the station, a driver with horse and cart gathered their vacation gear and took them the short distance to a modest but comfortable house, one of the few in Skawa recently equipped with electricity. The internist was renting this cottage for the second year from its enterprising owner, a farmer who gladly moved his family to the loft of his barn for the month.

His military bearing, formal goatee, and piercing eyes made Dr. Czarnek, fifty-two, seem taller than his actual height of five feet seven inches. He had come to Skawa to unwind from the demands of his busy practice in Kraków, and to give his family a firsthand feel for life in the Polish countryside. He cared little for resorts, preferring quiet, out-of-the-way villages where his family could enjoy one another's company.

His marriage to Janina Czaplińska, who was four years younger, was one of opposite attractions. She balanced his reserve with openness, his authority with warmth and affection, and his traditionalism with a flair for self-expression and resourcefulness. They had met at the Jagiellonian University in Kraków, one of Europe's old and great citadels of learning, while he studied medicine and she Romance languages. He had found in her a remarkable streak of independence, yet despite his conservative nature, their attachment had deepened because of it. Both were brought up to be devout Catholics and passionate Polish patriots, and to have a sense of noblesse oblige.

They married on August 2, 1914, just after he finished medical school. Two days later, World War I began and the young physician from Galicia, the area of Poland thrown by the 1795 partition to the Hapsburgs, was immediately called into service by the Austrian army.

His request for transfer to Piłsudski's famous Galician Legions—paramilitary Polish insurrectionists organized before the war under the guise of a gun club—was denied. Later, he was lightly wounded in a riverboat explosion. During his recuperation, Zbigniew and Janina—only in private or among close friends did they indulge in the tender diminutives "Zbysiu" and "Jasia"—were reunited, and continued through the rest of the war working together as a doctor-nurse team. Their first child, Maria, was born as the war ended in 1918. A son, Stanisław, followed in 1919, then two daughters, Agnieszka in 1922 and Magdalena in 1926.

With Polish independence, the young physician declined a lucrative offer to enter private practice, accepting instead a position in the new Polish army. He held a number of important posts, including the command of the army tuberculosis sanatorium at Zakopane from 1928 to 1932, and later that of the military hospital at Chełm Lubelski. A heavy smoker, Dr. Czarnek suffered a heart attack at age forty-five, and was forced because of declining health to leave the army. He accepted the decision stoically, but his retirement came as a great shock and injustice to the family. A delegation of concerned citizens came to him shortly afterward to urge that he accept appointment as mayor of Chełm Lubelski, but he politely declined, packed up the family, and returned in 1936 to his beloved Kraków to begin private practice.

Although he quit smoking after the heart attack, Dr. Czarnek never fully regained health—a continuing concern to his family. The deep paternal respect Janina always encouraged in the children became almost reverential as Dr. Czarnek's impaired health continued. Vacations were especially prized by the family as a time when he could unwind from the pressures of medical practice. Generally he avoided all undue effort, even excusing himself from family hiking expeditions to nearby points of interest. He spent most of the days reading and listening to the radio. In the evenings, he and Janina often played bridge with other couples who had rented houses nearby.

During their first year in Skawa, Stanisław ("Staszek"), who bore a striking physical resemblance to his father, hiked and biked through the surrounding countryside, at one point climbing Babia Góra, a nearby mountain that took its name from its shape—wide like a peasant woman. Maria, Agnieszka ("Jaga"), and their mother spent hours reading by the banks of the Skawa River and wading in the shallow stream. Magdalena ("Magda") plunged into farm life, pitching in with the village children as they herded cattle on nearby pastures. She played endlessly with the farm children and came to envy their outdoor life.

All this, just as the parents intended, deepened the family's feeling for
Polish village life with its colorful customs and folklore, where time
ebbed and flowed with the seasons.

The family's enthusiasm for the 1939 holiday was tempered considerably by the knowledge that Stanisław, called Staszek by his adoring
sisters, would be away in artillery school. After earning his advanced
high-school certificate, the *matura*, in 1938, Staszek decided to complete his compulsory military service before entering medical school.
Now stationed at Zambrów, a large base seventy-odd miles northwest
of Warsaw, he had just attained the rank of *podchorąży*, or junior
officer.

The family had barely unpacked when, on August 2, a telegram from
Staszek arrived wishing his mother and father a happy twenty-fifth
wedding anniversary. These greetings were the highlight of an otherwise quiet and uneventful observance dampened somewhat by compar-
isons of the current international tensions with those on the eve of
World War I. A premonition that history might be repeating itself—
that a new era might be beginning—prompted Janina Czarnek to walk
alone to mass the next morning.

Such worries gradually receded in the August haze of lazy days of
reading by the river and long walks in the countryside. Magda, now
thirteen and maturing rapidly, was attempting Henryk Sienkiewicz's
epic trilogy describing the Poles' seventeenth-century struggles against
the Cossacks, Tartars, Swedes, and Turks. Immensely popular in
Poland, Sienkiewicz had won the Nobel Prize for his works, including
Quo Vadis, a novel about Rome under Nero. Young Poles everywhere
whetted their intellectual curiosity on his work.

Magda and her friends frequently walked to the village station,
where they congregated on the platform with families who had rented
cottages in and around Skawa and were returning from vacation to
Kraków. These visits became an everyday attraction. At some point, in
a parting gesture, a few passengers leaned from the train windows and
began throwing brightly wrapped, inexpensive fruit candy; this caused
a great stir with the youngsters, who scrambled for catches, often
making acrobatic recoveries in the process. The lighthearted gesture
of candy tossing quickly became a popular daily ritual, an exciting
scene that prompted Magda to imagine her own departure as a time
when she would throw fistfuls of candy to her friends of two
summers.

In the third week of August 1939, Magda was sent about an hour
west by train to visit the family of Colonel Marian Bolesławicz, close

friends from Dr. Czarnek's army days who spent August vacations at an elegant ancestral home in the picturesque brewery town of Żywiec. In the early thirties the army had assigned the colonel, an artillery officer who had fought with Piłsudski's Legions, to Kraków, where both families had been housed in the same apartment complex. His daughter, Iwa, and Magda were the same age and became best friends. Their families periodically arranged for them to visit each other. Magda arrived in Żywiec expecting to spend the rest of August with the Bolesławiczes.

Strolling about the elegant estate with its formal flower gardens, the two girls spent hours inventing tales from which they later derived an endless string of paper-doll characters. Iwa had obvious artistic talent, and Magda watched in amazement as she quickly sketched a variety of subjects. A week flowed by and the outside world seemed far removed, holding only the certain and unwelcome threat of a return to school. The thought of ending these perfect days prompted Iwa several times to voice the universal August lament of adolescents, "I wish something would happen so that we wouldn't have to go back to school."

Less than a week of vacation remained when Maria came without warning to take Magda back to Skawa. The radio was full of startling reports that indicated war might be imminent. Germany and the Soviet Union were suddenly partners in an unusual nonaggression pact that could give the Nazis a free hand in settling matters with the Poles. This news was causing an eruption of headlines around the world. Moreover, there were widespread reports of German troop movements along the borders with Poland, and the Polish government was frantically mobilizing reserves.

By the time Maria and Magda reached Skawa, bags were packed and the family was ready to leave. They hurried to the station for the return trip to Kraków. On the platform, the scene of so much recent carefree excitement, the mood was somber and gloomy as vacationers conversed in a murmur of wonder, doubt, and concern. It was not the scene Magda had imagined—no candies were thrown and no happy farewells shouted as the train edged away from the platform. A few village children and young people waved shyly, uncertain about the abrupt change, the subdued and melancholy atmosphere.

The Czarneks waved back with fondness for Skawa and the platform assemblage, but also with irritation, worry, and apprehension that the on-again-off-again war had punctured an otherwise timeless summer. It was good, they felt, that Warsaw was responding firmly to the German pressure. Colonel Beck had probably known all along that something like this would happen. He and the rest of the government would know what to do about these latest developments.

In a fog of confusion, the Czarneks settled back for a nervous and brooding train ride back to Kraków and home.

Half a century later this scene seems improbable. Could the Poles possibly have been so oblivious to the realities of their situation? Certainly they knew that Hitler was more than a neighborhood bully. Piłsudski's adamant warnings about danger from the East were far from forgotten. What, then, explains their predicament? Was Beck's appeal to honor utterly lacking in realism? Certainly he knew that British and French military leaders could provide little immediate relief in the face of a German attack on Polnd. In the week before the Germans attacked, the British and French, remembering the provocative mobilizations just prior to World War I, persuaded the Poles to temporarily halt their frantic mobilization efforts. Partially as a result, thousands of Polish reserves were still milling around train depots when the Wehrmacht struck.

Was the Polish strategy all based on wishful thinking, or did the Allies mislead the Poles? In truth, elements of both were involved. Poland and France did have formal and long-standing agreements to defend each other. And on May 19, 1939, the two countries had signed a military protocol committing the French army to attack Germany within fifteen days if the Germans attacked Poland. However, political agreements to implement the protocol were never signed. On August 25, 1939, in response to the signing of the Nazi-Soviet Nonaggression Pact, the Anglo-Polish Mutual Assistance Pact of April 6 became a formal alliance. At a minimum Beck and the Poles had a right to expect some show of force from the British and French, enough to force the Wehrmacht to commit more than the skeleton force left so brazenly in the west. The French did mobilize, but then began their famous *Sitzkrieg*. They probably never intended an immediate attack—which meant that Beck and his colleagues had based their strategy on false expectations from the beginning. In July 1939 General Sir Edmund Ironside, then chief of the British general staff, said, "The French have lied to the Poles in saying they are going to attack. There is no idea of it."

Not only was Ironside right, but after Hitler attacked on September 1, the French and British waited until September 3 even to issue a declaration of war. Both countries hesitated to act, hoping that Mussolini could persuade Hitler to stop the invasion. Even with the tardy declaration, to the Poles it appeared that the two great powers that had defeated Germany in World War I were about to rescue them from unprovoked German aggression. No one bothered to explain that the Allies would impose a naval blockade, nothing else. A gradual troop buildup was planned, but nothing that could relieve the Poles' desperate situation. Moreover, no one had foreseen that Hitler would continue to gamble so boldly in the face of the Allied war declaration. None of the Wehrmacht divisions were shifted back to the west. Instead, Hitler threw the full weight of the Wehrmacht against Poland to gain a quick victory.

The real cause of the calamity that befell the Poles in September 1939 was geography. They occupied the central plain of Europe, between Berlin and Moscow. No strategy and no alliance could change this basic fact of their lives. Centuries of conflict from both directions had taught 'the Poles to fear both their neighbors. This history made them unable to choose the lesser of two evils, to consider either country as a potential ally. In 1937 and again in 1938, the Poles had tacitly refused to join Hitler's Anti-Comintern Pact to fight the Soviets. Three years later the Western Allies gingerly raised the possibilities of a linkage with the Soviets. Why not, they suggested, use the Red Army to reinforce the Polish army? The Poles bristled at the very idea. If the Soviets came in, what would ever induce them to leave? they emphatically replied. "With the Germans we risk losing our freedom. With the Russians we shall lose our souls," Marshal Edward Śmigły-Rydz, head of the Polish armed forces, had said on this occasion.

Such inflexibility resulted to some extent from military overconfidence and the fear that once the Soviets came they would never leave. The Poles still savored their 1920 victory over the Soviets and entertained the notion that this triumph could be repeated. Piłsudski's legacy of nonalignment with immediate neighbors also increased Polish rigidity. Poland was not a member of the Little Entente, a defensive alliance set up with the help of France after World War I to protect Czechoslovakia, Romania, and Yugoslavia from German aggression.

Thus, false expectations, overconfidence, and inflexibility contributed to the Poles' predicament and accounted for the surreal atmosphere that pervaded the country on the eve of the war. In hoping that there would be no war, the Poles were no different from most other Europeans. But for them most of all the rumblings were apocalyptic. A sense of the moment is captured in William L. Shirer's *Berlin Diary*. His entry for August 20 from Warsaw observed:

All in all, the Poles are calm and confident and Berlin's gibes and Goebbel's terrific press campaign of lies and invented incidents leave them cold. But they are too romantic, too confident. You ask them, as I've asked a score of officials in the Foreign Office and the army this past week, about Russia and they shrug their shoulders. Russia does not count for them. But it ought to. I think the Poles will fight. I know I said that, wrongly, about the Czechs a year ago. But I say it again about the Poles.

Despite their short-range miscalculations, in the long run the Poles *were* right: Eventually Hitler was caught in a suicidal two-front war. The conflict did not unfold as the Poles expected. But it was the Poles' willingness to fight—their refusal to go the way of the Czechs and Austrians—that embroiled Hitler in the general European war that finally destroyed him. En route to his destruction, Poland's Second Republic was also destroyed. In its place came another nightmare—a communist regime dominated by Moscow. In 1939, this outcome was not foreseeable, but it was almost certainly inevitable.

In retrospect, fighting was the best of several unattractive alternatives for the Poles. At least it put them on the eventual winning side and gave them the moral high ground in arguing for their continued independence. True, their alliance with the West might have been improved by more specific guarantees, but such changes could not have affected the outcome materially. Had they capitulated to Hitler's demands, there is little reason to believe that they would have fared any better than they did. Sooner or later, he would have occupied and dismembered Poland, applying the same lethal policies of racist imperialism. Had they aligned themselves with the Soviets, their independence would have been threatened by Hitler *and* Stalin. That Hitler would eventually attack the Soviet Union was a foregone conclusion. Linking Poland's future with a country that, in 1939, was considered militarily weak offered little apparent advantage. In the absence of German aggression, what would check Soviet designs on Polish territory? History emphatically told the Poles that to cooperate with the Russians meant risks that were simply unacceptable.

Again, the Poles could not escape their geography. The conflict began as a war to save Poland, but quickly became a war to defeat Germany. The vast resources of the Soviet Union were essential to that victory. As the tide began to turn, the Western Allies were poorly positioned to alter Stalin's contention that what the Red Army had won, the Soviet Union should keep. Only then was the tragedy of the Poles clear: that they had fought and won and still lost. Despite their heroism, despite their important role in the winning coalition, they would not regain their independence for another fifty years.

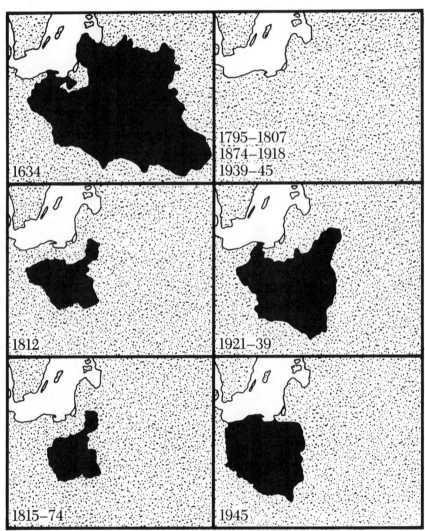

1795–1807
1874–1918
1939–45

1634

1812

1815–74

1921–39

1945

Poland's Changing Territory: 1634–1945

CHAPTER 2

Hitler's Command

<<<<<<<<<<<<

From the huge picture window in the living room of the Berghof, his Obersalzberg retreat, Hitler could see Untersberg across a deep valley of the Bavarian Alps. There, according to legend, Frederick Barbarossa, ruler of the Holy Roman Empire, slept inside the mountain guarding his nation's destiny—ready to rise and lead her from defeat to glory if ever needed.

To Hitler this was no mere fable, and it was no mere accident that many of the conferences and decisions that marked his rise to power and Germany's resurgence had occurred at Obersalzberg. Chamberlain, then sixty-nine, came to Germany three times during the Czech crisis, once subjecting himself to a grueling day-long trip by plane, train, and car to plead with the Führer for sanity. Most recently, Count Galeazzo Ciano, the Italian foreign minister, had come on August 12 to spend two days vainly searching for ways to dampen the war fever that gripped Hitler and his inner circle. Instead, Hitler confirmed to Ciano for the first time his intention to invade Poland. In his diary, Ciano wrote that Hitler had cushioned the shock with more startling news: The Reich and the Soviet Union were on the verge of a rapprochement based on a joint solution to problems in Eastern Europe.

The news astounded Ciano. For six years the Nazis and the Soviets had constantly excoriated each other, portraying each other's contrasting systems as evil incarnate. The first break in these torrents of abuse came in a March 10, 1939, radio address by Joseph Stalin, who noted a "kinship" between National Socialism and communism. He soon backed the statement with concrete action. For some time the British, French, and Soviet governments had been trying to devise a collective-security plan to forestall Hitler. These negotiations had amounted to little so far. Foreign Minister Maxim Litvinov, a Jew with close ties to the West and an advocate of collective security, was representing the Soviet side. Suddenly, on May 3, 1939, Stalin fired

15

him. A concession to Nazi anti-Semitism coupled with declining interest in the concept of collective security—not the slow pace of negotiations—had motivated the decision.

Litvinov was replaced by Stalin's closest confidant, the blunt and
uncompromising Vyacheslav Molotov, a man Lenin once called "the
best file clerk in Russia." With this appointment, Stalin signaled in the
spring of 1939 a sharp turn in Soviet policy away from the West and
toward Germany. How much longer could he wait? The Western Allies
seemed immobilized, unable to make up their minds. Where would
they be when it counted, when and if the trouble really started?
Chamberlain's spineless performance at Munich a year earlier was no
cause for encouragement. Caving in to Hitler's demands on Czechoslovakia, the British prime minister had declared: "I believe it is peace
for our time." In six short months, Hitler had turned his demands on
Poland. True, the British and French had offered a guarantee of Polish
independence. But it was vague, lacking in concrete military commitments—mere posturing as far as Stalin was concerned. All this, on top
of the fumbling negotiations with Litvinov, was a sign of debilitating
weakness, of partners who could not be counted on in a confrontation
with Germany.

Publicly, negotiations with the British and French appeared to be
edging forward, but secretly, under the guise of trade talks, the Soviets
began a slow mating dance with their totalitarian archenemy—a dance
that gathered in intensity as the summer wore on.

A powerful seduction was at work on both sides. Stalin was allured
by the prospects of a guarantee against German aggression and of the
extension of Soviet hegemony into eastern Poland, Bessarabia, and
along the Baltic. For Hitler, a pact with the U.S.S.R. was a way to
settle matters with the Poles without fear of Soviet intervention. He
had already convinced himself that the British and French leaders—
"little worms," as he called them—were unlikely to fight over Poland
even with Soviet support, and even less likely to do so without it. An
agreement with Stalin thus became the last piece of insurance Hitler
needed to begin a war that promised maximum spoils at minimum cost.

In the spring of 1939 Hitler had ordered the Oberkommando der
Wehrmacht (OKW, or High Command of the Armed Forces) to prepare Case White, the code name for plans to invade Poland. Hitler
himself had stipulated that the attack should be no later than September 1, to keep armored vehicles from bogging down in the fall mud
on Poland's notoriously bad roads. A fast-ticking clock now cast him as
the ardent suitor.

Hitler's startling comments to Ciano on August 12 were based in part on a report from the German foreign office that the Soviets were willing to broaden the scope of ongoing trade discussions to include such political concerns as the current difficulties with Poland. In typical methodical fashion, the Soviets added that these discussions should be undertaken "by degrees," and only after a trade agreement had been concluded.

But with Case White's September 1 deadline looming ever larger, Hitler could not wait. Already, German submarines and pocket battleships were preparing to sail for British waters. So on August 14, the Führer notified the Soviets of his readiness to send Foreign Minister Joachim von Ribbentrop to Moscow immediately to define a long-term German-Soviet accord. Receiving this news the following day, the wily Molotov again stressed the need for careful preparation for negotiations, then deftly asked: Would the Reich be willing to sign a nonaggression pact with the Soviet Union?

The Führer's response, wired back on August 16, was a predictable and unconditional yes. Knowing that Hitler planned to invade Poland, Molotov and Stalin now teased at their next reply. General Franz Halder, chief of the German general staff, later wrote that the tension at Obersalzberg rose almost to the breaking point. Finally, on August 19, Molotov met the German ambassador, Count Friedrich Werner von der Schulenburg, at the Kremlin only to state bluntly once again that until a trade agreement was signed there could be no nonaggression pact. Shortly after the meeting, Stalin apparently changed his mind, because Molotov phoned Schulenburg to arrange a second meeting. Surprisingly, at this session Molotov produced his own draft of a nonaggression pact, and agreed that if the trade treaty was signed, Ribbentrop could come to Moscow to finalize matters as early as August 26 or 27.

But even a week's delay could disrupt the Case White timetable, and Hitler now took matters directly into his own hands. Suppressing his pride, he appealed on Sunday, August 20, for a personal favor from his once irreconcilable foe, telegraphing Stalin personally to ask that Ribbentrop be permitted to come to Moscow on August 22, or at the latest the twenty-third.

Stalin's reply came back on Monday morning, indicating that he would see Ribbentrop on the twenty-third. In the meantime, Hitler had cleared Molotov's draft of the Nazi-Soviet Nonaggression Pact. The only matter that remained for Ribbentrop to clear up was a special secret protocol that the meticulous Soviets were insisting on as a way to specify clearly the division of spoils in Eastern Europe. Pressed by his invasion timetable, and knowing that sooner or later he planned to invade the Soviet Union anyway, Hitler was in no mood to quibble over fine points. He dispatched Ribbentrop with full authority to negotiate a final agreement.

As Ribbentrop's Condor flew to Moscow on the morning of August 22, a steady procession of OKW brass and high-ranking Nazis began arriving at Obersalzberg. Their large sedans and touring cars left a trail of dust on the valley floor as they passed the market town of Berchtesgaden, then slowed for the steep climb to Obersalzberg. On its outer slopes, they passed two identity checkpoints at high barbed-wire fences, the outer one looping for nine miles around the mountain, the inner one almost two miles long. Hairpin curves, in places blasted through sheer rock, marked the drive up to the Berghof, which sat at an altitude of 3,300 feet. Nearby were the chalets of Hitler's inner circle—Luftwaffe commander and future Reich Marshal Hermann Goering, Reichsleiter Martin Bormann, and architect Albert Speer—all in a 2.7-square-mile compound of confiscated state forests and forcibly bought farms.

On a distance peak called the Kehlstein sat the Eagle's Nest, a remote retreat used on rare occasions to impress important visitors. Built in 1936 as a birthday present for the Führer, it was approached up a winding asphalt road, four miles long, which ended abruptly at huge bronze portals set in rock. A brightly lit tunnel burrowed five hundred feet into the heart of the mountain, where marble walls, dampened by the inner-mountain moisture, framed an elevator of polished brass. Its shaft pierced 370 feet skyward to the top of the mountain. There, bathed in light, at an altitude of 6,400 feet, sat a rustic teahouse—a dreamlike aerie, a repose of pretensions, all befitting the legendary reawakening of Frederick Barbarossa.

As members of the OKW and high party officials gathered below at the Berghof, Hitler planned to impress them not with scenery but with his vision of Greater Germany—a thousand-year *reich* based on military conquest and glory. He had called them together to announce his "irrevocable decision to act" and to steel their confidence for the impending invasion of Poland. The speech began in the usual cloud of megalomania, according to a composite account taken by William L. Shirer from the diaries of General Halder and Admiral Hermann Boehm, Chief of the High Seas Fleet:

> Essentially, all depends on me, on my existence, because of my political talents. Furthermore, the fact [is] that probably no one will ever again

have the confidence of the whole German people as I have. There will probably never again in the future be a man with more authority than I have. My existence is therefore a factor of great value. But I can be eliminated at any time by a criminal or lunatic.

He reminded them of his inspired risks, all taken in the face of his listeners' timidity—and all resulting in bloodless triumphs: the occupation of the Rhineland, the taking of Austria and of the Sudetenland, Moravia, and Slovakia. These successes, he said, had been built by bluffing the leaders of England and France, who had proven weak and hesitant at every turn. Now, he gloated, he had severed their last hope,

that Russia would become our enemy after the conquest of Poland. The enemy did not count on my great power of resolution. Our enemies are little worms. I saw them at Munich.

I was convinced that Stalin would never accept the English offer. Only a blind optimist could believe that Stalin would be so crazy as not to see through England's intentions. Russia has no interest in maintaining Poland. . . . Litvinov's dismissal was decisive. It came to me like a cannon shot as a sign of a change in Moscow toward the Western Powers. . . . Now Poland is in the position in which I wanted her. . . . A beginning has been made for the destruction of England's hegemony. The way is open for the soldier, now that I have made the political preparations.

As the conference broke for lunch, Goering rose to assure the Führer that German's military forces would not disappoint him. Despite deepened concern among several of the senior commanders present that the blitzkrieg Hitler proposed could quickly turn into a worldwide conflagration, not one doubt was expressed, nor one word of opposition spoken. Returning from lunch, Hitler gave his peroration.

The destruction of Poland has priority. The aim is to eliminate active forces, not to reach a definite line. Even if war breaks out in the West, the destruction of Poland remains the primary objective. A quick decision, in view of the season.

I shall give a propagandist reason for starting the war—never mind whether it is plausible or not. The victor will not be asked afterward whether he told the truth or not. In starting and waging a war it is not right that matters, but victory.

Close your hearts to pity! Act brutally! Eighty million people must obtain what is their right. . . . The stronger man is right. . . . Be harsh

and remorseless! Be steeled against all signs of compassion! . . . Whoever
has pondered over this world order knows that its meaning lies in the
success of the best by means of force. . . .

His harangue completed, the Führer concluded by saying that the
invasion would probably begin on August 26 and certainly would come
no later than September 1.

By nightfall on August 23, Ribbentrop, Molotov, and Stalin were
redrawing the map of Eastern Europe, establishing spheres of German
and Soviet influence on a vast arc stretching from the Baltic republics
into Romania. Under the agreement, Poland was split along a boundary
approximately formed by the Narew, Vistula, and San rivers. While
the main text of the nonaggression pact was to be announced jointly
by both governments, these details were defined in a separate protocol
to be kept in strictest secrecy.

While the agreements were being prepared for the formal signing
ceremony, the former antagonists—now united by their shameless and
expedient territorial lust—toasted each other with banalities. The
German people welcomed an understanding with the Soviets, Ribbentrop said. "I know how much the German nation loves its Führer,"
Stalin replied.

The pact was dated August 23, but was not signed until the early
morning hours of August 24, 1939. With its signing, Poland was about
to disappear from the map of Europe. Her fourth partition since 1772
was about to begin. Russian and Prussian royalty had carved up the
country up three times previously. On two of those occasions, Austria,
too, had helped. Now the carving was being done by autocrats of a
new kind, totalitarians wielding the brutally efficient power of the modern police state. With them would come destruction, cruelty, and bar-
barism on a scale never before experienced.

CHAPTER 3

A Failed Escape

<<<<<<<<<<<<

Dr. Zbigniew Czarnek was among the minority of Poles who believed in 1939 that war was likely. His medical experience and World War I service in the Austrian army both told him that it made no sense to wait passively for its outbreak. After the mid-March flare-up over Danzig and the Polish Corridor, he quietly warned his family: "We have to prepare for the worst."

During one of my visits to Blacksburg, Magda told me that she, her sisters, and her mother were surprised by this warning. "None of us believed that the war was coming, but we could tell how worried he was. We were proud of his military background and felt that it made him worry more than he should."

Dr. Czarnek's main fear was gas. The Germans had initiated its use on April 22, 1915, releasing many cylinders of chlorine, which were driven by the wind toward British and French forces in an attack on the Ypres salient in Flanders. The new weapon had not been decisive in the overall offensive, but it had caused casualties in the thousands—far more than expected—and subjected many of its victims to a horrible, choking death. The specter of ghastly attacks against civilian populations soon followed. Not only had the Germans used gas first, they were said to have restocked under Hitler with new, more lethal toxins—all adding to the fear of gas as the silent, efficient scythe of modern warfare. There was even talk of a revenge motive since Hitler, a corporal during World War I, had been temporarily blinded by mustard gas near the village of Wervik in Belgium on October 14, 1918.

In the spring Dr. Czarnek began holding periodic after-supper drills to ingrain in his family a clear knowledge of how to react to this dreaded killer. Janina, Maria, Jaga, and Magda each had her own mask, and periodically practiced using it. Seated around the living room of their apartment with their faces covered, members of the family alternated between fear that such drastic steps were necessary and amuse-

21

ment at their absurd appearance. These sessions generally included lengthy readings from defense manuals and other safety literature published by the Polish government. As Dr. Czarnek read, his daughters' attention soon drifted toward less monotonous topics. Relaxed on a sofa, Janina stole catnaps, still alert to the possibility that her husband might ask a question about what he was reading. To such inquiries—much to the daughters' amusement and Dr. Czarnek's consternation—she invariably repeated the last two or three words he had spoken.

"To us, these moments could be hilarious, and they could also be frightening," Magda remembered. "But Tata [the Polish equivalent of "Dad"] never seemed to waver in his determination to get the points in these manuals across to us."

The Czarneks returned from vacation to their apartment at 82 Kazimierz Wielki Street, finding Kraków's atmosphere completely changed. War finally seemed imminent. Radio reports from Warsaw during the last few days of August 1939 described a number of border raids by Abwehr foreign-intelligence units. In one of the most serious incidents, an attempt was made to seize a key railroad station and tunnel near the Jabłonka pass in the Carpathians. Repulsing the attack, the Poles promptly blew up the tunnel. The Germans were also increasing high-altitude reconnaissance flights over Polish territory. On Wednesday, August 30, Marshal Edward Śmigły-Rydz and the government in Warsaw called for a full-scale mobilization. Because the British and French objected strongly that this step could provoke the Nazis, a recruitment and mobilization campaign using posters was briefly stopped, then resumed the next day. Individual call-ups by mail continued.

On Thursday, August 31, Jaga and Magda came back from the station in the early evening from a walk downtown. Dr. Czarnek, who had resumed seeing patients, came home from a round of house calls. The family ate a quiet supper and once again reviewed safety procedures under the doctor's watchful eye. Afterward, he walked across the living room and sat down at the piano. Both he and Staszek played frequently—mostly popular music and mostly by ear. Often, before Staszek left for the army, they played duets while the others sang and danced. Tonight, when Dr. Czarnek sat down to relax and unwind, he ranged over many of the old standbys in his repertoire. As he finished, he came to his favorite, "The White Roses Are Blooming," a tune popularized by Piłsudski's Legions. Its lyrics told the story of a young girl waiting for her fiancé to come home from the war—waiting to give him a white rose of summer. In the final verse, she learns that white roses are already blooming on his grave.

"I could never forget how he played that song," Magda told me. When he had finished, Dr. Czarnek rose from the piano. By ten-thirty, their usual time, the Czarneks had retired for the evening.

In the predawn darkness at Langenau Field, a Luftwaffe base in German Silesia, Dornier 17s and Heinkel 111s were being prepared for takeoff. Both were medium-range bombers with machine guns mounted in the nose or cockpit, the belly, and the dorsal area. Because of its thin fuselage, which limited payloads to a thousand pounds, the Dornier was also known as the Flying Pencil. The more devasting Heinkel, nicknamed Totenkopf, or Death's-head, carried a payload almost twice as large.

The launch began at 4:45 A.M. Roaring down the runway, the planes climbed into a clear early-morning sky and began banking slowly toward the dawn. Gathering into formation, two attack groups of sixty planes headed toward Polish airspace at a speed of more than two hundred miles per hour. They expected to reach their target in less than forty-five minutes.

On the horizon at 5:20 A.M. the German pilots could see Kraków in light mist. At this point they began dropping sharply to strafing altitude. Boring in on the outskirts of the city, the formation finally leveled out at 150 feet, where it seemed to graze the treetops.

The primary target was Rakowice Airfield, where a row of bombs was laid down the center of the runway, leaving craters twelve feet wide and six feet deep. On the aprons leading to the main runway, twenty-eight disabled aircraft were destroyed, but deployable planes of the Polish air force were not to be found: These had been dispersed from Kraków, and from other sizable airfields around Poland, to secret fields to avoid such a surprise attack.

The Czarneks were awakened by the steady humming of the planes passing their apartment on their way to the center of the city. Magda said her parents were already at the window of their bedroom when she and her sisters came rushing in from the adjoining room. As the family crowded at the window, it seemed they could almost touch the passing planes.

"Why the black crosses? Why not checkered crosses [the emblem on Polish planes]?" blurted Maria.

"The war has started. These are German planes," their father replied with calm resignation. The thud of the bombs could now be heard in the distance.

Dr. Czarnek quickly turned on the new Phillips radio at his bedside. An excited announcer was reading a patriotic appeal from the government. Then—just as they had practiced—the family hurried to the janitor's apartment two floors below in the basement to wait out the attack.

Finally, well past 6:00 A.M., the all-clear siren sounded. People began swarming into the streets to find that overall damage was light, confined for the most part to broken water mains and windowpanes, and gaping craters along several of the main thoroughfares, including the Planty, the city's parklike promenade.

Near the center of Kraków an army barracks, the railroad station, and the convent of St. Stanisław Kostka were all hit. There were pockets of devastation: A structure at the corner of Ogrodowa and Warszawska streets was demolished; seven persons there were killed and fifteen wounded, among them women and children. Nearby one house was collapsed, and the roof of a multistoried building had been blown off. A policeman stood at the entrance waiting to direct rescue workers.

The damage was still being assessed when a second group of planes arrived to bomb and strafe the city. Over the course of the day, five air strikes were directed against Kraków, the Dorniers and Heinkels being joined on several occasions by Junkers 87s, or Stukas—dive bombers equipped with sirens that made an ear-piercing whine as they plunged earthward. Inflicting minimal casualties and property damage, these strikes still achieved their primary objective of terrorizing the civilian population.

Added to these surprising and demoralizing attacks was even more alarming news: four panzer divisions had swept east into the industrial regions of Upper Silesia less than a hundred miles away, while infantry and armored units were slicing through the Carpathians from the south. Poland's largest army—Army Group South, or Army Kraków, which bore responsibility for the former capital's defense—initially was holding its ground, but still faced a potentially devasting pincer movement. The flat terrain along the Vistula River near Kraków offered few natural defenses, forcing military authorities to conclude, reluctantly, that a second line of defense must be established well to the east of the city.

Fearing that the city might quickly fall to the Germans, the Czarneks spent Friday night and most of Saturday preparing for an evacuation. Each member of the family packed essential belongings, including clothes, a blanket, a gas mask, and toiletries, into two suitcases. The weight of these two containers, Dr. Czarnek warned, must not exceed what they could realistically carry for several miles. Into one of her suitcases, Janina carefully placed two or three of her best dresses, and in the other, a metal case that could be locked, she stored the family jewelry.

While the packing and other preparations were under way, Dr. Czarnek learned that military families, including those of reserve officers, would be evacuated east by train 180 miles to Lwów on Sunday morning, September 3. Still holding the reserve rank of lieutenant colonel, he carried standing orders to join his unit in Lwów no later than the fifth day of mobilization. These orders and the hope of moving to an area well beyond the fighting brought the carefully packed Czarneks to the freight station at daybreak on Sunday. There they, the other families, and the reservists climbed aboard a long line of stuffy *towarowe*, or boxcars, and waited.

For reasons no one could explain, the train sat the entire day on the siding where the families had boarded. Air-raid alarms sounded several times during the day, prompting the waiting passengers to scramble for refuge beneath the boxcars. Few German planes could be seen or heard, but on several occasions bombs struck with earsplitting impact only a short distance away.

By dusk, when the train finally began to move, the stifling heat inside the boxcar, the sudden rush for cover at each alarm, and the endless waiting had given Magda a migraine. The creeping and creaking of the old boxcars magnified the tension. Passengers dozed, half asleep and half awake, through periodic stops and starts all through the night. After several hours, Dr. Czarnek complained that all sense of direction escaped him. At dawn the train stopped once again, and as surprised passengers peered out they could see that they were back in the outskirts of Kraków.

Hardly were bearings established and cramped muscles stretched when the whine of approaching aircraft sounded. The bombs crashed as people scrambled to safety beneath the train. The Czarnek daughters huddled tightly against each other, waiting for the attack to pass. It was over in seconds, and as people dusted themselves off, word came that the track had been severed in both directions. The train could go no farther.

A cluster of reserve officers debated excitedly whether to return to Kraków or press on toward Lwów on foot in the hope that transporation by rail or truck could be secured en route.

"I don't think there is any choice," Dr. Czarnek interjected. "I can't go back. I have orders in my pocket that tell me to be in Lwów by the fifth day of mobilization. It's less than two days from now. . . ."

On the fringe of this conference, Magda remembered her mother pleading, "You can't walk to Lwów!"

"There's no choice in the matter," her husband calmly and emphatically replied.

Worried that more planes might attack the train at any moment, he hurried his wife and three daughters toward their luggage, providing last-minute instructions for their safety. Do not return to the apartment, he told them. Go instead to a nearby home for the elderly, the House of Helchów, a place he visited on his daily round of house calls. The nuns in charge there would gladly take the family in, and the structure, with its old and exceptionally thick walls, would provide much greater safety.

Janina, sensing futility, implored her husband to stay. He simply shook his head.

The final good-bye was tearless. Despite his disdain for public displays of affection, the doctor and each daughter hugged in a firm, lingering embrace.

Turning back to Janina, he clasped her shoulders and half-whispered, "I'll be back soon. Tell Staszek when you see him that I know he will be brave."

Then he quickly turned and was gone.

CHAPTER 4

Case White

‹‹‹‹‹‹‹‹‹‹

Count Ciano flew back to Rome from his mid-August meeting at Obersalzberg convinced that Hitler was dragging Italy into a potentially disastrous adventure. Breaking this unpleasant news to his father-in-law, Benito Mussolini, Ciano stressed that Italy, with its weak army and sputtering economy, was in no position to be associated with such a reckless gamble. For almost two weeks, Il Duce wavered between the Führer's lure of cheaply won plunder and his fears of an uncontained fire. Finally, on August 25, he made his decision, writing Hitler that Italy could not provide military support if the invasion of Poland should cause a counterattack on Germany. The reason, he stressed, was "the present state of Italian war preparations, of which we have repeatedly and in good time informed you, Führer, and Herr von Ribbentrop."

This letter, read over the telephone by Ciano to the Italian ambassador in Berlin, arrived at the chancellery like a thunderclap at 6:30 P.M., with zero hour for the invasion a scant ten hours away. Final preparations for Case White, set in motion at the August 22 military conference on the Bavarian mountaintop, were nearing the point of no return. To complicate matters further, Hitler had learned at 4:30 P.M. that the British had strengthened their commitment to Poland by turning their April 6 mutual-assistance pact into a formal alliance.

Under the cascading pressure, the Führer blinked. At 8:30 P.M. he brought the massive invasion gears to a grinding but imperfect halt. Officers in some areas rushed to the border to stop forward detachments already on the move. A scout plane landed at the frontier just ahead of the motorized columns of General Paul Ludwig Ewald von Kleist to wave off their advance. Communication breakdowns all along the 1,750-mile border resulted in clashes, such as the one at the Jabłonka pass, caused by German units who failed to receive Hitler's last-minute order to halt. The Germans had been provoking border incidents

27

for days, and the Polish general staff continued to hope that this rash of incidents was not the gathering for a full-scale invasion.

Following the postponement, Hitler set about immediately to steel Mussolini's courage and to probe the depth of Britain's commitment to Poland. Reconfirming his belief that he could fight a localized war, less than twenty-four hours after the delay he set a new zero hour for 4:45 A.M. on September 1, and never again wavered in his commitment to attack.

During the fortnight before the invasion, a steady drumbeat of Nazi propaganda cynically fanned anti-Polish sentiment. The headlines of German daily newspapers warned: "POLISH SOLDIERS PUSH TO EDGE OF GERMAN BORDER!" "THREE GERMAN PASSENGER PLANES SHOT AT BY POLES." "IN CORRIDOR MANY GERMAN FARMHOUSES IN FLAMES!" "WHOLE OF POLAND IN WAR FEVER!"

Operation Canned Goods was the centerpiece in this campaign of deception to provide justification for the attack on Poland. It featured an attack on the night of August 31 on the German radio station at Gleiwitz (now Gliwice) near the Polish border in southwestern Silesia by SS troops dressed in Polish uniforms. Seizing the transmitter, the imposters appealed to the Polish minority in eastern Germany to take up arms against Hitler, sang a rousing chorus, fired a few pistol shots, and left. The "canned goods"—the bodies of several condemned concentration-camp victims outfitted in Polish uniforms—were left behind as proof for foreign correspondents. The incident was portrayed to the world as an unprovoked attack by the Poles on Germany—just the sort of propagandist pretext Hitler had promised his generals at the Berghof on August 22.

In the face of the Reich's staged provocations, the British and French continued to urge the Poles to delay general mobilization, claiming that such action might goad the Germans into attacking. Prompted by vivid memories of how the mobilization process had stretched tensions to the breaking point on the eve of World War I, these fears had not, however, deterred a secret call-up of Polish reserves in the summer. By the end of August, Polish troop strength—still short of full mobilization—reached 700,000. The Poles had 35 infantry divisions compared to 55 for Germany. But the disparities were even greater in armor and combat aircraft. Germany had 2,511 tanks to Poland's 475, and 2,085 bombers and fighters to her 313. German reserves also had been fully mobilized for weeks, while many of the newly mobilized Polish units had barely suited up and were poorly integrated with regular forces.

These disadvantages were magnified considerably by the Polish general staff's questionable decision to defend the nation's entire 1,750-mile border with Germany and German-occupied Slovakia. Thinly dispersed along this three-sided frontier, the Polish army faced Hitler's bristling arsenal with a flat landscape at its back that afforded few natural defenses—a perfect proving ground for an apocalyptic form of warfare called blitzkrieg.

The so-called lightning war involved tactics—based on surprise, speed, and the massed firepower of tanks, motorized artillery, highly mobile infantry, and planes—designed to create psychological shock and disorganization among enemy forces and civilian populations. By concentrating on a narrow front, the blitzkrieg was designed to bypass or quickly knife through main enemy positions, then follow with wide armored sweeps to disrupt supply lines, cut off reserves, and create large pockets of entrapped or immobilized enemy forces. Its primary architect was General Heinz Guderian, who had been heavily influenced by pioneering British work with armored divisions in the 1920s. In Hitler, always the gambler, Guderian found an enthusiastic sponsor for novel ideas that orthodox military planners in Germany and elsewhere were slow to accept.

The blitzkrieg against Poland quickly proved that Guderian was right. At zero hour on Friday, September 1, five German armies—a combined force of a million and a half men—began a simultaneous assault. Two of these armies attacked in the north, the Fourth Army striking west across the Corridor, and the Third Army piercing south from East Prussia. Guderian's Nineteenth Panzer Corps provided the spearhead for the Fourth Army. Riding in a specially equipped half-track, he was the first corps commander to direct a battle from a mobile radio-communications vehicle. The basic plan called for the Fourth and the Third Armies to link as soon as possible in northern Poland for a powerful thrust south between two major arteries, the Vistula and Bug rivers. If successful, this movement would isolate the large Polish forces committed to the defense of the Corridor and those centered opposite Germany's western frontier.

In the south, the Eighth, Tenth, and Fourteenth Armies—the combined forces of Army Group South under the able and aristocratic General (later Field Marshal) Gerd von Rundstedt—pushed north and east, cutting wedges between the largest Polish defense forces, armies Kraków, Łódź, and Poznań. In the far south, the German Fourteenth Army struck through and along the Carpathians, its objective to drive south below Kraków toward the oil fields near Lwów, the major rail center in eastern Poland. In central Silesia, the German Tenth Army

headed straight east, opening a big wedge between armies Kraków and
Łódź. On the northernmost flank of Army Group South, the Eighth
Army headed east toward the Bzura River, opening a gap between
armies Poznań and Łódź. In the grand strategy, elements of all five
armies were eventually to converge in giant pincers aimed at Warsaw,
leaving in their path isolated, encircled, and contained pockets of Polish
resistance.

The Poles fought courageously, but not as recklessly as one enduring
myth, that of brave cavalrymen with lances charging German tanks,
would have it. An incident on the evening of the first day of combat
in the Corridor provided the basis for this piece of folklore. Two Polish
cavalry squadrons under Colonel Kazimierz Mastelarz mounted a saber
charge against a German infantry battalion in a Tuchola Forest clearing
near the Brda River. Just as they wiped out the German formations,
several armored cars arrived and opened fire, killing about twenty
troopers and Mastelarz. The next day Italian war correspondents were
brought to the scene and were told that the troopers had been killed
while charging tanks. The Germans subsequently perpetuated this
myth to illustrate Polish backwardness, while the Poles themselves
cited it as an embellished example of their bravery.

The success of the German strategy, which surpassed all expectations, needed no embellishment. In the south, the German Tenth
Army brushed by Polish border positions in the first two days, and by
the fourth day had routed the Seventh Infantry division of Army Łódź
and was putting the right flank of Army Kraków under extreme pressure. That same day, Guderian breached the Corridor and was leading
the Fourth Army toward its planned junction with the Third Army,
then moving south from East Prussia.

On September 6 Kraków, Poland's fourth-largest city, fell and the
government in Warsaw was forced to flee a hundred miles southeast
to Lublin. That same day the Polish High Command was forced to
abandon all efforts to defend the frontiers, initiating massive withdrawals toward the east in hopes that stronger defensive positions could be
established beyond the Vistula River. To buy time the Poles launched
their one major counteroffensive on September 9, along the Bzura
River, a southwestern tributary of the Vistula. The battle turned out
to be a rare opportunity: The Poles briefly enjoyed numerical superiority and for a time were able to inflict heavy losses on the Germans.
But by September 12 reserve elements of the German Eighth Army
had rushed up from the south, encircling Polish forces and dooming
the counteroffensive.

Encountering stiff early resistance, the Luftwaffe quickly established its dominance and after the first few days of the invasion roamed the skies freely, bombing bridges, derailing trains, and strafing refugees along clogged roads. Toward the rear, Nazi Action Groups, or Einsatzgruppen, terrorized the civilian population, often arriving in towns and villages with lists of the Polish intelligentsia, who were rounded up and shot on the spot.

By the middle of the invasion's third week, Guderian had raced far to the east and south, making contact for the first time with elements of the Twelfth Panzer Corps of Army Group South some fifty miles south of Brześć nad Bugiem (now Brest Litovsk). Now, most of the Polish army was trapped in huge double pincers. The Polish government, dodging Luftwaffe bombs and machine-gun fire for most of the way, escaped across the Czeremosz (now Cheremosh) River into Romania.

What the Poles could have done to avert this disaster is hard to imagine. They could claim a victory of sorts: Their army was fighting a fierce delaying action, still waiting for the British and French to open a second front. But after issuing a declaration of war on September 3, the Western Allies did not fire a shot in Poland's defense; despite their pledges of support, despite the huge numerical advantage they enjoyed in the west, the long-promised offensive never came. Once again Hitler's intuition seemed remarkable; this was precisely the response he had expected.

On September 16, with their capital in flames and their government in flight, the Poles were about to encounter yet another devastating blow: a stab in the back from the east. While twenty-five Polish divisions made last-ditch stands on three large battlefields—at the Bzura River northeast of Łódź, near Tomaszów Lubelski between the Vistula and Bug rivers and on the outskirts on Lwów in southeastern Poland—the Red Army had massed for the coup de grace.

At this moment, even though the Poles were hemmed in by the Wehrmacht, they were far from capitulating. Mobilization was still under way despite the disruptions at the outset caused by last-minute Allied diplomatic maneuvers and the pandemonium caused by the German invasion. Hundreds of thousands of Polish reservists were still milling about train depots and at military installations, waiting to be moved to one of the fighting fronts. Horribly tangled or nonexistent lines of communication made it impossible for many of these men to find their units, and the High Command was hard pressed to use the disorganized mass to plug even the most obvious gaps on the major fronts. Any chance the Poles had to get these men into action ended with the intervention of the Red Army, which came just as German supply lines were stretched dangerously and munition supplies dipped to the point of exhaustion.

Just as Hitler had done on September 1, Stalin resorted to a transparent excuse as justification for sending his troops across the border. He was anxious to avoid being identified with German aggression, and hoped to portray the Red Army's intervention to Soviet citizens as an action to protect the Ukrainians and Byelorussians in eastern Poland from the German advance. Stalin was surprised by the Wehrmacht's rapid progress, and his delay in sending troops into eastern Poland soon led to rising concerns in Berlin. At one point Molotov advised the German ambassador in Moscow that intervention by the Red Army would be explained publicly as a step necessary to safeguard the interests of Ukrainians and Byelorussians. Berlin objected to such an explanation, suggesting instead that the two powers issue a joint communiqué excusing the invasion as a police action to restore order in Poland. Fearing that he would be too closely identified with Hitler, Stalin rejected this proposal. Finally, he decided to use the fuzzy excuse that the action was necessary to prevent third parties from capitalizing on the public disorder in Poland. Molotov told the Germans that intervention could not otherwise be explained to the Soviet or world public.

At 2:15 A.M. on September 17, the Polish ambassador to Moscow, Waclaw Grzybowski, was still fiddling with his radio dial hoping for late-breaking news from home when his telephone rang with an ominous summons to a 3:00 A.M. meeting at the Ministry of Foreign Affairs. The arriving ambassador was not even offered a chair to cushion the shock as a virtual death sentence was read on his country. The brusque note he heard, signed by Molotov, asserted that "the Polish State has ceased to exist." The Red Army, it continued, was crossing the Polish frontier to stretch out "a brotherly hand . . . to extricate the Polish people from the unfortunate war into which they were dragged by their unwise leaders, and to enable them to live a peaceful life." The stunned ambassador recovered enough to refuse Molotov's warped concoction, but by 8:00 A.M. Radio Moscow had announced that units of the Red Army were moving into eastern Poland.

That morning small planes flew over eastern Poland dropping leaflets signed by General Semyon Timoshenko, Red Army commander in chief for the Ukrainian front, telling Polish soldiers:

> Soldiers, what is left to you? What are you fighting for? Against whom are you fighting? Why do you risk your lives? Your resistance is useless.

Your officers are light-heartedly driving you to slaughter. They hate you and your families. They shot your negotiators [sic] whom you sent to us with a proposal of surrender. [A completely confusing statement since Soviet intervention was unexpected, and war had neither been threatened nor declared.]

Do not trust your officers! Your officers and generals are your enemies. They wish your death. Soldiers, turn on your officers and generals! Do not submit to the orders of your officers. Drive them out from your soil. Come to us boldly, to your brothers, to the Red Army. Here you will be cared for, here you will be respected.

Remember that the Red Army will liberate the Polish people from the fatal war and after that you will be able to begin a new life.

Believe us, the Red Army of the Soviet Union is your only friend.

Conditioned by centuries of deep distrust and dislike for the Russians, the Polish rank and file were not swayed by this typically Bolshevik class-line appeal. In many areas, however, advanced units of the Red Army spread the rumor that they were coming to Poland's aid in the fight against Germany. Since the Poles were cut off from their main command centers, with no way to clarify the situation, confusion prevailed. Some Polish units passively agreed to turn over their weapons, while others, such as the Frontier Defense Corps, offered stubborn resistance.

With its promises of freedom fluttering from the skies, the Red Army's main thrust west began along the Dniester River in southeastern Poland above the Romanian border (an area that today is part of the Ukraine). Its primary objective was to cut off the Poles' main escape route. In northeastern Poland, above the Pripet Marshes, large numbers of Soviet troops were pouring across the Niemen River on a wide front. Along the entire frontier of more than five hundred miles, thirty infantry divisions, twelve mechanized brigades, and ten cavalry divisions of the Red Army were on the move. Under the weight of this second avalanche, all semblance of an organized Polish resistance began to collapse.

The mop-up operations continued through the last half of September and into early October. Warsaw did not finally capitulate until September 28, with many parts of the city still burning out of control. The Royal Castle, the Cathedral of St. John, and the Old Town overlooking the Vistula at this point were reduced to rubble. The last Polish unit still fighting surrendered at Kock on October 5.

The blitzkrieg cost the Germans fifty thousand casualties and about a third of their tanks and planes. In contrast, more than sixty thousand Polish fighting men perished and another 140,000 were wounded. Many more civilians were killed and wounded. The Germans took 587,000 prisoners, who were fanned out to a large number of makeshift barbed-wire compounds set up for new prisoners of war. On September 28, a second German-Soviet treaty was signed that partitioned Poland along the Bug and the San rivers. Under the agreement, the Germans kept central Poland and turned Lithuania over to the Soviets. The Wehrmacht had penetrated well to the east of Bug in many places, but withdrew in accordance with the revised agreement.

At the expenditure of fewer than a thousand lives, the Soviets gained more than a third of what formerly had been Poland. More than 230,000 Polish soldiers, including at least eight thousand officers, were captured. Their status remained unclear since war was never declared.

On September 18, one day after the Red Army crossed the Polish border, a *New York Times* editorial denounced the attack:

> Germany having killed the prey, Soviet Russia will seize that part of the carcass that Germany cannot use. It will play the noble role of hyena to the German lion. . . . Hitlerism is brown Communism; Stalinism is Red Fascism. The world will now understand that the only real ideological issue is one between democracy, liberty, and peace on the one hand and despotism, peril, and war on the other.

These sentiments were representative of world opinion's overwhelming sympathy for the Poles and impotent outrage at the aggressors as the carving of the carcass began.

The Poles gave a good account of themselves in the September campaign, despite the farfetched notion that their defense consisted mainly of brave but hopeless cavalry charges against modern German tanks. Many German generals scorned the Polish High Command, but they had a high regard for the Polish fighting man. Despite the disadvantages of overwhelming German superiority in manpower and equipment, the unfortunate deployment of their troops, and the late mobilization, the Poles still held out for five weeks against a new form of warfare that no one, as it turned out, was prepared for. In the spring of 1940, when the Germans unleased their blitzkrieg in the west, they were outnumbered by the French, British, Belgians, and Dutch in men, tanks, and aircraft. There, they could not attack from three sides simultaneously as they had in Poland. Yet the Wehrmacht's victory in the west took only three weeks longer than the conquest of Poland. Without Soviet intervention, the Poles no doubt would have held out even longer.

The conflict has often been dismissed as a mere eighteen-day war in which the Germans achieved their objectives virtually unscathed. On September 18, 1939, the Wehrmacht and the Red Army staged a joint victory parade in Brest Litovsk, where twenty-one years earlier a barely organized Bolshevik government had signed an ignominious peace with Germany and made its exit from World War I. Now General Guderian, whose panzers were the spearpoint of the blitzrieg, sat on the reviewing stand; beside him were Soviet commanders whose troops, as the *New York Times* editorial said, would serve as hyena to the German lion. In important respects the celebration was premature. Wehrmacht casualties were far from over. Three fourths of the German casualties in Poland would be sustained by Army Group South—and more of its men would fall after the parade than before it.

Despite Poland's military collapse, the nation's legal continuity was preserved. When the Soviets invaded on September 17, the government's highest civilian authorities crossed the border into Romania in order to continue the struggle and represent Polish interests abroad. The Romanians interned Foreign Minister Beck, who was caught attempting to escape on October 21, 1939, using a British passport. It was clear that Beck's policies had failed and that new leadership was required. The Polish constitution delegated war powers to the president, which made it possible for him to appoint his successor. President Ignacy Mościcki used these powers to name Władysław Raczkiewicz, chairman of the World Association of Poles Abroad and a former speaker of the Senate, then in Paris, as the new president of Poland. On September 30, Raczkiewicz assumed the post and then named General Władysław Sikorski prime minister and commander in chief. Sikorski's army division had performed with great distinction in the 1920 Russo-Polish War. From 1924 to 1925, he had served as minister of war. In 1926 he left the army in protest over Piłsudski's coup. Gradually, he had emerged as Piłsudski's most important rival. By 1939, he was the most outspoken opponent of Beck. Before his untimely death in a plane crash in 1943, he would establish himself as one of the most effective leaders of World War II.

Sikorski's first action was to organize a truly representative coalition government from four major prewar opposition groups: the National, Peasant, Socialist, and Christian Labor Parties. He immediately dissolved the prewar parliament and formed a new one with the famous pianist Ignacy Jan Paderewski as its titular head. Then nearly eighty, Paderewski donated his fortune to the fight for Polish independence.

The transition from Piłsudski's authoritarian legacy to representative power sharing caused many stresses in the new Polish government.

The shock and trauma of defeat put the Piłsudski faction decidedly on the defensive. The methods it had employed to preserve the legality of the Polish government were severely criticized. Although the Poles themselves did not question the new government's legitimacy, there were vehement internal arguments about its composition and policies. Later the Soviets would claim that it was made up of "fascists" and lacked legitimacy with the Polish people.

The government's flight to Romania was not a total disaster. Almost $80 million worth of the nation's gold reserves, which might have fallen into Nazi hands, was whisked to safety, initially in Istanbul and then to Dakar in the part of French West Africa that is now Senegal. When France fell in the summer of 1940, the gold was later shipped to Canada and then to London. These important resources afforded the Polish government-in-exile a degree of financial autonomy that it otherwise would not have had.

Earlier in the year, the Poles had whisked an even more important possession to safety. It was a decoding device developed in the late 1930s by mathematicians at the University of Poznań, and capable of reading the Germans' complex "Enigma" machine. The historian Paul Kennedy later described it as "one of the greatest contributions to the eventual Allied victory."

CHAPTER 5

Capture

❮❮❮❮❮❮❮❮❮❮

Magda Czarnek is unsure what happened to her father in the days immediately following the Luftwaffe train-strafing. Minutes after the September 3 attack, Dr. Czarnek bade a painful farewell to his family and left. Magda has vivid memories of him shrinking into the distance as he walked east alone that day, beside the railroad track, which was severed in both directions. The orders in his pocket told him to join the Polish Army Health Service in Lwów, the largest city in eastern Poland, by the fifth day of mobilization. How far he got, what happened next was unclear. But Magda knew how to find out. "Our cousin Staszek [who shared her brother's first name and was her father's nephew] will know," she told me. "He and my father met each other accidentally somewhere between Kraków and Lwów during that first week of September. They were together for several weeks after that. I'm sure he will have the details."

A few weeks later, while in Poland, I took the express train south from Warsaw to Kraków to see Staszek Niewiadomski, a retired physician living near the center of the city. Magda had arranged everything. Dr. Niewiadomski spoke no English, so Magda asked her eighteen-year-old niece, Natalia, a student at the Jagiellonian University, to provide translation. Natalia and I arrived promptly for our 8:00 P.M. appointment at 35 Siemiracki Street, a once-elegant turn-of-the-century building now crusted, like most of downtown Kraków, by pollution. Dr. Niewiadomski welcomed us on an expansive landing at the top of the first flight of stairs. His bearing and appearance were patrician. He was tall, slender, and ramrod straight, with high arching eyebrows and a thin, trimly manicured mustache. At seventy-six, he seemed to be in excellent health. Inside the Niewiadomski apartment, the rooms were large. Its high ceilings, heavy furniture, and drapes of thick brocade emitted a formal, even stately atmosphere. We all sat over coffee at a large table in the center of the drawing room. Almost immediately

37

Dr. Niewiadomski reached in his pocket and pulled out a small black book.

"My uncle would like for me to tell you that he kept a diary during the war." To my great satisfaction, I learned that the small black book was a compendium of personal experience, one man's record of the September campaign. With the detached approach one might expect of a medical man, he had charted in September 1939 the observable data about him: What the weather, food, and company were like; his first encounter with the enemy; the high degree of confusion in the civilian population; the boredom of endless waiting. All this he had recorded with painstaking care. And yes, he told me, he knew exactly what happened to Magda's father.

At the beginning Dr. Czarnek got nowhere. Like other important thoroughfares, the first highway he reached was choked with fleeing civilians, all straining for the Romanian border, all hoping to evade the onrushing Wehrmacht. To continue toward Lwów, there was nothing he could do except inch along with the mass of humanity heading east. Peasants, villagers, and city dwellers all shared the same road with every conceivable conveyance: carts drawn by horses and some drawn by people, bicycles, cars, trucks, even baby buggies. For the next two days the fifty-three-year-old physician walked, hitchhiked, and caught trains wherever the track was clear. When the September 5 deadline in his mobilization orders passed, he had reached Przemyśl, an important railroad junction 130 miles east of Kraków, but still more than fifty miles short of Lwów. He planned to press on, until hearing on the outskirts of Przemyśl that the speed of the German advance made it doubtful that the three thousand physicians and nurses of the health service could be organized in Lwów.

The country's transportation and communications infrastructure was collapsing fast. Instead of attempting to go on to Lwów, other physicians in Przemyśl were organizing a volunteer medical corps. The military situation was so unstable that no one seemed to know what could be organized, or how long they might function in such a vulnerable location. Przemyśl sat on the banks of the San River and served as a major railroad gateway through the Carpathians. In this position, the city lay directly in the path of General (later Field Marshal) Wilhelm List's Fourteenth Army, the right wing of German Army Group South, which was moving north and east from Slovakia toward Przemyśl.

The city was already in a high state of confusion when Dr. Czarnek arrived and sought out other physicians who were already setting up a voluntary health service. At the army command center, he learned that an important field hospital had been heavily damaged in a Luftwaffe bombing raid. Because of his experience in managing large military hospitals, the acting commander of the health service asked him to try to put the facility back in operation. Dr. Czarnek agreed to try.

It was at this point that he and Staszek Niewiadomski bumped into each other. Staszek had always been a great favorite of Dr. Czarnek's. He was known as a good doctor and a bit of a daredevil. After finishing medical school at the Jagiellonian University in 1934, Staszek had practiced in Kraków. He was an "air doctor" in the Polish air force reserves. His duties required that he provide medical care both in flight and on the ground. When general mobilization began on August 31, Staszek was sent immediately to Przemyśl, where an airfield was being put into operation. For several days he had been waiting there with a number of other pilots, but there was no sign of when the field would be operational. Moreover, because the Luftwaffe had gained control of the skies, no one knew when or if there would be planes to fly.

"Since you are stranded anyway, why not help me?" Dr. Czarnek had immediately asked Staszek, explaining his task of putting the field hospital back in operation. Staszek agreed and they immediately began work on the project. Two days later it was obvious that they had no chance to succeed. Bomb damage, a shortage of supplies, and the high state of confusion in Przemyśl presented overwhelming obstacles. It was clear that the facility could not be reopened in the foreseeable future.

A lack of time had doomed their task from the outset. They had hardly begun when, on September 8, all members of the voluntary medical service in Przemyśl were ordered to leave. The group included 263 physicians and 17 chemists, all of whom were to be evacuated toward Lwów. Kraków had fallen on September 6 and Przemyśl was almost certain to be overrun by the Wehrmacht any day. The physicians were told that an attempt would be made to set up the health service in Lwów, where a number of modern medical facilities were located. Casualties were mounting rapidly by the day. If the medical staff could not get to Lwów, the health service would be organized in Tarnopol (now Ternopol) another seventy miles east of Lwów on what was then the Soviet frontier. Tarnopol, well beyond the presumed path of the German army, was also an important rail junction and had a modern medical institute.

Most of the physicians left Przemyśl on foot. A few, including Staszek, rode in cars and trucks that the army assigned them to transport supplies. Only a few miles from Przemyśl, they learned that heavy fighting and severed transportation arteries would make it impossible to get to Lwów. Tarnopol was their new destination. On a direct line, it lay approximately 120 miles east. But no one, at this point, was traveling in a direct line. Over the next eight days, the column zig-zagged over back roads at an agonizing pace. These roads were most jammed of all as the flood of refugees funneled into Poland's southeast corner, attempting to cross the border into Romania. Reports of German atrocities caused widespread panic. The people along these roads were scrambling through a fast-closing trap door along the San River between the giant pincers of Guderian's panzers in the north and the *panzergruppe* spearhead of Army Group South under General Paul von Kleist. The physicians decided it was safest to travel at night to avoid random strafings by the Luftwaffe. But even at night progress in many places was so slow that the entire column often sat and waited for hours on end.

At 3:00 A.M. on September 17 the physicians came to yet another halt about five or six miles from Tarnopol. This time word came down the line that they could go no farther. Shortly afterward, a senior officer personally walked back along the convoy with a startling order: "Gentlemen, the Soviets are coming to help us. Do not shoot! You will be asked to give up your weapons. Hand your weapons over as requested."

A half hour later Soviet T-26 tanks and armored personnel carriers came rumbling up. Several of these vehicles were flying white flags. Soviet soldiers began passing along the line, ordering the physicians and chemists out to give up their weapons. Most of the Poles were unarmed. A few carried revolvers, but because of their deep suspicion of the Soviets, many quickly tossed their weapons into the weeds along the roadside. Staszek carried his pistol, not an army issue. He hated to give it up, but wisely threw it away. One man concealed a pistol in his clothes. It was a mistake he may later have paid for with his life.

Within minutes it was obvious that the Soviets were not coming to help the Poles but to capture them. Soviet soldiers quickly moved into position about ten paces apart. Their bayonets were fixed. A few even carried a rifle in each hand. Grenades dangled from the belts of most of the Soviet soldiers. While the Poles stood at attention, the Soviets moved quickly up and down the line demanding watches, pocket-knives, and other personal possessions. Orders were loudly barked. Word quickly spread that the column was proceeding on foot to a nearby brickyard. Just as they left, there was a chilling warning: Anyone straying out of formation would be shot on the spot.

As the column began to move, the guards suddenly started firing their weapons in the air, urging and coercing the Poles into a double-time trot. Before leaving the truck, Staszek had hidden his watch inside one of his socks. As he ran, he was sure it would fall out, but somehow the timepiece kept its place. At the brickyard, the Poles were subjected to a thorough search. The hidden pistol was quickly found. Its owner was roughly pushed aside, then marched toward the back of the brickyard. A few minutes later, shots were fired. The physicians were shocked. Had he been shot for something so minor? No one was sure. But Staszek and Dr. Czarnek never saw him again.

Dr. Czarnek, Staszek, and their fellow physicians stayed in the brickyard for three days without food. Their only source of water was a single spigot. On September 20, the men were all herded to Tarnopol prison for interrogation; in the process, Staszek and Dr. Czarnek were separated. Questions, questions, and more questions from the Soviet secret police, the NKVD (People's Commissariat of Internal Affairs). What, they wanted to know, was Staszek's true rank? His papers, hastily issued when he volunteered on the eve of the German invasion, had not clearly designated his rank. In truth he was a second lieutenant. Yet his uniform bore the insignia of a cadet. The NKVD officer conducting the investigation could not decide whether Staszek should be classified as an officer or a cadet. Finally, he decided to return Staszek to the group as a cadet.

As he left, Staszek asked why he and the other physicians were being treated like prisoners. "Your government has not issued a declaration of war against us," he told the NKVD officer. "You really have no right to arrest me!"

"Get out of here, you fool," the NKVD officer shot back. "You are all prisoners of war."

After their interrogation, most of the physicians were marched toward the Soviet border. Staszek and a few others were driven at 3:00 A.M. on September 22 from the Tarnopol prison to meet the column of marching physicians near the Soviet frontier. They crossed the border around 6:00 P.M. the next day. At this point, Staszek and Dr. Czarnek had rejoined each other. They discussed the interrogation incident in detail. Both fully agreed that it was foolish to entertain further illusions that the Soviets were not mortal enemies.

Finally, there was food: a kilo loaf of bread for every five men and something called *kipiatok* by the Russians. *Kipiatok* was nothing but boiling water, drunk straight or with tea when available. Despite their intense hunger, the physicians ceremoniously divided each loaf of bread into five equal portions. Their spirits remained high.

Then they waited almost two days at a small railroad station on the
Soviet side of the border. On September 24, Staszek wrote in his diary:
"It is a nice Sunday. The whole of September has been spectacular.
Departure from Woloczyska [Volochisk]. By train, direction unknown,
into Russia." Later, under heavy guard, the group boarded freight cars,
sixty men to a car, for a slow trip east. A large number of Soviet guards
rode in passenger carriages; and, as an added precaution, one guard
was stationed on top of each wagon containing prisoners. Before departure, a grim-faced NKVD officer told the Poles that periodic rest stops
would be made and that anyone who strayed more than a few steps
from the trackside would be shot. He gave no hint of direction.

"These men are primitive, but if we stay calm, they won't be quite
as rough," Dr. Czarnek confided to Staszek.

Behind the sullen stares exchanged by the Soviet guards and Polish
prisoners lurked old and deeply felt animosities caused by centuries of
friction and conflict between their two countries—irreconcilable foes
who sought on many occasions to dominate each other. In 1611, at
their political zenith, their country then the largest in Europe, the
Poles occupied the Kremlin and burned much of Moscow. The Russians
exacted a large measure of revenge from the end of the eighteenth
century to the end of World War I when, except for a few years during
the Napoleonic conquests, they ruled Warsaw and a large part of
Poland, brutally repressing periodic uprisings and exiling thousands of
Poles to years of forced labor in Siberia and other remote parts of
Russia.

The Russians' and the Poles' common Slavic heritage developed a
deep fissure during the long struggle for ascendancy over Christianity
between the popes of Rome and the patriarchs of Constantinople. The
stage was set for a split when the emperor Constantine founded a new
capital of the Holy Roman Empire at Byzantium in 330. While the
Eastern church flourished, the papacy began a long period of decline.
Its revival in the Middle Ages brought Christianity in its Latin form
to Poland in 966; and gradually Poland became the easternmost
defender of the Western faith. In contrast, Russia was Christianized by
the Eastern, or Orthodox church, which spread its way north along the
great river systems of the Eurasian land mass. By the time Constantinople fell to the Turks in 1453, the metropolitan of Moscow had become
the most powerful figure in the Eastern church. Soon thereafter, Moscow proclaimed itself the third and last Rome.

Because of their Western orientation, the Poles' political, economic, and cultural development was much more rapid. They had produced an elected monarch in 1385, established its first bicameral parliament in 1493, and articulated the principle of "nothing new about us without us" (a forerunner of "no taxation without representation") in their constitution of 1505. From the fifteenth to the seventeenth century, the grain trade along the Vistula River was one of Europe's most profitable. A Polish astronomer, Nicolaus Copernicus, shattered Christian dogma and propelled the rise of modern science by publishing in 1543 his demonstration that the earth rotated around the sun. The Renaissance, with its new intellectual freedom, brought to Poland a burst of artistic expression in painting, music, and literature.

But the sea change that swept over Western Europe between 1400 and 1600 barely touched Russia, which remained inward-looking and transfixed by Orthodox piety. Modernization did not begin in earnest in Russia until 1697, when Peter the Great personally conducted members of his court on a tour of several European capitals to observe technological and economic development in the West and to recruit Western artisans and technicians.

These divergent paths of development profoundly affected how the Poles and the Russians felt about each other. To the Poles, the Russians were a backward and inferior people, as evidenced by the fact that Polish had served as the language of culture and refinement at the Russian court in the sixteenth and seventeenth centuries. During this same period, Poland was one of the great powers of Europe, before a long period of decline precipitated by costly wars, erosion in the strength of the central government, changes in land tenure, and prolonged agricultural depression. Poland's decline ran parallel to Russia's rise to great-power status in the eighteenth century, but it brought about little or no decline in the hubris and condescension that characterized Polish attitudes toward the Russians.

As real differences in relative development became more and more obvious, the Russian sense of inferiority not only grew, it also engendered essentially defensive Russian explanations and reactions. The Poles, according to the Russians, were decadent materialists who had succumbed to rampant Western hedonism. In becoming oriented toward the West, they also had betrayed the ideal of pan-Slavic union, a nebulous concept of Russian nationhood as the mechanism for achieving Slavic unity. Worst of all, the Poles, according to the Russians, were schismatics who, in accepting the pope as their ecclesiastical leader, had turned their backs on the real Vicar of Christ—the metropolitan of Moscow. This defensiveness was reflected, to a degree, in the work of great Russian authors such as Count Leo Tolstoy and Feodor Dostoyevsky, who portrayed a Russia anchored in the innocence and simplicity of its peasantry as the healthy core of Europe.

Even the nations' languages reflected a common Slavic heritage with divergent paths of development. Written Russian and Polish bear no similiarity. St. Cyril had derived the Russian characters from the Greek alphabet, while Polish had evolved from the Latin alphabet. Yet in spoken form the two languages are quite similar—so much so that the general sense of the Russian guards' orders could be understood by the Polish prisoners as they boarded the train on September 24.

The nine-day journey took Dr. Czarnek and his nephew Staszek four hundred miles, to the settlement of Kozelshchina, between Poltava and Kharkov many miles east of the Dnieper River. The Poles were permitted to leave the train infrequently, generally once a day or less. The heavy guard continued, with soldiers stationed approximately ten paces apart at trackside. The subsistence diet of bread and *kipiatok* did not change. Acute hunger prompted a few prisoners to exchange watches with peasants for fruits and vegetables. One prisoner traded a timepiece for a watermelon, which he cut into small slices and passed among his companions.

The settlement of Kozelshchina was nothing more than a compound surrounded by barbed wire. It was one of more than a hundred transition camps set up by Soviets where Poles captured during the September war were interned before being distributed to the forced-labor camps of the gulag system. Inside the compound at Kozelshchina were the barns and outbuildings of a collective farm. Together with a neighboring Orthodox church built at the end of the first millennium after Christ, the whole place had been converted into a temporary prison camp. When the physicians marched in, fifteen thousand Polish soldiers were already present. All were assigned quarters in accordance with class-conscious Marxist dogma. In the farmhouses and church— the most comfortable quarters of all—stayed ordinary soldiers. Several thousand officers and policemen were sleeping in tents. The Bolsheviks considered the physicians to be bourgeois exploiters of the working class, so they were assigned to a large, dilapidated shed where pigs had once been housed. There the physicians slept on the floor, packed so tightly together that turning or shifting during the night was almost impossible. The physicians grumbled that apparently the Bolsheviks considered the pigsty unsuitable for pigs, but plenty good enough for Polish officers.

Boredom quickly became the dominant feature of camp life. The physicians stamped in the early morning cold for hours as two Soviet guards conduced a cumbersome roll call. As each man's name was called, he replied by giving his birthdate and the name of his father. Each of the guards laboriously wrote this information down. They then exchanged the information for what seemed like endless checking and rechecking.

"I know why this is taking so long," Staszek joked to Dr. Czarnek early one morning. "They can't read each other's writing."

Religious services were banned, although Father J. L. Ziołkowski, a chaplain who held the rank of major, organized one secret Mass. Father Ziołkowski had the appearance of a soldier, not a clergyman. He was of peasant origin and radiated an unshakable inner faith that appealed to Staszek and Dr. Czarnek. He would later play a prominent role in the religious life of many of the Polish officers once they were moved to a more permanent place of internment.

The Soviets divided the men into mess squadrons, which were responsible for preparing their own food. With the addition of salt fish and cereals, camp provisions were markedly improved over those provided en route. The doctors set about building a makeshift kitchen from scrap materials, and had cooked only a few meals when word spread that theirs was the best food in camp. Other officers began showing up at mealtime at the hog shed, which soon became a center of camp social life.

On one occasion the hog shed received a supply of obviously tainted herring. The hungry men were extremely reluctant to forgo an important component of their regular food allowance, but were also afraid that eating the fish could cause food poisoning. They were about to dispose of the herring when Dr. Czarnek was struck with an inspiration: Soak the fish in potassium permanganate, he said. The solution was a standard disinfectant in Eastern Europe and the physicians had brought large quantities with them. His colleagues readily agreed; the fish were soaked, and the hog shed dined without complaint or after-effects on the tainted herring.

Dr. Czarnek's nerves were worn severely by the idle time. Coupled with the deplorable living conditions, it prompted him to propose the organization of a health clinic. He approached camp authorities with the idea, and within a short time a few medicines and dental extractors were delivered to the hog shed. These were of no use in combating a rampant infestation of lice, the prisoners' greatest cause of discomfort. Their cramped sleeping arrangement offered some protection against the October cold, but it also offered a hospitable environment for the parasites. Finally, after much urging, the camp administration delivered insecticides and several huge wooden boxes with iron tops in which delousing baths could be provided. A mass bathing operation followed under the painstaking supervision of Dr. Czarnek, and the problem abated considerably.

The problem of Staszek's rank—whether to classify him as an officer or an enlisted man—surfaced again soon after his arrival in camp. He insisted that he held the rank of second lieutenant, but because his uniform indicated otherwise, the Soviets made a final determination to list him as a cadet. Staszek was disappointed with the decision, but his spirits quickly soared when he learned, toward the end of October, that he might be sent back to Poland. Rumors were circulating that the Soviets and Germans were exchanging captives. The Soviets apparently were planning to turn over prisoners from German-occupied Poland, and the Germans planned to reciprocate by returning their captives from the Russian-occupied zone. There were reports that the exchange would take place near the Bug River, the demarcation line between the German and Soviet zones of occupation.

The rumors were confirmed in the last week of October when Staszek and five others—all from the area controlled by the newly designated German General Government, and all newly classified as cadets—were called together and told by a Soviet officer, "We are going to let you go home, but we don't know what the Germans will do to you."

On October 27, while he waited to be taken to the transport, Staszek met Dr. Czarnek for the last time. They speculated about why the exchange involved cadets and enlisted men but no officers.

"They must be planning to send you later," Staszek said.

"I'll be coming back soon," Dr. Czarnek replied. "Be sure to tell Janina that I'm fine—that actually I'm doing quite well under the circumstances."

They smiled and shook hands. Staszek hesitated for a moment and said, "Be sure to keep warm." He tugged at his uncle's thick navy sweater, which he had given Dr. Czarnek a few days earlier.

"I know. The winter lasts forever," Dr. Czarnek replied. "I am glad you are getting out of this godforsaken place."

The sudden commotion of commands barked in German and heavy footsteps in the corridor brought an instant, nervous hush to Magda Czarnek's classroom a few days later. Whispered warnings of "Police!"

swept instantly from desk to desk. Her lesson preempted, the teacher made a calming motion to the twenty or more thirteen-year-old school-girls before her, ordering them to stay in their seats. In the uneasy quiet that followed, all eyes strained toward the door, but it never opened. The bedlam beyond, loud as an evacuation drill, continued. Then, as quickly as it began, the noise stopped.

The students wondered aloud if classes were being suspended. A few weeks earlier, the Germans had taken over their prestigious high school, turning the impressive new building into an army barracks. A few days later, classes reopened at Jagiellonian University, which had been shut down by German authorities. There were rumors that all Polish schools would soon be closed. The cause of the commotion was clear moments after the noise subsided. Rushing to the classroom windows, the girls were shocked to see large German army trucks parked on the sidewalks between flower beds. Climbing aboard were members of the university faculty, who were soon hauled away.

Within minutes an explanation buzzed through the building: German authorities had summoned the faculty to a meeting on the pretext that their views would be solicited on procedures to be used in reopening the university. Many of the professors felt a professional responsibility to attend and provide input. Once they arrived, they were arrested and herded away. In all, 183 were taken. Later it was learned that they had been taken to Sachsenhausen Concentration Camp, near Berlin, where most perished.

A neighbor of the Czarneks, Dr. Feliks Kopera, a professor of art history and chief curator of the National Musuem of Art, narrowly avoided arrest. Kopera, a Catholic, began dressing to attend the meeting, but his Jewish wife insisted that the Germans had set a trap. She made her case so convincingly that he finally agreed not to go. Hours later, he learned what had happened to his colleagues, that his wife's fears were well founded.

Mrs. Kopera was a classmate of Dr. Czarnek's in medical school. A close friendship between the Koperas and the Czarneks developed in the years that followed. Dr. Kopera died of natural causes before the war ended, but his wife survived the conflict without moving from their elegant villa only a few blocks from the Czarnek apartment.

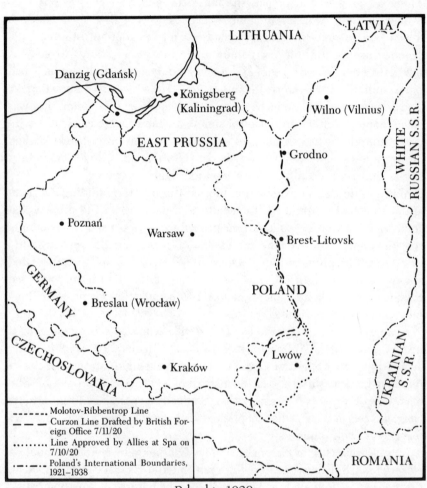

LITHUANIA

LATVIA

Danzig (Gdańsk)

• Königsberg
(Kaliningrad)

• Wilno (Vilnius)

EAST PRUSSIA

WHITE
RUSSIAN S.S.R.

• Grodno

• Poznań

Warsaw •

• Brest-Litovsk

POLAND

GERMANY

• Breslau (Wrocław)

CZECHOSLOVAKIA

Lwów •

UKRAINIAN
S.S.R.

• Kraków

- - - - - Molotov-Ribbentrop Line
- - - Curzon Line Drafted by British Foreign Office 7/11/20
. . . . Line Approved by Allies at Spa on
7/10/20
- . - . - . Poland's International Boundaries,
1921–1938

ROMANIA

Poland in 1939

CHAPTER 6

Diabolical Schemes

<<<<<<<<<<<

To the Bolsheviks, Dr. Czarnek epitomized the enemy. Many aspects of his background made it unlikely that he would ever leave the land he had called a "godforsaken place." His status as a high-ranking officer in a capitalist army made him a "political criminal." As a professional he was considered "antiworker." His high standard of living made him "bourgeois" and a "social danger." His conservative views typed him as an "enemy of the people." Even his trips abroad suggested contact with foreign spies. These were all offenses that placed his life in jeopardy. But one last "crime" sealed Dr. Czarnek's doom. In 1920, he had fought in the Russo-Polish War. This made him a "world counterrevolutionary" and an object of revenge.

What made this offense so important? On the night of the World War I armistice, Churchill told prime minister David Lloyd George: "The war of the giants has ended; the quarrel of the pygmies has begun." A generation after the last shots were fired, it was virtually forgotten by all but the combatants. Yet the origins of the Russo-Polish War and its outcome explained much about Poland's downfall in 1939, about Dr. Czarnek's fate and that of the 250,000 other Polish prisoners who sat that autumn in Soviet transition camps.

Interwar Poland had risen from the ashes of three empires that collapsed in exhaustion at the end of World War I. The eastern front in that conflict had raged back and forth over Polish soil, causing much destruction. More than a million Polish soldiers had been forced to fight on one side or the other. Men from areas partitioned by Russia fought for the czar and the Western Alliance. Others, from territory partitioned by the Austrian and German empires, fought for the Central Powers.

The first hints that Poland might be reborn began to glimmer in 1915. At that point, the Central Powers had driven the Russians out of Warsaw and the rest of czarist Poland. The ethnic Poles now found themselves reassembled under one rule, albeit still foreign. The military allegiance of a united Poland was potentially decisive. First Russia promised limited independence. Then, in 1916, the Central Powers proclaimed a Polish kingdom without defining its frontiers or naming a monarch. In January 1917, with the United States yet to enter the war, President Woodrow Wilson told Congress that an independent Poland with access to the Baltic must be established. This proposal later became Point Thirteen of his famous Fourteen Points. Britain, France, and Italy all backed the general notion of independence for the Poles.

The bidding for the Poles' allegiance introduced a touchy question: What frontiers should the new nation have? An independent Poland had not existed since 1795. Yet in their past, the Poles had ruled a vast part of Central Europe. Polish political institutions were broadly appealing. Polish nobility ruled many parts of Byelorussia, the Ukraine, and as far east as Smolensk, deep into Russia itself. In many of these areas, Polish had been the language of elegance and refinement for centuries. Important cities like Lwów (now Lvov), Pińsk (now Pinsk), and Wilno (now Vilnius) were islands of Polish culture surrounded by an ethnic amalgamation. The cities and countryside were interlaced with a high percentage of all the Jews of the European continent. Under the old empires, they had developed a largely autonomous but separate society. Sprinkled into the ethnographic stew were Germans who had scattered thinly over a wide swath from the Baltic to the Black Sea as colonists and industrialists. As if all these complexities in the east were not enough, in many areas on the western edge of historic Poland Germans were heavily concentrated and tended to dominate commerce. The old empires provided a structure that permitted ethnic diversity, but they barely kept a lid on a constant bubble of animosities resulting from struggles for political power and racial or ethnic identity. Against this diversity and competition, new Polish frontiers were formulated at the end of World War I.

Even the Poles could not decide where their frontiers belonged. For several years prior to independence, two core ideas dominated their debate on this question. One was the concept of an ethnically united nation state, a "Poland for the Poles." Its chief proponent was Roman Dmowski, leader of the conservative National Democrats, whose ideas were particularly offensive to Jews. At the other end of the spectrum was a concept proposed by the revolutionary faction of the Socialist Party, led by Józef Piłsudski. It envisioned a Polish-led multinational federation that would accommodate the region's ethnic diversity and stretch from Finland almost to the Black Sea. In many ways the proposed federation represented a revival of the pluralistic Polish empire that had dominated Eastern Europe in the fifteenth and sixteenth centuries.

In seeking Poland's rebirth, Dmowski and Piłsudski followed strategies that were as different as the ideas they advocated. Dmowski spent his life abroad cultivating foreign support, lobbying the statesmen of the Triple Entente in the belief that his "Poland for the Poles" eventually could emerge as a true partner with Russia. While Dmowski emphasized persuasion and diplomacy, Piłsudski relied on military force and organization from within. At one point he financed revolutionary activities with the spectacular robbery of a czarist mail train. Later, he moved to the part of Poland held by the Austrians, where there was less repression of Polish independence activity. There he organized a paramilitary gun club, later known as the Legions, and trained its members as future officers of an army to rid the country of its oppressors. Piłsudski saw socialism as the right path for Poland, but had no use for the Russian strain of international revolution.

Larger events overtook the debate late in 1918. The position of the Central Powers began to unravel in October, when soldiers in the Austro-Hungarian army simply packed their bags and headed for home. A fleet mutiny in Germany quickly spread to the cities. Revolutionary riots broke out in Berlin. German soldiers in Warsaw began forming Soviet-style councils. All this came, of course, on the heels of the Russian revolution. The Red plague seemed to be spreading to the industrial West. Amid the turmoil, the great powers agreed to an armistice on November 11, 1918. That decision left German authorities in Warsaw in an explosive situation. Polish independence was now inevitable, but anarchy threatened. A hasty exit from Warsaw was the safest German option. At the time, Piłsudski was at Magdeburg Fortress, imprisoned for refusing to swear an oath of brotherhood in arms to the German and Austrian armies. The Germans knew that Piłsudski was the one man with enough stature to control the situation. On November 10, 1918, one day before the armistice was signed, they released him, hoping that he would cooperate with them if he became head of the Polish state. In *God's Playground*, his excellent history of Poland, Norman Davies captures the atmosphere of Piłsudski's accession to power:

> He proposed to the German Command that they should simply lay down their arms and take the first train out, before civil commotion erupted.

The Germans readily agreed. Hardened stormtroopers handed over their rifles to schoolboys. The Citadel was abandoned to a gang of youths. . . . In truth, Piłsudski's appointment was neither "legal" nor "illegal." He had arrived in Warsaw from prison and exile with no precise knowledge of what he would find. Like Lenin in Petrograd the previous year, he had "found power lying in the street." As he stooped to pick it up, the Polish phoenix fluttered from the ashes of war which lay at his feet.

Three months later, in February 1919, the Germans also withdrew their troops from the Eastern Front, relinquishing large parts of Lithuania, Byelorussia, and the Ukraine. In the vacuum created by their departure, skirmishes broke out almost immediately between Polish and Bolshevik forces. In April 1919, Piłsudski seized on the situation to take his hometown, Wilno, and Minsk, the capital of Byelorussia. Months earlier, at the first sign of the German collapse, the Ukrainians attempted to capture the city of Lwów and eastern Galicia. The hostilities lasted from 1918 to 1919. During that time, the city's large Polish majority repulsed the attackers and eventually drove them east of the Zbrucz (Zbruch) River. To the south, the departing Germans had set up a new Ukrainian government. Piłsudski then turned his forces toward Kiev and forced that government to concede eastern Galicia to Poland despite its large Ukrainian majority. Over the next year, Polish military successes seemed to substantially increase prospects that Piłsudski's concept of federation might succeed.

These results set off alarm bells in Moscow and in Paris, where the Versailles Peace Conference had begun in January 1919. To Lenin and other prominent Soviet leaders it was suddenly apparent that Piłsudski could pose a threat to their own revolution. They were trying desperately to consolidate their hold on the czar's empire, yet provinces on its western edge were breaking away. The Bolsheviks complained that Piłsudski had responded to their friendly gestures on the question of Polish independence with menacing rhetoric and military aggression. In the flush of success, the Poles hinted to the Western statesmen that if German war matériel were put at their disposal they could take Moscow in a month. Poland, they promised, was the dam that would hold back the Red tide. Their capture of Kiev on May 7, 1920, made these boasts seem realistic.

The Poles' quick victories had gained them no appreciation in the West. Statesmen in Paris were appalled by the expansionist actions of the upstart state. A flood of Polish spokesmen had descended on the peace conference in January 1919 with many conflicting claims. Their presence would later prompt Count Carlo Sforza, the Italian foreign minister, to comment that "according to [the Poles] half Europe had been Polish and might become Polish again." The Allies were further dismayed by the border conflicts that were erupting on all sides of Poland. The country faced obvious domestic difficulties. It had inherited six currencies, four official army languages, different railway gauges, and three legal codes. To make war on all fronts in the midst of such difficulties seemed impossible. Often the Allies unfairly blamed the Poles, ignoring the fact that a power vacuum on all sides forced the Poles to fight for their survival. Concerns about the "Polish problem" prompted Western statesmen to attempt a succession of commissions, token military expeditions, and plebiscites. The failure of these actions contributed to a general souring in Western attitudes toward the new nation.

Shortly after the capture of Kiev, Polish fortunes plummeted. The threat from the "Whites" had begun to subside and the Soviets were finally free to turn their attention westward. Finding that Piłsudski's lines of communication and supply were greatly overextended, a cavalry force under General Semyon Budyonny quickly severed them. There began a Polish retreat that was as fast as the earlier advance. In pursuit was a huge Soviet army, assembled in the summer of 1920 under a remarkable young general, Mikhail N. Tukhachevsky, who was only twenty-seven at the time. Tukhachevsky pursued Piłsudski back toward the west, but stopped when he reached the frontier of ethnic Poland. The Politburo then faced a difficult decision: Should they risk overextending the Red Army supply and communication lines to further punish the Poles and, more importantly, carry their revolution into the heart of Western Europe? Stalin among others cautioned strongly against any further advance. He warned that fighting the Poles in Poland would be much harder than fighting them in the Ukraine. He also rejected Lenin's dream that Polish peasants and workers would flock to the Red banner, noting that "it is easier to saddle a cow than to establish communism in Poland." During this same period, he wrote Lenin proposing the establishment of a belt of states like Poland and Hungary under Soviet control. These were countries that according to Stalin would not agree to become Soviet republics. On the more immediate question of whether to advance, Lenin finally succumbed to the lure of igniting a truly international revolution. The attack against Poland proceeded with Tukhachevsky's ringing marching orders, signed on July 2, 1920: "Over the corpse of White Poland lies the road to worldwide conflagration."

While the Politburo was mulling strategy, the Poles had appealed for Western mediation. The Allied response was a proposal for a frontier along ethnic lines; it would run south from Grodno, east of Białystok, through Brest Litovsk (known to Poles as Brześć nad Bugiem), then along the Bug River, and finally south beyond Przemyśl to the Carpathians. This boundary, known as the Curzon Line because Lord George Curzon, the British foreign secretary, happened to convey the proposal to the Soviets in 1919, had been rejected the previous year by both sides. The Soviets now set extraordinary terms for their acceptance of the Curzon Line: Poland must become a communist satellite; its army must be reduced to fifty thousand men; and a militia of workers would provide for public order and safety in Poland. The Poles must also permit the Red Army to cross their territory at any time.

These terms were not acceptable to the Poles and were not intended to be. The proposal was then shelved until 1943, when an approximation of the line would be proposed as Poland's eastern frontier. Stalin would cleverly emphasize the line's British origins. But in 1943, he made no mention of the questionable manner in which the line had been drawn originally. Either through a clerical error in the British Foreign Office, or through intentional falsification, Lwów was placed on the Soviet side of the line. This "slip of the pen" was particularly galling to the Poles. The city's cultural identity was strongly Polish. In its long history as the halfway point on the trade route between the Black Sea and the Baltic, Lwów had never been under Russian rule. Yet at the end of World War II it became a part of the western Ukraine.

On July 28, 1920, Białystok became the first important Polish city to fall to the Soviets. Two large forces continued their advance west on a broad front. A group of armies in the north, under Tukhachevsky, the commander in chief, expected to seize Warsaw no later than August 12. A second group of southwestern armies, under General Alexander Yegorov with Stalin as commissar, veered south to capture Lwów because of its strategic importance and to guard against possible Romanian intervention. During the advance a dangerous gap opened between the forces under Tukhachevsky. On August 5, he demanded that Yegorov send reinforcements to protect his left flank, but Yegorov hesitated. There was a remote chance that one remaining force of "Whites" under General P. N. Wrangel might break out of the Crimea and attack from the rear. Yegorov's forces would then, potentially, be trapped between the Whites, the Poles, and the Romanians. Yegorov finally agreed to send reinforcements to Tukhachevsky anyway, but Stalin, as commissar, refused to sign the order. Without his consent, it could not be put into effect.

By August 14, the Red Army had reached the outskirts of Warsaw. Units of Red cavalry had already crossed the Vistula north of the city. But the Poles' defenses were stiffening. As Stalin had predicted a few months earlier, Polish peasants and workers—in fact, shopkeepers and intelligentsia, as well—were rallying to the defense of their country. Meanwhile, Polish intelligence had made an important discovery. A young mathematics professor at the University of Warsaw, Stefan Mazurkiewicz, had broken the Soviet communications code. His intercepts revealed the dangerous gap between Tukhachevsky's forces. A colonel named Tadeusz Schaetzl took the news to Piłsudski, who told him: "Listen, Schaetzl, if this report turns out to be false, I will have you shot."

Almost overnight, the Poles made a daring and brilliant series of maneuvers, shifting thousands of troops over the entire front to take advantage of the Soviet gap. On August 16, they counterattacked across the entire front. The telling blow came against Tukhachevsky's unprotected left flank and was directed northward toward East Prussia. Polish cavalry and infantry poured through the gap, quickly surrounding a large number of Tukhachevsky's men. More than a hundred thousand were taken prisoner and the rest were put to rout in a battle which has achieved enduring fame among the Poles as the "Miracle on the Vistula." In chasing the Red Army home, the Poles decisively won the last great European cavalry battle, at Komarów near Zamość, on August 31, 1920. Polish independence was saved and Europe was spared the threat of communism. In a description of the Battle of Warsaw written in 1920, Lord Edgar V. D'Abernon, the British ambassador to Berlin, said:

> If Charles Martel had not checked the Saracen conquest at the Battle of Tours, the interpretation of the Koran would now be taught at the schools of Oxford, and her pupils might demonstrate to a circumcised people the sanctity and truth of the revelation of Mahomet. Had Piłsudski and [Maxime] Weygand [a French general and adviser to the Poles who had nothing to do with the victory] failed to arrest the triumphant advance of the Soviet Army at the Battle of Warsaw, not only would Christianity have experienced a dangerous reverse, but the very existence of western civilization would have been imperiled. The Battle of Tours saved our ancestors from the Yoke of the Koran; it is probable

that the Battle of Warsaw saved Central, and parts of Western Europe
from a more subversive danger—the fanatical tyranny of the Soviet.

Lord D'Abernon's assessment, while inflated, was more accurate
than Churchill's prediction of "a quarrel of pygmies." The war had
involved more than one and a half million men. Its rapidly shifting
fronts made it one of the most mobile in history. The Polish victory
had probably spared the Germans a Bolshevik invasion. But after
Komarów, both sides were so exhausted that negotiations for a settlement began on October 12, 1920. The frontier agreed on at this point,
reflecting gains from the last Polish offensive, was more than 150 miles
east of the Curzon Line. The new line, incorporated into the Treaty
of Riga signed by both countries in 1921, represented humiliating territorial losses that would never be forgotten by Stalin or the Red Army.

Their victory contained the seeds of tragedy for the Poles. Their
newly won eastern frontier provided neither the federation dreamed
of by Piłsudski, nor the compact ethnic boundaries advocated by
Dmowski. Instead, territory belonging to the Lithuanians, Byelorussians, and Ukrainians was now split, causing bitter resentment among
its inhabitants. An interwar Poland emerged with twenty-four million
Poles, almost five million Ukrainians, 1.1 million Byelorussians, and
almost three million Jews. It also included large numbers of Lithuanians, Russians, and Germans. Ethnic Poles represented barely two
thirds of the total. The clash between Piłsudski's and Dmowski's views
had also contributed to deep divisions. Many Jews had been genuinely
frightened by supporters of Dmowski, who suspected Jews of being
sympathetic under the partitions to the Russians or Germans. Because
of its appeal to universalism, Marxism had attracted many Jewish intellectuals in Poland, who were appalled by the idea of "Poland for the
Poles." As a result, the leadership of the Polish Communist Party was
primarily Jewish. Many Jews had supported the Soviet invasion and
were accused of being traitors. (Overall, however, the Jewish population of Poland was quite conservative and only a small fraction was
attracted to communism.)

Under these circumstances, the new Polish nation was left with few
friends abroad and a lack of cohesion at home. Worst of all, the fall of
the czar was a moment when Russians and Poles, who were, after all,
Slavic brothers, might have initiated an era of cooperation. With the
signing of the Treaty of Riga in March 1921, that opportunity had
vanished.

Because of their defeat, the Soviets turned to the Germans for help.

No consequence of the Russo-Polish war was more ominious for Poland. In December 1920, Lenin explained why the Germans would be asked to help modernize the Red Army. His words contained a strong element of prophecy:

> I am not fond of the Germans by any means; but at the present time it is more advantageous to use them than to challenge them. . . . Germany wants revenge, and we want revolution. For the moment our aims are the same, but when our ways part, they will be our most ferocious and greatest enemies. Time will tell whether a German hegemony or a Communist federation is to arise out of the ruins of Europe.

Lenin's opinion was remarkably similar to that of General Hans von Seeckt, who ran a covert German general staff in violation of the Versailles Treaty. With the dust of World War I still settling, Seeckt wrote: "Only in firm cooperation with a great Russia does Germany have a chance of regaining her position as a world power. . . . It is quite immaterial whether we like or dislike the new Russia. . . ." Later, Seeckt said: "The re-establishment of a broad common frontier between Russia and Germany is the precondition of the regaining of strength of both countries."

Seeckt gladly accepted Lenin's invitation to help modernize the Red Army. He organized a secret unit called Special Group R to foster collaboration between the German and Soviet armies. These efforts, well hidden from the Western Allies, continued until Hitler came to power in 1933. During this time, the Germans established a secret air base in Russia, at Lipezk, where Soviet pilots were trained and where new, experimental German planes were tested and developed. Officers who would later form the core of the Luftwaffe, for a time the world's finest air force, were also trained at Lipezk. A school for gas warfare was also established at Saratov and a tank training center at Kazan. Among the future German and Soviet military leaders who trained together at Kazan were Heinz Guderian, who pioneered Germany's blitzkrieg tactics, and Semyon Timoshenko, whose tanks spearheaded the Soviet invasion of Poland in 1939.

While secretly cooperating in military matters, the German and Soviet governments gave the Western Allies a public jolt in 1922 at the Rapallo Conference (held near Genoa, Italy). Western statesmen had organized the conference to involve all the major powers, including the U.S.S.R. and Germany. Its purpose was to deal collectively with Europe's growing political and economic difficulties. The Western Allies were surprised and angered when the Germans used the occasion to announce their first postwar diplomatic agreement. In it, they granted recognition to the Soviet government and agreed to cooperate with it in economic development. Both governments also renounced all war-related claims and counterclaims against each other.

The relationship between the Soviets and the Germans was full of anomalies. In 1923, during their secret collaboration, the Bolsheviks publicly encouraged revolution and insurrection in Germany. Likewise, the Prussian military establishment publicly held the Bolsheviks reprehensible, but privately cooperated with them in establishing a comprehensive program of weapons research and development. Publicly the German and Soviet antagonisms seemed irreconcilable. Yet privately both countries were determined to recover the lost territory between them.

When Hitler came to power in 1933, he terminated the secret military collaboration between Germany and the Soviet Union. For the next six years, he and Stalin publicly excoriated each other, so severely that reconciliation on any basis seemed farfetched. But like the inflammatory rhetoric between the two countries in the 1920s, that of the thirties did nothing to diminish their revanchist designs. It was first and foremost the opportunity to make good these claims that paved the way for the shocking nonaggression pact of August 23, 1939. The September campaign that followed provided only partial revenge. Both sides were determined to dismember Poland completely.

The new lords of Poland bore little resemblance to the conservative sovereigns who had partitioned the country on three other occasions. Harsh oppressors were not new to the Poles, but none previous could compare to the barbarians who beset the country in 1939. With them came the methods of the modern totalitarian state—industrialized extermination, mass deportations, and police-state terror. Horror came on a scale never before experienced.

Complete subjugation was the ultimate aim, and no facet of that challenge was pursued with greater diligence than the destruction of the Polish intelligentsia (the Polish word has a broader sense than the English: roughly "educated class"). That policy was an attempt at "beheading" the nation to make it "an inert and amorphous mass of humanity," as Poland's most famous World War II general, Władysław Anders, later asserted. It set in motion a process of persecution in which millions of the intelligentsia lost their lives, were forced to flee, or were forcibly removed from the country. The savagery began in 1939 under joint Nazi-Soviet rule, continued from June 1941 to early 1944 under Germany alone, and proceeded after 1944 solely under Soviet rule.

Hitler's command of August 22 at Obersalzberg—"Close your hearts to pity! Act brutally! Be steeled against all signs of compassion"—was heeded with enthusiasm and, except for the dismay of a few generals, met little objection. Similar words by Stalin are nowhere recorded, but his deeds left little doubt that he shared Hitler's sentiments completely.

The immediate cause of the violence unleashed against Poland and its intelligentsia was the nonaggression pact of August 23, 1939. Its signing left the Western democracies in a state of shock. Leaving a meeting with the Führer, Sir Nevile Henderson, the British ambassador to Berlin, was "so wrought up he was speechless," said the *New York Times*. "Not trusting his memory to repeat the exact shadings of Herr Hitler's answer [to a formal British request for clarification of the pact's purpose], he asked that it be put in writing and he returned for it a half hour later." Henderson's surprise reflected the general failure of Western statesmen to appreciate the depth of German and Soviet determination to recover the territories that became Poland at the end of World War I. The West's failure to contain German and Russian revanchist aims was acidly illustrated by British cartoonist David Low's famous cartoon of Hitler and Stalin bowing toward each other and doffing their caps over the corpse of Poland. "The scum of the earth, I believe," says Hitler to Stalin. "The bloody assassin of the workers, I presume?" is Stalin's rejoinder.

With the signing of the August 23 agreement, large constraints were removed and the despots were freed to do as they pleased with the territory between them. Painful memories of World War I still plagued most Germans. In that conflict, an Allied naval blockade had seriously damaged Germany's economy while a two-front war chewed deeply into her manpower. Hitler acknowledged that these mistakes must not be repeated; his pact with Stalin seemed providentially inspired to accomplish that aim. For Germany the agreement eliminated the threat of a prolonged conflict on its eastern frontier and opened up a boundless source of raw materials that could largely nullify the effects of any blockade. Most of all it eliminated any hope of Allied intervention in Poland. For the Soviets, the agreement also offered compelling inducements: the opportunity to settle old scores with the Poles; a freer hand along the Baltic; and the conversion of a formidable potential adversary, Germany, into a political and economic ally. The pact was especially satisfying to Stalin. Recent actions of the Western Allies smacked of weakness. He was convinced that Hitler was going to war. Why risk facing him alone? Better yet, why not join him in carving up Eastern Europe?

The stage had already been set with the signing on August 19 of a German-Soviet trade agreement, under which large quantities of Soviet raw materials such as grain, cotton, oil, iron, and certain strategic commodities would be exchanged for German manufactured goods, industrial processes, and war matériel. Stalin was so anxious to please Hitler that he agreed to make substantial deliveries prior to the shipment of German goods. He also agreed to act as a buyer of metals and raw materials in third countries.

From its inception the nonaggression pact was a temporary arrangement for Hitler, a way station on the road to his ultimate goal of a Thousand-Year Reich. It meant the temporary sheathing of his most flamboyant rhetorical swords, the rantings against the communist "world conspiracy" and the old dream of German *lebensraum*. But these were momentary inconveniences made necessary by an expedient deal with an old adversary and, as such, represented no departure at all from his deepest convictions. Stalin also had visionary expectations. Knowing that the Poles would be quickly disposed of, he expected that Hitler would soon turn on the West and thereupon enmesh himself in the very kind of protracted conflict that had been Germany's undoing in World War I. In that event, Stalin envisioned the creation of a power vacuum in the center of Europe that only he could fill.

Two consummate opportunists thus were joined in a marriage of convenience in the treaty of August 23. Its secret protocol—the existence of which the Soviet Union would not acknowledge for half a century—split the projected spoils into German and Soviet spheres. Poland was halved west of its center along the Vistula, territory east of the river being allocated to the Soviets and lands west of it to the Germans, who also took Lithuania. The Soviets' sphere also included Estonia, Latvia, Bessarabia, and Finland. The spurious claims to these territories were to be exercised by coercion and naked force under the authority of an agreement that contained not one bellicose word. Even the secret protocol alluded to the impending invasion in euphemistic terms: "In the event of a territorial and political rearrangement . . ."

There could be no doubt that such a rearrangement would soon occur. The speed of the German advance caught even the Soviets by surprise. Having been urged to intervene at the outset, the ever-cautious Stalin insisted on waiting for a moment in which he could demonstrate loyalty to the new partnership while at the same time appearing as the guarantor of safety and order in eastern Poland. By mid-September the Wehrmacht had penetrated east of the Bug River, more than a hundred miles beyond the line specified in the secret protocol as the western boundary of the Soviet sphere. Stalin could wait no longer. Fearing that Hitler might refuse to withdraw to the line agreed on, he sent the Red Army across the frontier on September 17 under the pretext that it would restore public order and defend Poland's large Byelorussian and Ukrainian minorities. In many villages, these minorities, believing that repression at the hands of the Poles was at an end, warmly welcomed Soviet troops. In this they were correct: the Polish cavalry's occasional foray's into their communities to find nationalist guerrillas would not recur. But any relief was to be short-lived, as harsh policies to Sovietize the region soon followed.

At 6:00 P.M. on September 27, Ribbentrop's Condor touched down in Moscow bearing the German foreign minister to a new division of spoils, this time under greatly changed circumstances. Until the August 23 agreement, Stalin had been the arbiter of Europe's future, patiently hearing out British and French overtures for a second Triple Entente while dangling before Hitler the prospect of a nonaggression pact. But the blitzkrieg's success left Stalin shaken. Would the Wehrmacht return to the Vistula? Perhaps not, he fumed. On September 19 Ribbentrop wired reassurance, saying that the agreement stood "as the foundation stone of the new friendly relations between Germany and the Soviet Union." The aces were now, of course, in Hitler's hand, but Stalin masterfully played the lesser hand. First, he would collect for services rendered. Had he not made much of the German success possible? Where would Hitler be without him? He knew the Germans could not forget the British and French declaration of war. Under these circumstances how pushy could they be? As Ribbentrop arrived, a tough, shrewd bargainer waited, ready to gamble that his share of the spoils could be increased in the new agreement about to be negotiated.

Stalin's designs centered on a clever swap. At first both parties had considered creating a puppet Polish state, but Stalin soon turned against the idea, feeling that it would be better to obliterate the country completely. His strategy then became to give as many Poles as possible to the Germans. After all, why should he keep these unruly people? They would never acquiesce in the loss of their independence. The czars had seen that through 150 years of turmoil in which Russia had shared in Poland's governing. Let the Germans keep the land between the Vistula and the Bug rivers, territory the Wehrmacht now occupied anyway. In exchange Russia would take Lithuania, which belonged to Germany under the August 23 agreement. With Lithuania, Soviet control would extend all the way down the Baltic to the Prussian frontier. Future relations with the Reich could always sour. Should that ever happen, Lithuania would be a valuable buffer between Germany and the most direct routes to Moscow and Leningrad.

Stalin put these proposed changes to Ribbentrop between 10:00 P.M. and 1:00 A.M. on September 27 and 28. He craftily presented his design as a plan in which the Poles would be less able to "create sources of unrest from which discord between Germany and the Soviet Union might arise." At 4:00 A.M. Ribbentrop wired the proposed boundary adjustments to Hitler and got his concurrence. Such trifles were of marginal concern to the Führer; sooner or later he expected to attack Stalin anyway. With a few deft strokes of the pen, millions of people were shifted from one sphere to another. Twenty-two million Poles and 72,866 square miles of Poland were now to come under German authority. Thirteen million Poles and 77,620 square miles of their territory would be left to the Soviets. But what real difference did that make to Hitler? It was only a matter of time before all the territories in question would be under his control. Even in the matter of Poland's oil-rich area, south of Lwów, Germany acquiesced. The Soviets had vast oil deposits while the Reich had none, as Ribbentrop pointed out. But Stalin noted that the Ukrainians were strongly pressing their claims to the area. Why not permit Russia, he asked Ribbentrop, to trade oil to Germany for coal and steel tubing? On this point also he won.

The parties resumed talks from 3:00 P.M. to 6:00 P.M. on September 28, recessing for a state banquet at the Kremlin. Before meeting again at midnight, Ribbentrop attended one act of *Swan Lake* while Stalin and Molotov met with a delegation from Latvia. Stalin smiled benignly while Ribbentrop and Molotov signed the treaty, dated September 28, at 5:00 A.M. on the twenty-ninth. Throughout, few details escaped Stalin. Using a thick blue pencil, he had himself drawn the line of partition on one large map. He had personally signed and approved a technical correction along the Bug River south of Zamość.

Like the predecessor agreement on August 23, the announced version of the "German-Soviet Boundary and Friendship Treaty" sounded innocuous. In doing so it scaled new heights of cynicism: The two governments were trying "to re-establish peace and order" following "the collapse of the former Polish state." Their goal was to enable its people to live "a peaceful life in keeping with their national character."

Confidential attachments again were the heart of the agreement. This time there were three secret protocols. Most important among them was the new territorial split, moving the line of demarcation in Poland to the Bug River and giving Lithuania to Russia. Another of these protocols gave German nationals under Soviet jurisdiction the right to migrate back to Germany or to territories newly occupied by the Reich. Germany conveyed similar rights to persons of Ukrainian or Byelorussian descent residing in territories under its jurisdiction. The last of the protocols was emphatic and ominous:

> Both parties will tolerate in their territories no Polish agitation which affects the territories of the other party. They will suppress in their territories all beginnings of such agitation and inform each other concerning suitable measures for this purpose.

Once again Poland disappeared from the map of Europe. About half the territory taken by Germany—Poznań, Danzig, and Polish Silesia—was annexed to the Reich. The remainder under German jurisdiction, called the General Government, included Warsaw and Kraków and held the largest number of ethnic Poles. It was expected to serve as a dumping ground where cheap labor and local resources would be exploited completely. The day after he became Poland's governor, Hans Frank declared that the Poles "shall become the slaves of the German Reich."

At this point the German campaign against the Polish intelligentsia was well under way. Squads of Einsatzgruppen, or special extermination units, had followed the Wehrmacht into Poland. On September 19 Reinhard Heydrich, second in command to SS Reichsführer Heinrich Himmler, said such units were undertaking a "housecleaning of Jews, intelligentsia, clergy and the nobility." Thousands in these categories were shot, arrested, and terrorized. In the areas annexed to the Reich, a huge program of colonization was planned. The eight million to nine million Poles in these provinces were to be forced out, making room for Germans—especially those returning under the nonaggression pact's secret protocol on exchange of nationals. The annexed areas were to be Germanized completely. The Polish language was banned in public, education for Poles beyond elementary school was prohibited, and special shopping hours for Poles were imposed. Throughout German-occupied Poland, the Nazis imposed harsh and demeaning regulations. It was against the law for Poles to ride in taxis, carry briefcases, walk in public parks, make calls from phone booths, or even have their teeth filled with gold. The flurry of absurd edicts later even included a general ban on dancing in territory administered by the General Government.

The chilling thrust of these policies was noted by General Franz Halder in his diary entry for October 18:

We have no intention of rebuilding Poland. . . . Not to be a model
state by German standards. Polish intelligentsia must be prevented from
establishing itself as a governing class. Low standard of living must be
conserved. Cheap slaves . . .

Total disorganization must be created! The Reich will give the
Governor General [Frank] the means to carry out this devilish plan.

Policies to eliminate the intelligentsia in the Soviet sphere were not
so well documented. Germany's eventual defeat and the trial of their
leaders at Nuremberg exposed in revolting detail the Reich's monstrous
crimes against humanity. The fortunes of war assured that no such
tribunal would call the Soviets to account for their crimes against the
Poles. At Nuremberg the Soviets themselves were in charge of indictments for war crimes in Eastern Europe. They perverted that responsibility, as we shall later see, by attempting to blame the Germans for
the Soviets' own most flagrant atrocity against the Polish intelligentsia.

Almost immediately after Poland's defeat, local officials in the Soviet
sphere were rounded up and deported. Then there was a brief respite
while the machinery of Sovietization was put into place under the
personal direction of Nikita Khrushchev, First Secretary of the Ukrainian
Communist Party. On October 22, 1939, sham elections were held in
Soviet-occupied Poland. Voters were given no choice in electing two
so-called popular assemblies. The names of persons elected were never
made public.

As might be expected, the assemblies immediately requested union
with the Soviet Byelorussian and Ukrainian republics. The Supreme
Soviet voted in the first two days of November to approve these requests. Prior to its vote Molotov gloatingly told that body: "One swift
blow to Poland, first by the German Army and then by the Red Army,
and nothing was left of this bastard of the Versailles Treaty."

With annexation the Poles and other inhabitants of Eastern Poland
became citizens of the U.S.S.R. in the eyes of the Soviet government.
The implications were ominous. Why should the Poles be treated differently from other Soviet citizens, millions of whom had already been
deported to the gulag archipelago or to the far reaches of Kazakhstan?
The U.S.S.R.'s new Polish citizens were soon to be victims of the same
social engineering. From October 1939 up until the eve of the June
22, 1941, German attack on the Soviet Union, an estimated 1.2 million
Poles were deported to the Soviet Union. This estimate is based on a
detailed survey conducted in 1942 by the Polish government-in-exile
of deportees who were permitted to leave the Soviet Union. Its

research showed that 52 percent of the deportees were ethnic Poles, 30 percent were Jewish, and 18 percent were Ukrainian and Byelorussian. The treaty signed by the Germans and Soviets on September 28, 1939, had left only about five million ethnic Poles under Soviet jurisdiction. Most were concentrated in Lwów, Wilno, and other cities and towns. The removal of such a large number of ethnic Poles and Polish Jews meant that the annexed territories were practically stripped of their educated people.

For many, deportation was tantamount to a death sentence. Only a few would survive the harsh conditions of life in Siberia or in the forced-labor camps along the Arctic Circle. Many, dumped on collective farms on the steppes without food or adequate clothing, died during the first winter. Only a fraction of these people would ever leave the Soviet Union, even after the Soviets and Poles joined forces to wage war against Hitler. These deportations and other harsh repressions in the annexed territories caused irreconcilable conflict between the Soviet Union and the Polish government-in-exile. That conflict was never resolved and persists to this day as a source of continuing friction in Russo-Polish relations.

The German and Soviet governments collaborated closely in their efforts to eliminate the Polish intelligentsia. The secret protocols in their September 28 agreement on exchange of nationals and suppression of dissent set the stage for careful cooperation between the NKVD and the Gestapo. Over the winter of 1939–1940, the intelligence service of the Polish army-in-exile reported that senior officials of the German and Soviet secret police met several times at Kraków, Lwów, and Zakopane. These sessions had a twofold purpose: first, to coordinate so-called resettlement policies in the German and Soviet spheres, as well as other plans to eliminate the Polish intelligentsia; and second, to devise effective policies for combating the Polish underground. Khrushchev acknowledged that Gestapo representatives came to Lwów several times to coordinate matters with Ivan Serov, head of the Ukrainian NKVD. Tadeusz Bór-Komorowski, head of the Armia Krajowa, or Home Army (so named because it was coordinated from abroad by the Polish government-in-exile), in Kraków and later for the entire territory held by the General Government, also described such meetings in his book, *The Secret Army*:

In March, 1940, my staff received information that an NKVD mission had come to Krakow to work out with the Gestapo the methods they were jointly to adopt against Polish military organizations. The NKVD was already aware that Polish military resistance was centralized and directed from one headquarters. The consultations in Krakow lasted for several weeks. I received reports of the discussions, the names of those present and their addresses. Apparently the NKVD methods for combating our Underground were greatly admired by the Gestapo, and it was suggested that they should be adopted in the German zone.

These gatherings represented a fraternity of miscreants who shared similar goals but used different methods. Gestapo admiration of the NKVD was understandable. The NKVD permeated every aspect of Soviet life. Its tentacles could strangle or caress. They spread mutual distrust and bent the nation to Stalin's every wish. The NKVD's terrorism radiated from the Kremlin to the remotest corners of the land. No one escaped the fear it engendered, and millions died at its hand. From the late twenties to the early thirties, massive resettlement had transformed Soviet society as Stalin sought to industrialize through collectivization. The relentless brutality used by the NKVD to carry out this policy is well documented. Over the years a separate empire emerged, a state within the state, operating a vast system of slave-labor camps and enterprises. No one knew how many millions mined NKVD gold, harvested NKVD lumber, produced NKVD cement, operated NKVD barges, drove NKVD tractors, or worked in NKVD knitting mills and shoe factories. Later, Soviet author Aleksandr Solzhenitsyn would describe the NKVD's ubiquitous presence as a "Gulag Archipelago" with millions of prisoners. These camps and collectivization may have claimed as many as sixteen million lives between 1929 and 1936, according to a Soviet demographic study by Iosif G. Dyadkin.

In contrast, the German police-state apparatus was never so pervasive. Nor were the Gestapo's methods as effective. The Polish underground and Home Army became occupied Europe's largest and most effective resistance by far—but only in the German sphere. The resistance's system of cells spread rapidly throughout German-occupied Poland and became a powerful extension of the London government-in-exile. It ran schools, dispensed justice, and blew up German supply trains on a comprehensive scale. But nothing comparable existed in Soviet-occupied Poland.

Russians did have certain advantages over their German counterparts. Language was less of a problem. As Slavs, many Russians understood Polish and conversed in it easily, but few Germans spoke the language. For a while, the Russians also had the collaboration of the large anti-Polish Ukrainian minority in their zone. But neither of these advantages was nearly as important as one other factor: In approach, the Gestapo and the NKVD were fundamentally different. Bold, impulsive, reckless, and careless—each of these adjectives characterized the Gestapo. In contrast, the NKVD was slow, patient, cunning, and thorough. One played poker, the other played chess. Gestapo suspicions often led to immediate liquidations that cut off leads to other suspects or to underground leaders. The NKVD, in contrast, methodically built networks that often pervaded entire offices and factories. Plots, schemes, and troublemakers were much more difficult to hide from its all-pervasive eyes.

Rhetoric also played a part in the relative effectiveness of the Gestapo and the NKVD. With their half-baked theories of Germanic racial and cultural superiority, the Nazis were instantly detestable to occupied peoples, the Poles in particular. The Poles had an old and attractive culture. Through all the partitions they had nurtured distant glories, both their military victories and their contributions to political pluralism. The Poles regarded the Germans, who had only been unified for a few decades, as political upstarts. German infatuation, under the Nazis, with the concept of a "super race" that would colonize the Slavs was, of course, thoroughly revolting to the Poles.

Soviet rhetoric did not assault Polish culture and was much less offensive generally. Goals fully as imperialistic as the German ones were camouflaged by high-sounding slogans and ideals. Soviet communism's appeal to international brotherhood and the fraternal cause of workers won some converts. Greater ethnic diversity and factionalism in the Soviet-occupied zone were also skillfully exploited by the NKVD and by Soviet propaganda. In retaliation for many real and perceived wrongs, Byelorussians and Ukrainians often helped the NKVD compile its lists of ethnic Poles to be arrested or deported.

While the Gestapo and the NKVD were meeting at Kraków and Zakopane, massive deportations were already under way in the Soviet-occupied zone. These contributed to fears that NKVD eyes and ears already observed the entire society. The mixing of brutal and subtle methods left the man in the Soviet-occupied street wondering whom, if anyone, he could speak with in safety.

CHAPTER 7

Camp Life

In the bone-chilling November sleet and drizzle, the onion dome of a long-defunct Russian Orthodox church towered, barely visible, above a sprawling complex of box-shaped two-story buildings covered in stucco. High, thick walls surrounded the rectangular compound, which measured about two hundred yards in length and a hundred fifty yards in width. Originally the Kozelsk Monastery, the cloister once served as a retreat where Tolstoy, Gogol, and other prominent Russian artists and intellectuals joined hermit monks for long periods of meditation and reflection. After the revolution, the Bolsheviks evicted the monks, closed the church, and began confining political prisoners at the monastery. Stork towers with machine-gun nests and barbed-wire traps had later been added. It was soon known to the local peasantry as a "forbidden place."

Three miles from the compound lay the small town of Kozelsk, the sixteenth- and seventeenth-century home of two Polish noble families, the Ogińskis and the Puzynas, who had once ruled the area, then a part of the Nobles' Republic of Poland and Lithuania. Kozelsk's location, about one hundred fifty miles south of Moscow on the main railway line between Smolensk and Tula, made it a convenient transit point for moving the almost five thousand Polish officers, Dr. Czarnek among them, who arrived here during November 1939. These prisoners came from a number of transit camps, like Kozelshchina, where more than 250,000 captured Poles were interned by the end of October. Early in November the Soviets began a culling operation in which more than fifteen thousand officers and others with "bourgeois tendencies" were withdrawn from the transit camps and taken to Kozelsk and two other monasteries: Starobelsk, about 140 miles east of Kharkov in the Ukraine, and Ostashkov, on Lake Seliger in the Kalinin Region, about two hundred miles northwest of Moscow.

At Ostashkov, the Soviets confined about 6,500 noncommissioned officers from the Polish intelligence service, the military police, frontier guards, state police, prison wardens, and a handful of priests, landowners, and court magistrates. The group included only about four hundred officers, most of them members of auxiliary police units from eastern Poland called up after Germany's September 1 invasion.

In contrast, the inmate rosters of Kozelsk and Starobelsk read like a *Who's Who* of Poland's armed forces, major professions, and intellectual life. About half the men were reservists mobilized in the last days of peace and the early days of the German invasion. At Kozelsk Dr. Czarnek was joined by more than three hundred peers from the medical profession, including a number of the country's preeminent surgeons. The camp held four generals; one rear admiral; twenty-one university professors and lecturers; several hundred lawyers, judges, prosecutors, and court officials; several hundred engineers and secondary-school teachers; and many journalists, writers, and businessmen. About 5 percent of the men were Jews. Among the high-ranking officers was Major Baruch Steinberg, chief rabbi of the Polish army.

About half the 3,910 men at Starobelsk were captured following the surrender of Lwów on September 22, 1939, after a fierce, but uncoordinated assault by the Red Army and the Wehrmacht. Interned in the fifteen-acre compound at Starobelsk were eight generals and the entire staff of the Antigas Institute of Poland, as well as chaplains of all major religious persuasions. Also among Starobelsk's prisoners were hundreds of physicians, engineers, lawyers, teachers, social-welfare workers, and politicians. Confined at both Starobelsk and Kozelsk were a number of officers who had been disabled in previous wars.

After the war, the Polish government-in-exile compiled many details concerning life in these camps and published them in an extensive report called *The Crime of Katyn: Facts and Documents*. It contained a number of personal accounts by a small number of men who survived the liquidation of the Polish officer corps that was undertaken in the spring of 1940. I was fortunate to find two of these survivors, who had arrived at Kozelsk as young cadets in late fall of 1939. I was surprised by the strong positive memories both men carried of their months within the walls of the monastery compound.

"At Kozelsk, I discovered Poland." There was a distant look in his eyes, the memory of a winter fifty years past, when Father Zdzisław Peszkowski told me this on October 2, 1989. We met at a home where he was visiting, on a high bluff along the Potomac River overlooking Washington. He had come to Washington for a special ceremony at the National Cathedral commemorating Poland's sacrifice in World

War II. What he meant was that at Kozelsk he met the best that Poland could offer. At twenty-one he had been thrown together with men from all parts of the country, a cross section of the nation's professional elite. Their accomplishments, their strong loyalty to Poland, and their mood of optimism made a deep impression on Peszkowski. After the war, he had gone on to Oxford, where he had earned a Ph.D. in Polish literature. In 1950 he came to the United States and in 1954 he was ordained as a Catholic priest.

Many of Father Peszkowski's observations were confirmed a few weeks later in my meeting with Władek Cichy. We met on November 10, 1989, at his comfortable apartment in Cresswell Gardens in London. That he was a gifted storyteller was immediately apparent. (In fact, as we shall later see, he became a widely listened-to interpreter of official Soviet news reports.) He reached Kozelsk at age twenty-six, a recent law graduate of the University of Poznań. For him, Kozelsk had also been an eye-opening experience. "You could not help but feel the esprit de corps," he told me. "There was a basic confidence that pervaded the camp that 'Somehow, we will all survive this.' "

Like many other *podchorążowie*, or cadet officers, Cichy and Peszkowski were not nearly as fortunate as Staszek Niewiadomski, whose rank confused his captors and led to his classification as an enlisted man. Luckily, Staszek was sent back to Poland and turned over to the Germans in a prisoner exchange at the Bug River on November 4. But Cichy, Peszkowski, and many others among the *podchorążowie*—including a number of recent graduates from Polish military academies—were classified as officers. About five hundred were sent to Kozelsk and fifty to Starobelsk.

Julian Bakon was fairly typical of many of these young cadets. He was Peszkowski's best friend. They were the same age and since childhood had been inseparable companions. Growing up in Sanok, a small town on the San River in southeastern Poland, near the Czechoslovakian border, they attended the same schools. Zdzisław was a bit taller at five feet ten inches, but Julian had a powerful, athletic frame. He especially excelled at soccer. They roomed together at Dęblin Cavalry Academy, and had just received their diplomas when the war broke out. The two companions went to the front together and were captured together north of Lwów on September 23, 1939. Their unit was surrounded by Soviet armor and after two days of resistance finally capitulated. They arrived at Kozelsk with all the exuberance that youth can muster, convinced that it was only a matter of time before an Anglo-French offensive would crush Hitler and his opportunistic

Soviet accomplices. I mention their relationship here because of the manner in which these inseparable friends parted several months later. It is a particularly moving story, one that we will come back to much later.

The officers at Kozelsk were part of an army that had tasted disastrous defeat only a few weeks earlier. Yet despondency was nowhere to be found within the compound. The officers knew their defeat was inevitable. With Poland wedged between two giants, no other outcome was possible. Yet they had acquitted themselves well. Only a few months earlier, Foreign Minister Beck had told the Polish nation: "There is only one thing in the life of men, nations and states which is without price, and that is honor." The officers at Kozelsk believed they had heeded Beck's words well. Almost to a man, they cherished a vision of eternal Poland. They savored the days of grandeur and glory when Poland stretched from the Baltic to the Black Sea. They reveled in the great victories: Grunwald, where the Teutonic Knights were crushed in 1410; the lifting of the siege of Vienna in 1683; and, especially, the stunning defeat of the Bolsheviks in the war of 1920. They even gleaned triumph from disaster. In the eighteenth century, three partitions had wiped Poland from the map of Europe. For more than a century, chain gangs periodically shuffled off to Siberia after violent but futile uprisings. But the Poles had proved their endurance, proved their ability to outlast oppression in many forms, and proved that in the worst of times they could even preserve a nation without a state. These images, glimpsed by the mind's eye, were powerful ones to the men at Kozelsk. They were the basis on which a powerful Polish concept of victory was formed. To the men of Kozelsk, victory was more than a matter of winning or losing. It was also defined by the triumph of honor over shame, of endurance over submission. In that sense, the fourth partition could be considered a uniquely Polish triumph, a vindication of Polish valor and endurance. Thus, the men confined within the ancient walls of the Kozelsk Monastery intended not only to endure, but to triumph in adversity. To them, Beck's words rang clear: The honor of Poland was priceless. And this they intended to prove.

Their high spirits and positive frame of mind combined with their appearance to give the Polish officers a mien of confidence. With their formfitting, elegantly flared riding pants; their *kurtki*, or short coats with high, tapered collars; their wide outside belts with straps extending over the right shoulder to counterbalance the pistol and holster on the left hip, the Poles contrasted sharply with the frumpy and disheveled look of their Soviet guards. Most distinctive of all were the Polish cavalry officers' high black boots made of soft calf leather. Rising to a point just below the knee, the pliable material maintained almost perfect shape because of a thin metal rib that extended from the heel to the top of the calf. These boots were polished with meticulous attention; they were the pride of every man who wore them and were much envied by the NKVD guards. Despite the large sums of rubles and generous quantities of vodka often offered in exchange, the Poles refused to part with their footwear or to otherwise compromise their appearance. Their bearing, demeanor, and overall appearance were outward reflections of the high levels of order, discipline, and respect for rank maintained by the captives.

Not all the captives were males. In the September war, Soviet artillery had downed a young woman named Janina Muśnicka Lewandowska, a second lieutenant in the Polish air force. Her father was General Dowbor Muśnicki, an outstanding Polish military leader who was said to be particularly hated by the Bolsheviks. For this reason, Ms. Lewandowska kept her kinship to him secret. She was an active member of the Poznań Aero Club. In the summer of 1939, she married a Colonel Lewandowski. After the war broke out, she was shot down over one of Poland's eastern provinces.

At Kozelsk she was provided separate accommodations. She was rather tall for a woman and wore her chestnut-colored hair closely cropped. Cichy remembered that she seemed striking in her air force uniform. She was permitted to visit friends and took an active, clandestine part in the vigorous religious life of the camp. Despite the Bolshevik ban on religious services, she made communion wafers, an activity that several times got her into trouble with camp authorities. She was subjected to repeated searches because of her involvement in religious activities.

The short days of the northern latitude typically began before dawn with a breakfast of soup and Russian bread of good quality, one feature of a sparse and bland diet that the men looked forward to. A shortage of toilet facilities and water made bathing and shaving an infrequent luxury. On most mornings, cleanup details would roam the monastery, tidying up the grounds and performing minor repairs. Others cleaned inside or performed kitchen duties. In the afternoons large details were often assigned to various projects on nearby collective farms. At Ostashkov the noncommissioned officers and frontier guards were engaged in building a high earth embankment with a wooden bridge to connect their island prison to the mainland. But here too there were relaxed pursuits. A music group, featuring violins made of scrap wood, played Polish folk melodies to a highly receptive audience.

Throughout the day the Poles were bombarded with the constant din of Bolshevik propaganda. Radio Moscow and Radio Smolensk were alternately piped into the camp and blared forth on loudspeakers. An assortment of Communist party newspapers and pamphlets was also readily available. The Poles eagerly filtered the Bolshevik media barrage, attempting to piece together an accurate version of reality in the outside world. Officers who were fluent enough in Russian to sift through the propaganda and provide a credible interpretation of international events often became instant celebrities. From time to time, camp authorities provided a Communist newspaper in Polish, but prisoners paid little attention to it. Its Polish was excruciatingly bad and difficult to understand.

Nightfall arrived between 4:00 and 5:00 P.M.; with it the camp became a hive of activity. Dinner was served early and generally consisted of some type of soup with potatoes and, on rare occasions, salt herring. The daily diet included few vegetables and no milk or fruit. Because of the severe shortage of vitamin A, cases of night blindness were common. Many of the men collected and ate blades of grass, or tree bark, to supplement their diet.

After the evening meal, the men were free to mix with each other and the life of Kozelsk assumed a rhythm all its own, especially in the nave of the old Orthodox church, where more than six hundred of the men were jammed together in bunks five tiers high. Despite the dim lighting afforded by a few naked bulbs, an occasional candle, and a few kerosene lamps, the atmosphere bubbled with organized activity: lectures by professional experts; classes in languages, history, and other subjects taught by prominent authorities; travelogues and chess matches were all part of the typical evening's fare. As a design for combating boredom and maintaining morale, it worked.

Their desire for freedom made the men willing subscribers to many rumors of their impending release and imminent return to Poland, no matter how ill-founded and optimistic the concoctions. Many such reports buzzing through the camp were originated by NKVD political agents as a means of keeping the officers off balance and confused. One popular theme was that an Anglo-French offensive to be launched any day would crush Hitler and his opportunistic Soviet accomplices. Others told themselves that since the Poles were allies of the British and French their presence was an embarrassment to the Russians. After all, the Soviets were not at war with the West and often seemed at pains to distance themselves from the Germans. Surely, the men reasoned, the Soviets would not want to antagonize the British and French. Remnants of the Polish air force in Syria were relatively close. The Western Allies might well, or so the reasoning went, authorize the Poles to knock out the Soviet oil fields at Baku. Others reasoned that at worst they would be sent back to their homes in Poland; for some this would mean being turned over to the Germans, but at least they would see their families and friends again. Almost to a man the Poles felt that Germany's defeat was inevitable, an outcome each hoped to hasten by rejoining Polish fighting men in the West.

The nave stirred in the early evenings as men circulated along the aisles touting the time, location, and subject of classes, lectures, and other events. "All sorts of promotions were going on," Father Peszkowski told me. "Someone would come by announcing, 'Tonight there will be a trip up the Amazon River.' Then he would give the aisle and bunk number where this lecture would take place. The speaker would be someone who had recently visited that part of the world. There were language classes, history classes, and others as well. What was incredible was who presented all this; they were the outstanding people of Poland."

Men who shared the same bunk area often took turns telling their life stories. Father Peszkowski remembered one Warsaw man who told of winning one million złoty in the national lottery shortly before the war. Unfortunately he was unable to enjoy his money and worried whether it would have any value once the war ended. He seemed embittered by his dubious gain.

Each night precisely at 9:00 P.M. the sharp cry "Silence, please!" pierced the air. The deeply religious Poles began three minutes of spiritual communion in direct violation of an edict by camp authorities banning religious observance of any kind. Within seconds the din of activity was transformed into an eerie silence as Roman Catholics, Protestants, members of the Orthodox Church, Jews, agnostics, and atheists all observed these quiet moments. Remote noise from the outside barely penetrated the thick church walls. The typical NKVD guard who happened on this scene might ask for an explanation, but the only reply would be the echo of his voice reverberating through the ancient and cavernous sanctuary.

Communal evening prayers, an old tradition in the Polish army, continued despite determined Soviet policies to uproot religious prejudices and reeducate the Poles. As prayers and surreptitious communion services continued, the persecution of chaplains escalated. Several were thrown into solitary confinement, but this did not stop the services. On Christmas Eve, 1939, all the chaplains of Kozelsk but one were suddenly removed from the camp. Only Father Ziółkowski, who had conducted a secret Mass at the Kozelshchina transit camp in October, remained. Like all Polish chaplains, he carried the rank of major and it was possible that camp authorities did not realize he was a priest. His down-to-earth approach was extremely popular with his fellow prisoners. He continued conducting secret services, including communion using ordinary ration bread, in remote reaches of the camp, away from the ever-watchful NKVD authorities. On most days, he could be seen walking for brief periods with different men as he heard their confessions. He was particularly busy in March 1940, hearing hundreds of confessions during the Easter season.

On the surface, prevailing Soviet political dogma seemed to provide clear-cut options for dealing with captured enemies: Either put them to work for the party or state, reeducate and convert them ideologically, or simply liquidate them. From a bureaucratic point of view, the process of evaluating which option to apply in the case of the men of Kozelsk, Starobelsk, and Ostashkov became a monumental undertaking. NKVD agents busily engaged themselves in exhaustive efforts to evaluate the prisoners. Each man was subjected to a series of interrogations. These were conducted at all hours and under circumstances that ranged from informal office chats to verbally abusive confrontations. Photographs were generally taken of each man from frontal and profile angles. Gradually the NKVD built individual personnel folders containing information on family origins, social connections, educational background, languages spoken, employment history, religious beliefs, and political affiliations and outlook.

Were these detailed interrogations a step in the Soviet legal process? They might well have been. Technically, all Poles from eastern Poland were considered Soviet citizens, not prisoners of war. These were semantic twists with a sinister side—a position that made the Poles vulnerable to criminal charges that were punishable by death. When the Red Army marched into Poland on September 17, 1939, the Soviet government did not issue a declaration of war. The action was justified as an intervention to restore public order following the "collapse" of the Polish government. Its "disintegration," according to the Soviets, left the Polish prisoners stateless. In these circumstances, the Soviets held that they were extending de facto Soviet citizenship to prisoners from eastern Poland. That position, of course, denied the Poles protection under the Geneva Convention on the treatment of prisoners of war. While the Soviets never signed that convention, its standards were widely accepted norms of civilized conduct and could be considered binding under common law. The Poles were thus left in the worst possible legal position. For having served in a "capitalist army," they were automatically considered criminals. They were vulnerable to the nebulous charge of engaging in counterrevolutionary activities injurious to the working class and the world proletariat. Generally, there were no extenuating circumstances for these charges, and "extreme punishment"—a death sentence—was required.

The interrogations also served as a screening process to identify possible espionage agents. For unexplained reasons, a small group of prisoners from Kozelsk was transferred to Smolensk prison in early March 1940. One of these men later escaped to the West and described the subtle line of questioning used by the NKVD. He described his interrogation in Smolensk by a *politruk*, or political officer, named Samarin. It probably typified the approach used at Kozelsk:

Samarin: "Let us imagine that the public prosecutor annuls your case. Let us suppose that your request to return to German-occupied Poland is complied with, that the Germans allow you to live at liberty in Warsaw in your apartment. What would you do?"

Prisoner: "I would rest after my exhausting experiences."

Samarin: "Supposing I turned up at your apartment for one day, would you give me a cup of tea?"

Prisoner: "I do not know if there would be any tea there."

Samarin: "And would you put me up for the night?"

Prisoner: "You have the large Soviet Legation in Warsaw. You would be better off and more comfortable there."

Samarin: "But if I did not want the Soviet Legation to know of my arrival; if I came incognito as a spy, would you take me in and report to the Gestapo that a Soviet agent had arrived?"

Prisoner: "I do not know the regulations in Warsaw about reporting. I do not know what has happened to my apartment. In these circumstances I cannot give you an answer."

Prisoners who gave answers similar to these faced a grim future.

A mysterious figure in the interrogations at Kozelsk was NKVD general V. M. Zarubin, who earned respect and a degree of confidence from the Poles. He was not the camp commandant, but clearly he outranked everyone. Detaching himself from the ongoing evaluation process, Zarubin exhibited a refined manner and made it a practice to hold private visits with officers to discuss a wide range of social, political, and philosophical topics. An obviously well-educated man, Zarubin was fluent in French and German and spoke some English. He brought a small library of five hundred books to the camp, and gladly lent volumes to the prisoners. He offered visitors good cigarettes, tea, cakes, even oranges—a rare luxury—and the feeling that he respected their views. As a result, the Poles decided that Zarubin alone, among all the NKVD men, deserved the courtesy of a salute.

No doubt Zarubin presented only one side to the Poles. He and his NKVD subordinates kept their prisoners under close observation. Among the documents turned over by Soviet president Gorbachev to the Poles on April 13, 1990, is one that dramatically illustrates this point. It was written as the Poles at Kozelsk were transported for liquidation. On April 22, 1940, an NKVD commissar at Kozelsk named Niechorochev wrote the following report to General V. N. Merkulov in Moscow:

There were no attempts to escape. A large number of petitions were sent from those prisoners left, asking to stay in the Soviet Union and not be sent to Germany or some other neutral countries. They were sent by mostly physicians, engineers, and teachers. Some examples of those petitions were:

"Please do not turn me over to any German or neutral authorities but allow me to stay and work in the Soviet Union. My request is motivated in the following ways: (a) Up until now I've been apolitical, but recently I've been able to learn the ideology of a socialist country and have been strongly attracted by it. I have no doubts that I can fulfill the duties of a Soviet citizen with honor; (b) By profession, I'm an engineer in the textile industry and I'm sure my knowledge and experience can prove to be useful to the Soviet Union; (c) I'm Jewish and up until now I've been under nationalistic oppression; that allows me to appreciate the policy of national freedom conducted by the Soviet Union."

"I asked why the camp is being disbanded. I'm asking to stay in the Soviet Union. I'm the son of a tailor. I don't want to go to Germany or any other country."

"When you empty the camps, please let me stay in the Soviet Union. I'm a doctor. For a long time, up until now, I've lived in a capitalistic country and saw the injustice of the system there. I saw what a terrible life poor people had and I've always been a sympathizer of the communist movement. I've always dreamed of living in a free socialistic country without any nationalistic oppression—which I've always felt, being Jewish."

Other requests are similar in form. The officers of Polish origin do not write requests to stay in the Soviet Union.

Most officers who were being shipped from April 3 on felt rather happy that they lived until the moment of being free. They would say that it's better to go wherever rather than stay in this camp. On the first day, there were some signs of nervousness since so many officers of the same rank were taken. But on the second day, officers of different ranks were taken and they felt better. Some guessed that they would be taken west—for example to Brest. There, special committees would ask them whether they would like to go to neutral countries or stay in the Soviet Union after signing some special declarations. In that connection, the Polish generals gave orders that the officers of POWs should not sign any declarations.

The majority of officers coming from the German territories do not wish to go to the Polish land occupied by Germany, but want to go to neutral countries such as France where they would volunteer for the French army and fight against Germany, then turn against the Soviet Union and restore Poland from the Oder to the Dnieper. Some officers dream of finding themselves in Romania, then joining the Weygand army and forming an armed detachment against the Soviet Union. . . .The soldiers whose families live in the Ukraine and Byelorussia [Western territories] showed panic and fear of going home. They explained the reason for this fear of returning home in the following way: "Here in the camp we're sitting quietly under the care of the NKVD and camp authorities, and as POWs no one can touch us. At home we won't be POWs anymore and as citizens of the Soviet Union, we'll be under its law. They can arrest us there, send us to prison because every one of us has committed some offense against the Soviet Union."

There have been signs of anti-Sovietism. Some offer the following opinions: "The Soviet Union is worried because there is danger from their allies," "The Soviet Union is very large but it has feet made of clay. It's enough to touch it and it will fall." The POW officer Birnbaum, a journalist, makes anti-Soviet speeches. During the political indoctrination talks, the audience is very passive and one can often hear: "Why do you feed us with those speeches? Our heads are busy thinking where we are going from here." Some others challenge us. For example, "You have nothing. You spend everything on arms. You gave us a knife in the back. Poland is going to exist anyway and it will pay you back. You're going to be our prisoners."

Lieutenant Birnbaum, in his speeches, proved that an attack from the Turkish border against the Soviet Union is being prepared by the army of General Weygand. This attack is aimed at taking over the oil fields of the Caucasus, and in this way depriving the Soviet Union of fuel, which will stop industry and mechanized units of the Red Army. Necessary steps have been taken to stop those anti-Soviet slanders.

Some officers spread the news that the POWs, no matter where their families come from, are being sent to Germany, and in this connection they threaten those who showed loyal attitudes toward the Soviet Union. Those who were loyal are not anti-Soviet. Some of the officers do not believe they are going to be sent home, due to the fact the convoys that go out are being searched and they are being taken out in prison cars. The prisoners are trying to find out, from the person in charge of them, where they are being shipped. In this regard, the personnel was strongly warned. It's been found that some information was leaked by film projectionists.

Some officers say they're being transported to Smolensk. They are not sure about it. They guess that maybe they're being taken out to Smolensk to be fed. The source of this information has not been precisely found. However, after returning to the camp the political officer Fiodorov told some personnel that the prisoners were taken to Smolensk. The commander of the battalion, Commander Stiepanov, was informed that Fiodorov is talkative. Senior Polish officers among the prisoners have ordered those in the first transports to write their destination on the carriage walls so those following will know where they are being transported to. In one of the carriages an inscription in Polish was found on April 7: "Second group, Smolensk, April 6, 1940."

Also almost all the walls of the cars were covered with inscriptions, probably made during earlier transports, with the most anti-Soviet slogans; under many of these were additions in Polish supporting those statements. Orders were given to wash all the walls and to inspect all cars in the future.

In order to isolate the POWs from the personnel, the latter was reduced to a minimum in the camp. The rest have limited access to the camp. However, the majority of the POW officers are convinced they're going home. There's a feeling that it's better to go as fast as possible, and some officers are asking the administrator of the camp to put them in the earliest transport.

On the seventh of April, Generals Minkiewicz and Smorowiński tried to use their authority to convince the other POWs that they should demand transfer to neutral countries. They gave an order that none of the officers should sign any declarations at the transition point obliging them to go to Germany or stay in the Soviet Union. Anyone who signs this type of declaration will be considered a deserter from the Polish army. Some of the officers were conveying this order to others. However, it does not have a strong influence.

In connection with a certain break in transport due to a clerical problem the mood of the POWs got worse. There were speculations that because of the complications on the western front, Germans refused to accept POWs. Prisoner Piekłowski on April 13 expressed his view that no one would be taken out of the camp again. According to him, some more space was made in the camp and that's it. The rest will stay. Those conversations were very depressing to the majority of the POWs. Some of them asked the camp administrator if they would be transported. After obtaining a positive answer they came away happy and told the others about it. However, some of the POWs, because of these breaks in transportation, decided they should try to escape [names given].

In connection with the departures from Ostashkov camp the attitude of the majority of POWs was excitement, especially among the lower-rank police functionaries who are convinced they are going home. Some doubt it. Prisoners from territories of Germany say they wouldn't like going there.

While leaving the camp, deportees throw out matchboxes with little pieces of paper on which they write: "During the search, weapons are being sought. Our personal belongings and things we value are not taken away. It's hard to guess where we are being taken." Deportations are well organized and take place peacefully.

This report provides specific documentation of the meticulous care exercised by the NKVD in transporting the prisoners to their final destination. Few details of how the men reacted to these operations escaped NKVD observation.

Despite the busy atmosphere of camp life, the men remained in a constant state of anxiety about the welfare of their families and loved ones back in Poland. Letters from home seemed to arrive only sporadically and after long delays. Despite a severe shortage of paper, the men began writing home soon after they arrived in camp.

Dr. Czarnek wrote his family on November 1, 1939, asking, "What is happening with you? How is Staszek [his son]? Worry about you is the most painful of all!" Describing his harrowing trip from Kraków to Przemyśl in the first few days of the war, he mentioned the "great relief" he felt over his chance meeting with his nephew Staszek Niewiadomski: "I spent a lot of time with him—he was very good to me."

He reassured Jasia that he was surviving "in a peculiar good way [well, under the circumstances]. I've lost weight during the first few weeks—marching a lot. Still I am in pretty good shape, although I started to smoke again. But I will give it up soon. I can't walk fast, but I couldn't earlier either." He went on to note that at Kozelsk he had been playing chess with Colonel Marian Bolesławicz (father of his daughter's summer playmate), and that the colonel had heard nothing about the whereabouts of his wife and children.

Worries about his own family also flowed forth: "What about the apartment? How do you pay for it? . . . I'm worried about winter. You are left without coal. Jasia, do not think about sending me a parcel!" To combat financial difficulties, he advised his wife to try to collect 250 złoty that the health department owed him for August.

In closing he promised to write again before Christmas and expressed the hope that by then he would be home, adding, "But we had better be more patient!" He asked for a picture of the family and then offered "A big, big hug and kiss for all of you—I keep thinking about you."

From correspondence such as this letter from Dr. Czarnek to his family, the NKVD almost certainly compiled arrest lists. Later, many of the Polish officers' families in the Soviet-occupied zone of the country were rounded up and deported to collective farms and forced-labor camps in Siberia and other remote parts of the U.S.S.R.

Dr. Czarnek's letter reached a wife who had changed remarkably in his absence. After parting with her husband on September 4, 1939, moments after the Luftwaffe strafed their train and blocked the escape route east, Janina Czarnek had followed his emphatic instructions. She had hurried with her daughters to the House of Hełchów, a former convent then being used as a home for the elderly. Dr. Czarnek's routine had involved daily visits to the home, where he provided pro bono care for indigent patients. The nuns were deeply grateful for his services and he knew they would gladly provide refuge to his family. Over the next few days, as the war front swept east past Kraków, the Luftwaffe attacks subsided and Janina resolved to take her daughters home. With that decision, she began to assert herself as head of the Czarnek household and, over time, would display remarkable gifts of ingenuity, judgment, and courage.

The change in Janina was dramatic. Before the war, she had been a lady of leisure, preoccupied with her children, friends, shopping, bridge, and supervising the two servants who cooked and cleaned for the family. That persona was replaced in the first week of the war by a woman who scrubbed her own floors and led the rest of the family by example. She entertained no despair, and confidently told her daughters, "We will survive and we will control our own lives as much as we can."

Immediately she sensed that her husband's absence might be lengthy—and could mean economic catastrophe, since he was the family's only breadwinner. The price of gold skyrocketed in the aftermath of the invasion. Many families like the Czarneks supported themselves in the first few months of the war by selling their jewelry. The Czarneks were not so fortunate. In the panic of the September 3 train-strafing, the metal storage case containing Janina's jewelry had been lost. Thus early in the war she was forced to improvise to support her family.

Her first efforts centered on a home baking enterprise. She had long prided herself as a dessert maker, and shortly before the war she had put aside a large supply of baking ingredients. Within a few weeks after the invasion she was supporting the family by baking cakes. Jaga helped in the kitchen while Magda made deliveries to small stores and restaurants. Tight supplies forced Janina to give up the business after a few months. But in that short time, she had proven her ability to act decisively and shown her determination to hold the family together by whatever means possible.

Declining income forced Janina to put her daughters to work. She quickly placed Magda as a math and Latin tutor. She urged Maria, then in medical school, to work part-time as an extern at a nearby hospital. The combined pay of both daughters, however, was only a pittance.

A big break came in mid-1940 when Janina bumped into a distant Viennese relative who had been sent to Kraków to work for the German General Government. Through him she placed Jaga as a sales clerk at Mienl, a Vienna-based food chain located on the city's main square. A sign on Mienl's front door proclaimed, "NUR FÜR DEUTSCHE," or only for Germans. These words, so thoroughly repugnant to Poles, gave little hint that inside the huge store the Czarneks would solve their pressing income problems.

Mienl's prices were heavily subsidized by the German government. Most of its merchandise sold at a fraction of the market rate. Though in theory only Germans could shop there, in practice Poles also made purchases. At any given moment, many Poles were milling about the store making purchases for German employers. Others, ostensibly there for the same purpose, were attempting to purchase merchandise illegally for their own use or for resale. Those involved in such schemes faced severe punishment if caught.

The store delegated responsibility to its clerks to determine who was eligible to buy. In becoming one of these clerks, Jaga thus gained a position of great strategic importance to her family. With careful discretion she could and did begin selling merchandise at nominal prices to members of her family and, later, to close acquaintances. Her family, in turn, resold most of the merchandise purchased at Mienl at or near its market value. The profits gave the Czarneks enough to live on, but the risks, especially for Jaga, were quite high. And those risks would increase as the war continued and made shortages of basic foodstuffs a feature of everyday life.

In carrying out their small-scale crimes against the German economic system, the Czarneks were greatly aided by one critical skill: They all spoke fluent German. That made them less conspicuous inside the store. And as subsequent events would prove, these same skills would also render their German masters more vulnerable to good alibis well told.

CHAPTER 8

House Calls

The abrupt pounding at the front door began about eleven P.M., just as the occupants of the comfortable three-story house at 69 Zadworzańska Street in Lwów's villa district were preparing for bed. For days, rumors of arrests and deportations had swirled through the city, so the late-night commotion on Saturday, April 13, 1940, sent a rush of fear throughout the household.

Moments earlier, Zofia Neuhoff Hoffman, at thirty-four a woman of regal bearing and striking good looks, had taken her eighteen-month-old daughter upstairs to the third-floor apartment of her brother, Zbigniew, and his wife, Anna. They were keeping Ewa, who was battling a bad case of flu, overnight so that Zofia could keep an early-morning appointment. In the last few months, Zofia's world had turned upside down. Maksymilian, her law partner and husband, had been called to active duty with the Polish army when the war began on September 1. As a reserve captain, he was involved in heavy fighting outside Lwów and was captured by the Soviets in late September. Later the Soviets had taken Maks and many other Polish officers to Starobelsk. There had been little word from him since. The Soviets occupied Lwów in early October 1939 and immediately closed all the courts. The Hoffman law firm became moribund. As the occupation wore on, the firm and its clients—a large oil company and a number of upper-middle-class professionals—faced a bleak future.

Zofia was just returning to the second-floor apartment she shared with her fifty-nine-year-old mother, Maria, when the knocking began. Hurrying down to the first floor, Zofia composed herself before opening the front door, unsure what to expect on the other side. Waiting on the front steps were five uniformed men carrying rifles with fixed bayonets. The blue band above the visor of their spokesman's cap identified him as an officer of the NKVD. He curtly announced that they had come to arrest Zofia Bożena Neuhoff Hoffman and Maria Włodziemiera

Neuhoff, her mother. He then said, "You have one hour to pack your things, no more."

"Where are you taking us? Why are we being arrested?"

"We are taking you to join your husband. You should pack his things as well as your own," said the officer.

He would say little else, except that they would be taken to the train station in the truck parked in front of the house.

He escorted Zofia back to the second floor, where she quickly explained the situation to her mother: "They are taking you, too, because we are sharing the same apartment." The dazed women struggled to collect their thoughts, wondering what could be done, what should be packed for their unexpected journey.

Rushing down from upstairs, Zbigniew was shocked that his mother was being arrested. He implored the men to reconsider, to take him in her place. The soldiers stared back impassively as he emotionally argued his case.

"Why are you taking her?" he implored. "There must be some mistake. There is no reason to take her. I can go in her place."

"Don't worry—you will go too," the NKVD officer replied..

"But this is my mother . . ."

"If they ordered me to shoot my mother, I would do it without any discussion," the NKVD man replied.

Zbigniew knew his pleading was futile. The NKVD officer was implacable. He left no doubt that their orders would be carried out to the letter. Yet there was no verbal or physical abuse. While the packing continued at a feverish pace, the soldiers stood by, watching nonchalantly.

In the scant time available, the women ransacked chests and closets, grabbing garments at random. They filled suitcases, pots, and pans. Many of these possessions were rolled up inside two mattresses. Just as the packing was finished, Maria remembered a purse in which several valuable pieces of jewelry were stored: a diamond pendant, two large diamond earrings, and Zofia's diamond engagement and wedding rings. She tucked the purse inside their luggage, thinking that if worse came to worst the jewelry could be sold. Neither woman thought to pack food. Still wearing the same light dresses they had worn during the day, Zofia and her mother were about to leave, then hesitated at the thought of the cold evening air of the Polish early spring. Both quickly went back to fish full-length fur coats from the closet. The coats were afterthoughts, but they later proved to be the most important possessions taken that night.

The Soviets were divided on the question of what to do about Ewa.

Their orders were to arrest everyone in the second-floor apartment, including Ewa. When they learned that the child was on the third floor, not the second, two or three of the soldiers went up to take a look. Anna confronted them at the door of the bedroom where Ewa slept.

"She is much too sick to leave," she warned.

An animated discussion ensued among the men. They ranged back and forth over the pros and cons of whether the child should be taken or left behind. Finally one of the men insisted to Anna that he must take a look at Ewa to make sure that she was indeed sick. Anna nodded in agreement. Then, sheepishly, the soldier tiptoed across the room to peek into Ewa's crib. After a moment's look, he tiptoed back toward his companions to confirm that, without question, the child was too sick to be taken. Then he turned to Anna: "Swear that you will take care of her." "Of course," said Anna, who was white as a sheet.

By this time the luggage was being hauled to the truck. Zofia anxiously provided Anna with a quick rundown of last-minute instructions about Ewa. Then she and her mother bade Zbigniew and Anna affectionate farewells. Stolidly, under armed guard, the two women walked down the spiral staircase, out the front door, past the lilac bushes along the front walk, and past the brick-colored wire fence to the NKVD's waiting truck. Helping her mother aboard, Zofia turned and bade Zbigniew a last good-bye. Looking back toward the house, she had good reason to wonder when, if ever, she would see her child again.

Ewa Hoffman Jędruch told me a great deal about the NKVD's late-night arrest of her mother and grandmother when we first met in May 1989. I had heard about Ewa's story through friends of friends. Tom Wolanin, the staff director of a congressional subcommittee and a man with many Polish contacts, had heard that her father was among the missing Polish officers from World War II. He, in turn, put me in touch with Janina Jaruzelski, counsel to the House of Representatives, whose family knew Ewa personally and introduced us. Our first meeting was at Hunter College in New York, where Ewa was attending a meeting of the Polish Institute. The story of how her mother and grandmother were arrested was one of the first things she told me. She was hazy about certain details, but told me that many of these could be quickly cleared up by talking to her uncle and aunt, Zbigniew and Anna, then in their mid-eighties. They had emigrated to Argentina after the war and were living in Buenos Aires. Ewa herself had grown up there. She had studied chemical engineering at the University of

Buenos Aires and gone to work for the multinational food giant CPC International immediately after her graduation. In 1969, she had moved to Boston, where she met her husband, Jacek, a nuclear physicist. For the past five years, they had been living in Summit, New Jersey, a suburb of New York.

Jacek also had an interesting past. He had fought with the Polish underground at sixteen and was shot in the arm on one occasion while successfully eluding arrest. As an adult, he had developed a keen interest in Polish constitutional history. In 1982 he had published *Constitutions, Elections and Legislatures of Poland, 1493–1977*, one of the most scholarly and definitive works in the field.

Many conversations with Ewa, supplemented by information from her aunt and uncle, made it possible to reconstruct the story of her family's war years. At our first meeting, it was clear that talking about these matters was not easy for Ewa. "The way it all happened still makes me angry—very, very angry," she told me. "It is the sort of anger we have—but shouldn't have—against fate; I don't know what else to call it. There are few things that can rouse me to this sort of emotional anger, but that is one of them. It seems surprising because I was very small. I don't remember my father. I'm told that I resemble him quite a bit. But I guess I grew up with this tragedy—my mother's tragedy. They were a very happy couple. They were very well matched. . . ."

There were polonized Germans on both sides of Ewa's family. The long period in which the city was part of the Austro-Hungarian Empire brought many such upper-middle-class families to Lwów. From 1912 to the end of World War I, her maternal grandfather had served as an adviser to the ministry of transportation in Vienna. Her father, Maksymilian Adolf Hoffman, spent three years in the Austrian army during World War I. He had also fought in the 1920 Russo-Polish War in the pivotal battle of Lwów. In 1925, he had earned a doctorate of law from the University of Lwów. Soon afterward, he opened his own practice. He met Zofia during her university years, and although she was twelve years younger, their romance quickly blossomed. Soon after Zofia finished law school, they married and she joined his law practice. Ewa was born nine years later.

Maks Hoffman was an avid tennis player and a mountain climber. With their law practice flourishing, the couple enjoyed a large circle of friends and traveled widely throughout Europe. Maks was forty-five when the war began and might have avoided military service. "He had a strong sense of obligation," Ewa said. "It wasn't just him, it was his entire generation. There were lots of reasons why he might have avoided going to the front, but that would have been considered dishonorable. His generation had such pride in the country."

The arrests at 69 Zadworzańska Street were one ripple in a tide of disaster that swept across Lwów and the rest of Soviet-occupied Poland that evening. Thousands of families were being wrenched from their homes for deportation to remote parts of the Soviet Union as a result of a meticulously planned NKVD roundup of the intelligentsia. Prime targets were families of persons who had escaped to the West during the collapse of the Second Republic, families of prisoners of war in Germany and the U.S.S.R., and families of persons who had been previously arrested or deported. Families of captured Polish officers were singled out for special attention. To round up the families of the men imprisoned at Kozelsk, Ostashkov, and Starobelsk, the NKVD is likely to have compiled address lists from the post cards and letters exchanged by the men and their families. Prisoners in each place were encouraged to write home soon after they reached camp.

These arrests were by no means an isolated affair. Viewed in their totality, they represented a modified extension of the brutal economic restructuring, social engineering, and mass terror that Stalin had used to transform the Soviet Union from a backward peasant society into a world-class industrial power. Between 1929 and 1939, forced collectivization, mass deportations, famine, and political purges may have claimed twenty million or more Soviet lives. These staggering losses were roughly offset in 1939–1940 when the U.S.S.R. acquired approximately twenty-three million in new population through the annexation of eastern Poland, the Baltic states, Bessarabia (taken from Romania), and portions of Finland.

The great prize among these conquests was what the Russians called the western Ukraine, or eastern Poland. Ukraine meant "borderland" for good reason: The region contained an admixture of Poles, Ukrainians, Lithuanians, Byelorussians, and others who had vied for centuries to control the vast, flat, and fertile expanses rimmed by the Carpathians in the west and the Black Sea in the south. Mongols and Tartars had launched invasions into the heart of Europe from this open and accessible plain. Born in Kiev, the Russian state had been forced in the thirteenth century to retreat a thousand miles to the northeast by Genghis Khan and his Golden Horde. The Tartars were driven out in the fifteenth century by a coalition of Ruthenian and Lithuanian principalities. A union between Poland and Lithuania followed. With the first partition of Poland in 1772, part of Byelorussia was reunited with Russia. Part of Ruthenia was incorporated into the Austrian Empire. During this period Lwów became the administrative center and capital of Austrian Galicia; its new, germanized name was Lemberg. Many of its most prominent families, like the Hoffmans and the Neuhoffs, were people of German extraction who after several generations in Poland had been thoroughly polonized. In its long history, the Russians had never controlled the city, but they gave it the Russified name "Lvov" when they took over in 1939.

Despite the centuries of external domination, the Ukrainians developed a strong sense of national identity, and were able, as the old empires collapsed, to briefly establish an independent state at the end of World War I. It was born in a period of great regional instability. Much of the Russo-Polish War in 1919–1920 had been fought on Ukrainian soil. By the time the Treaty of Riga settled this conflict in 1921, the Ukraine once again had been divided between Russia and Poland.

During the interwar period, ethnic conflict often flared openly. Ukrainians and Byelorussians represented a clear majority in many areas of eastern Poland, but tended to be concentrated in small villages and the countryside. Ethnic Poles dominated the life of cities such as Lwów, Wilno (Vilnius), and Tarnopol. Because the government in Warsaw tolerated some dissent, while that in Moscow brooked none, Ukrainian nationalists were much more vocal and visible on the Polish side. Soviet propaganda cleverly exploited occasional crackdowns by the Polish government to fan Ukrainian nationalist sentiment, just as it stirred ethnic resentments elsewhere along its border between the Poles and the Lithuanians and the Poles and the Byelorussians.

The Soviets cynically portrayed their intervention in Poland in 1939 as the long-awaited liberation and unification of the Ukraine and Byelorussia, when in fact the primary motive was extension of the U.S.S.R.'s western frontier and defenses by almost two hundred miles. As a member of the Politburo and First Secretary of the Central Committee of the Ukrainian Communist Party, Khrushchev took personal responsibility for overseeing the Sovietization process. He moved from Kiev to Lwów in October 1939. With him came Deputy Commissar Ivan A. Serov, a former Red Army officer who was Khrushchev's personal choice to head the Ukrainian NKVD. Serov would later direct the NKVD's successor agency, the Committee for State Security (KGB). Over the next year, the ruthless, unemotional, but able Serov developed a well-earned reputation as the Soviet Union's master deporter, a Soviet Adolf Eichmann in a sense.

The plundering—euphemistically called nationalization of commerce—began almost immediately after Khrushchev and Serov arrived. Factories, laboratories, even doors and windowframes in private homes were dismantled and carted off to the U.S.S.R. Some 6,500 shops in Lwów were stripped of their goods and closed. Meanwhile essential commodities such as grain, timber, sugar, tobacco, hides, pig iron, cement, drugs, and textiles were collected and sent back to the U.S.S.R. Robbed of basic raw materials, many firms employing skilled labor were quickly put out of business. The region's pauperization became a fait accompli when the złoty was withdrawn from circulation. Individual savings were wiped out overnight, inflation soared, and a thriving black market quickly emerged.

Hundreds of judges, attorneys, policemen, civil servants, local officials, university professors, priests, and businessmen were arrested, jailed, and held for deportation by Serov's agents just prior to the Soviets' sham plebiscite. In his memoirs, Khrushchev presented an account of these elections that is remarkable for its distortion:

> But while these men [those elected] were well known to us, they were by no means our stooges or our planted agents. They were communists by conviction.
>
> The assembly continued for a number of days amid great jubilation and political fervor. I didn't hear a single speech expressing even the slightest doubt that Soviet Power should be established in the Western Ukraine. One by one, movingly and joyfully, the speakers all said that it was their fondest dream to be accepted into the Ukrainian Soviet Republic. It was gratifying for me to see that the working class, peasantry, and laboring intelligentsia were beginning to understand Marxist-Leninist teachings and that they all wanted to build their future on that foundation. Such was the power of Lenin's ideas! Despite all the efforts of the Polish leaders to distort our Leninist doctrine and to intimidate the people, Lenin's ideas were alive and thriving in the Western Ukraine.
>
> At the same time we were still conducting arrests. It was our view that these arrests served to strengthen the Soviet State and clear the road for the building of Socialism on Marxist-Leninist doctrine; but our bourgeois enemies had their own interpretation of the arrests, which they tried to use to discredit us throughout Poland. But despite this intensive slander campaign, the people of the Western Ukraine welcomed the Red Army in the way a laboring people should welcome its liberators.

At about the same time some thirty thousand workers were arrested and deported as slave labor to the coal mines of the Donets Basin in the eastern Ukraine. Those arrested prior to the elections were deported with thousands of others beginning on February 8, 1940, under the notorious Order 001223, signed by Serov on October 11, 1939.

Between the plebiscites and the deportations, escaping from Soviet-occupied Poland became extremely hazardous. One man who succeeded in fleeing was Paweł Zaleski, an active organizer for the Peasant Party in Lwów before the war began. In my research on the atmosphere in eastern Poland during arrests and deportations, I heard Zaleski's name mentioned many times. His war years spanned a remarkable breadth of experience, from the underground to important responsibilities in the government-in-exile. During the first of our many discussions, beginning early in 1990, I was struck by his thoughtful, carefully framed answers. His quiet reserve and self-effacing nature gave no hint of a dramatic past that had put him at the center of many of Poland's most important war-year struggles.

The son of a farmer, Zaleski grew up in Podole and had just received degrees in law and diplomatic sciences from Lwów University when the war began. During his university years he had served as chairman of the student wing of the Stronnictwo Ludowe, or Populist Party, which was known in the West as the Peasant Party because of its strong support among the Polish peasantry. Zaleski's student group was so small that its numbers were a closely guarded secret. Because of their outspoken opposition to the government in Warsaw, the student populists attracted much greater attention than their small numbers might otherwise have commanded. Their efforts centered on organizing for their party among peasants and villagers in southeastern Poland. A lifelong association between Zaleski and Stanisław Mikołajczyk, the head of the Peasant Party and a future prime minister of Poland, developed during this period.

By early December 1939, it was evident to Zaleski that the Soviets were undertaking "a systematic destruction" of the eastern territories. He decided to try to cross the border to Romania and go on to France to join the Polish army-in-exile. He established contact with a prominent Pole named Wincenty Kmiecik in the town of Horodenka. Kmiecik put Zaleski in touch with a railroad man who was leading groups across the border. On December 13, Zaleski, two of his friends, and Kmiecik's son-in-law, Judge Bolesław Piłaciński, went to a cemetery at the edge of Horodenka to meet the railroad man. They arrived about 7 P.M. and hid, as instructed, behind the large headstones. A short distance away, Russian soldiers strolled casually on patrol along one of the main roads through Horodenka. As Zaleski's group waited, other people began slipping into the graveyard, crouching quietly behind headstones. When the guide arrived around 10:00 P.M., about forty men and women had gathered in the cemetery. He told them to follow him in pairs and to say nothing; the border was six kilometers away through hilly, open country.

For two hours, the serpentine procession moved through deep snow and rolling country. Wet snow was falling. At each farmstead they passed, dogs yelped incessantly. Nearing the border about midnight, the procession was moving up a gradual incline when the trouble started. At the crest, about a hundred yards up, a few Soviet soldiers suddenly appeared from nowhere.

"For a moment, both groups froze," Zaleski told me. "They may have thought we were armed." He remembered a woman in the middle of the line screaming, "Jesus, Maria!" One man near Zaleski had a pistol. Zaleski told him to fire the gun in the air and said, "Let's run for the border." The man with the pistol agreed and raised the gun, but it misfired.

At that instant the first flare exploded directly overhead, bathing the group below in light. Then the Soviet platoon opened fire with automatic weapons.

"Don't go back, run for the border," Zaleski shouted to those around him. He and his friends dashed for the crest of the hill, slanting to the side of the Soviet platoon as they rushed forward toward freedom. Bodies dotted the slope as the fleeing Poles continued.

"Davai! Davai!" the Russians shouted as the Poles ran by them.

Zaleski and eight others, including the guide, made it across. About thirty had been shot down or caught on the Polish side of the border. Among them was Judge Piłaciński, who was sent to a forced-labor camp in Siberia. Two years later he was able to leave the U.S.S.R., but his health was broken and he died shortly thereafter in Iran.

"Our guide from the railroad apologized profusely on the other side," Zaleski said. "He told us, 'I never expected something like this.' But we were in Romania and I can remember how extremely happy we were that somehow we had made it across." Zaleski's group slept that night on the earthen floor in the cottage of a hospitable Ukrainian peasant. The next day his group was arrested by Romanian soldiers. They were later tried and convicted of illegal entry into the country. A light sentence ordered them to stay for the duration of the war in Buzău, a small town in southeastern Romania. Within weeks, Zaleski had gone on to France, where he joined the Polish army-in-exile.

*   *   *

The mid-April 1940 roundup involving Zofia Hoffman and her mother was the second of four mass deportations involving a total of at least 1.2 million Poles. The number may have been considerably higher—as high, perhaps, as two million—but few clues to the total were left by the NKVD and no one else knew. According to a study undertaken by the Polish Foreign Ministry, 52 percent were ethnic Poles, 30 percent were Jewish, and 18 percent were Ukrainian and Byelorussian. In some cases entire villages were deported. So were children in summer camps and orphanages. A group of high-school boys from Drohobycz (now Drogobych), like many other youths, were shipped off without any opportunity to bid farewell to their families. Almost 10 percent of the region's population and perhaps two thirds of its intelligentsia were taken away. These deportations continued up to the eve of the German invasion of the Soviet Union on June 22, 1941. Added to the 250,000 fighting men already held in the Soviet Union, the civilian deportations represented yet another systematic effort to destroy the intelligentsia in Soviet-occupied Poland.

Serov issued explicit, detailed instructions to district troikas for the administration of these complex and massive operations. He warned that the task must be carried out swiftly and quietly "to avoid demonstrations or panic among the local population." Most of the deportees were to be arrested at night. They were to be given twenty minutes to an hour to pack, and could take no more than a hundred kilos of belongings including clothing, bedding, cooking utensils, and a month's supply of food. Farmers were to be permitted to take implements, but these were to be stored separately to prevent their use as weapons. Serov ordered that heads of households be segregated in separate cars, and that the trains be prepared for departure at dawn on April 14.

On one of our first visits, Ewa Jędruch told me about Maria Pawulska Rasiej. She, too, came from Lwów and her father, also, had been captured by the Soviets and taken to Starobelsk. Ewa said, "She is a gold mine of information because she was there and she saw what happened." I found that Maria, like Ewa, frequently attended seminars on cultural and political topics sponsored by the Polish Institute. We arranged to meet at one of the institute's functions, at Washington, D.C.'s Georgetown University in June 1990. In several telephone conversations beforehand, Maria had kindly consented to tell me a good bit of her story. As I listened to these experiences, I was often curious how she and her family had summoned the endurance to survive. So I was quite surprised by her diminutive, almost girlish look. Now the

mother of five, she had met her husband, Kazimierz, in London in
1951. Kazimierz had flown with the Royal Air Force and after the
war received a degree in electrical engineering from the University of
London. They had married in 1951 and on borrowed money emigrated
to the United States the following year aboard the S.S. *Neptune*. Kazimierz quickly landed a job as a draftsman with the consulting engineering firm of Syska and Hennessy, progressed with the firm, and
never left. Since coming to America, the Rasiejs had never left the
New York metropolitan area.

Maria remembered vividly the atmosphere in Lwów in mid-April
1940. "I will never forget," she told me, "the feeling of dread that
seemed to permeate everything. . . ."

With tens of thousands of victims targeted for arrest, part of the big
sweep began as a gray dawn broke across Lwów twenty-four hours
before the departure stipulated by Serov. Heavy footsteps and strange
voices from the apartment above awakened Mrs. Maria Pawulska at
six-thirty that morning. She and her three children, Maria, twelve,
Tadeusz, eleven, and Jerzy, eight, slept in the same room—one of two
they still occupied since a flood of squatters from war-ravaged Łódź in
western Poland had begun pouring into their building and neighborhood the previous fall. The sounds upstairs caused the boys to stir in
their sleep. A half-awake Maria looked quizzically at her mother.

"Shush," Mrs. Pawulska whispered, holding a forefinger to her lips.
"I think the Russians are upstairs in the Ojaks' apartment."

Maria and her mother waited quietly for several minutes in the half
light of morning, listening to the tramping on the parquet floors above.
They were not dressed yet when their doorbell rang. They cracked it
open and found Mrs. Ojak and her three children waiting in the hall,
in the company of an escort of militia and NKVD.

"We have been arrested," Mrs. Ojak told the Pawulskis. "They say
they are taking us to Siberia."

The stunned mother and daughter stared back in disbelief.

"Please, would one of you go to second mass? My mother will be
there. Would you tell her what has happened?"

Of course we'll go," Mrs. Pawulska responded. "Is there anything
else we can do?"

Mrs. Ojak simply bit her lip, tears swelling in her eyes as the escort
led her and her children away.

For years Mr. Ojak, an appellate judge, and his family had occupied
the apartment directly above the Pawulskis in the fashionable building
at 12 Ziemiałkowska Street near the center of Lwów, one block from

Kościuszko Park and a short walk to the University of King Jan Kazimierz. The two families were close before the war, but their ties deepened when both fathers became Soviet prisoners within a matter of weeks in the fall of 1939. Captain Stanisław Pawulski, a former adjutant to the commandant of the Lwów garrison, had been serving in the Fortieth Infantry Regiment when captured at the battle of Lwów and eventually, like Maks Hoffman, he was interned at Starobelsk in the eastern Ukraine. After the Soviet occupation began in early October, Judge Ojak was among hundreds of eastern Poland's public officials and civic leaders who were arrested as so-called enemies of the people, or on trumped-up charges of engaging in anti-Soviet activity.

In the months that followed, Mrs. Ojak and Mrs. Pawulska often leaned on each other, exchanging news of their husbands and reassurances that both would eventually be freed. As recently as April 10 or 11, 1940, Mrs. Pawulska had told Mrs. Ojak that apparently the Soviets were transferring Stanisław. She had just gotten a call from Mrs. Gigieł, the wife of an officer also imprisoned at Starobelsk. A telegram from her husband had advised Mrs. Gigieł that letters, cards, and packages should no longer be sent to Starobelsk. Maria told me that the brief message said: "We are being moved in an unknown direction. About our new location, we will let you know." Mrs. Gegieł had promised to bring the telegram over on Saturday to let Mrs. Pawulska read it for herself.

The captain's absence deeply troubled the Pawulski children. Their father's confidence, warmth, and public prominence inspired their pride and admiration. They reveled in the moments when he led the Podhalański Riflemen, a popular infantry regiment, during patriotic parades and official ceremonies. At a shade under six feet tall, wearing his dark-green, ankle-length cape and the Podhale mountaineer's felt hat adorned with a tall eagle feather, the ruggedly handsome captain seemed larger than life.

The Ojaks' arrest left the two Marias standing at the door of their apartment in shock, engulfed by a flood of questions: "What have they done?" "Why are they being taken away?" "How will they live?" Behind them the boys, awakened by the commotion, stretched and yawned.

In several adjacent rooms—each part of an expansive suite once occupied entirely by the Pawulskis, but now taken over by squatters—they could hear people stirring. These were part of the mass of refugees flooding Lwów between October 1939 and April 1940, swelling the population of the country's third-largest city from 350,000 to 1.5 million. Many were poor Jews who feared Nazi anti-Semitism and hoped to emigrate to the Soviet Union—to *raj*, or paradise, as many of them called it. The previous fall thirty-six people had occupied a vacant apartment on the third floor above the Pawulskis. They came from Łódź, Poland's second-largest city, a huge textile center seventy miles southwest of Warsaw. Many were members of the Polish Communist Party, which had been officially disbanded by Stalin in 1938. Early in 1940, eight more people forced their way into the Pawulskis' apartment, taking over all but two rooms. Mrs. Pawulska protested to the militia, hoping the squatters would be removed. Instead she received a reprimand. Her new neighbors, she was told, were heroes who had come voluntarily to go to the Soviet Union (actually to Soviet-occupied territory); she should be proud to have them in her house; and, besides, "it is illegal to have so much space for just one family. You should forgive them for breaking in as they are under great tension escaping from Hitler."

Wishing to avoid the questions, opinions, and advice of these new neighbors, Mrs. Pawulska gave a hushed, curt command to her daughter: "Quick, Maria, let's get dressed so that we can attend to Mrs. Ojak's request."

Before they could begin dressing, their doorbell sounded several persistent rings. Peeking out they found two Soviet soldiers with rifles and fixed bayonets, a Ukrainian militiaman, and two political agents in plainclothes. Maria told me that the men pushed their way into the apartment, telling her mother that she and her children were under arrest and would have thirty minutes to pack before being taken to the train station.

"Where are we being taken?" Mrs. Pawulska asked.

"Siberia," was the blunt reply.

The intruders ordered Mrs. Pawulska to dress in the bathroom while one of the men watched through the open door. The others began ransacking the apartment, expecting, they said, to find a large cache of guns since the head of the household was an army man. While they searched the basement, one of the refugee women, overcome with curiosity, came in and began examining the Pawulskis' possessions.

According to Maria, she held up Stanisław's best leather boots and said: "Let me have these for my husband; you won't need them in the Soviet Union."

Remembering her luggage in the attic, Mrs. Pawulska asked to retrieve it, but the soldiers refused to let her leave the room. "Use these," said one of the squatter women, spreading two huge Persian

quilts on the beds. She and the Pawulskis quickly began piling belongings in the center of the bedcovers. Surveying her kitchen cupboard,
Mrs. Pawulska began reaching for canned and packaged foods, but the
squatter quickly interjected, "Don't take these things; you won't need
them in *raj*." The food stayed behind. In the haste and confusion
several useless possessions were thrown on the pile, including Stanisław's briefcase and a folk costume outgrown by Maria years earlier.

Suddenly a horrifying thought struck Maria. She knew her father
was being moved to an unknown destination. Now she, her mother,
and her brothers were moving to "God knows where." How could they
possibly find each other again? This thought caused her to burst into
tears, crying uncontrollably.

The pro-communist squatter chose this moment to allude haltingly
to her complicity in the Pawulskis' arrest, indicating cryptically that
someone among the starving refugees had acted as an informer to the
NKVD. "You will understand why this was done when you arrive in
the Soviet Union," she said. "We need the apartment, and we know
that nothing bad will befall you." Ironically, thousands of idealistic Jews
like her would also be deported to the Soviet Union, where a harsh
fate awaited them. Eventually Stalin forbade their return to the West,
and most died in the Siberian wilderness.

Maria was still sobbing when she reached the truck in front of the
apartment building. One of the political agents, perhaps in his mid-
twenties and quite young for the job, tried to console Maria. He
insisted that she ride in the cab of the truck.

Maria said he told her, "You are going to the same place where your
father is. Don't worry. Even though it seems that you are leaving
everything here, you are going to a place where you and your father
will meet and stay together." Even though the promise seemed dubious to Maria, the young political agent kept repeating it over and over;
gradually she began to feel calmer.

With their belongings piled in the back of the truck, the Pawulskis
waited while their captors hauled a mother and her son and their
possessions from a nearby building. The young man, probably in his
late teens or early twenties, quickly discovered how to buy time to
pack and how to gain advice on what to take. Fetching glasses, he
began pouring vodka for members of the arrest team. Suddenly their
interest in leaving waned, and they began advising the young man and
his mother on the real necessities for their journey. "Take jewelry,
table silver, furs, and men's clothing. You'll be able to exchange these
for food," the guards advised.

About 8:00 A.M. while the truck was being loaded, an elderly nun arrived to have breakfast with the Pawulskis. Her life had been shattered months ago when her nunnery was shut down by Soviet authorities. On the occasion of its closing, soldiers were permitted to ransack and vandalize the premises. Parishioners were scandalized by one aspect of the incident in particular: The Bolsheviks took consecrated communion hosts and threw them into the garden, then laughed while the horrified nuns scrambled on their hands and knees to recover the small wafers.

The closing of the nunnery cast the sisters adrift with little or no means of support. Talk of this incident caused great sympathy for the nuns, prompting many parishioners to provide them with food and lodging. The elderly sister who happened on the arrest scene had an arrangement in which she taught French to the Pawulski children in return for breakfast. Faced with a new desecration that morning at 12 Ziemiałkowska Street, she simply stood watching in helpless and speechless horror.

Within moments the truck pulled away. Through the rear window of the cab Maria could see her mother and brothers sitting on a mound of belongings. Amik, the family chihuahua, was seated serenely on Mrs. Pawulska's lap. As they left Ziemiałkowska Street and the immediate neighborhood, they passed St. Elizabeth's, a Lwów landmark, which, though smaller, bore a striking resemblance to the cathedral of Cologne. Now boarded up, its twin spires crumpled by bombs, the old church was a desolate shell. The wide, normally busy streets through which the truck drove were empty and ghostlike.

Here, before the war, impressive two-horse fiacres still competed with taxis and tramways, clattering busily across the cobblestones with passengers bound for well-stocked shops, coffee houses, and sidewalk cafés or the university district. Near Lwów Polytechnic Institute, the mathematician Stefan Banach, founder of modern functional analysis, and his colleagues scribbled notes and equations on the white marble tabletops of the Scottish Café. If asked, a waiter would bring a large notebook called the *Scottish Book*, which contained advanced problems, solutions, and comments jotted down in casual conversation by members of the famous Lwów School of Mathematics. One of the contributors to this book was Stanisław Ulam, who later devised the famous "Monte Carlo" method, one of the big breakthroughs in the Manhattan Project. While visiting Lwów in the summer of 1939, Ulam was told by Stanisław Mazur, a prominent member of the Lwów Polytechnic University faculty: "A world war may break out. What shall we do with the *Scottish Book* and our joint unpublished papers? You are leaving for the United States and presumably will be safe. In case of a bombardment of the city, I shall put the manuscripts and the book in a case, which I shall bury in the ground." Mazur and Ulam agreed that the book would be buried near the goalpost on a soccer field just outside the city. Whether the plan was followed is unclear, but Ulam did receive a copy of the book after the war. He translated it in 1957 and distributed it to many of his mathematical friends in the United States and abroad.

Since its days as the primary stopover on the spice route between the Black Sea and the Baltic, Lwów was known as a city of diversity, excitement, and sophistication. By spring 1940, in a mere six months, it was stripped to a bare hulk of its former self. Long queues for bread and other staples were a fixture of daily life. Factories and other capital stock were being dismantled for shipment to the Soviet Union. Fear and uncertainty hovered at every corner. During Stalin's purges it was often said that there were only three types of Russians: those who were in prison, those who had been to prison, and those who were going to prison. The same could now be said of the Poles.

Where Grodecka Street, which split the center of the city, met elegant, tree-lined Marshal Foch Avenue, other trucks loaded with families to be deported were streaming toward the station. Most of the passengers, like the newly pauperized Pawulskis, carried their life's possessions in one or two bundles.

Turning left in front of the once-commanding station, its high glazed arches now bombed into shards, the truck made its way toward the freight yard. There a long line of trucks was already formed, waiting to transfer passengers to the waiting freight cars. Down the tracks, as far as the eye could see, the empty boxcars lay waiting for the human cargo at hand.

The mass deportations from eastern Poland in 1940 and 1941 went virtually unnoticed in the West. Men like Paweł Zaleski who escaped to the West provided detailed reports to the Polish government of steps to Sovietize the territories occupied by the Red Army. The Polish government had accurate information defining the scope and the brutality of the Soviet actions being carried out in this period, but had little success in activating Western concern.

On February 9, 1941, a year and a day after the mass deportations began, the *New York Times* reported that Poles were being taken to Siberia and "dumped there to get along as best they can or to perish if they are not strong enough to survive. . . .Due to the rigid ban on all communication between Russianized Poland and the outside world, it is only now that the facts concerning the deportations and the terrible condition of the victims in their new environment are coming out." The *Times* article said its report had been gleaned from letters sent by deportees in Siberia to the United States and to Polish consular offices in Tehran, Stockholm, and Shanghai. Similar fragmented reports appeared in the Western press, but during this period world attention was riveted by two of the most important stories of the century: the German blitzkriegs of May 10, 1940, in the west and June 22, 1941, in the east.

CHAPTER 9

The Liquidations

<<<<<<<<<<<

In NKVD slang, the event was *mokraya rabota*—literally "wet work"—or a bloodletting assignment. The liquidations began on April 3, 1940, and did not end until May 13, more than five weeks later. There were no survivors and no eyewitnesses. The executioners almost certainly congratulated themselves on a complete and unqualified success, hardly expecting that their work would later be proven careless, even amateurish.

Only one man, a prominent economics professor named Stanisław Świaniewicz, was taken by the NKVD to the edge of the forest where many of the victims were shot, and lived to tell about it. He witnessed a scene that explained much about the way the *mokraya rabota* was conducted and later, in his memoirs, recorded a fleeting portrait of what he saw. His close brush with death and his intimate account of the event made Professor Świaniewicz something of a celebrity to the Poles as the massacre's symbolic significance grew in the postwar years.

Because of his central role in the tragedy, there were questions that only he could answer. For that reason, I began to wonder in early fall 1989 if he was still alive and how I might find him. From the Eastern European section of the Library of Congress, I learned that he was living in London in 1976 when his book *W cieniu Katynia* (*In the Shadow of Katyń*) was published. I was told that the Polish Library in London might know how to find him.

"Yes, he lives near here at the Polish Home in Chislehurst," the director of the library, Zdzisław Jagodziński, told me by phone. He said the professor was about ninety years of age, but still in good health. "I think he might enjoy seeing you," he added.

In mid-November 1989, I took the train from Victoria Station to suburban Chislehurst, about an hour's ride. I had talked to Professor Świaniewicz and he said he would be glad to see me. He was waiting in the lobby when I arrived and greeted me warmly. He insisted that we talk in his room, where he kept many of his books and papers. He used a cane and bent over it noticeably from the waist as he walked, but otherwise he seemed animated and eager to discuss his experiences.

"You know, of course, that I was one of the czar's subjects." Professor Świaniewicz smiled sarcastically when he said this. His life spanned an enormous period of change. He was born on October 23, 1899, and was a student at Moscow State University in 1917 when the Russian revolution began. He told me that in his student years he joined the Polish Military Organization (POW), a secret group set up by Józef Piłsudski to collect information on the czar's army. "We tried to keep track of where various military units were located," he said. The information was then relayed to insurrectionists who were plotting to rid Poland of czarist authority. "My father was an engineer on the czar's railroad. He had no idea that I was involved in such things. I'm sure if he had known he would have been quite upset; it certainly would have cost him his job, perhaps more."

The professor fought in the infantry and later with an artillery regiment in the Russo-Polish War in 1919 and 1920. In the early twenties, he finished his studies at the university in Wilno (now Vilna in Russian, or Vilnius in Lithuanian) and became an assistant professor and later a full professor of economics. In the interwar years he traveled widely in England, France, and Germany. Gradually he developed a worldwide reputation as an authority on forced-labor economics, specializing in the application of such policies in the Soviet Union. In 1965, Oxford University Press published his book *Forced Labor and Economic Development: An Inquiry into the Experience of Soviet Industrialization*. It is still considered one of the most authoritative works in the field and is frequently cited in academic works.

From earlier conversations with Father Zdzisław Peszkowski and Władek Cichy, both of whom were cadets at Kozelsk, I knew that in March 1940 the spirits of the prisoners were soaring with optimism. Professor Świaniewicz also confirmed that the first hint of spring seemed to add to the buoyancy, the widespread belief at Kozelsk that freedom was near.

The men were all aware of Foreign Minister Beck's deal in the spring of 1939 obtaining a British and French guarantee of Polish independence. They knew about the Anglo-Polish Mutual Assistance Pact of April 6 of that year and the military protocol with France that followed in May. The latter committed the French army to begin an offensive on the fifteenth day after any German attack on Poland. Since the men's arrival at Kozelsk and at the other two camps, these commitments had been the subject of constant discussion and speculation. When the Western offensive failed to materialize in 1939, many of the men theorized over the winter months that surely the British and French were merely waiting for spring to mount their attack.

These expectations gained credence when the British and the French began beefing up their forces in the Middle East early in 1940. One of the prisoners' most optimistic theories was that the Soviets would be cowed by the increasing presence of the Western Allies so near to the giant Soviet oil fields at Baku on the Caspian Sea. After all, according to this theory, the French air force was within striking distance of the Soviet oil-tank farms and could easily blow them up.

To further fuel the optimism, in early March constant rumors buzzed about the camp that the Soviets had reached a definite decision to close the camps. Many of the men inferred from these rumors that when the camps were closed, they would be sent home.

Suddenly, on April 3, 1940, at Kozelsk and on April 5 at Ostashkov and Starobelsk, the rumors came true. Using the same detailed procedures at each location, the Soviets began shifting men out of the camps, encouraging their hopes of repatriation while transporting them in small groups to secret execution sites. For unknown reasons, the NKVD decided to spare 448 men from a total of 15,400. Świaniewicz, Cichy, and Peszkowski were among them. Of those spared, 245 came from Kozelsk, 79 from Starobelsk, and 124 from Ostashkov. Had these men not survived, the circumstances under which the *mokraya rabota* was conducted might never have been known.

In his memoirs, Świaniewicz gave an excellent account of the moment when he first learned that some of the men were being removed from Kozelsk. He and a number of officers were waiting in their bunk area for the midday meal when an NKVD rifleman arrived to summon one of their companions for the first transport. He was a twenty-six-year-old lieutenant who had arrived in camp the previous autumn still nursing a leg wound. Even though he had no crutches and was forced to hobble about with the aid of his companions, the lieutenant exuded an infectious optimism.

Since men were frequently called to the camp office for interviews, Świaniewicz and the others assumed that the lieutenant's summons was routine until the guard ordered, "Take your things with you." These words—instantly familiar in Soviet prisons and camps—meant that the prisoner was being separated and taken to some unknown destination. Świaniewicz wrote:

Something strange was reflected in the eyes of this young man who had up till then endured all the blows of fate and physical suffering with equanimity and faith in his lucky star. It was not fear, but as if he had seen a bottomless abyss suddenly open in front of him. Yet he gradually regained control of himself and began to take his leave in his usual jocular manner. His was an exceptional case in that, amongst all who were departing for Katyn, he was the only one who seemed to have some premonition of the fate awaiting them the next morning.

Meanwhile the camp was buzzing with reports that officers from other buildings were being rounded up for departure. Even men housed just outside the monastery walls, in huts where hermit monks once lived, were involved. These men, who hailed from areas of eastern Poland annexed by the U.S.S.R., had been strictly segregated in the past—a policy widely interpreted as a sign of Soviet determination to impose a new state allegiance on these men. Their mixing with those from within the monastery itself seemed solid evidence that the Soviets were experiencing a change of heart toward the men and their country.

The curious crowd of onlookers already gathered in front of the "clubhouse," a large hall otherwise used to show propaganda films, made way for the departing men as the NKVD escorted them inside. As they walked past, there were loud and confident shouts of encouragement. Some of the departing men—particularly those who had fought in September to the bitter end—carried nothing more than an overcoat or a blanket. Others, including several of Dr. Czarnek's colleagues from the medical corps, carried suitcases. Inside the clubhouse, the men were subjected to a thorough search before being treated to a special meal, far better and more generous than the usual fare. The departing men and the crowd outside both reasoned that this comparatively sumptuous repast represented a Soviet attempt to create a favorable last impression before non-Soviet authorities assumed custody of the prisoners.

Further compounding all these surprises were the provisions provided to each man for his journey: eight hundred grams of bread, some sugar, and three herrings wrapped in new gray paper. To prisoners who had scrounged for months for scraps of paper to write letters on, to roll tobacco in, and for use in the latrines, the new paper was, indeed, a luxury—indicative, as one prisoner put it, that "they probably want to produce the impression that there is culture in the Soviet Union."

The men left that afternoon under heavy escort. Because this first group included Kozelsk's four generals, the men remaining behind formed a long honor guard in facing rows. The generals passed through these rows to exuberant cheers. Even the NKVD guards joined in the ovation. Two days later at Starobelsk a military band bade a touching farewell to the first departing group, which included eight generals.

"There was not the slightest suspicion," according to Świaniewicz, that these events were "taking place in the shadow of Lady Death. . . ."

Subsequent transports were organized in a similar way. Each morning about 10:00 A.M. a telephone call came from NKVD headquarters in Moscow with a fresh list of names for the camp commandant. It was a long call, initiating what the men jokingly called the "roulette hour." Many of the strange-sounding Polish names required spelling and respelling, and often there were 250 or more on the list. News that Moscow was on the line spread quickly through the camp, and eavesdroppers listened through the ventilation panes of the commandant's office windows as the names were read. As soon as the first page of names had been written, NKVD guards scurried away to find these men, who were then isolated and searched carefully before receiving their special farewell meal. They too received three neatly wrapped herrings, eight hundred grams of bread, and sugar for their journey.

Much impressed that their names were coming from Moscow, the men interpreted this fact as an indication that the Russians were seriously concerned about their welfare. Rumor had it that a joint French, British, and Russian commission was deciding which officers were to go abroad. Such speculation was encouraged by camp officials, who continued to encourage the idea that the men were leaving the Soviet Union. From time to time an NKVD officer would comment, "You are going toward home" or "to the west." And for the men of Kozelsk this was true: Katyń Forest lay less than 150 miles away, almost due west.

As each group left, those who remained were as perplexed as ever about the criteria Moscow might be using to select the composition of each transport. There was no discernible pattern; age, rank, peacetime occupation, membership in the reserves or the regular army—all were mixed. It seemed that officers with the strongest leadership traits were among the first shipped out, but even this was unclear.

Eyewitness accounts by Świaniewicz and others, like Cadets Cichy and Peszkowski, who were spared can be combined with incriminating circumstantial evidence to establish what happened once the men left Kozelsk.

The festive atmosphere of departure took a sinister turn just outside the camp gates. Waiting out of sight a short distance away were new NKVD guards with truncheons, machine guns, and dogs. Why such harsh measures for a repatriation detail? the men wondered. The infectious optimism of the camp quickly faded as the grim-faced guards roughly ordered the men into cars or trucks without explanation. Carefully detouring the village, they were driven through the woods to the railroad station about five miles away. On a siding there, a section of *Stolypinkas*—windowless prison wagons named for Piotr Stolypin, the conservative prime minister who introduced them during a wave of repression under Czar Nicholas II—waited like huge coffins. Some of the men were severely beaten as they were herded aboard. Inside, as many as sixteen men were jammed into compartments designed for six to eight persons.

As the trains moved out, their carriage doors chained, the prisoners craned to see through small slits near the ceiling, hoping to catch any inkling of direction. Fleeting images gave some cause for encouragement: Shadows from the late-afternoon sun unmistakably read west, toward Poland and home; hope again surged that they were being repatriated.

On through the night the trains rumbled, stopping briefly or at length, depending on the volume of higher-priority rail traffic. On a fast run the church spires of Smolensk would appear with the first rays of sun. A slow run might take two days or more, adding greatly to the discomfort of prisoners who had limited access to toilets.

Eight miles west of Smolensk the trains stopped for good—at a small station called Gniezdovo, a destination noted in the carriage-wall scrawlings of fellow prisoners on previous shipments. The wall notes said "We are getting off at Gniezdovo" but gave no reason why. Gushing steam and boots tramping in dirty patches of spring snow preceded the first shouts of "We are getting off here!" Even so, several hours might pass before the last of the men were unloaded.

The men left the train in groups of thirty, stepping directly from the carriage doors into the rear of an autobus commonly known as a black raven, which had been backed into place by the NKVD. Passing for these few seconds through daylight, the Poles could again see dogs beside the tracks, which were lined with NKVD guards, their bayonets fixed. Inside the vehicle, its windows splashed with lime, the prisoners entered a small passageway flanked on each side by many narrow, low doors opening to cramped individual compartments. Space inside these isolation chambers was so tight that the men were forced to back inside, assuming an uncomfortable crouched or hunched position. Many of the men balked at entering these dark, foreboding holes, fearful that an unusual form of torture might await them. Those who hesitated were roughly shoved inside by an NKVD guard in the passageway.

Świaniewicz was the only prisoner to witness this moment and survive. He told me that his group had been summoned for transport on April 29 and reached the siding at Gniezdovo early on the morning of April 30. Men from other cars were already being off-loaded when an NKVD colonel (this rank was equivalent to that of general in the Red Army, an indication of the high priority of this assignment) came to the door and ordered Swianiewicz outside, then took him to an empty carriage where he was locked in one of its compartments. Although a guard was stationed at the door, he paid little attention to Świaniewicz, who soon discovered a small hole in the wall near the roof of the compartment. Climbing on the upper rack used to stow luggage, Świaniewicz pretended to nap while watching the NKVD remove his companions from the train. In his memoirs, he wrote:

> I saw a fairly large open area with patches of grass. . . .The NKVD colonel who had picked me out from my group stood, with hands in the pockets of his greatcoat, in the middle of the area: he was a tall, stout, middle-aged man, with dark hair and a ruddy face. He was obviously directing the whole operation. I wondered what kind of operation it was. Clearly, my companions were being taken to a place in the vicinity, probably only a few miles away. It was a fine spring day and I wondered why they were not told to march there, as had been the usual procedure on arrival at camps. The presence of a high-ranking NKVD officer at what was apparently the simple operation of transferring several hundred prisoners from one camp to another could be explained if we were actually going to be handed over to the Germans. But, in such a case, why these extraordinary precautions? Why the fixed bayonets of the escort? I could think of no reasonable explanation. But then, on that brilliant spring day, it never even occurred to me that the operation might entail the execution of my companions.

A short time later, Świaniewicz was transferred to a prison van and driven to an NKVD prison in Smolensk. He was held there for six days without explanation, then driven to Lubyanka prison in Moscow and charged with espionage.

The bus he saw shuttling back and forth to the woods beyond the station traveled southwest along the main road between Smolensk and Vitebsk for about two miles, then turned left onto a curving, heavily wooded lane sloping south toward the Dnieper River. This wooded region, from Smolensk to the town of Katyń about four miles further west—the whole valley of the Dnieper including its tributary the Olsha—was known locally as Katyń Forest.

At the end of this lane, three quarters of a mile from the main road and just above the river marsh, was the Little Castle of the Dnieper, a summer house, or dacha, built by the NKVD in 1934. On the right, about halfway between the main road and the Little Castle, a small clearing appeared; here, large open pits waited to claim new victims.

No doubt many of the men sensed the worst on the drive out from the train station. The last words written by Major Adam Solski in the diary recovered from his body noted:

April 9: Ever since dawn it has been a peculiar day. Departure in lorries fitted with cells; terrible. Taken to forest somewhere, something like a summer resort. Very thorough search of our belongings. They took my watch, which showed time as 6:30, 8:30; asked about my ring, which was taken; ruble belt, penknife.

In this clearing, near the edge of common graves dug deep in dry, sandy soil, death was swiftly dispensed with assembly-line efficiency. Forced to their knees near the edge of the pits, the Polish officers were quickly shot behind the head at close range, probably with a German-made pistol—the light 7.65 mm Walther. The smooth-firing Walther was considered the finest police pistol in the world. It had been exported in large quantities before the war to the Baltic states, where NKVD agents could have easily seized them. A few victims may have been pushed into the pits, or even forced to lie on bodies already in the graves before being shot. Many younger men resisted and were stabbed with bayonets, often several times. The NKVD reserved a macabre death for those most difficult to subdue. Their mouths were stuffed with sawdust and gagged; their overcoats were then yanked above their heads and fastened with choke knots about the neck. Their hands were lashed tightly behind the back and pulled sharply toward the shoulder blades. Finally, a cord connected their raised hands to the choke knot around the neck. If these victims continued to struggle, they strangled themselves to death.

It is difficult to imagine proud Polish fighting men meekly kneeling, at the request of NKVD agents, before pits where their companions had already been executed—and it is doubtful that they did so. Instead, the final seconds of their lives were controlled so completely by the NKVD that struggle was clearly futile, if not virtually impossible. For the victims these last seconds were marked, almost certainly, by disorientation and helplessness. It seems likely that their thoughts—geared so recently to hopes of repatriation—suddenly swirled in fear and dismay as the first shots were fired outside the bus. Alone and immobilized inside cramped cubicles, the officers' only companions now were shock, a gnawing dread, and, for some, resignation. After each execution, those who remained could probably hear the guard's footsteps in the passageway as he came back to fetch a new victim. As the guard opened each victim's door in turn, he barked orders to move out and probably used his bayonet as a prod to force the victim toward the door. Their muscles tight and aching from the cramped ride, many of the prisoners must have stumbled down the corridor toward the door, blinking there in momentary blindness at the exterior light. As their feet hit the ground, NKVD agents stationed on either side of the door would have quickly grasped each arm and begun dragging the victim a short distance to the edge of the pits. There, a sharp blow behind the legs would have knocked the men to their knees while another member of the NKVD team stepped forward, Walther in hand, placing the muzzle six to ten inches behind the victim's head before squeezing the trigger. The last member of the NKVD team, the reloader, probably stood a few paces to one side, calmly preparing another weapon for the next round of victims. No doubt the executioners managed this abattoir with ruthless detachment, processing the daily quota of victims so efficiently that the "black raven" could make a round-trip run from the train station to the forest in thirty-five to forty minutes. While the driver returned to the train station, the team at the scene neatly stacked the newest victims like cordwood on those already in the pit. It is quite possible that the execution team itself was exterminated in mid-May when the job was complete.

Only the bullets were merciful at this scene of slaughter. They pierced like estoques to the occipital bone, coursing upward from this small protrusion at the base of the skull, then passing through the brain to a point of egress between the nose and hair line. This angle suggests that each victim's head was bent forward and that the executioner stood close behind him, firing slightly downward. A shot thus aimed offered two practical advantages: It caused instant death and minimal loss of blood. It was a vintage Bolshevik technique developed in the early days of the revolution when Lenin's secret police, the Cheka, routinely shot so-called enemies of the people in basements of prisons and public places throughout Russia. Wishing to avoid a bloody aftermath with half-dead victims writhing on the floor, the Cheka perfected what the

Germans would later call the *Nackenschuss*, or shot in the nape of the neck. By the 1930s it had become the standard method used by the NKVD to dispatch Stalin's purge victims and others.

The 4,143 victims—all from what the Soviets called Camp 13, or Kozelsk—were buried in eight common graves ranging in depth from six to eleven feet. The largest of these was L-shaped, eighty-five feet by twenty-six feet at its longest and widest points. Its twelve layers of bodies were neatly stacked so that the heads of those in each new row were placed facedown on the feet of the men below. This grave held approximately 2,800 men. The weight and compaction of tons of heavy sand used as fill between the surface and the men on the top layer was so great that it served to compress the bodies; as fluids began to leak in the decomposition process, a bacteria-free seal was formed that helped mummify the corpses. The finishing touch on this *mokraya rabota* was a tidy landscaping job: Small birch trees were transplanted onto the surface of each grave. The NKVD made its last deposits in the gruesome bank below on or about May 13, 1940, with no reason to expect that the world would witness sensational withdrawals three years later.

The site of the shootings was a wooded compound known locally as Kozie Góry ("Goats' Hills") because of the small hills near the main road on its northern and western boundaries. Kozie Góry was a private preserve of the NKVD and a venerable execution site. Agents of the Cheka had shot several hundred men and women here shortly after the revolution. These victims lay in a common grave only a few paces east of where the Polish officers were buried. During the twenties, the only visitors to the wooded area were villagers from nearby who came for berries, mushrooms, and kindling. But in 1929, the NKVD posted signs forbidding trespassers. A barbed-wire fence was erected in 1931. Three years later the NKVD built the Little Castle on the high grounds just above the marsh of the Dnieper River. To the peasants of the surrounding area, there was much mystery attached to this building. Little was known about those who came and went there. The place became even more secluded in 1940, when the NKVD initiated dog-escorted patrols around the perimeter fence of the compound.

Here, near the source of Europe's third-longest river, in a remote forest five hundred miles from his beloved Kraków, Zbigniew Czarnek was probably murdered on April 8. He departed, according to Colonel Bolesławicz, who survived, in the transport of April 7, which included mostly senior officers. Bolesławicz handed Dr. Czarnek a letter to his wife as he departed that afternoon.

Why Dr. Czarnek was liquidated is still difficult to say. The Bolsheviks charged him and his companions with being bourgeois enemies of the people. It was an abstraction that he, no doubt, regarded to the moment of his death with amused contempt. His good qualities, multiplied many times over by companions who shared the same fate, explained much about subsequent Polish bitterness. Dr. Czarnek and the others were part of the Polish elite; their destruction was an irreparable loss to Poland. Staszek Niewiadomski told me that his uncle was admired by his fellow officers because of his strong sense of duty, his perseverance in adversity. They respected him both as a physician and as a man of considerable knowledge and experience in military matters. By his family and friends, he was seen as quiet, introspective, and thoughtful, a doting husband and father, a skillful and committed internist. Even taking into account possible embellishments by his companions and family, these assessments make his death seem not just cruel, but senseless—which it was. Why were Dr. Czarnek and his companions not sent to the gulag system and simply worked to death like so many millions of others? Revenge, possible bureacratic blunder, Stalin's determination to suppress Polish independence by eliminating its leadership class—all these have been cited as possible explanations for why the Polish officers were murdered. But even today, half a century later, the truth is still unclear.

Whatever the motive, the Poles were determined never to forget. Unlike millions of Stalin's Soviet victims, who moldered anonymously in graves all across the U.S.S.R., Dr. Czarnek and his 4,143 companions gradually became immortalized in the eyes of their countrymen. Their deaths appealed to that peculiarly Polish concept of triumph which is earned through endurance, the victory of honor over shame. To the Poles, the men of Katyń represented a national elite, heroically sacrificed on the altar of freedom. Their deaths symbolized the death of the interwar Second Republic, a fleeting period of independence between the third and fourth partitions. The qualities of these men were later idealized by yet another generation of Poles in revolt, striving again to regain the nation's lost state.

The path from Kozelsk to Katyń Forest was clearly documented by Swianiewicz, Peszkowski, Cichy, and 242 others who, for still unexplained reasons, were "saved" by Soviet authorities. While their companions were being murdered, these men were transferred to a camp called Pawlishtchev Bor and survived. More than two hundred men from the camps at Starobelsk and Ostashkov were also transferred to Pawlishtchev during the period of the executions in April and May

1940. Subsequent accounts provided by these fortunate few presented a clear picture of what life in the camps was like, how the liquidations began, and how these operations were carried out—up to, but not including, the final moments of the victims' lives.

Almost fifteen thousand men from all three camps were murdered. Of these about 4,400 had been imprisoned at Kozelsk. Much less is known about what happened to the men from the other two camps—the 3,920 prisoners of Starobelsk and the 6,500 men at Ostashkov—on the way to Katyń. From the small number of men from each camp who were spared, it was learned that Starobelsk's victims were first taken to the Kharkov railroad station about 125 miles west of the camp. Stanisław Pawulski, Maria's father, was almost certainly among the victims who traveled this path. Maks Hoffman, Ewa's father, may have traveled it as well, although there is some evidence that he was transferred to Vorkuta, which is near the Arctic Circle. From Kharkov the victims were driven away in automobiles. The men from Ostashkov who were spared saw some of their fellow prisoners taken to the railroad station at Bologoye, about seventy-five miles northeast of the camp; others, they believed, were taken on to the railroad station at Vyazma, about ninety miles south of the camp. These eyewitness reports are consistent with other evidence, such as the notes listing these destinations that the men themselves wrote on the carriage walls of their trains. The fate of these victims remained unknown for half a century until Soviet president Gorbachev acknowledged on April 13, 1990, that the NKVD had murdered the men from all three camps. Two months later, Soviet authorities disclosed that the men from Starobelsk were probably buried in a park outside Kharkov, and that the men from Ostashkov were buried in a forest near Miednoye, a village on the Moscow–Leningrad highway.

Over the years, the lack of information spawned many groundless rumors about the fate of these men. In September 1941, Polish deportees from the Kola Peninsula reported that a boat bearing prisoners from Ostashkov had been towed into the White Sea and sunk with artillery fire. Later, one missing man's wife, Catherine Gaszciecka, reported that in June 1941, as a passenger on a transport crossing the White Sea to a labor camp, she talked to two Russians who claimed to have seen two barges, containing seven thousand Polish prisoners, towed from Arkhangelsk and sunk. She said one of the Russians, a young guard, "mocked me and said that they [the Poles] had all been drowned there, in the White Sea." She said an elderly Russian from the barge crew overheard this conversation and later came to her to express sympathy, but confirmed that he too had seen the barges sunk. The vagueness of these rumors, coupled with sudden amnesty for Polish prisoners following the German invasion of Russia on June 22, 1941, caused the Polish authorities to quietly let the matter drop; any chance of clearing up the rumors was quickly lost.

We now know that the men from all three camps were liquidated during the same six-week period in the spring of 1940. Because the men from two of the camps disappeared without a trace, these NKVD operations have often been described as thorough, completely efficient. This, as we shall later see, was far from the actual case. Many important details were carelessly handled and would subsequently cause the Soviet government acute embarrassment.

The Soviets made one lame attempt to explain the executions as a bureaucratic mistake. Stanisław Mikołajczyk, General Władysław Sikorski's successor as premier of the government-in-exile, reported that an officer attached to the Soviet embassy in London gave the following explanation of the executions about a year after the war at a private party in that city:

Early in 1940, the Red Army sent a staff officer to the Kremlin to find what Stalin planned to do with the Polish officers. A planned swap in which the officers would be turned over to the Germans in return for 30,000 Ukrainians had just fallen through. The Ukrainians were Polish Army conscripts captured by Germany in the previous September and interned in two camps in eastern Poland. The Germans at first agreed to the exchange, but backed out at the last possible moment, telling the Soviets to take the Ukrainians and keep the Poles. Then came rumors in Moscow that the Ukrainian conscripts and the Polish officers would be organized into special units of the Red Army. Senior commanders were aware of such talk, but had nothing specific to go on. The staff officer was sent to get Stalin's clarification.

The staff officer saw Stalin and briefly explained his superiors' question. Stalin listened patiently. When the staff officer finished, Stalin supplied him with a written order. Such orders were common, often requested by subordinates as a matter of self-protection. In this case, Stalin took a sheet of his personal stationery and wrote only one word on it: "Liquidate."

The staff officer returned the one-word order to his superiors, but they were uncertain what it meant. Did Stalin mean liquidate the camps, or liquidate the men? He might have meant that the men should be released, sent to other prisons, or to work in the gulag system. He might also have meant that the men should be shot, or otherwise eliminated. No one knew for sure what the order meant. But no one wanted to risk Stalin's ire by asking him to clarify it. To delay a decision was also risky and could invite retribution. The army took the safe way out: it turned the whole matter over to the NKVD.

For the NKVD, there was no ambiguity in Stalin's order. It could only mean one thing: that the Poles were to be executed immediately; that, of course, is exactly what happened.

No Soviet embassy official would ever have passed on such comments as idle cocktail gossip. The story may have been an unofficial attempt to defuse the controversy by blaming the deaths on an overzealous NKVD. If so, there was one element of consistency in the presentation. In 1940, shortly after the executions, NKVD chiefs Lavrenti Beria and V.N. Merkulov met with a few of the survivors from Kozelsk and Starobelsk. They told these men that "a great mistake" had been made with the others from these camps. The comment was unclear at the time, but later would cause deep concern among Polish leaders.

One thing seems certain: The liquidations were not carried out by mistake. In the Soviet Union, any decision of such magnitude and sensitivity could have been made by one man alone: Joseph Stalin.

While the liquidations in Katyń Forest were under way, a mass roundup of the intelligentsia began in German-occupied Poland. Among those arrested up was Dr. Czarnek's younger and only brother, Witold, a prominent lawyer in Rzeszów. Witold's concern about his brother's wife and children had prompted him to travel to Kraków in late 1939 to make sure they were safe and able to provide for themselves. After his arrest the following spring, Witold, then fifty-one, was taken briefly to Auschwitz, where overcrowded conditions resulted in his immediate transfer with five hundred other prisoners to the Sachsenhausen concentration camp near Berlin. (In a strange turn of events, Iwo Pogonowski, who, seventeen years later would marry Witold's niece Magda, was on the same transport.)

The conditions of forced labor at Sachsenhausen took a terrible and immediate toll on Witold. Working on a starvation diet, he and his fellow prisoners were forced to run with bags of cement weighing more than a hundred pounds from river barges to nearby construction sites. Sadistic guards often beat prisoners who were breaking down under the severe regimen. In the fall of 1940, Witold was struck by a guard and fell face forward in the mud. The guard stepped on Witold's neck, forcing him down in the gooey mess. Within minutes Witold had drowned.

News of his death reached the Czarneks in Kraków at the end of 1940, coming as a great and bitter shock. By then the Czarneks were already involved in the underground. But with Witold's death, those activities took on a new and grim element of urgency. Of the five hundred men in the transport that took Witold from Auschwitz to Sachsenhausen, Iwo Pogonowski could count only thirteen others besides himself who had survived at the end of the war.

The fate of the Czarnek brothers—one murdered by the Germans, the other by the Soviets—symbolized the fate of the Polish nation.

CHAPTER 10

Trains to the East

‹‹‹‹‹‹‹‹‹‹‹

The fear, dread, and despair of a forced departure into the unknown all came crashing home to the Poles being deported from Lwów as the huge metal-framed doors scraped shut and the heavy iron bars were locked into place from the outside. No czar ever boasted a more practical prison or a more degrading chamber of private horror than the massive green-and-rust-colored boxcars in the Lwów freight yard, their human cargo ticketed collectively by the authorities for a cavernous maw known simply as "the East." Nothing drove home with such finality to those inside their helplessness, their utter inability to resist, as the spiking of these doors.

As they slammed shut, the fifty or sixty desolate souls inside were plunged into immediate darkness and stunned silence, dumbstruck by the chaotic, noisy calamity of arrest, frantic packing, the hysterical crying of children, the frantic shouts of families being separated at the freight yard, the bewildered milling throng there—all under the prod of well-armed NKVD agents. Slowly the blackness diffused into gray as eyes adjusted to the glimmer of light strained through four small grates on each side and at each end of the boxcar near the ceiling. These apertures, about two feet wide by one and a half feet tall, were just large enough for one or two people to peer out and were generally reachable only from the third tier of the slats that had been attached to the interior walls as makeshift bunks. There the more agile, generally younger deportees squirmed and strained to catch sight of any familiar face below, and to toss out notes hastily scrawled on scraps of paper—urgent messages to family and friends, names and addresses of people to be contacted, expressions of love and farewell, prayers for mercy and protection.

Zofia Hoffman and her mother, Maria Neuhoff, were herded with their hastily assembled possessions into one of these crates of gloom around midnight on April 13, 1940. The NKVD had been busy that

entire day and evening with human freight consolidation. Thousands
of people from Lwów and surrounding villages and towns in eastern
Poland had already been brought to the freight yard and were loaded
by the time Zofia and her mother arrived. Hundreds of boxcars now
waited, row after row, disappearing into an infinity of darkness.

As the passengers' eyes adjusted to the dim surroundings, they
quickly surmised just how primitive this journey would be and could
only assume that their destination would be no more hospitable.
Mounds of luggage and personal effects—pillow cases stuffed with bedding and clothes, boxes with pots and pans, containers of food, and
a wide assortment of other items—were strewn, like their traveling
companions, across the entire floor of the freight car, because neither
shelves nor seats were provided. The few planks attached as bunks to
the walls would only accommodate a few people and were devoid of
bedding. A dilapidated iron stove, once fueled by coal or wood, sat
rusting in disuse. Toward the center of the car, behind a blanket that
afforded a minimum of privacy, a pail sat beside a large round hole in
the floor—a crude arrangement for the disposal of excrement, and the
source of breath-arresting foulness.

The air itself seemed captive, hovering over the rectangular, unven-
tilated pit with a dank, stale, and cloying presence. Sharing it were
people of all ages being thrown together for the first time: the old and
infirm, young mothers with infants and toddlers, school-aged children,
adolescents, and a few, very few, able-bodied adult males—a jumbled,
jostling, and uncomfortable cargo. The discomfort made real sleep
almost impossible. Passengers who dozed were periodically awakened
by the shrieks and sobbing of the small children. Huddled against their
things, the passengers waited and wondered when the journey would
begin and where it would take them.

Elsewhere in this vast caravan, as the morning light slowly filtered
through the iron gratings above their heads, the Pawulskis also waited.
Maria told me that it was barely daylight when her mother broached
a delicate subject with the children. Mrs. Pawulska was having second
thoughts about taking Amik, their small chihuahua, on what promised
to be a long and difficult journey. The guards had raised no objection
when they climbed into the boxcar with the dog. It seemed unlikely
that they would be prevented from taking Amik, but how well the
animal might fare was another matter. By morning, Mrs. Pawulska had
decided that the dog would be better off staying in Lwów.

"We will have a very hard time taking care of him," she warned her
children. "Amik will be miserable. We must consider what is best for

him." Her two sons, Tadeusz and Jerzy, sat in dejected silence, but Maria reluctantly conceded that caring for the dog would be difficult.

The previous afternoon the Pawulskis had been visited by Captain Pawulski's cousin, Wanda Tomaszewska, who managed to find them despite the mass confusion in the freight yard. Wanda came to say good-bye and to find out what, if anything, she could do to help the family. Mrs. Pawulska confided her deep concerns about the food situation. She was embarrassed to admit that a pushy neighbor had dissuaded her from bringing food that the family obviously needed—canned goods and other nonperishables that lined the pantry in her apartment. She also regretted that a pot of tripe had been left sitting on the kitchen stove. The two women agreed that the neighbors might already have eaten the tripe, and Maria, who detested the dish, secretly hoped that they had. Perhaps the other things could be retrieved, Mrs. Pawulska speculated. Wanda promised to go back to the apartment to look into the matter and bring to the train whatever food she could find early the next morning. Before leaving she also expressed reservations about the dog, and offered to take him home with her if the family so wished.

Early the next morning, as promised, Wanda arrived at trackside carrying several bundles of food. The guards agreed to open the doors so she could pass them inside. Standing at ground level, a foot or so below the top of the track bed, Wanda could barely lift her packages high enough for Mrs. Pawulska, leaning out the door of the freight car, to grasp them.

"This is the best I could do," Wanda reported.

"Thank God you could do it," Mrs. Pawulska responded.

They spoke for a few minutes more about family matters. Then Wanda asked about the dog.

"We are going to leave Amik here with you," said Maria, cradling the small animal in her arms. Tadeusz and Jerzy stood by quietly, still far from certain about this decision. Not wishing to belabor the matter, Mrs. Pawulska quickly wrapped part of Amik's leash several times around his body and used the rest as tackle to lower him carefully into Wanda's arms. The boys and Maria observed these delicate maneuvers with intense interest, offering muffled good-byes when the exchange was complete. Sensing that it would be unwise to prolong the farewell, the two women exchanged a few last words. Their outstretched hands barely touched as they said good-bye.

A short time later the caravan began to move. The first forward lurches caused the throng of friends and relatives still at trackside to surge toward the cars, reaching out with their hands, holding on to the sides, as if, somehow, they might hold back the massive convoy. A final flurry of paper scraps—last-minute notes and appeals—descended from the grates. At this moment, an immutable fate clearly upon the passengers, a few voices, haltingly at first, sang the "Serdeczna Matko" ("O Loving Mother of All"), a deeply moving hymn sung by generations of Poles in times of difficulty. In the Pawulskis' wagon and all up and down the line, the scattered voices welled into a massive chorus as an emotional dam burst open, flooding the freight yard in song.

The train lumbered for the first hundred miles toward the Soviet border through relatively flat farmland, halting in only a few places, where sympathetic bystanders waited to offer tidbits of food and words of comfort. Most were harshly fended off by the guards. New faces appeared constantly at the window grates as passengers took turns briefly capturing gulps of fresh air and glimpses of the passing landscape. Once they were across the border, speed began to build, the cars rocked more rhythmically, sparks flashed brightly in the tunnels as the caravan thundered through the fertile and gently rolling lands of the western Ukraine.

The train did not stop at either the giant railyards of Kiev and Kharkov or other large terminals. Instead it stopped on sidetracks or, often, in open country. As they passed through the big stations, the Poles were struck by the indifference of the people on the platforms. As the deportees would later learn, the sight was not new or unusual, and the Soviets could hardly be expected to turn their heads toward what for them was simply a normal occurrence.

Irregularly, at stops such as these, some food and liquid were distributed among the passengers. The typical fare, passed out at two- or three-day intervals, consisted of black bread and an occasional bucket of fish soup or vegetables; heads, entrails and bones often floated on the surface. *Kipiatok*, or boiling-hot water, was generally provided. Young mothers in particular depended on it to make porridge for their infants. Passengers in many cars received no hot food during the entire journey. Hunger was rampant and thirst even more acute. Discomfort from cold was so severe that slats from the sleeping bunks were ripped off the walls and used as firewood. Occasionally the train stopped for the night in open countryside, or to allow passengers to climb down to relieve themselves. While the long row of men, women, adolescents, and children squatted awkwardly in unison, their armed guards frequently shouted and jeered at their predicament. From a commanding perch on the last car of the train, a machine gunner watched impassively, an ever-present reminder that at any sign of disturbance the entire row might be raked by a withering hail of bullets.

From the moment of their boarding, Maria was glad to see that their companions on the truck ride from the apartment to the train station, a Jewish woman and her son, were assigned to her wagon. She soon learned that the young man who had poured vodka for their captors was named Ryszard Horowitz, that he was just finishing high school, and that he planned to enter Lwów University in the fall. Ryszard was leanly built, of medium height, quick-witted, and intelligent. He had dark curly hair and a thin face and exuded an air of confidence. Although his mother seemed overbearing, Ryszard manipulated her skillfully. Ryszard's father, a banker, had disappeared soon after the Soviet occupation began. Since then, Mrs. Horowitz had become increasingly dependent on her only son.

To a girl still short of her thirteenth birthday, flattered only recently by any attention from the opposite sex, Ryszard seemed a paragon of sophistication. At first, Maria felt skinny and awkward in his presence and was quick to make verbal stumbles. At four feet six inches tall and seventy-five pounds, she was delicate and small-boned, had bright and inquisitive eyes, carried herself with perfect posture, and usually displayed the strong assurance of an eldest child. But her instincts left no doubt: Her fascination with Ryszard was not to be disclosed to anyone—least of all her mother. Weeks earlier, while queuing for sugar, she had spent two hours talking to a boy her own age. Later, walking by her apartment with friends, the same boy passed Maria a note saying he hoped they could meet again. Maria innocently tucked the note inside the sleeve of her dress and forgot it. That night at home the note fell on the floor, where it was discovered by her mother. After reading the contents, a mildly shocked Mrs. Pawulska announced, much to Maria's embarrassment, "I think you are carrying on a secret life, and let me tell you that I am certainly not amused!"

On the nights when the train rolled on late into the evening, Maria and Ryszard inched their way toward the upper slats nearest the grate, where they could look out together at the vast countryside. They spent hours in hushed conversation, talking about what the future would bring. Ryszard speculated enthusiastically about limitless professional possibilities, describing how difficult it would be to select one and stick with it. Maria listened attentively, interjecting an infrequent question here and there, mainly content to smell the fresh evening air and observe. Once when Ryszard asked her what she planned to do, she hesitated before saying, "Maybe I'll sing." It was not a thought she dwelled on, but Maria had been complimented many times on her voice and knew she had talent. Music was a passion in her family. Her mother had trained briefly as a mezzo-soprano and had sung as a young adult in choirs and with small opera groups. In recent years, her mother and father had liked nothing better than taking an overnight trip to the opera in Warsaw. Ryszard agreed that music could be a spectacular career but pointed out that reaching the top would involve a long and arduous struggle.

The weather on most of these evenings was clear and crisp, with skies so bright that the stars seemed barely beyond the passing fields. After Kharkov, the route began bending north in a wide arc toward Kuybyshev, where the mighty Volga River reaches a confluence with the Samara. A short distance to the east, the caravan began ascending the western slopes of the Ural Mountains, the traditional boundary between Europe and Asia. Here the huge, flat expanses of eastern European plain gave way to a spine of low-lying, tree-covered peaks extending longitudinally for 1,640 miles from arctic marshes to semi-arid pasturelands. Beyond lay the vast Siberian wilderness, belted from east to west by tundra, taiga, and steppe, a mysterious land of extremes where the pilgrimage would end.

On the first leg of the journey through the Urals, the train entered a small plateau near Ufa, a new center of industrial activity. Here along the Belaya River people first congregated around a fortress designed to protect the trade route through the mountains. In recent years development had been stimulated by the development of the Volga-Urals oil field, bringing large refineries and a petrochemical complex. Peering through the window grate, Maria and Ryszard were impressed by the endless flow of smoke from Ufa's factories, which stretched for twenty-five miles along the high bank of the river.

The train now labored along the Trans-Siberian Rail Road leaving the Urals behind at Chelyabinsk, a large steel center and home of the largest tractor factory in the Soviet Union. Here the landscape abruptly changed into virgin forests of pine, fir, spruce, and birch that continued for eight hundred miles to Novosibirsk. This massive expanse of taiga is drained by the Ob and the Irtysh rivers, which form one of the world's largest river systems. En route, at Omsk, the Soviets began detaching a few wagons at a time, sending deportees in different directions.

The train had crossed the Irtysh at Omsk, almost at the midpoint on the journey through these endless virgin forests. It met the Ob at Novosibirsk, the largest city in Soviet Asia. As one of the U.S.S.R.'s new cities, it was well lighted. Its huge radio tower, one of the world's largest, could be seen for miles around. Here the caravan turned sharply south for the last leg of the journey. The route kept to the banks of the Ob for about a hundred miles, then bent back westward as it left the taiga and entered the treeless and arid steppes. About three hundred and fifty miles to the south, the route once again came to the Irtysh near Semipalatinsk, Siberia's gateway to Central Asia, where the great caravans from Mongolia once stopped. From Semipalatinsk at the river's southernmost reaches, the train headed straight south across the steppes for another hundred miles to Zhangiz-Tobe.

There, after three thousand miles and seventeen days, the journey by train ended. Along the way the passengers had had no chance to bathe and were generally dehydrated from an acute lack of water. Hunger verged toward starvation. Diarrhea, dysentery, fevers, and convulsions were rampant, yet doctors and medicine were nowhere to be found. In the midst of great accumulations of filth, babies were born and death became a daily companion, preying mainly on the young and the old. Many of the dead lay lightly covered by straw in ditches along the route; others were dumped on the open ground at trackside. If the train stopped long enough, relatives gouged out shallow graves with any available instrument. The prospect of being left behind, unburied or in one of these nameless graves, was most horrible to the elderly, who also sought desperately to avoid becoming a burden to the able-bodied.

Zhangiz-Tobe was an exotic rail junction where Maria was astonished to see camels lazily pulling carts along the thoroughfares. The depot retained the flavor of a small bazaar where merchants, livestock, and colorful visitors with the look of nomads milled about.

The train had barely arrived when many deportees were reloaded on trucks to be distributed among one of two types of cooperative or collective farms scattered across the steppes. One type, the kolkhoz, was ostensibly owned by the workers and run on a democratic basis. Theoretically, each member of the cooperative shared equitably in the overall output of the enterprise. The second type, the sovkhoz, was state-owned; its workers were paid wages like employees of other state-owned enterprises. As a rule, sovkhozy tended to be somewhat larger than kolkhozy. However, on the steppe, kolkhozy were more numerous.

As the last truckload of deportees left the Zhangiz-Tobe railyard, the guards told the passengers in the Pawulskis' wagon that they would not leave until the following day. A short time later, Maria and Ryszard observed the annual May Day parade proceeding along a dusty street.

Amid squalor at every turn, they watched as a strange procession of military and farm vehicles went by. Marchers carried banners proudly proclaiming socialist ideals and the inevitable triumph of communism. The young Poles convulsed in laughter over the parade's improbable rear guard. There, following the last of the musicians, ambling nonchalantly down the center of the muddy street, were a sow and her piglets.

Early the following morning the Pawulskis learned that no more trucks were available, and that the passengers who remained would be transported south on oxcarts to several kolkhozy. Later that day the family and all their belongings were piled into a wagon filled with straw and drawn by two large oxen. For about five days, as they traveled southeast deeper into the undulating steppe, the vegetation grew thinner and thinner. Along the way their cart plodded across several shallow, unbridged, but fast-moving rivers and streams. Halfway across one of these, the wheel on one cart lurched suddenly into a deep hole, and its axle snapped, causing an eighty-year-old woman, her nurse, and all their belongings to be dumped in the stream. People from the carts nearby leaped into the water and raced after the women as the current swept them downstream. The nurse finally found her footing and began making her way unaided to shore, but the old woman was too frail to resist the current and floated rapidly downstream for several minutes. Finally one young man came splashing in from the bank, caught the old woman, gathered her in his arms, and then carefully inched his way back to the bank. There a crowd quickly gathered and watched anxiously as he placed the dazed and completely soaked old woman on a level patch of ground. The nurse knelt quickly by her, expecting to find a patient in shock, probably with broken bones. But slowly the old woman, almost unaided, righted herself to a sitting position, and asked what caused her predicament; she had escaped the mishap unharmed.

Otherwise the journey by ox cart on the open steppe was unexciting and uneventful for the Pawulskis. Totally unprepared for rural life by their previous experience, they arrived in one of the earth's most inhospitable environments. There anonymous authorities expected them to fend for themselves.

CHAPTER 11

The Remnant

<<<<<<<<<<<<

For unknown reasons Soviet authorities spared 448 of the prisoners at Kozelsk, Starobelsk, and Ostashkov. These men began arriving at an empty camp called Pawlishtchev Bor, in pleasant, rolling countryside about fifty miles northwest of Kozelsk, between April 26 and May 20, 1940. None of these men had any inkling that among more than fifteen thousand prisoners at all three camps, they alone had survived. Pawlishtchev Bor was a transit camp for these men. They arrived there in seven groups—two each from Kozelsk and Starobelsk and three from Ostashkov. The largest shipment included 150 men, the smallest only nineteen.

The men were surprised and initially delighted by their new surroundings. The camp administration seemed more relaxed. Food portions were increased, and though many of the men were housed in stables and outbuildings belonging to a prerevolutionary estate, they were less cramped and had access to a bath.

"Maybe the Bolsheviks are human after all," Cadet Władek Cichy remarked to one of his friends after taking a hot bath, donning a clean new shirt, and tasting his first white bread in months. His sentiments were representative.

Barbed wire now replaced monastery walls, and the men were generally free to roam over the camp's eleven sprawling acres. Optimism radiated, fed in part by an unusually beautiful spring and in part by the widely held belief that freedom would soon be granted after a brief "psychological quarantine."

This mood was punctured on May 10, when Soviet radio announced Germany's invasion of the Low Countries and France. In the days that followed, Moscow Radio gloated over a succession of stunning Wehrmacht successes. These reports shattered convictions—nurtured by the prisoners, since their own defeat, in countless discussions of the coming confrontation in Western Europe—that the Allies

127

would quickly demonstrate overwhelming superiority in any showdown.

Spirits were further dampened by a new round of interrogations that got under way shortly after the last party from Kozelsk arrived. Quick on the prisoners' heels came a horde of political agents from Kozelsk— freed for this duty in such large numbers, as they put it, by the release to the Germans of all other inmates from Kozelsk. They emphasized that once a few remaining details were cleared up, liberation would be granted. But it quickly became apparent that the interrogations were aimed more blatantly than ever at converting the Poles to Bolshevism.

The great majority of prisoners remained uninfluenced in any way by these sessions. Two vocal minorities, however, began to emerge. About thirty men who had earlier declared themselves "Volksdeutsche" (those who considered themselves "racial" Germans) now became more noticeable and outspoken. They conversed ostentatiously in German and agitated vigorously for their return to Germany. Meanwhile, a group of about fifty men began openly espousing pro-Soviet sentiments. In the larger camps, where these factions represented less than one percent of all the inmates being held, they were careful not to reveal their sentiments. Among the remnant of Pawlishtchev Bor, they were 12 percent. Emboldened by their increase in relative numbers and the strong backing of camp authorities, these men triggered a degree of internal tension and bickering not known before.

The leader of the pro-Soviet faction was Lieutenant Colonel Zygmunt Berling, a man quickly thrust to the forefront by vanity and strongly held geopolitical convictions. He was once a rising star among regular-army officers, but his career had been tarnished on the eve of the war by a formal reprimand stemming from a romantic dalliance. Privately, Berling seethed with feelings of unjust treatment and determination to recover lost prestige. Suddenly and openly he began excoriating the Polish government's ineptness and pigheadedness in opposing both the Soviets and Germany. He claimed—with considerable accuracy, as subsequent events proved—that conflict between the two military giants was inevitable, and that Polish security interests could only be achieved through an accommodation with the Soviets. Berling seems to have remained a patriotic Pole with considerable skepticism about communism, but at heart he was an opportunist. His aspirations of leading a military force capable of reestablishing Polish independence under the Soviet aegis were naïve at best.

While debate among the prisoners grew increasingly rancorous, doubts also began to emerge that the other prisoners from Kozelsk, Starobelsk, and Ostashkov had been sent home. A large quantity of planks arrived in early June, and camp authorities ordered the men to begin building tiers of bunks for the prison dormitories. Many regarded this as clear evidence that their former companions would soon be rejoining them.

Suddenly, in mid-June, the prisoners were further puzzled by an order to prepare for departure. Authorities provided no explanation of their destination. Again the men were loaded onto trucks and then entrained for transport. Crisscrossing and backtracking over a wide area, they wondered if the Soviets were confused about where to send them. During the journey they received demoralizing news at a small railroad station north of Moscow. Soviet radio reported that France had fallen to the Nazis and that the British army was being forced to evacuate the Continent at Dunkirk.

Under this dark psychological cloud, the men reached the land of the midnight sun, arriving about a third of the way between Moscow and Arkhangelsk at a camp called Gryazovets near the large city of Vologda. The camp was centered around the ruins of an ancient Orthodox church that the Bolsheviks had dynamited. The Soviets regarded the camp as a model facility to house prisoners they expected to use politically. For that reason, more privileges and greater autonomy were offered at Gryazovets, where prisoners were even permitted to run their own kitchen and to grow vegetables on camp grounds.

Despite the improved living conditions, a puzzling and disturbing question began to trouble the men at Gryazovets deeply: Where were their fellow prisoners from Kozelsk, Starobelsk, and Ostashkov? Not one word had been heard from them since the camps had been broken up. Letters from their relatives in Poland were arriving at Gryazovets daily asking for news of their whereabouts. Obviously the men had not been sent back to Poland. In August, Cichy received a letter from his sister in Poland asking why one of the men from Kozelsk—the fiancé of one of her close friends—had not written. "I wrote back in good faith," Cichy told me, "and told her that I had not known this officer at Kozelsk, but I was sure he was in a camp similar to mine and would write home soon."

Always a favorite among his companions, the gregarious and optimistic Cichy was appointed chief cook for the prisoners, and assigned three cadet helpers. Generally they served the main meal in an open-air area adjacent to one of the main buildings, where the kitchen was housed on the first floor. The new food arrangements were satisfactory for a time, but some of the men soon began grumbling about a lack of meat in the soup.

As the men ate one evening, Cichy could not help overhearing a comment through the kitchen window. "Everyone who has meat in his soup, please raise your hand," a senior officer asked. Quickly peeping out, Cichy saw very few hands being raised. "Now," the senior officer intoned, "everyone who has no meat in his soup, please raise your hand." A forest of hands shot up. A dumbfounded Cichy exploded, interpreting the horseplay as an accusation that he and his helpers were withholding meat. Cichy and his helpers immediately turned in their resignations to camp authorities. The senior Polish officers were surprised to learn of this decision, and summoned Cichy to account for his action.

"You have rendered a great disservice to our cause by leaving the kitchen," one officer scolded.

"Sir, when I saw this type of vote being taken, I took it as a vote of no confidence. I had no other way open but to resign from the kitchen."

After a brief conference, his superiors agreed that he had suffered an affront and that his decision to quit the kitchen should stand.

It was not the only time that Cichy ran into trouble with the hierarchy. Though he spoke with a heavy accent influenced by his knowledge of German and Czech, Cichy, a law graduate of the University of Poznań, worked hard to master Russian speaking skills. To increase his proficiency, he avidly listened to radio reports and carefully studied the Russian newspapers provided by camp authorities. Gradually he emerged as the camp's favorite interpreter of Soviet news reports.

Most of the prisoners did not speak Russian, and they generally stood by patiently each evening as five- to ten-minute newscasts were piped into the camp from Radio Moscow or Radio Smolensk. At the end of these reports, Cichy, short of stature at five feet five inches, would stand on a stool or chair to provide both translation and his interpretation of what the Russian announcers had reported. Often two hundred or more men would be gathered for Cichy's translation and interpretation.

During the fall of France, Cichy relayed straightforward reports of the Russian broadcasts even though the news was highly disturbing. On more than one occasion Cichy's superiors chided him for the negative effect his reports were having on morale.

"I don't like reporting these things," Cichy told me he noted on one such occasion. "These are not my views; these are events that are happening. What else can I tell them?"

"You are undermining the morale of the men," one senior officer growled.

"Sir, we cannot maintain their morale with lies. We can only be prepared by the truth—whatever the truth may be."

After a brief discussion, the hierarchy agreed that Cichy's news reports were generally harmless and should not be terminated.

Months of depressing news and pessimistic prospects made the men wonder if their fortunes would ever change. The first break came in late summer. Speculation was building that the Germans were preparing for a cross-Channel invasion. On August 8 the Luftwaffe launched an all-out effort to break the back of the British Royal Air Force. For days the prisoners listened in rapt attention to Cichy's interpretations of Soviet broadcasts on the pivotal Battle of Britain. On August 15 they were amazed to learn that more than a thousand German planes were involved in a massive strike that ranged as far north as Scotland. Because Soviet radio dutifully acknowledged heavy British retaliation in raids on Berlin, Düsseldorf, Essen, and other German cities, Cichy characterized the reports as credible. The prisoners knew that most of the Allied hopes of stopping the Nazis rested with the RAF. They swelled with pride at the knowledge that a large number of RAF pilots (almost 20 percent) were Polish airmen who had escaped to the West the previous fall. Through the end of August and early September the men waited tensely for a decisive turning point in the great air battle.

On the evening of September 15 they detected a sharp edge in the Soviet announcer's voice, sensing that news of momentous importance might be in the air. Impatient voices in the huddled crowd hissed, "What does he say? What does he say?"

All eyes were riveted on Cichy standing on a stool in the center of the gathering, his ear cocked toward the loudspeaker. There was absolute silence as the announcer finished and Cichy began to speak. "Gentlemen, a great air battle took place earlier today over England. The Soviets are quoting official bulletins from the German government and from the British government. Both governments are basically saying the same thing: The RAF apparently has shot down an unusually large number of Luftwaffe planes while suffering only light losses. The RAF has demonstrated a clear superiority. Our men have come through. Our men have come—"

A wild roar cascaded across the room, drowning out Cichy and setting off raucous whooping, backslapping, hand shaking, and bear hugs. Pent-up emotions burst as voices cracked and eyes glistened. The Poles all sensed that a great victory was at hand and intended to savor it fully.

Finally the crowd calmed. Cichy resumed with his interpretation of fragments of the Russian report on the pivotal confrontation. He concluded with ebullience: "Gentlemen, this is our first good news—a great turning point. Today, for the first time we can say hooray; we are not going to lose this war!"

On July 7, 1940, the Germans occupied Romania. Twelve weeks later, on September 27, Germany, Italy, and Japan signed a ten-year military and economic security agreement in Berlin, called the Tripartite Pact. It committed each party to assist any one of the others should it become embroiled in a new military conflict. To Stalin and his closest advisers, the pact was evidence that Germany was contemplating war against the Soviet Union. Stalin remained deeply attached personally to the idea of cooperation with Germany, his determination to fulfill obligations under the Nazi-Soviet Nonaggression Pact never wavering. But with the signing of the Tripartite Pact, exploiting Polish manpower to serve Soviet security interests became a more attractive and important strategic objective.

In early October, political agents at Gryazovets deliberately began to circulate rumors that a Polish army might be formed in the Soviet Union. On October 10, Berling and six other senior Polish officers at Gryazovets were summoned to Moscow. They were followed the next day by twenty-one more Polish officers from a group of 2,500 prisoners recently transferred from the Baltic area to Gryazovets and to the empty camp at Kozelsk. (These troops had crossed into Lithuania after the Soviet attack on Poland on September 17, 1939. Later, when the Soviets occupied the Baltic states, they had been captured and interned there.) The small groups sent to Butyrki prison in Moscow were kept separately and treated not as prisoners but as "guests" of the NKVD. All were targeted by interrogators as potentially willing to cooperate with the Soviets.

On their first evening in Moscow, Berling's group was treated to good food, a bath, and a visit from a deputation of senior NKVD officials including General V. N. Merkulov, second in command to General Lavrenti Beria. Merkulov and his associates were anxious to know how willing the men were to fight the Germans. They also carefully probed the Poles' attitudes toward the Polish government-in-exile in London. Merkulov and his entourage adamantly held that the London government was illegitimate, that power had been transferred illegally when senior officials of the Second Republic escaped into Romania following Poland's collapse the previous fall. One of the Poles took exception to this interpretation and was quickly isolated from the group. Berling and the others were then transferred to Lubyanka prison, where they were constantly grilled by the NKVD's top men over the next three weeks. Beria himself participated in some of these sessions, at one point entertaining the men over dinner.

Toward the end of October a concrete proposal was advanced for the formation of Polish units within the Red Army. The NKVD hierarchy, including Beria, held a final meeting with Berling and his companions. Beria emphasized the importance of quality over quantity, and proposed the formation of a panzer division "as strong as an armored fist."

"And where will we get the officers?" Berling asked. "I would want to have my officers from Starobelsk and from Kozelsk."

Beria offered a shocking reply: "We made a blunder—we *did* make a blunder." (His actual words in Russian were "*Zdielali oshibku— oshibku zdielali.*")

The Poles were startled by the remark, but did not risk demanding clarification. They left the meeting completely mystified, mulling over several possible interpretations. Late that evening Lieutenant Colonel Gorczyński asked the one member of the group who had not attended the meeting with Beria to meet him in the washroom, where he related the entire incident. In this and in subsequent conversations, none of the men could come up with a plausible explanation of Beria's comment.

That evening Berling and the others accepted the NKVD's invitation to form a Polish division and agreed to undergo ideological and political training. Soon thereafter they were transferred from Lubyanka to what the Poles called the "Villa of Delight," about thirty miles from Moscow in the vicinity of Malakhovka. Here the men enjoyed good food, well-furnished rooms, a well-stocked political and military library, access to a radio, a car to take them to the cinema—even a good-looking and well-dressed maid. They remained under nominal surveillance by the NKVD while being reeducated.

A few days after their arrival, one of the six men told Soviet officials that he doubted he was doing the right thing. He was immediately sent back to prison in Moscow. In mid-November, six more Polish officers identified by Berling as potential recruits for the project arrived from Gryazovets. Around the first of the year, the villa received a final group of four junior Polish officers chosen from the group of twenty-one originally taken to Moscow one day after Berling's group.

Shortly after their arrival at the villa, these men were treated to an elaborate evening meal. Later, Berling, in uniform and carrying the rank of a full colonel, informed the men that he would be their leader, and that a great task awaited them. Would it be possible, one of the men asked Berling, to leave the villa? Berling's response was that they were free to leave at any time; but if they did, they would be put in a place where they "would not be able to see the light of day."

For the next six months, this cadre was prepared for leadership of what would later become the Kościuszko Division—a Red Army unit manned by Poles and named for General Tadeusz Kościuszko, hero of the American Revolution and Poland's commander in chief in the War of the Third Partition. Berling and his coterie faced many difficulties in organizing Poles under the Bolshevik banner—not the least difficulty being the assigned organizational slogan: "Red Poland, the Seventeenth Soviet Republic." The prospect of a Poland entirely dominated by the U.S.S.R. was almost universally repugnant among the rank and file Berling's group sought to enlist.

Almost a century and a half earlier, Kościuszko himself had warned against Moscow's subversive intrigues. At the time, he was head of state and commander in chief of Poland's armed forces. On May 7, 1794, on the eve of a war that would lead to the nation's third partition, he wrote:

> On so many occasions when Poles fought the Muscovy clan of robbers, the Muscovites did not win a single honest victory. However, at the end, despite the bravery of the Poles, the enemy has always returned to put his yoke, temporarily loosened, back on the victor's neck. Why such a bad turn of events for Poland? Why did the Polish nation suffer without any means to free itself? Because Muscovy's cunning intrigues were stronger than military weapons and they always ruined Poles with Polish hands.

The Wehrmacht's stunning success in the west seemed to change the Soviet hierarchy's attitude toward the remnant of officers still alive in the summer of 1940. Stalin had assumed all along that Hitler would attack in the west. He expected that a long war of attrition would follow, much like the trench warfare of World War I. If the Germans were bled white, a power vacuum would develop in Eastern Europe— one that the Soviets could then fill. The Wehrmacht shattered these illusions. With the ordinary Polish soldiers already in captivity and others being deported at the time from eastern Poland, there was a huge pool of manpower to draw on in forming Polish units of the Red Army. The officers at Gryazovets could be used to command such units.

This likely change of strategy carried with it a chilling implication: that the fifteen thousand men from Kozelsk, Starobelsk, and Ostashkov who were liquidated in the spring of 1940 were also victims of timing. Had they lived for a few more months—until the Wehrmacht had completed its lightning victory in the west—they might well have survived.*

Janina Czarnek and her daughters had just seated themselves for dinner one evening in November 1940 when they heard someone enter the unlocked front door of their apartment. Moments later, a thin, gray-faced, disheveled young man walked into the dining room. Gasps of disbelief preceded a salvo of shouts: "Stasiu!" "Stasieńku!" "Staszecz-ku!" Sheepishly, Staszek Czarnek basked in these endearments offered by his ecstatic mother and sisters. A torrent of concerns, questions about his fourteen months as a German prisoner of war, quickly engulfed him: "When were you released?" "How were you treated?" "How did you get here?"

Finally, Janina waved her daughters away, insisting that Staszek sit down at the dining-room table and eat immediately. Her son's physical weakness was obvious to her. Within moments she had set a huge plate of food before him. But Staszek, whose diet for months had barely exceeded a starvation level, could hardly eat any of it. His spirits also seemed subdued. Like his father, he was normally quiet and reserved. But a quick wit, marked by a sparkling sense of irony, had always lurked just beneath the composed exterior. Now it was missing.

As he picked at the food, Staszek finally was able to pose a question: "What have you heard from Tata?" A pall of silence settled immediately over the table. At last his mother replied: "Just this one letter from last November, and not a word since."

---

*It is also interesting to note that Berling's Kościuszko Division was expanded in 1944 into the First and Second Polish armies. By the end of the war, its ranks included some sixteen thousand Soviet officers. These men in Polish uniform replaced, in a sense, the victims of Kozelsk, Starobelsk, and Ostashkov.

CHAPTER 12

Life on the Steppes

≪≪≪≪≪≪≪≪≪

Many of the 1.2 million Poles deported to the Soviet Union after the Nazi-Soviet invasion of their homeland in 1939 were taken beyond the Ural Mountains and scattered across the steppes of Kazakhstan on large collective farms. Had they awakened on Jupiter or Mars, their new surroundings could hardly have seemed more alien.

Kazakhstan's semiarid tablelands stretch for almost two thousand miles from the edge of China to the Caspian Sea, an area larger than Greenland but so dry that entire rivers vanish into the saltbeds and sand of its interior. In every direction the steppes roll like a sea, unbroken by trees or other substantial vegetation except for karaganjnik, a rounded, prickly bush like tumbleweed. A few lapwings and bustards and an occasional pigeon dart about above these bushes; otherwise the landscape seems barren of life. And not without reason: Few species can survive the climatic extremes that descend on this empty wilderness, from lows of minus 40 degrees Fahrenheit—or below—in winter to 113 degrees or above in summer. Hurricane-force storms called *burany* drive blinding snow or choking dust across these wastes, depending on the season. In the driest spots, a trickle of eight to twelve inches of rain falls annually, in the wettest no more than twenty inches.

Until collectivization, nomadic tribes—mostly Kazakhs and a few Kirghiz and Uzbeks—roamed the steppes freely, looking for pasture for their horses, sheep, goats, cattle, and camels. They lived in felt-covered, dome-shaped tents called yurts and sustained themselves on a diet of milk and milk derivatives, supplemented by meat, berries, and a few vegetables and fruits, such as potatoes and melons. After the 1917 revolution in Russia, many of the wealthier Kazakhs fled with their herds across the border into China. By 1934 almost all who remained in the Soviet Union were forced onto livestock-breeding collective farms where the bitterly resentful Kazakhs gave up their traditional yurts and free-roaming ways for clusters of clay and mud huts and the life of settled farmers. Many of these new collectives were unconnected by roads or other means of communication. Agents of the state routinely arrived to provide political indoctrination and to collect the farm's output. The villagers were left with barely enough to survive on and deepened convictions that nothing good ever came from the outside.

Mrs. Pawulska and her three children, Maria, Tadeusz, and Jerzy, arrived in one of these wretched communities less than two hundred miles from China during the first week of May 1940, after a five-day trip by ox cart from the rail junction of Zhangiz-Tobe. Kalinin was a village of less than seven hundred people, where the life of each inhabitant centered around one large cooperative, or kolkhoz. Its population planted and harvested its grain, fed and managed its livestock, milked its cows, made its butter, maintained and repaired its equipment, and undertook many other tasks on several thousand acres of cooperative land surrounding the village.

Moscow's planning ministries and Soviet propaganda described collectives like Kalinin as shining examples of the socialist dream and democracy in action at the village level. In theory the members of the kolkhoz elected management and shared equitably in collective output. In practice, this was all a sham. The cooperative hierarchy was empowered to extract every ounce of production possible from the local community. Kalinin's Kazakh chairman and other cooperative leaders were hand-picked by party apparatchiks. Their job was to procure crops and livestock on behalf of the state at the cheapest possible price—in short, to enforce the unpopular idea of high delivery quotas at very low prices. They also saw to it that Kalinin received production materials, such as feed, seed, and fertilizer, at inflated prices. Stalin's plan to modernize the Soviet Union was painfully clear in communities like Kalinin. He was financing industrial growth by squeezing everything possible from the local population for export to the cities and abroad. The result—reflected in almost every aspect of daily life—was that Kalinin and similar communities lacked the elements for survival.

When they arrived, the Pawulskis and about ten other Polish families were lodged in the auditorium of a square, squat building near the center of the village. Beds were made by spreading blankets on piles of straw in the space where members of the cooperative generally met to hear political lectures, watch propaganda films, and receive reports on cooperative business. The auditorium was the hub of Kalinin's social life, so the newly arrived families could stay there only briefly. Authorities stressed that each new family was responsible for finding its own permanent housing. To do this they would have to convince a local family, in a community already critically short of shelter, to take them in. They were also told that every able-bodied person would be required to work, and that fair compensation would be provided from the proceeds of the collective harvest.

Mrs. Pawulska was immediately ordered to work in a crew of women who spent long hot days making *kiziaky*, or fuel bricks. Because the steppes were devoid of firewood, livestock manure was collected and hauled to a central point where a room-sized pit had been created by removing topsoil down to the hardpan. Manure was spread across the depression, where it could be mixed with straw and water into a gooey mass. The mixing was done by eight to ten women, who, skirts held shin-high, stamped ankle-deep through the pit's unsavory contents. Once the ingredients had been churned to the right consistency, they were shoveled into wooden forms and then set in the sun to dry. After several days, the forms were removed, leaving a brick the size of a cement block that would burn slowly, giving off intense heat in the form of a small, blue, odorless flame. The bricks were then neatly stacked and jealously guarded because of their primary role in combating the steppe's bitterly cold winter. Stealing one of these bricks was considered a serious crime and might well earn the perpetrator a sentence in a forced-labor camp.

Mud construction bricks were also made in a similar way. Other menial jobs were undertaken once an adequate supply of *kiziaky* had been prepared. Mrs. Pawulska was soon ordered to clean sediment from the bottom of a watering hole for cattle. Standing waist-deep in the hole, she lifted out bucketfuls of silt pushed into the water by the cows as they drank. The work caused her severe back strain that became a recurring problem for the rest of her life.

At age twelve, Maria was considered old enough to work and was put in charge of fifty or more calves that were being weaned from their mothers. At sunup she herded the animals to sparse pasturelands several kilometers from the village, and brought them back at sundown after their mothers had been milked. For performing this task, she and her mother were told, the family would be credited for payment after the harvest. Maria was warned that she would be penalized severely if any of the calves succeeded in rejoining their mothers before nightfall. Because of the difficulties of keeping track of fifty rambunctious yearlings, Tadeusz, ten, was often sent with Maria. Their days in the relentless sun with nothing to do except chase occasional strays seemed endless. The youngsters anxiously awaited dusk, when they could return to the village and the calves would be fed a little of the skim milk that remained from the day's production. Occasionally some of the skim milk was given to the youngsters to take home.

After a few weeks in Kalinin, the Pawulskis were finally able to secure lodging in the Russian section of the village. Most of the people there had been sent to Siberia in the early 1930s, when collectivization had just begun. Their own harsh experience made many of them sympathetic to the Poles. Finally one elderly, kindly Russian woman agreed that the Pawulskis could have a cramped corner of her house that adjoined a room where she kept an old cow. It was the only space Mrs. Pawulska could find and she was glad to get it.

Finding enough food for survival was a constant, pressing problem. The Pawulskis arrived in Kalinin with few assets. Knowing that they would not be paid for their assigned work until after the harvest, they were forced to search out odd jobs in addition. Maria earned a few pieces of bread and, occasionally, cabbage, melons, or cucumbers for an unusual kind of child care. Most of the infants she watched were left by their mothers on a small stretcher-bed suspended on a spring from the ceiling. When a child in one of these contraptions cried, Maria simply tugged on the spring, causing a rocking motion that calmed the baby. Her earnings from such work added little, however, to the family food supply.

Initially the Pawulskis survived by bartering clothes and other possessions for flour and other staples. A few people owned their own cows and could be persuaded to exchange whole milk for Western-style garments. After skimming the cream, Maria and her brothers would then shake it in a bottle until they got butter. Because of her mother's long hours, Maria learned to prepare simple dishes like vegetable soup, fried potatoes, and onions and porridge. Although it was a short-range investment, one of Mrs. Pawulska's first exchanges turned out to be especially astute. She traded a flowery nightgown of Maria's to a Kazakh woman for a hen and ten eggs. The hen sat on these eggs only a short time before hatching nine chicks. These offspring could soon forage for themselves and by late summer were sufficiently grown to grace the Pawulski dinner table as rare and highly prized delicacies.

Shortly after they arrived, Mrs. Pawulska began receiving from relatives and friends in Lwów small amounts of money as well as packages of food and other items that could be bartered. Most of these packages contained jars of pork fat called *słonina*, which could be spread on bread to make a filling sandwich. Flour, sugar, coffee, cereals, and pressed bricks of tea were also generally included. The tea was especially popular with the Kazakhs, who drank it constantly and would often trade a good-sized chicken or sack of potatoes or a couple of pounds of flour for a small quantity. With careful bartering and rationing, the food and money from Lwów were just enough to keep starvation at bay. Maria and her brothers dreamed frequently of food. One day Maria observed to her mother: "At least the dream makes me feel like I've had more to eat." Because of their almost constant hunger, the children were transfixed by the appearance of tiny morsels of food. Even the small pieces of bread Maria earned for her occasional baby-sitting were carefully divided into four equal pieces as each member of the family watched intently. Then each person retreated into a corner, like a dog with a bone, to consume his or her piece crumb by crumb.

Because Kalinin had no post office, Mrs. Pawulska had to walk more than four miles to the postal depot of a larger cooperative to pick up her packages from Lwów and get other mail. Before leaving, however, she was required to obtain a travel permit from authorities in Kalinin. Often she arrived to find letters but no packages. Her relatives in Lwów generally described the contents of each package in a separate letter. Their correspondence, which arrived without fail, clearly indicated that many of the packages were being either lost or stolen. Questions or complaints to postal authorities yielded no information and turned up none of the missing packages.

Even more distressing for Mrs. Pawulska was that not one word arrived from her husband, Stanisław. Where was he, and why was there no news of him whatsoever? Only days before leaving Lwów she had learned that he and his fellow officers at Starobelsk in the Ukraine were apparently being transferred. But where? And why no word of their whereabouts? She had continued writing Stanisław at Starobelsk, expecting that her letters would be forwarded, but not one letter had been returned or acknowledged. Surely, she felt, some word of him should have reached her by now. As mystifyingly, their relatives in Lwów had heard nothing from him either. These long trips to the postal depot, on which Mrs. Pawulska left with the hope of receiving some word from her husband and returned with no news at all, were deeply painful to her. She continued, however, to make the long trek as often as possible, believing each time that a letter would finally be waiting.

(We now know that her letters were among thousands from the victims' families that were burned by the NKVD. Among the documents turned over by President Gorbachev on April 13, 1990, was a report to the NKVD in Moscow from officials named Klok and Kuriachiy, who were in charge of camp administration. They noted on July 23, 1940, that incoming correspondence addressed to the men—and received, presumably, after their liquidation—had been destroyed. In the NKVD's typically methodical fashion, they reported the destruction of 422 registered letters, 562 regular letters, 148 registered postcards, 3,102 regular post cards, and 79 telegrams.)

While Kalinin had no central market, the nearby town of Bolshaya Bukon offered one of considerable size. Its prices and supplies were much better, and Mrs. Pawulska went there when she could afford to buy small amounts of food, especially fresh vegetables. On one trip she had just bought a bag of onions when a Kazakh woman informed her that it was bad luck to travel with onions. Mrs. Pawulska knew that the Kazakhs were deeply superstitious and willingly suscribed to an endless number of old wives' tales. Hearing this warning, she nodded courteously and promptly forgot it. While she was walking back to Kalinin, two trucks came roaring up from behind, then slowed to a stop as they approached her. She noticed that the drivers—men in their mid- to late twenties—appeared to be Russians and that a young woman accompanied each of the men. Would she like a ride? one of the drivers asked Mrs. Pawulska. She gladly accepted and climbed into the rear of one of the trucks. The journey had barely resumed when Mrs. Pawulska realized that she would have to hold on for dear life. The two trucks were racing along the rough dirt road at breakneck speed. At times the drivers swerved their trucks directly at each other, cutting back at the last possible moment. A cloud of dust billowed high on the road behind as the vehicles bounced along at top speed across the jarring ruts and furrows of a road that amounted to little more than a track across the steppe.

Finally the trucks rolled safely into the village, and with great relief Mrs. Pawulska set her feet on secure ground. Then she learned that the drivers, well-laden with vodka, had agreed in Bolshaya Bukon to exchange wives for the return journey to Kalinin. The apparently harmless gesture had quickly turned ugly when one of the drivers tried to pass the other. Not only had Mrs. Pawulska received the most frightening ride of her life, she now had good cause to wonder if she should ever travel with onions again.

In the group deported to Kazakhstan with the Pawulskis were several people from small villages who knew something about farming. They expressed amazement at the beauty and quality of the wheat produced in the dry, virgin soil of the steppes. The stalks grew chest-high to a man of average height, and their heads were full enough to provide exceptional yields.

During the summer harvest the huge fields were cut mechanically. Crews of men, women, and children then gathered the entire stalk, with head intact, into shocks for transport to the threshing operation near the village. There a long line of horses and carts piled high with wheat waited to reach the huge machines that separated the grain from the stalk. At the end of this operation, kernels poured out in mountains of gold that often sat for days drying in the summer heat. Often the horses waiting in line at the thresher fed leisurely at these piles. No one seemed to care, though with Kalinin's delivery quota to the state already set, the horses were eating village grain. There were limits, however. Once Maria was sharply rebuked when her calves veered dangerously close to one of the mountains of corn.

Again the Polish women were assigned the worst work in grain processing. They cleared away the chaff that billowed from the huge separators. At the end of these long days, Mrs. Pawulska came home caked with dirt and debris. She wore a mask, but it afforded little protection against the tiny particles that penetrated into her nose and made breathing quite difficult.

A small tributary of the Irtysh flowed past Kalinin. It was wide and dangerous in the spring, but became a meandering brook by the end of summer. In places where the stream's path made a sharp turn, high banks and deep pockets or pools had developed. From one of these banks, ten feet or more above the water, village children came on hot summer days to dive and swim. As often as she could, Maria came as a spectator, watching the headfirst dives with particular admiration. Standing one day on top of the bank and too near the edge, she was pushed. She disappeared into the middle of the pool, then came up thrashing wildly. For a few moments, the surprised bystanders did not realize that the prank's victim could not swim; finally someone pulled her to safety. It was Maria's last visit to the diving bank.

The harvest season concluded with corn picking. There was not enough moisture to produce this crop on the steppes without irrigation. However, enough water could be diverted from the stream to produce several large fields of corn, which served as an especially valuable supplement to the diet of Kalinin's livestock, particularly its dairy cows. The corn was picked by hand by crews who pulled the ears from the stalk, then tossed them into horse-drawn carts. Later, some of the corn was fed to the livestock unshelled, and other amounts were shelled mechanically and bagged.

With the last of the crops in, cooperative authorities gave Mrs.

Pawulska and other Polish families devastating news: Kalinin was broke and none of their accumulated wages would be paid. The Poles were told that they would be transferred to other collective farms. Moreover, Mrs. Pawulska now was told that as unrestricted deportees—that is, those confined to a general area rather than to a prison or work camp—her family had been entitled to nothing from the outset. In early November she requested permission to go to Kokpekty, the nearest town of significant size, to seek work. It was clear that she and her three children might not survive the winter in Kalinin. The political commissar who listened to this request seemed unusually callous. He warned her to forget any idea of returning to Poland. If she left Kalinin, he said, Jerzy, her youngest, could go with her, but Maria and Tadeusz must remain as hostages.

There was no choice in the matter. In late November, with the first flurries of light snow and freezing rain blowing across the steppes, Mrs. Pawulska and Jerzy left Kalinin for Kokpekty, about twenty-five miles away. The administrative center of the region, Kokpekty had a population of about twenty-five thousand people. Mrs. Pawulska's plan was to take any available job that would enable her to send money for food back to Maria and Tadeusz. Before leaving, she moved the two youngsters to an abandoned house recently occupied by several Polish families, who planned to remain in Kalinin until spring. Mrs. Pawulska had been told that her Russian landlady was too elderly to help Maria and Tadeusz; she knew that the Polish families would at least take a general interest in their welfare.

Maria and Tadeusz were not reduced to beggary, but they quickly learned that only by being resourceful could they survive. Their mother had left them only a small amount of food. Babysitting and other odd jobs earned bits of food and a few kopeks. Sympathetic Poles shared meals occasionally, but such invitations were irregular and unpredictable since most people did not know where their next meal was coming from. To quell their hunger, one cold but sunny day Maria and Tadeusz attended a wake in the Russian section of the village. The event centered around a feast at which the bereaved family and friends of the deceased set out their best available food. A large crowd was present. By Russian tradition, the event was open to all. Still, Maria had trouble summoning the nerve to walk in. Tadeusz was insistent and threatened to go inside without her. Finally, they walked in quickly together. In the room where the food was, no one seemed to notice their presence. On the table were steaming dishes of *lapsha*, thick noodles made from wheat. The youngsters expected to eat enough to last for a long time.

To their surprise they found that they could eat only a few spoonfuls because their stomachs had shrunk. The experience was too tense and embarrassing for Maria, who told Tadeusz it was the last time she would do such a thing.

Before Christmas Maria and Tadeusz received optimistic news from Kokpekty. Their mother had found work as the janitor of a school there. True, she wrote, the job would barely support her and Jerzy, but she still wanted Maria and Tadeusz to come just as soon as possible. According to Mrs. Pawulska's letter, she had also asked authorities in Kalinin to release her children. So far the plea had fallen on deaf ears. The authorities claimed that they had no spare horses to take the children to Kokpekty.

Most of the panes in the windows of the house shared by Maria, Tadeusz, and the other Poles were broken and had been replaced by cardboard. The house featured a huge open-hearth oven that no longer worked. It was said that in the worst part of the winter the Russians who previously occupied the house had removed the coals and slept in the hearth. The oven would have thrown off considerable heat to a rear wall, where bunks had been built to capitalize on the warmth. Maria and Tadeusz slept in two of these spots, but since the oven was never put back in operation, they found it impossible to stay warm. They had few bedcovers and by early December were sleeping with their coats and gloves on.

Shortly after Mrs. Pawulska's departure, tragedy struck the family of the political commissar who had so coldly ordered her away from Kalinin. His first and favorite son, about ten, came down with measles and died within days after the symptons appeared. The father was completely devastated. In his bereavement he was haunted by an incident that had occurred a few weeks earlier. He had denounced two Polish women for not working hard enough and taken them to court in Kokpekty, where they were sentenced to seven years in a labor camp. Because she knew the women, Mrs. Pawulska attended their trial. When it ended she heard one of the women tell the commissar: "God may not be fast, but He is just." The commissar had responded by sharply rebuking the women for their antistate, religious convictions. All this apparently came back to haunt him after his son's death. Gradually he seemed to undergo a remarkable transformation. The old bluster disappeared. He began seeking out the Poles on religious matters. Then one night early in January 1941, he came to the shack where Maria and Tadeusz were living. It was approaching midnight when he arrived.

"Listen," he told them. "I am going to take you to Kokpekty." Maria was shocked that the commissar would do this. He seemed nervous, anxious that no one know where he was taking them. He told Maria and Tadeusz to gather their things quickly and say nothing of their departure. Within a short time the young Pawulskis' few possessions were packed onto a small one-horse sleigh and they were headed across the snow-covered steppe toward Kokpekty. The children rode on a seat made of bands of rope covered by straw, huddled under their tattered bedcovers against the bitter cold.

They arrived near noon the next day, finding Kokpekty blanketed in snow so deep that chimneys and rooftops barely peeked through the highest drifts. Most chimneys were "corked" at night to keep the snow out and the heat in. As an administrative center, Kokpekty boasted a few stores, a restaurant, a cinema, and other amenities rarely found on the steppes. It had a fairly large population of Russians and Ukrainians, who had been forcibly settled there during collectivization. The Russian and Ukrainian section was drab and shabby, but seemed modern compared to the decrepit parts inhabited by the Kazakhs and Mongolians.

The commissar took Maria and Tadeusz to a small inn, in the Russian section, where their mother was staying. Mrs. Pawulska was at work when they arrived. When she returned that evening, she was shocked that the commissar had shown such kindness to her children.

Shortly after that the Pawulskis moved in with a Russian family willing to rent them the corner of one room. Finally, the family fortunes were improving. Mrs. Pawulska had a paying job, a tiny but warm place to live, and enough food to survive on. Except for Stanisław, everyone was, at last, reunited. On the steppe in 1941, these were blessings for which any Polish mother could indeed be grateful.

Nothing in her previous thirty-four years had prepared Zofia Hoffman for the life that awaited her and her fifty-nine-year-old mother, Maria Neuhoff, when they arrived in Semipalatinsk about May 1, 1940. Zofia had been born to a life of privilege. Since her birth, servants had performed most of the menial tasks in her home. She attended and excelled in Poland's best schools, traveled widely in Europe, spoke several languages, and, at a time when few women worked outside the home, established herself in a professional career. While a student at Jan Kazimierz University, she danced at a carnival ball with Maks, who by then held a doctorate in jurisprudence. A romance between the two soon flourished despite the twelve-year difference in their ages. He was a successful young attorney with a thriving law practice in Lwów, and she was studying law. In October 1930, she and Maks married and she joined his law practice. After several years of apprenticeship, she became eligible to take the bar exam, and on February 1, 1936, she became the third woman to be admitted to the Polish bar.

Her arrest for deportation in the big roundup of April 13, 1940, was not a suprise. The Bolsheviks already had made clear their intention to purge eastern Poland of "antisocialist" elements. Zofia knew that every professional was a prime target for deportation. Being the wife of an army officer made her even more vulnerable. Many immediate family members of the officers and noncommissioned officers at Kozelsk, Starobelsk, and Ostashkov were arrested in the April 13 sweep. The army, more than any other institution, unified Poland. By eliminating all traces of its leadership, the Soviets expected to decapitate the country, rendering it helpless and compliant.

Those being deported feared that all contact with their captive husbands, fathers, and sons might be lost. Even six months after the capture of these men, little was known about their welfare or future. Their cards and letters, which came back in a trickle, expressed guarded optimism for an early release. Finally, in early April, word seeped back that transfers to an unknown destination were beginning. Coming just prior to their own deportation, this latest word was deeply troubling for the families of the captive officers. Zofia had received only one post card from Maks since his arrival at Starobelsk. (In it, he said: "I am healthy but anxious about you and Ajka [a nickname given their daughter, Ewa, because of the sound she made crying]. I have everything I need; don't deprive yourself of anything. Please don't send me any parcels, dearest.") Under normal circumstances, she knew he would write often. Suddenly she herself was being sent to an unknown place. Under these circumstances, she feared that all contact with Maks might be lost.

The NKVD exploited these fears to calm the families of the captured men. During the arrest of her family, Maria Pawulska had been quieted with the promise that she would see her father again. Zofia was told that she would be reunited with her husband. Unknown to either family, as their transports left for Siberia, the captives of Kozelsk, Starobelsk, and Ostashkov were daily being moved by the Soviets to secret sites for execution. By the time the deportees reached Siberia, virtually the entire population of these camps had been murdered. No news of the captives, therefore, awaited their families on the steppes. Days in that remote land blurred from summer into fall and from fall into winter as wives, mothers, and children hoped for any word that the missing men were alive. Many feared that they were being held among the faceless millions of the gulag archipelago, in any one of hundreds of forced-labor camps that dotted the Soviet Union. They might well have been sent to the remote north, along the Arctic Circle, to Kotlas, Vorkuta, Kolyma, or Magadan—places from which there was no escape and from which no news reached the outside world. Perhaps, the families hoped, a spring thaw would finally bring word that the missing men had been released. Three long years would pass before even these faint hopes would be crushed by the discoveries in Katyń Forest.

"Shortly after she arrived in Semipalatinsk, my mother was taken south near a place called Georgiyevka. She went to work nearby in a stone quarry, where she drove a cart pulled by two small oxen," Ewa told me during one of our meetings. "Her job was to load the cart by hand and haul the stone to the local railroad station. She and my grandmother were housed in a vacant sheep barn that offered very little protection against the severe winter in that godforsaken region. My mother said the conditions in those barns were such that in the winter people's hair would freeze to the walls. There was no heat at all. The scene was really quite absurd. Here these two women sat huddled against the cold wearing full-length fur coats in the middle of nowhere." Did the fur coats save their lives? I asked Ewa. "Well, certainly there were survivors who did not have fur coats, but there is no doubt that some type of heavy protection was essential. If they had not taken those coats, who knows what kind of protection they might have had?"

In the worst of the *burany*, the snow was totally blinding. It was possible to lose all sense of direction after taking a few steps outside. Living and working in these conditions quickly exacted a harsh toll. In the fall, Zofia became infected with a rare, near-fatal illness. The long days of handling sharp-edged stones left her hands raw and bleeding. Since she slept in the barn, contact with sheep manure was unavoidable. Suddenly Zofia began to experience chills and high fever. At night her temperature began to rage out of control. As the infection grew worse, her long hair, which she generally wore rolled in a braided knot at the nape of her neck, began coming out in handfuls. Finally her mother convinced authorities in the labor camp to take her daughter to a hospital in Georgiyevka, about five miles away. Its only doctor, an elderly Tartar, guessed that Zofia had either malaria or brucellosis, a disease common in animals and humans. Like malaria, it is characterized by extremely high fever.

"My mother told me that the old doctor seemed to take a special interest in her case," Ewa said. "Her temperature would run up to 104 or 105 degrees at night, and every night she would become unconscious. The doctor had no drug of any sort other than quinine, which was used to treat malaria. So he decided to use the one drug he had, on the assumption that if it worked, it meant she had malaria, and if it didn't, it meant she had something else. The quinine had no effect, and this situation went on for about thirty days until my mother finally simply outlasted the fever. Even though the quinine didn't work, my mother felt that she owed her life to the old doctor.

"My mother was in no condition to go back to the labor camp," Ewa went on. "So she and my grandmother were permitted to rent a corner of a room in Georgiyevka from a young Russian couple. The husband was a truck driver and was on the road most of the time, leaving his wife and small child alone a lot. His wife, Lena, was brought up during the revolution and was obviously a communist born and bred. That first Christmas Eve she saw my mother and grandmother praying and said, 'I want to show you something.' She took them to her bedroom where there was a portrait of Lenin which she took down from the wall. She turned it around and there, glued on the back, was an icon of the Virgin with Child. She said, 'If you want to pray, then you can pray here.' It was obvious that she was not a believer, but she didn't want to destroy the icon, so she kept it by gluing it to the other side of the Lenin portrait. I think this simple little incident tells how complex that whole system was. You never knew who believed and who didn't."

The beautiful jewelry Zofia's mother had hidden in a handbag when arrested proved useless. Cigarettes—not diamond and emerald pendants and earrings—were the Kazakhs' precious gems. Fortunately, Zbigniew, Zofia's brother, sent packages of cigarettes as frequently as possible and the two women used them to bargain for food. Once cigarettes became plentiful, nobody would exchange them for food. At this point, Zofia began smoking to kill her hunger pangs.

"One day my grandmother heard that a small store nearby expected a shipment of tea, which was greatly prized but always in short supply on the steppes," Ewa said. "She decided to see if she could buy some. She waited all night with a huge crowd in front of the store. The next morning when the store opened, people were packed around the door. The crowd began to surge inside and she was crushed between two big Kazakhs and had two of her ribs broken. Even so, she managed to get inside and get some tea."

The hardships suffered by the Hoffmans and the Pawulskis were hardly unusual. Forced labor, starvation, illness, and exposure to the elements were common for almost all the deportees. Many did not live through their first winter in the Soviet Union. Only a small fraction of those deported would ever leave the isolated kolkhozy, mines, and lumber camps where Stalin's decision to Sovietize eastern Poland had taken them.

CHAPTER 13

Bad-Faith Agreements

<<<<<<<<<<<

A blood-red sky drenched the western horizon of the steppes for several afternoons in mid-June 1941. In the part of Kokpekty where the Pawulskis lived, Russian women spoke nervously in small groups at the roadsides about the meaning of the deep red sun. Many saw it as a bad omen. Listening at the edge of one of these groups, Maria heard someone say, "A great war coming." The words were spoken with conviction and impressed her deeply.

"I don't know why, but I believed it," Maria told me in one of our conversations. "The prediction wasn't based on anything the woman knew. It was just what she felt. I'm sure it was only a short time before the Germans invaded. For us it was not such a great surprise. I think we all felt that it would happen."

Many Poles greeted the news of the German attack with elation, feeling that they could only benefit. The day it began, Sunday, June 22, 1941, Władek Cichy and another prisoner were sitting at noontime beside a small stream that ran through the middle of Camp Gryazovets. They were half listening to the classical music on Radio Moscow, piped into the camp on loudspeakers. The music stopped and a lengthy pause followed. Then came a terse announcement: German forces, in an act of treachery, had crossed the frontier early that morning. The patriotic forces of the Soviet Union were repelling the invaders and would avenge the act of perfidy.

The camp erupted in pandemonium. Cichy and his friend leaped to their feet congratulating each other that Poland's two greatest enemies had attacked each other. Cichy gave an animated account of that moment during our visit in his London apartment. He said his reactions were "instinct. Pure instinct. My first thought was that it could only be good for Poland. Here, at last, were our ancient enemies fighting each other. My hope was that they would kill each other off. But most of us resented the Bolsheviks so strongly that, deep down, we hoped

151

the Germans would destroy them. We all felt that the attack would certainly hasten Polish independence."

Amid Gryazovets's momentary jubilation, Cichy remembered the perplexed reaction of the NKVD guards. One of them asked Cichy, "Why are you so happy? Hitler is your enemy, too."

"Yes, but so are you," Cichy shot back. At the moment, it did not occur to him that the German attack would change relationships overnight, that Poland and the Soviet Union would have little choice but to join forces.

The prisoners of Gryazovets were not celebrating alone. On the banks of another stream roughly seven hundred miles to the west, reactions were similar. Staszek, Magda, and Jaga Czarnek, and Jaga's boyfriend, Jurek (who later became her husband), were sitting on a sandbank along the Vistula River below Kraków's stately Wawel Castle. It was a perfect afternoon for sunbathing and idle conversation. The small group was teasing Jurek about his escape, several months earlier, from the Germans. He had been held, at the time, under minimum-security conditions with hundreds of other reservists. No prisoner lists had been compiled, which meant anyone who escaped might not be missed. Somehow Jurek had found a schoolboy's uniform, put it on, and walked away from the camp without being stopped. On the sandbank, someone joked that Jurek probably looked so adorable in his makeshift disguise that the Germans were ashamed to keep him.

About that time shouts came from downstream. A couple was paddling furiously toward the sandbank in a kayak. The sunbathers quickly recognized a Girl Scout friend of Agnes, Rena, and her brother, Witek. The two of them were shouting, "The Germans have attacked Russia! The Germans have attacked Russia!" Jumping out of the kayak, Rena and Witek gulped for air and relayed what they had just heard on Radio Kraków. The news set off a small celebration on the sandbank. "We all felt this was a great day for Poland," Magda told me. "We felt we could only gain as a result of our two worst enemies fighting each other. We were so sick of the Germans—what they were doing on an everyday basis." Magda pointed out that Rena and Witek had even taken a serious risk in obtaining the news. Their family owned a radio— an offense, for a Pole, punishable by death under the German General Government.

The peasant women of Kokpekty had proven more adept at reading signs than Stalin was. Despite staggering evidence to the contrary, he refused to believe his ally, Hitler, would attack him. By the spring of 1941, the danger could no longer be ignored. The Wehrmacht had begun a huge buildup, dispersing 70 percent of its strength across the Soviet Union's western frontier. Luftwaffe reconnaissance overflights had increased noticeably, yet Stalin refused permission to fire on them. These were bluffing actions, he said, to camouflage the long-expected cross-Channel invasion of Great Britain. Besides, Stalin pointed out, where were Hitler's new demands? His big chess moves were always preceded by bold claims, and none had been made so far.

In March the Soviets received specific evidence of Hitler's invasion plans through United States diplomatic channels. Then, on May 12, Soviet superagent Richard Sorge relayed disturbing news from Tokyo. He had intercepted a message from Hitler to the Japanese government describing Operation Barbarossa, the code name for a massive invasion of the Soviet Union. About this time, families of German diplomats began leaving Moscow, documents were being burned at the German embassy, and German ships set sail from Soviet harbors. Stalin continued to dismiss the snowballing evidence as simple provocation. Then, on June 18, a German deserter told a field command in the western Ukraine that the Soviet Union would be attacked at dawn on June 22. Stalin greeted this news with the comment: "Haven't the German generals sent this defector over to provoke a conflict?" That same day, a Soviet secret agent in Switzerland finished radioing Moscow many details of the invasion, including the time and date it would commence. To the very end, Stalin refused to believe the invasion would take place. He remained determined to stay in Hitler's good graces. On the eve of the attack, he purchased U.S. copper for transshipment to Germany and stepped up deliveries of other strategic commodities.

With the invasion, Hitler planned to carve open for the Reich a gigantic new area of *lebensraum*—everything west of a line running from Arkhangelsk on the White Sea south to Kazan and then down the Volga River to its mouth at Astrakhan on the Caspian Sea. A population of 140 million people and most of the Soviet Union's agricultural and industrial resources lay to the west of this line, all ripe for exploitation in what the Führer called The Thousand-Year Reich. Still intoxicated by the quick victories in Poland and France, Hitler and many in his inner circle expected the campaign would end in eight to ten weeks, or well before Russia's bitter winter began. Confidence was so high that the Wehrmacht left without winter clothing.

Barbarossa was the last and greatest blitzkrieg. It thundered forward, as scheduled, at three fifteen A.M. on June 22, 1941, smashing into a thoroughly confused and woefully unprepared foe. The attack covered a two-thousand-mile arc from the Arctic Ocean to the Black Sea and involved 190 divisions totaling 4.6 million Germans, Romanians, and Finns. At their disposal were 3,700 tanks, 5,000 aircraft and 50,000 cannons and mortars.

Although the Red Army numbered about five million men at the beginning of the war, only 2.9 million, or about 58 percent, were concentrated along the western border. Their arsenal included 1,800 late-model tanks, 1,540 late-model airplanes, and 34,700 cannons and mortars. Where the Wehrmacht's heaviest blows fell, it often enjoyed a two-to-one advantage in manpower and significant advantages in matériel. These were margins that the experienced German officer corps, well trained in the techniques of modern warfare, knew how to exploit.

In many places, assault teams raced across vital bridges, seizing them intact before defenders could detonate demolition charges. Planes bombed targets from Murmansk to Odessa. The Luftwaffe wiped out eight hundred planes on the ground, and a total of 1,200 in the first day's action. Big guns along the border destroyed railroad terminals, communications complexes, and army installations. Soviet supply dumps, for some unknown reason located too close to the frontier, were seized or destroyed. All this prepared the way for the panzer divisions, which raced deep into Soviet territory, penetrating in places thirty-five to forty miles on the first day.

Stalin was alerted to the disaster in a 4:00 A.M. phone call. At the Kremlin an hour later he ventured that the assault still might be a provocation. These hopes were dashed when Molotov arrived with the German declaration of war. Stalin's impetuous reaction was an absurd order that Soviet forces drive the enemy back to the frontier and wait for further clarification. But calamity was now spreading all along the front. Why weren't Soviet troops advancing? a panicky Stalin demanded. Then, at 9:15 P.M., came a truly murderous decision: an order that the German invasion force was to be "surrounded and annihilated." The result was that many Soviet front- and second-line troops began advancing into the teeth of the Wehrmacht, whose jaws quickly snapped shut, wiping out entire divisions and causing huge pockets of troops to be encircled, captured, and slaughtered.

A rout was in progress. Before Stalin and his high command could sort out the damage caused by these orders, the Germans had dashed in places ninety miles beyond the frontier. After three weeks, advanced thrusts of the Wehrmacht were 130 miles inside Soviet territory. Latvia, Lithuania, Byelorussia, and all of the Ukraine west of the Dnieper River were in German hands. Smolensk, which blocked the path to Moscow, was about to fall. Even in the Napoleonic deluge, the country had never experienced a disaster of this magnitude.

The Sovietization of eastern Poland was still in full swing when the German attack began. A fourth mass roundup of deportees probably began on June 20 and continued even after the Wehrmacht bombardment of rail lines commenced. In his excellent study of the Soviet occupation of eastern Poland, *Revolution from Abroad*, Jan T. Gross estimates that between sixty thousand and eighty thousand Poles—about half the number taken in each of the first three roundups—were taken to the Soviet Union. Among those in the fourth wave were a large number of children from summer camps and orphanages.

The first German bombs had barely fallen on Lwów when the slaughter began. At two large prisons, the NKVD began herding prisoners into cellars and shooting them. These murders were well documented after the war in extensive testimony before the U.S. House of Representatives Select Committee on Communist Aggression. The shootings continued for several days. When the NKVD men finally fled, all but six hundred to seven hundred of the prison's estimated thirteen thousand inmates had been murdered. It appears that the first to be murdered were political prisoners.

Once the Germans arrived, friends and relatives of the prisoners quickly entered the huge compounds and were confronted with a sickening sight. Bodies were heaped in piles. Doors to cellars full of corpses in many cases were bricked up. Many bodies were mutilated.

The NKVD rampage was by no means confined to Lwów. Prisoners in many smaller towns fared even worse. Inmates were scalded in boiling water. Noses, ears, and fingers were cut off. Even the corpses of children were found. Near Dobromil, many bodies were recovered from the shaft of a salt mine. NKVD sadists had been given a free hand to murder prisoners at will before fleeing the eastern territories. With the Wehrmacht pressing at the door, the NKVD had still gone about its work in a thorough, methodical way.

Stalin was not nearly so self-possessed. In the moment of greatest crisis, he apparently deserted his post. After issuing the suicidal order to advance on the evening of June 22, he vanished to his retreat at Kuntsevo. Little is know about his whereabouts or state of mind over the next seven days. It is widely believed that he was overcome with nervous exhaustion. Newspapers made no mention of his name and his voice was not heard on Soviet radio during this period. A rudderless ship of state foundered and no one stepped forward to challenge the toadies left nominally in charge.

The years of escalating terror, bloodshed, and blundering had caused a deep crisis of leadership, particularly within the state's military hierarchy. In 1937, the NKVD had instigated a sweeping purge of the Red

Army's officer corps. A Byzantine plot had been used to liquidate many outstanding military men, including Marshal Tukhachevsky, a hero of the revolution and a boy-general during the Russo-Polish War. Using double agents, the NKVD induced the German intelligence service to develop fake evidence of treason against Tukhachevsky and several other senior commanders. Their show trials scandalized the Soviet public and led to massive purges between May 1937 and September 1938. There is general agreement that the purge victims included nearly half of U.S.S.R. regimental commanders, nearly all brigade commanders, most military district and army corps commanders, and a great many of the army's political commissars. These purges contributed heavily to the Red Army's unpreparedness for and devastating initial losses following the German attack on June 22.

Stalin's absence on June 28 at a meeting between Ambassador Sir Richard Stafford Cripps and an arriving British military mission was a sure sign of his continuing disability. There was still no word of him in official reports. The Soviet public was befuddled by the strangely worded news from the front. Newspapers and radio were filled with clumsy verbal concoctions designed to conceal the frightening territorial losses or to encourage the fantasy that the Germans were being repelled.

At last, on July 1, there was word of Stalin. According to a brief announcement, he would head a new State Defense Committee. Two days later he was able to collect himself for a radio address to the Soviet people. "It came out badly," according to the Soviet ambassador to Great Britain, Ivan Maisky. "Stalin spoke in a dull, colorless voice, often stopping and breathing heavily. . . . He seemed ailing and at the end of his strength."

While Stalin gathered himself, his people's desperate military situation forced a complete reorientation of Soviet foreign policy. The barely muted pro-German bias vanished overnight. So did the thinly veiled antagonism toward the West. The Soviets desperately needed food and military equipment from the West and were anxious to reconcile with the British. Even under these circumstances, Stalin still drove a hard bargain. The British empire was cracking at the seams and he knew it. The sheer size of the Soviet Union gave him time. If the Wehrmacht could be fended off until winter, the Soviets could regroup behind the Volga River and the Ural Mountains. Russia was absorbing the full might of the German war machine. The West would have no choice but to help in the struggle against the common foe.

Churchill wasted little time in laying out the framework for an Anglo-

Soviet alliance to fight the Germans. The Poles were crucial to that strategy. They already had a large number of fighting men in the West and perhaps as many as three hundred thousand men in Russia who could be formed into combat units to fight beside the Red Army. The problem was British public opinion. The Molotov-Ribbentrop Pact and the subsequent plundering in Poland, the Baltic States, Finland, and Romania had caused an extremely negative view of the Soviets in Great Britain. Nazi-Soviet collaboration had hurt Poland more than any other country. The British public both sympathized with the Poles for their losses and keenly appreciated their contribution to the war effort. Polish pilots had performed heroically in the pivotal Battle of Britain. One seventh of all the German aircraft shot down had been destroyed by Polish pilots. Even the Luftwaffe accorded them grudging respect. Churchill knew that the Soviets' standing would be improved if the Poles accepted them as allies. It would help bring about the speedy realignment of relationships needed to structure a strong coalition to fight Germany. Sensitivity on this point prompted the prime minister to tell Parliament, "If Hitler invaded Hell, I would make at least a favourable reference to the Devil in the House of Commons."

One day after the German attack, General Władysław Sikorski, the Polish prime minister and commander in chief, made a radio address to Poland telling his countrymen that Russia was to be welcomed to the common struggle against the Nazis. He said the Poles were willing to put aside the past, and called on the Soviet Union to renounce the 1939 treaties with Germany that resulted in the partitioning of Poland. Sikorski also called for restoration of the Russo-Polish frontier of 1939 and the release of Polish prisoners of war and deportees in the U.S.S.R.

With Stalin still in seclusion, Moscow did not respond for ten days. It finally answered on July 4, initiating a flurry of exchanges. The Soviet position was surprisingly hard-line, especially for a country in such desperate circumstances. The Soviet ambassador in London, Ivan Maisky, conveyed the position of his government to British foreign secretary Anthony Eden, who in turn relayed it to the Poles. The Soviets suggested the formation of a Polish National Committee in the U.S.S.R. and said they would help such a committee in organizing military forces to fight alongside the Red Army. Maisky estimated that there were no more than twenty thousand Polish fighting men to be freed in Russia. Furthermore, he said, Poland's future boundaries should be "ethnographically" (sic) based, or pared back to the area populated principally by ethnic Poles. Clearly the Soviets intended to keep the western Ukraine and western Byelorussia, territories gained as a result of the Molotov-Ribbentrop Pact. Moreover, Maisky hinted, the Polish government was regarded as reactionary and fundamentally hostile to the U.S.S.R.

Shortly after receiving them, Eden phoned the proposals to Sikorski, who rejected them immediately. He was stunned by Maisky's estimate of available manpower for the army, pointing out that the Soviets themselves had published an estimate that 190,000 Polish soldiers were captured in September 1939. Sikorski emphasized that any agreement approved by his government must include recognition of the Polish government-in-exile; annulment of the Soviet-Nazi agreements of August 23 and September 28, 1939; establishment of a Polish embassy in Moscow with authority to care for all Polish citizens in the U.S.S.R., including war prisoners and deportees; and, finally, establishment of a Polish army in Russia under the authority of the Polish government-in-exile.

Eden advised Maisky of these terms immediately and all three parties met face-to-face the next day, July 5. It was clear then that the Soviets did not intend to budge on the question of territory. The settlement imposed after their defeat in the 1920 Russo-Polish War had left a bitter aftertaste. The Treaty of Riga, signed in 1921, had pushed Poland's frontier 150 miles east of the Curzon Line, which had been proposed by the Western Allies as the frontier of ethnic Poland. It bore a remarkable similarity to the line of partition established in the Nazi-Soviet Nonagression Pact of 1939. Maisky said that the Soviets were willing to renounce their 1939 pact with Hitler, but would not give up the territory gained as a result. Once again he emphasized that Poland's future borders must be defined on an ethnic basis. Sikorski protested, pointing out that the Soviet Union itself was a multinational, multiethnic federation. Maisky suggested that the boundary question could be left open, but reiterated Soviet determination to preserve the territorial status quo of June 22, 1941.

The citizenship status of the deportees was almost as controversial. On October 22, 1939, a few weeks into their military occupation of eastern Poland, the Soviets had staged a sham plebiscite. The population was forced to vote for candidates, handpicked by the NKVD, who ran without opposition. A turnout of between 92 and 96 percent of eligible voters was achieved through force and intimidation. Those elected became members of so-called popular assemblies, which promptly and dutifully requested unification with the Byelorussian and Ukrainian Socialist Republics. On November 1 and 2, 1939, the Supreme Soviet of the U.S.S.R. had approved the requests. The Polish government had protested that these actions were illegal. The Soviets, in turn, claimed that the annexations were justified by the will of the people of these territories. Over the next twenty months, as the Soviets had deported those citizens, their Polish identification documents were replaced by Soviet citizenship papers.

Through its intelligence network in eastern Poland, the Polish government-in-exile estimated that between 1.2 and two million persons had been deported. It had little specific information, however, about the whereabouts, living conditions, or legal status of these people. In their negotiations with the Soviets, Polish authorities proposed that freedom and civil rights be restored to all persons detained in the U.S.S.R. who held Polish citizenship on September 16, 1939, the day before the Red Army had advanced into the eastern territories. Such a specific definition was unacceptable to the Soviets. They insisted that any agreement contain language specifying that the problem "shall be solved in a constructive spirit after the resumption of diplomatic relations." As far as the Soviets were concerned, until the territorial dispute was settled the citizenship problem could not be resolved.

The two sides agreed that an autonomous Polish army would be formed in the Soviet Union and subordinated in operational matters to the high command of the Red Army. But on the territorial and citizenship questions, they remained far apart. The negotiations continued to drag through July, while the Wehrmacht raced forward on the Eastern front. The British, who had hoped that a general agreement could be signed quickly, became increasingly frustrated with the pace of negotiations. On July 11, Eden snapped at Sikorski in Maisky's presence, telling him that an agreement must be signed and that specific concerns could be settled later. Four days later, Churchill told Parliament that he hoped an agreement was imminent. He asked Sikorski to exercise statesmanship, but made no such request of the Soviets. On the same day, Eden bluntly told Sikorski: "Whether you want to or not, an agreement with the Soviet Union has to be signed."

Under great pressure from his own cabinet, Sikorski still pressed for Soviet concessions. Then, on July 17, Maisky added an element of threat to the negotiations. He complained to Eden about Polish "obdurance." If it continued, he warned, the Soviets would organize a Polish National Committee. "There [are] large numbers of Poles who [have] no love at all for the Polish government," Maisky insisted. Once again he emphasized that the Soviet stand on the frontier question would not change.

Sikorski and a majority of his cabinet could not hold out much longer.

The desperate situation of the Poles in the Soviet Union added great urgency to their decision. They knew that another winter in Russia without relief would cost thousands of lives. Gearing up to help would take time, and every day lost would make their rescue more difficult. From the minister to the file clerk, every Pole in London seemed personally struck by the crisis. Almost all of them had relatives, close friends, or acquaintances among the deportees.

On July 24, the British War Cabinet told Eden to tell Sikorski that the pact, as proposed by Moscow, "would be in the interest of Poland." It was the final straw. Hoping that, as comrades in arms, the Poles and the Soviets could bridge their differences, Sikorski signed in the face of enraged opposition within his own Cabinet. Foreign Minister August Zaleski, Defense Minister Kazimierz Sosnkowski, and Marian Seyda, a third member of the Cabinet, resigned immediately. President Władysław Raczkiewicz refused to approve the agreement even though the Polish constitution required his signature.

What most incensed the minority was the handling of the two key issues. The territorial problem had not been resolved, and at the end of the agreement a protocol had been added, which read: "As soon as diplomatic relations are re-established, the Government of the Union of Soviet Socialist Republics will grant an amnesty to all Polish citizens who are at present deprived of their freedom on the territory of the U.S.S.R., either as prisoners of war or on other adequate grounds." These words sent a wave of outrage cascading through the Polish expatriate community. For what were the Poles being pardoned? What offense had the deportees committed against the Soviets? The phrase "other adequate grounds" was equally repugnant. It seemed to justify the Soviets' 1939 invasion, their capture of Polish soldiers, and the subsequent mass deportations of civilians. Sikorski had swallowed hard, but the language was simply unacceptable to most of the government's constituency.

The Polish-Soviet Agreement of 1941, containing this protocol, was signed on July 30, 1941. In announcing it by broadcast to Poland, Sikorski emphasized its practical value, saying: "It enables us to form Polish military units from prisoners of war now languishing somewhere in Russia and longing to fight for Poland. . . . It restores freedom to all Polish citizens, whatever the pretext for their detention on the territory of the USSR may be. . . ."

What choice did the Poles have except to cooperate with Stalin? The only practical way to regain their homeland was through collective action with his government. How else could freedom be gained for those in the U.S.S.R. who were living and dying in such wretched circumstances? British pressure added to the urgency. Since the British were hosts to the government-in-exile, their views could not be ignored. The Poles were thus in a weak and vulnerable position. The Soviets came to the negotiations determined that never again would Polish territory be used as a springboard to attack Russia. They professed support for a strong and independent postwar Poland, but it cost nothing to say this.

The agreement that emerged was unusually vague, certainly for one that bore Stalin's imprimatur. It did not guarantee the return of Polish territory taken by the Soviets in 1939. While promising amnesty to all Polish citizens on Soviet soil, it did not define the word "citizen." In marked contrast to his negotiations with Ribbentrop on the night of September 28, 1939, Stalin now insisted on vagueness. Were cooperative relations with the Poles ever intended? Events that soon followed clearly suggest that they were not.

The summer of 1941 marked the end of one bad-faith agreement and the beginning of a new one. Hitler had never intended to keep his pact with Stalin. At one point he said: "You know, Ribbentrop, if I settled with Russia today I would only come to grips with her again tomorrow—I just can't help it." The Hitler-Stalin agreement of August 23, 1939, lasted twenty-two months, long enough for Germany to settle matters in the west and gear up for Barbarossa. The agreement signed by Sikorski and Maisky on July 30, 1941, lasted for twenty-one months, long enough for the Soviets to take the steam out of the Wehrmacht, to reverse the course of the war, and to set the stage for their domination of Eastern Europe. During this period, the Soviets would repeatedly violate both the letter and spirit of their agreement with the Poles. These two agreements resulted in the destruction of Poland's Second Republic. The first drove that government into exile and caused the enslavement of its citizens. The second created conditions that eliminated any possibility of its return to Poland.

The first signs of fatal weakness in the Polish government-in-exile could be glimpsed as the agreement of July 30, 1941, was consummated. The coalition forces within the government had not bridged the deep divisions of interwar Polish society. These divisions led to stalemate, which made the exile government susceptible to British coercion. Many of its leaders would not accept an immutable reality: The war was no longer a fight for Poland's territorial integrity; overnight it had become an all-out struggle to defeat Hitler. The Soviet Union, the Poles' archenemy, would play the pivotal role in achieving that goal.

In airing their grievances against the Soviets, it later would seem that the Poles were undercutting the war effort. From July 30, 1941, forward, the Poles were "Little Allies" nipping at the heels of the "Big Allies," or so it seemed. A great tragedy was in the making, one the Poles themselves seemed powerless to prevent.

For a brief time, it appeared that the Sikorski-Maisky agreement might provide a basis for genuine cooperation between the Soviets and the Poles. On August 4, the Soviets released General Władysław Anders from Lubyanka prison in Moscow. The Polish government in London had named Anders commander in chief of the army it would be organizing in the U.S.S.R., and the Soviets had already approved the appointment. On August 12, the Soviet government published the amnesty protocol word for word as an *ukaz*, or decree. Procedures for the release of the deportees were also established. They were to receive special amnesty certificates that could be exchanged at the end of three months for passports. The deportees were to receive free railway tickets to a destination of their choice and a travel allowance of fifteen rubles a day. The Polish government would be permitted to name trustees to supervise relief efforts for the deportees. One or more joint commissions were to be set up to find Polish citizens, assist in their resettlement, and help provide for their livelihood. The two governments exchanged ambassadors and on September 4, the new Polish ambassador, Stanisław Kot, arrived in Moscow.

The amnesty decree was not the only hopeful message the Poles received on August 12, 1941. That same day Churchill and Roosevelt signed the Atlantic Charter, which committed the signatories not to seek territorial aggrandizement and not to countenance "territorial changes that do not accord with the freely expressed wishes of the people concerned." Although neither Parliament nor Congress ratified the charter, these words were quickly embraced by the Poles and other beleaguered peoples the world over as a moral covenant with the Western Allies. The Soviet Union and Poland were among ten nations that signed the charter in London on September 24, 1941. In signing the document, Maisky added the cryptic qualification that "the practical application of these principles will necessarily adapt itself to the circumstances, needs, and historic peculiarities of particular countries."

The Joint Polish-Soviet Commission to assist deportees held its first meeting on September 9, 1941. Here, for the first time, it was evident how far apart the governments were in their respective estimates of how many Poles were being held in the U.S.S.R. The Soviets estimated the number at 300,000 to 350,000. From their intelligence reports, the Poles were sure that these numbers represented no more than 25 to 30 percent of the real total. The Soviets said most of the deportees were living in free exile and that 107,933 persons had already been supplied with amnesty certificates. It was unclear whether these totals included the Polish minorities—Jews, Byelorussians, and Ukrainians—who accounted for nearly half the deportees. Soviet commission members were ambiguous about the citizenship status of these minorities. Polish members of the commission left the meeting concerned about this aspect of the discussion.

More complete Soviet figures were presented on October 6 at a meeting between Kot and Deputy Commissar for Foreign Affairs Andrei Vyshinsky, who had served as prosecutor at several of the famous show trials of the late thirties. Vyshinsky reported that 291,137 deportees were living in "free exile," that 71,481 were in prisons and work camps, and that 25,314 were prisoners of war. Kot objected that the numbers were far too low, and heated words were exchanged. Kot found that Vyshinsky's figures did not include the Polish minorities and did not account for deportees who had died in the Soviet Union. The number of deaths was known to be quite large. Kot felt this might account for some, but not all, of the discrepancy between his estimates and Vyshinsky's. The report presented by Vyshinsky was the last of its kind provided by Soviet authorities. One month later, on November 8, Molotov sent a note to the Polish embassy saying that the amnesty operations were complete.

On August 14, two days after the amnesty decree was issued, the Poles and the Soviets signed a special military agreement. It stipulated that the army to be formed as a result would be "supplied as far as possible" by the Soviets and by the Poles' own lend-lease program with the United States. Polish leaders estimated that they had enough manpower in the U.S.S.R. to organize an army of 300,000 men. They based their estimate on what the Soviets themselves said and on reports from Polish intelligence. On November 2, 1939, Molotov had said that 300,000 Polish troops had been captured during the Soviet invasion of Poland. On September 17, 1940, the first anniversary of the Soviet attack, the Red Army newspaper, *Red Star*, had boasted that almost 200,000 men and eight thousand officers had been captured on the Ukrainian and Lithuanian fronts. The Poles also knew that following the occupation of eastern Poland, between 100,000 and 150,000 men had been conscripted there into the Red Army and Soviet labor battalions.

Two days after the military agreement was signed, General Ivan Panfilov, assistant chief of the Soviet general staff, casually told General Anders that only twenty-one thousand Polish fighting men were available. Among these, he said, there were a thousand officers, all at Camp Gryazovets. Anders asked immediately about the more than fifteen thousand officers and noncommissioned officers who had been interned at Kozelsk, Starobelsk, and Ostashkov. Panfilov was noncommittal. Not wanting a confrontation, Anders did not press the issue. Representatives of both armies held a strategy conference on August 19 and agreed that the first Polish units would consist of two infantry divisions and support personnel, about thirty thousand men.

Anders writes in his memoirs that on August 22 he learned that his army would be based in the area around Buzuluk, a remote Russian town of wooden houses and muddy streets east of the Volga River, at the southern end of the Ural Mountains. Buzuluk was six hundred miles from Moscow, safely beyond the war zone. Anders was anxious to begin assembling his men, so three days later he headed north to Camp Gryazovets to prepare for the release of the officers being held there. Anders was flown first on an antediluvian Soviet aircraft to Vologda, about 250 miles north of Moscow. He was taken the rest of the way to the camp through deserted country on a hand-propelled railway trolley. At Gryazovets, Anders found 1,600 men, not a thousand as Panfilov had reported. Among them was a remnant who had been transferred there from Kozelsk, Starobelsk, and Ostashkov. A total of 448 had survived from these camps, but that number had mysteriously dwindled to 350 by the time Anders arrived. In addition to these men were more than a thousand officers who had escaped into Lithuania and Latvia after Poland's collapse. These men had all been captured after the Soviet occupation of the Baltic States in 1940. The 1,600 men at Gryazovets had no idea that, except for a few high-ranking officers already in Moscow, they represented most of the Polish officers still alive in the Soviet Union.

Władek Cichy was among those waiting for the general to arrive. Over the past year, since his electrifying translation of Soviet newscasts on the Battle of Britain, Cichy had continued to monitor Radio Moscow and Radio Smolensk, passing war news on to his companions. After the German attack, camp authorities had permitted him to prepare a bulletin with maps, which he drew by hand with colored pencils, depicting the front. A censor carefully reviewed each bulletin, often requiring changes, before Cichy could post the document on a large board in front of the barracks.

Cichy showed me a large, colorful map he had prepared only a day or two before Stalin's famous radio address of July 3. "I was basing my work on the Soviet news bulletins," he said. "Then, in this address on July third, Stalin finally depicted a situation much worse. The news bulletins were lying. After eleven days of the war, it was a great shock to find out how far the Germans had gotten." Later, Cichy had reported on the July 30 agreement and the general amnesty granted on August 12. His bulletin for Sunday, August 24, described Anders's pending visit and the formation of a Polish army in the U.S.S.R.

Cichy and his companions were lined up and had been waiting for some time when Anders arrived. The general himself had narrowly avoided being sent to Kozelsk or Starobelsk. He had been shot through the back in the closing days of the September 1939 campaign and captured by the Soviets. He was hospitalized still when the executions took place. "I remember how he limped along with a stick walking by me," Cichy said. Lubyanka prison had not been kind to Anders. His face was discolored and gaunt. He was tall and angular; he had been in peak physical condition before the war. Now, at forty-nine, he was hunched over and lacking vitality. Only his eyes communicated strength, according to Cichy. They warmed as they fixed, periodically, on the familiar face of an old friend or comrade in arms.

The general began by telling the men that he was their new commander in chief, and that they would become part of a new Polish army-in-exile to be formed among Poles in the Soviet Union. He called on each man to follow his country's lead in putting aside differences— no matter how bitter or justified—with the Soviet Union. The Poles and Soviets had no choice, Anders emphasized, but to unite in their common struggle against the Nazis. Anders told the men they would soon be heading south to Buzuluk, where units of the new army would be organized. The forming of a new army was welcome news, but the idea of joining forces with the Soviets was not. "We received it most unwillingly and with great apprehension," Cichy told me.

Before leaving, Anders demanded and received a commitment from the NKVD to remove armed sentries from the camp and to allow his men to leave the barbed-wire enclosure.

The amnesty decree of August 12 and the military agreement of August 14 set loose a human tide that neither Polish authorities nor the NKVD were prepared for. Transportation arteries, already strained to the limit because of the war, and hastily organized reception centers were overwhelmed by the sudden release of tens of thousands of deportees. Many left without obtaining the required amnesty certificate. Many who obtained the certificates had no idea what destination to list. Soviet authorities often filled in this blank arbitrarily. The deportees had been sprinkled in small groups over the entire territory of the Soviet Union, not to russify them, but instead to quietly exterminate them through one to two years of forced labor. Those in the harsh, unforgiving climate of the north sought to move south as quickly as possible. They immediately began funneling toward the giant Volga River. The barge and train lines that ran on and along it took this mass of humanity south toward Buzuluk, where the army was organizing. Cichy flowed with that tide, riding south from Camp Gryazovets on a coal train. He reported for duty at Buzuluk in early September covered from head to foot in coal dust.

Most of the deportees were physically unfit for an arduous journey and thousands died as a result. Their plight has been documented in hundreds of eyewitness accounts collected by the Polish army-in-exile and subsequently taken to the Hoover Institution at Stanford University. From these reports, it seems clear that almost all who made the trek south were emaciated from severe malnutrition and physically exhausted from the rigors of forced labor. They were clothed in rags. Many were barefoot or wore makeshift shoes. With them came raging epidemics that forced the quarantining of entire trains. Health hazards at some stations were so great that trains were forbidden to stop. Relief centers set up to assist the deportees were also forced to shut down. Many deportees died after finally reaching their destination. Amnesty thus mirrored many of the worst horrors of deportation.

The rate of voluntary enlistment for the new army exceeded all expectations. By the end of November, forty-six thousand men had been enrolled. Then came a roadblock on November 6. General Panfilov told General Anders that the Soviets could provide rations for only thirty thousand men and called for a halt in further enlistments. Anders was shocked by the news but was left with only two alternatives. He could either discharge sixteen thousand men, or divide the reduced rations among all his emaciated troops. Part of these rations were already being shared with Polish civilians who were beginning to congregate in great numbers near Buzuluk. Anders decided not to cut individual rations, knowing that to send men away at the beginning of the Russian winter would be to serve them with a virtual death sentence.

Many men were still on their way to Buzuluk when Panfilov curtailed rations. Word of the amnesty and the formation of a Polish army had yet to penetrate to many remote camps, prisons, and collective farms. Poles arriving to join the armed forces after November 6 found the Buzuluk train station and the nearby Totskoye station heavily guarded by Soviet troops. These men were forced at gunpoint to continue moving south, away from the army. No one knew how many passed in this fashion, but most who did probably perished during the winter of 1941–1942.

Among the lucky few permitted to enroll in the Polish army during this period were Zofia Hoffman and her mother, Maria Neuhoff. Despite their emaciation, they were able to get from Georgiyevka in Kazakhstan to Buzuluk by about December 1. Zofia weighed only a hundred pounds, about forty pounds less than her normal weight. Both women were sworn in as members of the Polish Women's Auxiliary Service. Colonel Leopold Okulicki, General Anders's chief of staff, known affectionately to the troops as the "Little Bear," personally signed their induction papers. Zofia was enrolled as a private and her mother, then sixty-one, as a "senior volunteer"—an ad hoc rank designed to afford Mrs. Neuhoff the army's protection. Both women began their military careers peeling badly decayed carrots in one of the camp kitchens.

With winter closing in, only a fraction of the Poles' available manpower in the U.S.S.R. had reported to Buzuluk. Those who had were living in appalling conditions. Many would not make it through the winter. Many others were being turned away as they tried to reach the army. All these were bitter disappointments. Most distressing of all, not one word had been heard from any of the men missing from Kozelsk, Starobelsk, and Ostashkov. General Anders's chief of staff in the 1939 September campaign, Major A. Solton, was among those missing. So was Anders's adjutant, Major Fuhran. Dozens of highly regarded generals and colonels were also missing. So were thousands of Poland's most prominent professionals who were among the reserves. There was also a vague, uncooperative, and worrisome aspect in the Soviet response to questions about these men.

Believing that such difficulties could only be resolved face to face with Stalin, General Sikorski decided to go to the Soviet Union in late November 1941, where he was received with the highest honors. Sikorski carried with him a heavy burden. Barely a hundred days after its signing, the agreement of July 30 was not providing a basis for cooperative relations with the Soviets. Many problems foreseen by his own deeply divided cabinet had, in fact, materialized. To Sikorski some of these difficulties were inevitable. What mattered most to him was the spirit, not the details, of the relationship. And on that count, there was increasing cause for concern. Sikorski knew that on the Soviet side only one man could call forth the spirit required at this critical juncture. For a brief moment, it seemed that he and Stalin might, after all, become comrades in arms.

CHAPTER 14

Crumbling Hopes

Where were the missing officers? By the time General Sikorski arrived in Moscow this question had become a paramount concern to the government-in-exile. A strong Polish army on the Eastern Front was desperately needed to help ensure Poland's future independence and to lead civilian deportees back to their homeland. Such a fighting force could not be organized without experienced military leaders, but many of Poland's ablest men had not been heard from for eighteen months or more. Over the winter of 1941–1942, letters and telegrams from anguished relatives of the missing men began pouring in daily to the Polish embassy. Among them were several inquiries about Captain Stanisław Pawulski sent by his wife, Maria, from Kokpekty in Kazakhstan. The embassy had nothing to tell her or any of the others who were writing. Its vague replies seemed unresponsive and caused a shower of continuing demands for more information from the families of the missing men.

A sense of foreboding began to pervade the issue. Long before his August 4 release from Lubyanka prison, General Anders had learned from a cellmate, a Captain Kuszel, about the three big camps at Kozelsk, Starobelsk, and Ostashkov, where thousands of Polish officers and noncoms had been held. Kuszel had been a prisoner at Starobelsk and later at Pawlishtchev Bor, an interim camp where a small number of men from Kozelsk, Starobelsk, and Ostashkov had all been taken in June 1940. These men had quickly discovered that the NKVD used similar procedures at all three camps. Kuszel told Anders about the mysterious transports of men taken daily from these camps in April and May of 1940. The evening of his release from Lubyanka, the NKVD had arranged for Anders to meet with Colonel Zygmunt Berling to discuss his efforts to form Polish units in the Red Army. Berling, who had been held at Starobelsk, confirmed to Anders many of the details related by Kuszel. Although Anders had a poor opinion of

Berling, suspecting him of being much too close to the Soviets, he found his comments about the missing men convincing.

Immediately after his arrival on September 4, Ambassador Kot, a feisty former professor of history and leader in the Peasant Party, began trying to track down the missing men. The new embassy was still being organized when the diplomatic corps, foreign correspondents, and many government ministries were moved out of Moscow on October 15. The possibility that the Wehrmacht might capture the Soviet capital appeared real. Stalin remained there as a symbol of Soviet determination to resist, but most of his government withdrew far from the war zone. The provisional capital became Kuybyshev, a city at the confluence of the Volga and Samara rivers five hundred fifty miles east of Moscow. Buzuluk, where the Polish army-in-exile was gathering, lay only ninety miles to the east. Despite the turmoil, Kot began writing and asking embarrassing questions. He refused to accept the standard Soviet response that all Poles in captivity had been released. On October 6, he told Vyshinsky that the Poles had scoured German POW camps in occupied Poland—"everywhere where they could possibly be"—and found no sign of the men. "I could understand it if it were a matter of a few dozen or even a few hundred people missing, but not thousands," Kot said. The two men exchanged hot words on November 2, when Kot complained bitterly about Vyshinsky's lack of follow-through. Vyshinsky pointed out the chaotic situation caused by the evacuation of Moscow, but Kot had the last word: "People," he said, "are not like steam. They cannot evaporate."

In preparation for Sikorski's visit, Kot met with Stalin and Molotov in Moscow for two hours and ten minutes on November 14. Minutes of the meeting, made immediately afterward by Kot, show that much of the discussion dealt with Stalin's decision to provide rations for only thirty thousand Polish soldiers. Stalin reminded Kot that "we are fighting on a widespread front and we risk to fail [sic] to supply our own armies." The Poles could form as many divisions as they chose, Stalin said, as long as they were supplied from abroad. Kot pointed out that Polish troops were being diverted away from Buzuluk, to the south where they faced an uncertain fate. He and Stalin agreed that new points of concentration should be established in the south for Polish troops and civilians and that the locations should be set after consulting with Sikorski. Stalin agreed to continue feeding the men at Buzuluk until foreign supplies could be obtained.

"After all, we are allies," he told Kot. "And who wants a weak ally? We will share with the Poles everything, like with brothers. We'll do for you whatever we can."

Near the end of the meeting, Kot raised the issue of the missing men. "Are there still any Poles in captivity?" Stalin asked.

Kot explained that the officers from Kozelsk, Starobelsk, and Ostashkov were missing and said, "We possess records of when they were removed from the camps."

"Are there any accurate lists?" Stalin asked.

Kot replied that the camp commanders had recorded the names of every prisoner and that NKVD files were developed on each man.

Stalin, pacing slowly with a cigarette in his hand, moved toward the telephone, fumbled with a switch, which Molotov fixed, then placed a call to the army or the NKVD.

"Stalin here. Have all Poles been released from prison?" he asked. There was a pause while Stalin listened. "I have with me here the Polish ambassador who tells me that not all have been." Again, Stalin paused to listen. Finally he put the receiver down and returned to the conference table and asked Kot when and where the Polish army expected to fight the Germans. Kot replied that the Poles did not want to be sent to the front in single divisions, but hoped to have a sector assigned to them. Stalin gave a noncommittal answer.

According to Kot's minutes of the meeting, the telephone rang at this point and Stalin got up to answer. He listened, apparently to the answer to his earlier question. After a few moments, Stalin put the receiver down and returned to the conference table without saying a word. Stalin then asked for details about Sikorski's pending visit before telling Kot, "I am personally anxious to be of help in the rebuilding of an independent Polish state, without being concerned with its internal structure."

Was this skillful acting on Stalin's part? Looking back on the scene in the harsh light of subsequent revelations, Kot thought so. He was convinced that in the highly centralized Soviet system the liquidations could not have occurred without Stalin's personal approval.

At the time, Kot came away convinced that lists of the missing men were urgently needed. "[That] was our weak point in these negotiations," he said later. On his return to Kuybyshev, he dispatched an urgent message to General Anders asking him to canvass his troops within a week for the names of missing men. The embassy staff worked all night the evening Sikorski arrived, putting a master list in order. It contained almost four thousand names.

On November 28, Anders flew in a Soviet aircraft from the provisional capital to Tehran to meet Sikorski. He writes in his memoirs that he left in subzero temperatures with three feet of snow on the ground. His men were huddled in light tents. Only a fortunate few

had stoves. His route took him over the sprawling Volga delta at Astrakhan, across the Caspian Sea, and over the slopes of majestic Mount
Demavend before landing at the sunny Persian capital, where roses
were blooming. Flying back, he and Sikorski found the Kuybyshev
airport festooned with Polish and Soviet flags. A military band played
the anthems of both nations. The Soviet writer Ilya Ehrenburg watched
the new Polish army parading before Sikorski in the deep snow and
wrote:

> These men who march past have come out of profound suffering. A
> human tragedy looks out of every pair of eyes; these men had lost every-
> thing. But they hold their rifles with joy and pride. I have seen grey-
> haired soldiers and young boys kissing the arms they had just received;
> holding the weapon tight in their hands, radiant with happiness as a man
> holds a beloved woman.

Stalin and Molotov received Sikorski, Kot, and Anders at the
Kremlin on December 3 for a meeting that lasted two and a half hours.
Kot took detailed notes, which he and Anders later used to create a
transcript of the discussion. At the outset, Sikorski bluntly told Stalin
that the terms of the amnesty were not being fulfilled, that "the most
valuable of our people are still in labor camps and prisons." Sikorski
described the list of four thousand officers just compiled and told Stalin
that underground sources reported that none of the men were in
Poland or in German POW camps. "These people are here; not one
of them has returned," Sikorski said.

"That is impossible. They have escaped," Stalin said.

"Where could they have escaped to?" Anders asked.

"Well, to Manchuria," Stalin replied.

Sikorski and Anders pointed out how impossible it would be for men
from three separate camps to make their way thousands of miles without being detected.

"They have certainly been freed, but have not yet arrived," Stalin
said.

Stalin's answer seemed to satisfy Sikorski, Anders, and Kot. These
words would later be the subject of much discussion among the Polish
leaders. They would inspire hope among some that perhaps local
authorities were still holding the men. Others felt that because of
Russia's vast distances and shortage of transport, the missing men simply had been unable, as yet, to get to Buzuluk.

A great deal of the discussion on December 3 focused on the plight
of Poland's civilian deportees. Sikorski complained bitterly about their

treatment, at one point telling Stalin, "These people are not tourists, they are people forcibly deported from their homes. They did not come here of their own will but have been deported and have undergone untold sufferings." He told Stalin that he was anxious to organize a system of delegates under embassy supervision to coordinate relief in areas where there were large concentrations of deportees. Large shipments of clothes, he said, were waiting to be sent by Poles in America on condition that Polish authorities would be permitted to distribute them. He said the delegates would also assist in moving the deportees to a milder climate.

Stalin agreed without objection to the establishment of the delegate system. He then gathered the group around a large map and began discussing possible sites to which the deportees could be evacuated. It was agreed that the areas of southern Kazakhstan around Tashkent and Alma-Ata were most feasible.

Because of the atrocious physical condition of his men, Sikorski then proposed moving the entire Polish army to Iran, where American and British food and equipment could be used to help them regain their health and prepare to fight. He promised to return to the Soviet Union as quickly as possible "and take over a whole sector of the front." He said the plan had Churchill's approval.

The proposal seemed to catch Stalin off guard and to irritate him greatly. He dropped a paper containing his notes on the meeting; Molotov swooped down obsequiously to retrieve it. "I am an old and experienced man," Stalin said. "I know that once you leave for Persia you will never come back here." Both Anders and Sikorski tried to reassure Stalin that they wanted to fight on the Eastern Front. He listened briefly, then spoke again in an irritated voice: "If the Poles don't want to fight, let them go. We cannot retain the Poles. If they wish, then let them go."

In an agitated voice, Sikorski told Stalin, "Please find me another solution, because here the conditions are such as to make it quite impossible to form an army and I do not want to let my men perish to no avail. This is not an ultimatum, but in the conditions of a severe winter when gales and frost decimate my men I cannot just watch and remain silent." Later Sikorski curtly added, "You have insulted me, Mr. President, by saying that our soldier does not want to fight."

Finally Stalin began to relent. "If you categorically insist, one corps—from two to three divisions—can leave. While if you really want, I will give you the place and the means to form seven divisions." At that point general Panfilov was brought into the room to participate in the discussion and Anders began a detailed listing of the army's difficulties. He said his men had not received all the food they were entitled to and that cases of typhus had been reported, but could not be treated because medicines were not available. The men were living without camp stoves in the middle of winter. No soap, tools, or vegetables had been available for several months. Anders reminded Stalin of his order to restore rations cut by General Panfilov on November 6, then pointed out that the camp at Tockim had received no food at all three days earlier.

Panfilov stood silently through this indexing of ills. "Who is responsible for all that?" Stalin barked. Panfilov said the orders had been given by someone else.

"When did I order to increase the number of food rations?" Stalin asked.

"Two and a half weeks ago," Panfilov replied.

"Then why have my orders not been put into effect till now? Are they to eat your instructions?" Stalin growled. Panfilov stood erect at attention, blushing deeply. Stalin then assured Sikorski and Anders that supplies would be restored to levels sufficient for the army to be organized in the Soviet Union. Molotov said little or nothing during the entire meeting. Each time Stalin drew a cigarette from a case, Molotov leaned forward quickly to light it.

That evening Stalin, who seemed in excellent humor, hosted the Polish delegation at a state dinner. Anders later said Stalin laughed and joked, "but it never seemed to be the kind of laughter that came from the heart." The status of the Polish minorities came up briefly when Sikorski and Anders asked Stalin about releasing Poles from the eastern territories who had been conscripted into the Red Army and into labor battalions.

"What is the case of the White Russians, Ukrainians, and Jews to you?" Stalin responded. "You want Poles, they are the best soldiers." His comment broached a sensitive subject. By a note on December 1, the Soviet government had informed the Polish embassy that it now considered the Polish minorities to be Soviet citizens. Sikorski knew that discussion of the note would automatically introduce the highly sensitive matter of frontiers, a subject both sides had avoided earlier in the day.

"No faits accomplis can be created by force," Sikorski said. Stalin then noted that the minorities had taken part in plebiscites that permitted them to become Soviet citizens. Sikorski questioned the conditions under which the plebiscites were conducted.

"We must fix our common boundaries ourselves, and before the peace conference, as soon as the Polish army goes into battle," Stalin said. "We should stop any talks on this subject. Be sure we shall not wrong you." Sikorski said he would like to come back to the topic later.

In the early morning hours, the two leaders signed a friendship declaration pledging that the armed forces of the two countries would fight side by side to defeat "German Hitlerite Imperialism."

The Polish delegation returned to Kuybyshev on December 5 in a special train, sensing that Stalin and Sikorski had developed a good rapport and that breakthroughs had been achieved on several difficult issues. The embassy could now organize a delegate system with local representatives to coordinate relief efforts for the deportees. Both civilians and the army were to be moved to a warmer climate. Rations would continue for 46,000 men, and any number beyond that would be evacuated to Iran. Stalin had indicated that eventually he would help the Poles form an army of nearly 100,000 men to fight on the Eastern Front. He had even agreed to a substantial loan to support the rehabilitation of the Poles in the U.S.S.R. Only two major issues had not been settled at the meeting, or so it seemed. The Poles themselves had been anxious to defer the sensitive frontier issue until their position improved. That left only the mystery of the missing officers. And even here Stalin had seemed to offer hope.

Sikorski wrote Churchill describing his visit as a complete success. He felt Stalin was "sincere" and that his visit had "resulted in a solution of nearly all the outstanding Polish-Soviet problems and also resulted in some benefit to the Allied cause."

Two days after the delegation had returned to Kuybyshev, the Japanese attacked Pearl Harbor. The United States entered the war the following day, December 8, 1941. That event seemed to remove the last bit of gloom for the Poles. The coalition to defeat Hitler and recover their homeland was finally in place, and apparently they would play a prominent role in it.

On December 23 the two governments signed an agreement that provided for the appointment, with joint approval, of nineteen embassy delegates to extend legal protection and relief to Polish citizens. This function was critical since most of the deportees had been forced to surrender their personal documents and accept Soviet passports or be designated stateless individuals. The delegates covered forty-six administrative districts containing some 2,600 settlements of Poles. About four hundred local representatives were named to coordinate most of the legal and relief work within these settlements. They began their work in February 1942 and continued it for approximately one year. During that time, prodigious results were achieved. Financial support was channeled to the desperately needy. A large number of orphanages, kindergartens, elementary schools, and child-feeding centers were established, as were hostels, workshops, and homes for invalids. Ten hospitals and many health clinics were set up. These facilities and the support they dispensed were all designed to make life in the U.S.S.R. more bearable for the Poles, to help them survive until Hitler could be driven from their homeland.

At first the relief effort met no objection from Soviet authorities. But slowly that attitude changed as complaints arose among ordinary Soviet citizens. Up to this point, the Soviet peasantry, which had endured untold hardship of its own, had empathized with the Poles. Individual acts of kindness were common. The Pawulskis, Zofia Hoffman and her mother, and thousands of other Polish families were the beneficiaries of such acts. But resentments began to boil early in 1942 as Polish relief supplies began arriving in the settlements. Who, among the local population, had ever been granted amnesty? Who among the millions of uprooted Soviet peoples had ever been given the choice of moving? These were shocking concessions. Then a trickle of tinned food, blankets, clothing, shoes, building materials, and other supplies began reaching the Poles in small settlements all over the U.S.S.R. A crescendo of grumbling arose: Why were these "luxuries" being given to the Poles? Why not to the Soviet people instead?

The relief effort also defied conventional wisdom. For more than a generation, Soviet propaganda had relentlessly driven home the idea that ordinary Soviet citizens were well off compared to people in the decadent West. The arrival of many goods that were simply unavailable in the Soviet Union posed a direct challenge to this myth. The groundswell of complaints alarmed Soviet authorities. One senior NKVD man told the Polish chief of staff, General Zygmunt Bohusz-Szyszko, "It will take us twenty years to efface the impression of your passage through our country."

By spring it was evident that the work of the delegates would not be tolerated on any significant scale much longer. Obstacles were raised in the most ordinary matters that made communication between the Kuybyshev embassy and the relief organization increasingly difficult. Paweł Zaleski arrived from Istanbul during this period and was assigned at the embassy to channeling relief supplies through the delegate system. In one of our discussions he described one of the simple but effective ways in which the NKVD stymied relief distribution.

"Very often I would place calls to one of our delegates," Zaleski said.

"These went through the local operator in Kuybyshev. Typically, I would ask to be connected with the office in a place such as Novosibirsk and the operator would put me through with no problem. I would begin talking to the person on the other end when suddenly we would hear one of Tchaikovsky's waltzes filtering louder and louder onto the line. We would try to shout above the noise, but it was impossible. Then the operator would come back on the line and say, 'Are you still talking?' We would explain that we could not hear each other and the operator would say, 'Please try again.' The same thing would happen all over again. Finally, while we still shouted back and forth, the operator would come back on the line and say, 'I'm sorry, your time is up.' Then we were disconnected."

In May, the NKVD arrested a number of local representatives of the relief program and charged them with engaging in activities hostile to the Soviet Union. The action seemed to target representatives who were achieving the most success. The problem came to a head on June 29, 1942, when the delegates and their entire staffs in Arkhangelsk and Vladivostok were arrested and charged with espionage. All relief supplies in both locations were impounded. The fact that the delegates carried diplomatic passports and identity cards made no difference. The embassy itself was not informed of the action and did not find out about the arrests for over a week. Kot lodged a vehement protest, and those arrested were set free on July 10, but Soviet authorities did not explain why they had taken the action.

Over the next few months, the relief effort became a shambles. Vyshinsky demanded that all the delegates be recalled to Kuybyshev, where they and the principal members of their staffs were arrested. Most of the delegates and representatives remained in prison until October 1942, when ninety-three were released. For unexplained reasons, sixteen of those arrested were never released. (What happened to them is unknown.) Meanwhile, on July 20, all remaining offices were closed and supply depots were sealed. These actions by Soviet authorities had disastrous consequences for thousands of Polish citizens who were still being detained in Siberian lumber camps, on remote kolkhozy, or in other work camps. Many authorities in these isolated places had disregarded the amnesty decree, keeping their most able-bodied workers in order to meet production quotas. One of the major objectives of the relief effort was to provide legal protection for Polish citizens under such circumstances. This part of the effort never really got off the ground. By early 1943, the entire relief effort had come to a virtual halt.

The army also began experiencing a new round of difficulties early in 1942. Further recruitment among the Polish minorities was abruptly prohibited. Despite strong protests, the Soviets would not yield on the issue. About the same time, Soviet authorities told Anders he could move his men south about 1,200 miles from Buzuluk to Yangiyul, a town near Tashkent, the capital of the Uzbek Soviet Socialist Republic. "Yangiyul" means New Road, and indeed the Polish army-in-exile was embarking on a long journey, which would eventually take it out of Central Asia, through the Middle East, and into Italy, where its Second Corps would lead the final assault at Monte Cassino.

While the army prepared to leave, the Soviets began pressuring Anders to send individual units to the front. Anders resisted. The British had only recently supplied his men with uniforms. Only one division had been armed. Its rations were being shared with a large number of civilians who had congregated near Buzuluk. Most of the men were in poor health and either suffered from or were susceptible to a variety of illnesses. The Poles had assumed that all units would go into action together. They expected to prove themselves on an entire sector of the front and believed that their contributions would give an important boost to morale in the Home Army in Poland. The Soviets were not satisfied with these explanations from Anders, who finally referred the matter to London. General Sikorski wired back an adamant response supporting Anders's position. Anders then told the Soviets that single units would not be dispatched to the front.

A further tightening of the screws followed. In early March, Anders was once again advised that rations for his men would be cut drastically. He was told that provisions could be continued for only 26,000 of the seventy thousand volunteers he had then assembled. If carried out, the decision could mean starvation for thousands of his men and for thousands of civilians who had become totally dependent on the army for food. The action was prompted, according to the Soviets, by Japan's entry into the war, which had cut to a trickle shipments of U.S. wheat to Russia. Anders flew to Moscow to meet with Stalin about the problem on March 18. As a result of their three-and-a-half-hour meeting, Stalin agreed to provide rations for 44,000 men and to permit Anders to evacuate the rest to Iran. Anders also succeeded in persuading Stalin to permit him to take a large number of women and children with him. Efforts to evacuate thirty thousand troops and ten thousand civilians began in late March. A reception depot was set up at Krasnovodsk on the Caspian Sea. Those being evacuated were taken there by train and crossed by ship to Pahlevi (now Bandar-e Anzalī) in Iran. The first of seventeen transports left on March 31 and the last on April 5. Many children and others recently released from prison died en route. Zofia Hoffman and her mother were among those evacuated during this period.

Those who remained faced a precarious future. Moving from snow-bound tents and huts at the base of the Ural Mountains to the semiarid heat of Uzbekistan left the army and the civilians who followed even more physically depleted. Contagious disease quickly began to rage out of control. Józef Czapski, who headed the army's Propaganda Service, documented these miseries after the war in a book called *Inhuman Land*. He wrote that 44 percent of the army's men were hospitalized at some point with typhus, typhoid fever, dysentery, or malaria. Some units were billeted near mosquito-infested rice fields and were totally immobilized by malaria. The few available hospitals, jammed with sick soldiers and civilians, had little or no medicines to fight the epidemics. More than two thousand in the armed forces died from contagious diseases, according to Czapski. Many more civilians and volunteers died attempting to reach the army. Czapski and his men in the Propaganda Service were forbidden by the NKVD to write about or photograph the army's disastrous health situation.

The problem of infectious disease continued relentlessly for as long as the army remained in the U.S.S.R. Almost every Pole's health was threatened by swarms of disease-carrying insects. "For most people, there was no possibility to wash and no soap if there had been," Paweł Zaleski told me. "Almost none of them [the deportees] could change clothes either. They were dressed so poorly that they slept close together to keep warm. The lice simply marched from one person to the next; there was no way to get rid of them. When someone died, their clothes were boiled and taken by someone else." Zofia Hoffman described these same problems in a report to her superiors shortly after she joined the army-in-exile. She noted that the stable where she and her mother were first housed was "host to an incredible amount of vermin, such as cockroaches, centipedes, and fleas. Fleas in particular were a real disaster. On one sleeping spot, at any one time, one killed fifty to eighty insects, without making a dent in their numbers."

In his March 18 meeting with Stalin, Anders had once again raised the issue of the missing men from Kozelsk, Starobelsk, and Ostashkov. The previous fall, he had personally assigned Czapski the task of tracking the men down. Czapski, who had achieved international acclaim as an artist before the war, had been a prisoner at Starobelsk. To conduct his investigation, he sought out top officials of the NKVD in Moscow and with great difficulty visited the headquarters of the

GULAG (an acronym for Glavnoe Upravlenie Ispravitel'no-trudovykh Lagerei, the central administration for labor camps and corrective facilities) at Orenburg, about two hundred miles southeast of Kuybyshev. His efforts resulted in complete failure, and left Polish authorities hoping that with warmer weather and improved conditions of transport, the missing officers would show up. Stalin reinforced these hopes with a comment he let fall in his March 18 meeting with Anders. At one point in that meeting, Anders said to Stalin: "Where can they be? We have traces of their whereabouts on the Kolyma River."

"I have already given orders that they are to be freed," Stalin replied. "They say [It is said] they are in Franz Joseph Land, but there is no one there. I do not know where they are. Why should we keep them? It may be that they were in camps in territories which have been taken by the Germans and were dispersed."

The importance of Stalin's comment that the men might have been captured by the Germans would not be revealed for more than a year. But his hint about Franz Joseph Land, far to the north of the Arctic Circle, served to fuel a strong undercurrent of rumors among the Poles that the men had been sent to the far north and would be returning in the warm-weather season. There were many instances in which Soviet authorities encouraged such speculation, probably in an effort to calm the continuing fears of friends and relatives. To many, it made sense that the missing men were still being held somewhere in the great mines along or above the Arctic Circle. Where else could they be? Word traveled slowly to these remote, ice-bound outposts. News of the amnesty could take a year or more to penetrate.

The possibility that the men might be in the far north was hardly cause for encouragement. Disasters in such desolate places might never be discovered by the outside world. One Polish lieutenant who returned from the far north reported that 1,650 deportees and 110 Soviet guards had frozen to death in a train in February 1941. The incident had been related to him by the head of the NKVD in Ukhta, who said snow had blocked a convoy on the Kotlas–Vorkuta line. Many passengers had left on foot only to collapse and die in deep snow a short distance from the train. It was rumored that entire camps in the far north had perished in snowstorms.

To the Poles, Kolyma seemed the most likely of all the godforsaken outposts where the missing men might be. Anders and those around him had established that about ten thousand Poles had been sent there in 1940. En route, these men had been taken by train to Vladivostok, then 1,500 miles north by steamer across the Sea of Okhotsk to Magadan. From Magadan some were sent to work in the lead mines of the Chukotski Peninsula, across the Bering Strait from Alaska. Others were taken inland to camps in the gold fields along the Kolyma River and its tributaries. Temperatures at Kolyma could plunge to 90 degrees below zero. In the gulag archipelago, the word "Kolyma" had become synonymous with death. Once sent there, even the guards rarely left. They knew too much. Kolyma's gold mines were chiefly responsible for tripling Soviet gold production between 1930 and 1937. A cruel system of slave labor and terrible suffering made these gains possible. Often an inmate who was ill or fainted was accused of sabotage and shot on the spot. Less than a quarter of the prisoners survived more than one winter. In principle, prisoners were excused from work when the temperature dropped below minus 51 degrees centigrade, but the rule was not always applied. Few of the men had shoes, so they wrapped their feet in rags from rubbish heaps. They worked in twelve-hour shifts, but those unable to do their work were usually forced to stay for the second shift.

Eventually, in the summer of 1942, 171 Poles, none of whom could shed any light on the whereabouts of the missing men from Kozelsk, Starobelsk, and Ostashkov, returned from Kolyma. They arrived in August as the last of the Polish army was leaving the Soviet Union. They had departed Kolyma on July 8, 1942, almost a year after the signing of the agreement of July 30, 1941. Nearly all these men had lost fingers and toes due to frostbite. Their bodies were covered with symptoms of scurvy. One of these men described a particular camp at Magadan. He said it was populated

> exclusively by cripples without hands and feet. All were crippled by frostbite in the mines. Even these were not fed for nothing, but had to sew sacks and make baskets. Even those who had lost both hands had to work, pushing large timber blocks with their feet. Others who had no feet worked at chopping wood. The most extraordinary sight was when these cripples made their way in fives to the *bania* (primitive Turkish bath).

Anders later wrote that the system was designed for "ruthless and intentional extermination of human beings." Conditions at camps in or near Kotlas, Vorkuta, Murmansk, Arkhangelsk, and many places in the north were about the same. When news of the amnesty reached some of these camps, no doubt it was ignored. Despite Magnitogorsk prison's location near the Trans-Siberian Rail Road, prisoners there did not hear about the amnesty until 1943.

By the summer of 1942, the Poles' hopes for the missing men were reduced to straws. Any chance that they would return from Kolyma, or places like it in the far north, were remote. If they did return, they would come back as human skeletons, hardly fit to lead the army's return to the homeland.

Since his return from the POW camp in Germany, Staszek Czarnek had been working in an institute in Kraków that made a typhus vaccine for the Wehrmacht. Each day he spent a few hours in a laboratory feeding his blood to lice. Arriving for work, he was given a strip of material to which several tiny cages containing lice had been attached. He then attached the strip around his thigh, opened the cages, and permitted the lice to feed. The job sounded awful, but Staszek was happy to get it. It paid well and took only a few hours a day, which gave him more time for the two great passions in his life: Krysia and the underground.

At twenty, Krysia was two years younger than Staszek. She was the sister of one his high school classmates. She was a tall brunette and a talented pianist. Once she finished her studies, she planned a career in music. Krysia and Staszek were both quiet, reserved even to the point of shyness. Their affection for each other was a secret, unknown to friends or family.

Staszek loved to sleep late and was difficult to wake in the mornings. In the spring of 1942, Janina Czarnek was astounded to see that her son had begun rising promptly every morning at six and soon after that hurrying away from the apartment. She assumed that he was off on some impossible-to-discuss mission for the underground. Later she would learn that Staszek's early-morning departures were part of his courtship of Krysia: He was rushing to her house and then walking her to work.

No one in the family asked about Staszek's role in the underground. Such questions were forbidden by the underground as a matter of self-protection.

Staszek spent his last night at home on June 24, 1942. It was the Night of St. John, a holiday celebrated as the first day of summer in Poland. That evening the Gestapo arrested hundreds of young people suspected of underground activity all over Kraków. The Czarnek family was asleep when Gestapo agents kicked in the front door of their apartment around midnight. Staszek, sleeping soundly as always, never heard the crash. He was awakened by a flashlight shining in his eyes and several Gestapo men standing beside his bed. He was given time to change from his pajamas to street clothes while the intruders searched the apartment. Within minutes they were leading Staszek away.

Magda told me that on his way out the door, he paused for a moment. "Here, Mama," he said. "Give this to Krysia." He was holding out his watch. Janina knew Krysia and her family well, but it was her first inkling of the romance.

A few days later, Staszek managed to send word to his mother that he had been subjected to "a light interrogation" and that he "was not forced to reveal anything." One of his first letters began with a line Magda would never forget: "Thus, I am in the famous Auschwitz." He went on to ask his mother to forgive him for the pain his arrest had caused her. Cards and letters from Staszek arrived intermittently over the next two and a half years from a succession of concentration and forced-labor camps.

The frightening sight of his departure in the hands of the Gestapo was the last that his mother and three sisters would have of him.

Corpses of Polish officers exhumed by Germans in Katyń Forest in 1943 await forensic examination.

Standard Bolshevik execution technique—shot at the base of the skull.

Stalin receives names of "missing" Polish officers from Generals Anders (left) and Sikorski, with Molotov looking on.

Among the murdered officers: Magda Czarnek's father, Zbigniew, a physician; Ewa Hoffman Jędruch's father, Maks, a Lwów attorney; and Maria Pawulska Rasiej's father, Stanislaw, a captain in the regular army.

Warsaw monument to Polish deportees.

Former U.S. Ambassador to Poland Arthur Bliss Lane (center) with Stanisław
Mikołajczyk and Paul Zaleski after their dramatic escape from Poland.

Right, Magda Czarnek, in
her mother's arms, and other
family members in 1929.
Below left, her mother, Janina
Czaplińska Czarnek, after
marriage to Zbigniew in 1914;
below right, at First Communion, age 8.

Left, Magda Czarnek with her father at the Grunwald Monument, Kraków, 1939. *Above,* on bike as a wartime courier.

Panoramic view of Lwów before the war.

Maksymilian Hoffman (standing, second from right) with fellow officers in the Austrian army in 1917.

Above, document certifying Zofia Hoffman as one of Poland's first female attorneys; *right,* Maks and Zofia in Lwów shortly before World War II.

Zofia Hoffman commanding Women's Auxiliary in Iraq after leaving the USSR.

Ewa Hoffman Jędruch and her husband, Jacek Jędruch, shortly before his death in 1995.

Maria Pawulska with her
family about 1937.

Above left, Maria Pawulska in Lusaka, the midpoint of her long journey, in 1945;
above right, Maria's husband, Kazik, who became an RAF pilot after surviving a
Russian forced labor camp.

CHAPTER 15

Exodus

<<<<<<<<<<<

News of the amnesty spread quickly on the steppes among the *svobod-naya sslylka*, or Poles living in so-called free exile. Soon after the August 12 decree, word came to Semipalatinsk, the gateway to Siberian Asia, that a spokesman for the new Polish embassy and the government in London would be coming to explain the surprising mandate. These tidings radiated far out onto the steppes and when the envoy, a Mr. Heitzman, arrived from Moscow on about October 1, 1941, a huge crowd was waiting to greet him.

The meeting took place in the open, on one of the city's mostly unpaved streets, with people pressed tightly together, each one straining anxiously to hear Heitzman's every word. At the edge of the crowd stood a young woman of nineteen wearing a sheepskin coat, a Kirghiz fur hat, and *botinki*, or knee-length boots made of pressed wool. She marveled at the envoy's attire, wondering if anyone had ever worn a camel-hair coat and a tailored suit on the steppes before. She felt drab, unattractive in comparison, but these were fleeting thoughts of the moment.

I first heard of Zofia Łaszewski described as "an exceptionally attractive woman," and when I met her in May 1990 I found the description in no way exaggerated. A childhood acquaintance of hers, Iwo Pogonowski, Magda Czarnek's husband, introduced us and after several talks by phone, we agreed to meet in Washington. "I'll be wearing a bright red suit," she told me as we made these arrangements.

Even though Iwo had prepared me, I was still surprised by her youthful good looks, her air of unstudied refinement. After the war, she had gone to medical school at the University of Aberdeen in Scotland, graduating in 1950. The next year, she and her husband moved to New York, where she specialized in rehabilitative medicine at New York University Hospital. Later she developed a private practice in Manhattan. More recently, she had practiced at the Veterans Administration Hospital in Greenville, Rhode Island.

185

Zofia Łaszewski's family background exemplified some of the complexity of Polish ethnography. Like that of Zofia Hoffman, her family on both sides—the Kinels and Schneiders—were polonized Germans. Despite his German ancestry, her grandfather became a Pole by choice and fought in the uprising against the czar in 1863. After its brutal suppression, he and thousands of other young revolutionaries had been sent to Siberia in chains. He served his sentence, but was forbidden to return to czarist Poland. He settled instead in Polish Galicia, a part of the Hapsburg Empire. There he raised Zygmunt, Zofia's father, as a Galician Pole and sent him to the University of Lwów. Zygmunt had opposed Piłsudski's coup in 1926 and his promising career as a regular-army officer was cut short as a result. Later he became a senior administrator in the Ministry of Post Office and Communication in Warsaw. One of Zygmunt's brothers was an administrative-law judge and another brother was a commander in the Polish navy. Many families of Germanic origin like Zofia's had found Polish culture appealing, were gradually absorbed, and eventually became an important part of the nation's social fabric.

On Sunday, November 26, 1939, Zofia and her mother came home from church to find five Soviet soldiers ransacking their house in Lwów. Her father had already been arrested and taken away. Zofia saw him for the last time in prison. Soon after that he was deported to the Soviet Union, where he disappeared and was never heard from again. She, her mother, and her brother were deported to Kazakhstan in the big sweep of April 13, 1940.

Seeing her in her elegant red suit, it was difficult to imagine Zofia, half a century earlier, standing in sheepskins at the edge of the crowd in Semipalatinsk.

"Up to then we had only heard fragments of news about the war breaking out," she told me. "There was such elation about this envoy coming to see us. Despite our imprisonment, there was a tremendous belief that we were going to get out of Russia eventually. We all had a deep inner feeling about it, like extrasensory perception—something in our subconscious minds. Maybe it was because we had survived all these hardships. As irrational as it seems, we had this overwhelming faith that we would make it. I think it has a lot to do with the historical background of the Polish nation. We believed in the unbelievable through our Romantic poets."

She said Heitzman's visit was "like Hollywood coming to the steppes. He was handsome—probably in his early forties—and he looked like he [had] just stepped out of Bergdorf Goodman. For building up the spirits of depressed people, you can't imagine what his visit meant to us. People were so excited that we almost smothered him. Everyone had questions because the Soviet newspapers only told what was allowed. From him we heard the truth, how things really were."

Heitzman explained the amnesty certificates and the legal rights of the deportees. He said the embassy planned a census of all the deported Poles and planned to set up a delegate system to channel support to Polish citizens. Zofia said his report that a Polish army would be formed in the Soviet Union was greeted with great enthusiasm. When a delegate office was established in Semipalatinsk about three months later, Zofia was hired, with food as her only compensation, to work there as a clerk preparing the new identity documents required by the amnesty. She later joined the Polish army and went south to Yangiyul in Uzbekistan.

"We thought our problems would soon be solved after Heitzman came," Zofia said. "But they were far from over. Many who were sure they would get out, of course, never made it."

News of the amnesty was slower reaching more remote Kokpekty, where the Pawulskis were living in a space three yards square in the house of a Russian family. The news came by word of mouth after the first snowfalls had begun to cover the steppes. The idea that the Poles were now being freed sent Mrs. Pawulska's hopes soaring. She felt that any day she might be seeing her husband, Stanisław. She heard that the new Polish army was gathering near Buzuluk and would soon move south. Since she was the wife of a military man, it would be wise, she felt, to move as close to the army as possible. Immediately she began inquiring about the documents needed to leave. At the same time, she began writing letters to the Polish embassy in Kuybyshev asking for any news they could give her about Stanisław. The replies were vague, irritating, and slow in coming. They prompted her to write back, demanding more specific information. Her relatives in Poland had heard nothing from Stanisław either. Their letters had offered one consolation: Certainly he would be far better off as a prisoner of war than in a forced-labor camp, where only a fortunate few survived. Then, with the German capture of Lwów, all correspondence with home stopped.

Nine months earlier, in late January 1941, Mrs. Pawulska had been overjoyed to come home from work one evening and find Maria and Tadeusz waiting for her. As has been related, Mrs. Pawulska was reunited with her children in January 1941 through the unexpected kindness of the Kalinin commissar. But the arrival of her children posed a serious problem for her. As the janitor at a school for orphans, she earned barely enough to provide for Jerzy and herself. Their clothes were tattered, her footwear hopeless. For months she had wrapped her worn-out shoes in layers of rags, but dampness still soaked through to her feet. Both were frostbitten and caused her much pain. Buying better shoes or clothes for herself or the children was impossible. It took more than she earned to keep starvation at bay. To get food, she had already bartered clothes, bedding, housewares, and many other items brought from Lwów. Even her wedding ring had been sold to the state jewelry trust. Only one or two items of value remained and these she intended to save for an emergency.

The harsh climate in Kokpekty often seemed unbearable. The small city was situated near the western slopes of the Altai, or Golden, Mountains, which separate the plains of western Siberia from the Gobi Desert. When Maria and Tadeusz arrived, snow was piled to the roofs of most of the houses. Even a simple task like drawing water from the well was dangerous. Accumulations of snow raised the mouth of the well several feet. Water spilt there often caused a permanent and treacherous sheet of ice. A long safety rope, anchored to a post near the front door, was used to keep those fetching water from slipping into the well. Only the foolhardy ventured out for water without belting themselves with this life-protecting line. It was also a homing device in the blinding *burany* when all sense of direction might vanish only steps away from the door. During the worst of the storms, snow often blocked the way out. To get water, ice was chipped from the door and melted on the stove.

At times, small cruelties were deeply painful. The children at the orphanage had been told that Mrs. Pawulska was Polish and, as such, an enemy of the people. They seemed to delight in complicating one back-breaking task she performed every few days. The school's earthen floors required frequent coating with a special solution of water, mud, manure, and straw. These applications, which were smeared on by hand, made the floors hard and kept dust under control. Often, while the solution dried, the children tore up small strips of paper and sprinkled them across the sticky surface. The blame fell on Mrs. Pawulska, whose supervisor threatened and publicly scolded her as a result.

Her financial difficulties forced Mrs. Pawulska to part with one of her prized possessions, a huge, finely embroidered linen tablecloth with matching napkins for twenty-four place settings. Its intricate pattern, designed by an artist, depicted clusters of bluish plums and other fruits. Embroidering the tablecloth had taken five years and Mrs.

Pawulska had formed a sentimental attachment to her imposing handi-work. But her determination to leave made her anxious to sell. She knew that a mammoth banquet linen had no practical value to the people who lived on the steppes. The Kazakhs, among others, ate sitting on the floor. But unusual objects sometimes attracted great curi-osity and could command exceptional prices. Cautiously she enter-tained the hope that her exotic tablecloth would pique stronger buyer interest.

"She was holding it for a rainy day," Maria told me. "It was kept in a small storage room because we had no place to put things—only enough room for our beds. When she made up her mind to sell it, she began rummaging around in the storage room but couldn't find it. She knew immediately that something was wrong—that someone had stolen it. I know she was very much crushed when she made that discovery."

The most likely suspect was her landlady's daughter. The young woman and her husband had moved out of the house only a few days earlier, in the spring of 1941. No one regretted their leaving. For months, the husband, a devout communist, had made fun of his mother-in-law and the Pawulskis whenever they prayed. More than once he had told them, "Your Bible is nothing but fairy tales." Maria said he spoke constantly of "a new way of life" under communism. "We were sure they had taken the tablecloth, but there was nothing we could say without taking the risk that we would lose our place in the house."

The stolen tablecloth forced Mrs. Pawulska to take a drastic step. She made up her mind to sell her last bit of gold: the bridgework in the back of her mouth. With great difficulty, she found a Russian dentist in Kokpekty who seemed competent enough to extract the denture. Maria told me that her mother "agonized over the decision but finally con-cluded that she had no other choice." When Mrs. Pawulska saw the dentist, he warned her that removing the bridge could cause serious problems later. Was it absolutely necessary that she take such a step? he had asked. Mrs. Pawulska explained that she needed the gold to buy food for her children and to make the trip south. Hearing this, the dentist reluctantly agreed to undertake the procedure.

Maria told me that her mother was careful to ask the dentist, "How much will it cost?" Maria said at this point the dentist responded gen-tly, "Madam, knowing your purpose, I could never look myself in the mirror again if I took one kopek for my services."

About this same time, Mrs. Pawulska received a reply, signed per-sonally by Ambassador Kot, to one of her letters to the embassy in Kuybyshev. The ambassador, a distant acquaintance of the Pawulskis, wrote back to express his regret that there was still no word on Stanisław's whereabouts. In his reply, Kot enclosed one thousand rubles and expressed the hope that the money would help Mrs. Pawulska get through her difficulties.

The dentist who removed Mrs. Pawulska's bridgework was not the only Russian who befriended her and her family. The summer after they arrived in Kokpekty, Maria and Tadeusz had gone house to house offering to take calves to pastures at the edge of town. Because of their experience in Kalinin, they persuaded several families to pay small amounts of money or food for this service. Looking for customers, they had knocked one day at the door of a new, modern-looking building in the outskirts of Kokpekty. A voice inside said, "Please come in. The door is open." These words carried the unmistakable inflection of a well-educated Russian. Cautiously pushing open the door, Maria and Tadeusz saw a man seated at a drafting board. He received them graciously, listened patiently to their offer, then explained that he had no calves to be grazed. Sensing their disappointment, he passed a bowl of candy to his guests. It was the first candy Maria and Tadeusz had tasted in many months. Then the man told them that there were other things they might do to help him. He was the chief engineer on a large railway project then being built through Kokpekty. His engineers congregated frequently at the small building where he worked. He would be glad, he said, to pay Maria and Tadeusz a small wage for preparing tea for these gatherings.

"I'm sure he understood our situation," Maria told me. "For some reason, he decided to take us under his wing. There was a sense of noblesse oblige about it. He gave us the feeling that he would do everything in his power to come to our aid."

Over the next few months, the chief engineer befriended the Pawulskis in many ways. More than once he brought bread and fish to where they were staying. Once he sent a subordinate to the post office to request packages of theirs from Poland that were being held arbitrarily. He succeeded in this and many other endeavors that helped the Pawulskis survive their final months in Kokpekty. But his last act of generosity was most important of all.

By the end of October, Mrs. Pawulska had what she hoped would be enough money to settle in Alma-Ata, Kazakhstan's capital, about 450 miles south in the center of a lush fruit-growing area. To get there, somehow she and her children would have to catch the train in Zhangiz-Tobe, where their journey by ox cart to Kalinin had begun eighteen months earlier. Zhangiz-Tobe was 125 miles from Kokpekty and, by this time of the year, impossible to reach on foot.

"If he [the engineer] had not agreed to help us, I doubt that we could have made it," Maria said. "There were very few trucks there [in Kokpekty] and he happened to have one of them. When he offered to have one of his men take us, my mother began packing immediately." The engineer arranged for the Pawulskis to be driven to the Zhangiz-Tobe train station on about November 1. He had helped them around a difficult obstacle. Thousands of other Poles far from train stations and barely alive at the end of forgotten ruts in the wilderness would not be so fortunate.

The train south did not come for three or four days. Even in wartime, with every car packed, the Soviet trains often ran at random. The Pawulskis slept on the platform of the squat, square station in the bone-chilling weather. There was nothing to do but wait—and yearn for the mild, near-Mediterranean climate of Alma-Ata. Finally a freight train stopped and the Pawulskis and a few Kazahks and Russians boarded. The stop-and-go journey south took two or three days.

They approached that city on a clear day, and from the train it seemed to Maria to sparkle in the sunlight. Alma-Ata's streets were wide and clean, and imparted a sense of order. An impressive number of cars were parked at the station. What the Pawulskis did not know was that Alma-Ata was used by Stalin as a showcase to impress foreign visitors. As the Pawulskis were leaving the train, they were stopped abruptly and asked to show their documents. The inquiring officer took one look at the Polish documents and sternly told the family that they could not stay in Alma-Ata.

"We were made to feel like riffraff," Maria said. "The officer told us that we could not even leave the station. Standing at the side of the track, we watched troop trains going to the front and others coming back with the wounded and soldiers going on leave. At first my mother had no idea what to do. We had only eighty-three rubles left. It wasn't much, but she went to the ticket window and asked how far it would take us. The ticket agent said, 'Dzhambul,' so she purchased tickets to go there."

Their new destination, about 250 miles to the southwest, was an unattractive city with a fascinating past. Dzhambul was once the midpoint on a long stretch of the Silk Road between Alma-Ata and Samarkand. Ancient caravans traveling between Europe and China had followed this route. So had fearsome hordes from Asia thundering west in search of new conquests. In the thirteenth century, the Mongols had destroyed Dzhambul. The city had been captured by the Russians in 1864 and had become an important center of phosphate production and sugar-beet processing.

Arriving at the Dzhambul train station, the Pawulskis were again stopped. This time they were told they could stay, but only if Mrs. Pawulska found work within a few days. Under the system, once work was found, a permit for residence could then be obtained. This document also served as the so-called "bread card," since it contained stamps that permitted the holder to purchase food. The Pawulskis' first few nights in Dzhambul were spent on the station platform with hundreds of other homeless Poles. They then occupied an abandoned *banya* in the garden of a Russian family. (The bath, long since fallen into disuse, had once thrown off an invigorating steam when water was poured over hot stone.) Mrs. Pawulska quickly found a job as a seamstress making quilts, which made it possible for the family to remain in the city. After a few weeks, however, distant relatives of their Russian landlord arrived and they were asked to give up the *banya*. Dzhambul's weather was much milder than that of Kokpekty, but finding shelter was still imperative. Instead of snow, the city's winter brought chilling rains that turned the streets into rivers of mud. There were few sidewalks or paved streets.

While looking for a new place to live, the Pawulskis once again were befriended by a complete stranger. Mrs. Pawulska was "completely dejected," according to Maria, when she met a tall Tartar woman who told her, "Come to me tomorrow for tea with your children. Maybe I can find something for you." The next day the woman sent the Pawulskis to a place where a small room was available. "When we got there," Maria told me, "we found that our rent had been paid for three months in advance." Such generosities, often extended with little or no explanation, were an admirable feature of Dzhambul's dominant Islamic culture.

Shortly after their arrival, Maria turned fifteen and was required to find work. Her first job was in a factory that produced pressed wool, a strong and durable fabric used widely in the Soviet Union. She worked twelve-hour days removing thorns, burrs, and other debris from the raw wool before it went to the steam room. The task was especially repugnant. The wool had a sickening smell and the prickly foreign matter often left Maria's hands badly nicked and bleeding. Even worse, the factory never, as promised, paid her. The job did enable her to keep her bread card and avoid being sent to a kolkhoz. By late spring she had been moved to a new job, gathering pebbles for use in road construction. She and other young people hauled small stones on stretchers from a streambed to a road-paving project. The pebbles were dumped along the road and mixed with adhesives to macadamize the surface.

Purely by happenstance, Maria achieved a degree of fame as a seer in her off-hours. In Kalinin and Kokpekty, she had watched endlessly how some Polish women used playing cards to tell fortunes. The superstitious Kazakhs were captivated by the exercise and gladly exchanged food or small gifts for the service. Gradually, Maria learned the simple system herself and began experimenting with it for fun. One evening a woman she had never met, the sister of the Pawulskis' landlady, asked Maria to tell her fortune.

After examining the cards, Maria told her, "You and another member of your family will soon be leaving the Soviet Union to visit a close relative." Several people who were watching laughed at the preposterous prediction. Ordinary people rarely, if ever, left the Soviet Union. Maria's bold divination was quickly forgotten. But two weeks later the woman came rushing back to tell Maria, "You told me the truth. I am getting papers to go to Iran."

Shortly after Maria's prediction, the Red Army had notified the woman that her husband, then with a small contingent of Soviet forces in Iran, had typhoid fever. Official permission had been granted to her to visit him for two weeks. This startling news became an overnight sensation, radiating Maria's name over a wide circle. The next day a steady stream of Kazakh women began coming to the Pawulskis' room, asking to have their fortunes told. Maria weakly disclaimed the reliability of her predictions, but the women were unconvinced. She acceded to their requests and shyly accepted their small gifts of food, much to the satisfaction of her family.

Early in 1942, many Poles hoping to join the army-in-exile began passing through Dzhambul on their way to Yangiyul, near Tashkent about 150 miles southwest. Many among this flood of deportees had stopped in Dzhambul, where a large coordinating center for the Polish relief effort, the *delegatura*, had been organized. By spring, the *delegatura* had received shipments of American food and secondhand clothing and was distributing these goods in Dzhambul. Maria herself received a sweater, socks, and a silk dress with a bright yellow floral design. Because no one else had feet so small, she also got a pair of saddle shoes, which had pleased her greatly. The garden behind the *delegatura* was packed with dozens of desperate Poles, among them people in the last stages of starvation. When free food was dispensed, many of the weakest could not stand in line. On several occasions Maria waited in the long queue on behalf of a one-legged man, who blessed her, saying, "God will repay you for your goodness." She also queued for a woman with a small child. The mother's stomach was already bloated and hair was growing on her face, sure signs that she could not live much longer. Sometimes the bread ran out before Maria reached the head of the line. The people she had been queuing for got nothing on these occasions. There were many complaints about the *delegatura*'s operations, even accusations that relief supplies were being sold on the black market. Some of the *delegatura* employees were arrested by the Soviets in the summer and charged with carrying on anti-Soviet activity. These actions were part of the general crackdown by the Soviets on the operations of the delegate system all over the Soviet Union.

About this time, Tadeusz left to join the Polish army as a *junak*, one of a group of young boys who would be prepared for cadet training. He was sent to Kermine, a camp near the headquarters of the army-in-exile in Yangiyul.

By midsummer, there was growing talk that the army would soon leave the Soviet Union. Such rumors set off a desperate clamor among civilians to get out at the same time. Information about who would go and under what circumstances was highly uncertain. Soviet decrees already barred the departure of Jews, Ukrainians, and Byelorussians. Gradually it became clear that only the families of those in the army were assured of leaving. Because her husband was missing, Mrs. Pawulska was unsure of her status and unsure how to get it clarified. Many military men who had been separated from their families were searching all along the train route south to find them. It was like looking for a needle in a haystack. Some of these men, giving up hope of finding their own families, were agreeing to list another family as dependents.

Mrs. Pawulska still believed that Stanisław might show up any day, but the fluid situation made her fearful that she and her family could be left behind. As the summer wore on, these same fears prompted Maria to begin searching the tracksides at the train station in Dzhambul, hoping to catch sight of her father among the hundreds of gaunt and haggard men who were on their way from northern Siberian labor camps to Tashkent and Yangiyul.

In early July, she noticed a cluster of officers near the passenger depot and heard one introduced as Captain Eugeniusz Kopeć, the officer in charge of civilian transports leaving with the army. She then heard the captain comment that his transport lists were almost full and would soon be closed. Alarmed by these words, Maria started to speak to the man but shyness suppressed the impulse. The captain's face, nevertheless, made a deep impression. He had light blond hair, eyebrows, and eyelashes—a look the Poles called pig-blond—and wore pince-nez.

On her way home, Maria felt ashamed at her failure to speak up and argued with herself about how to tell her mother that the transport lists were almost full. When she arrived, her mother quickly sensed her mood.

"I see you have bad news," said Mrs. Pawulska. Maria related what had happened at the train station. Her mother listened with apparent resignation until Maria mentioned the name "Captain Kopeć, Captain Eugeniusz Kopeć."

"Did he have light blond hair? . . ." Mrs. Pawulska continued with a perfect description of the man Maria had seen at the station. Then her voice rose in excitement: "Your father and Captain Kopeć are close friends!" The two men, she then explained, had been stationed together several years before the war. Immediately, Mrs. Pawulska wrote the first of several letters to Captain Kopeć asking him to help get her and her children on the transport list.

"One of these letters reached him only a few hours before the list for the last transport was closed," Maria told me. "He wrote back to say that he had put my mother down as his sister and that we should meet him in Lugovoy [seventy-odd miles east of Dzhambul], where it would be loaded." The captain's letter arrived in mid-August, only a few days before the transport departed. These transports ran west along the route of the old Silk Road. Once the train was loaded in Lugovoy, it would go to Dzhambul, Tashkent, and Samarkand. From Samarkand, it would head southwest along the base of the Alai Mountains. Several hundred miles from Samarkand it would cross the Amu Darya River, the Oxus of ancient times, which flowed 1,500 miles north to the Aral Sea. On the final leg, the transport would cross the Kara Kum, or "Black Desert," before reaching the port of Krasnovodsk on the Caspian Sea.

Even with the welcome news that their names were on the list, the Pawulskis faced one remaining hurdle: how to get from Dzhambul to Lugovoy, where those on the transport list were required by the Soviets to check in. Because of the problems at the *delegatura*, Poles in Dzhambul had recently been placed under "home arrest" and were forbidden to leave the city without a special permit. Obtaining such a document was almost impossible and train tickets to Lugovoy could not be purchased without it.

A Polish cobbler who lived across the street from the Pawulskis devised an ingenious solution to this problem. He and his family were also anxious to reach Lugovoy. With a bribe arranged through a Soviet accomplice, the man had managed to get both a truck and an NKVD uniform. The cobbler planned for his accomplice to pose as a member of the Soviet secret police, taking laborers to a kolkhoz to help with the harvest. If they stayed on back roads, it would appear that they were heading for the fields. Instead, he expected to take several Polish families to the transport in Lugovoy. Once there, his accomplice would return both the truck and the NKVD uniform.

When the cobbler knocked on her door and explained the scheme, Mrs. Pawulska agreed instantly that his idea was superb. She asked how much the trip would cost and was told five hundred rubles per person. Disappointed, she replied that she had only four hundred rubles in all.

"At that point the man told my mother, 'Don't worry, I have no use for the rubles anyway,'" Maria told me. "He said he wanted to help us because we had never looked down on his family. Although our families were not close, we played with his children and knew them fairly well. He ended up telling my mother, 'Madam, the truck is at your disposal,' and asking her if she knew other deserving families that should be taken along." The group left at night and picked up passengers on the way. It reached Lugovoy early the next morning without mishap.

When the Pawulskis arrived, a huge throng was already milling about the siding where the transport was being formed. People were scattered all along the track in a camplike atmosphere waiting for the transport's departure. Almost everyone had slept on the ground in the clear, comfortable late-summer air. Mrs. Pawulska found Captain Kopeć and thanked him profusely for listing her as his sister. He made sure that her family's papers were in order and told her that the train would leave, as scheduled, the next morning with about eight hundred people aboard.

Walking through the crowd, Mrs. Pawulska spied acquaintances from Lwów, a Jewish banker and his wife and daughter, a beautiful girl with long blond hair, slightly younger than Maria. After an exchange of pleasantries, the banker told Mrs. Pawulska that his family was not listed for departure on the transport. He said they had come to Lugovoy knowing that the Soviet decree denying amnesty to Jews made it illegal for Polish authorities to take them. He had hoped, nevertheless, that something could be done at the last minute to get them on board. The prospects were not encouraging. Apparently, he said, his family would not be permitted to leave. Words were not needed to explain their fate should that result occur. A deep sense of gloom settled over the conversation.

Mrs. Pawulska felt that surely some arrangement could be made to help the family and decided to discuss the matter with Captain Kopeć, who agreed that the family could board as stowaways. Their despair was transformed into elation with the delivery of this news. One practical question remained: how to evade document checks by the NKVD at important stations along the way. The only possibility was for the family to hide under the seats and luggage whenever the NKVD boarded. Maria would serve as lookout, sitting in the door of the vestibule at the end of the car. When the NKVD approached, her warning would be to say in a loud voice, "My mother has my papers."

The Jewish family left in elation, but the agony of the damned awaited many others as the train approached Dzhambul. Many on board had walked the entire seventy miles to Lugovoy. Heads of families listed on the transport were required to check in there personally, but because of the distance to Lugovoy, many who walked there left small children or elderly parents in Dzhambul. They planned to pick up their relatives when the train went through Dzhambul on its way west. Everything seemed normal approaching the city. It was a bright, sunny day and the train slowed as expected at the outskirts of the city. It came to a stop beside platform one, nearest the terminal building. Maria could see hundreds of people waiting behind the station's tall wrought-iron fence, no more than 150 feet away.

After the train stopped, the doors to the wagons remained closed. People assumed that there would be a momentary delay before debarking. Catching sight of their children or parents, many passengers leaned out the windows and began waving or clamoring for those beyond the fence. Then someone shouted, "The gates are blocked!" The gates had all been chained and soldiers stood guard at each. Then the outcry began. A chorus of demands came from all up and down the convoy.

"Let us off!" people screamed. "Open the doors!"

But nothing happened and no one seemed to know what was going on. The guards stood by impassively. The passengers could not get off the train and their relatives could not get on. While this impasse continued, the screaming back and forth from the train to the fence reached a higher pitch. For almost an hour the train sat at the platform engulfed in the din of parents and children screaming from both sides of the fence. It seemed like an eternity to Maria.

Then came the first lurch, as the train began to move. The angry shouts, long since modulated into a tone of beseeching, turned into anguished wails as the caravan slowly pulled away from the platform. Mothers leaned as far as they could from the windows, arms outstretched, as if somehow they could touch the hands of their children reaching through the fence. At this moment all knew: These frantic glimpses were the last they would ever see of each other.

"Jesus, Maria . . ." The prayers came last in a fever of agony that echoed over the expanding chasm, reverberating with the rhythm of the wheels as the train picked up speed. A mind-numbing madness convulsed the wagon where Maria was sitting. Slowly, a pall of gloom settled over the car, and the passengers rode for a long time in silence.

"I will never forget the horrible sight of the hands reaching through the fence," Maria told me.

Who had caused this moment of horror with its eternity of consequences? And why? No one on the train could answer these questions. It was possible, certainly, in the vast asylum that some called paradise, that no one knew. But this was not a mishap. The specter of hundreds of thousands of others—the quick and the dead—towered behind the few hundred screaming victims left at Dzhambul station. That specter, too, would fade in the distance as the last transport headed for the port at Krasnovodsk. Almost no one in the West knew; thus few could remember. For a world in flames, it was, at most, a fleeting image. A fraction of the estimated 1.2 million Poles taken to the Soviet Union was evacuated. Most of the others were, or soon would be, exterminated through forced labor, starvation, and neglect. These were colossal losses for a nation of thirty-six million. Hardly a Pole alive escaped losing family or friends in this debacle.

The steamer bearing the Pawulskis and others on the last transport left Krasnovodsk on August 26. Two days later it arrived at the Iranian port of Pahlevi (Bandar-e Anzalī), where, using small boats, passengers were unloaded by the Soviets and turned over at the beach to British authorities, who had set up refugee camps. When these last passengers stepped ashore, the number of Poles evacuated from the Soviet Union stood at 112,000. About thirty thousand soldiers and ten thousand civilians—a total of forty thousand—had left in late March and early April. About forty-two thousand soldiers and thirty thousand civilians—a total of seventy-two thousand—had left in August.

A few Poles would return to their homeland as soldiers in the Red Army in 1944; a few others would straggle back shortly after Stalin's death. Most who had been deported in the four big sweeps between February 8, 1940, and mid-June 1941 simply disappeared and were never heard from again.

*   *   *

In the fall of 1942, the Gestapo came calling once again at 82 Kazimierz Wielki Street in Kraków. One evening shortly after midnight, Janina and her daughters were awakened by the crashing sound of their front door being kicked in. Several men with skull-and-cross-bones emblems on their uniforms were already ransacking the apartment by the time Janina arrived in the living room. "Where are they?" shouted the officer in charge. "Where are those you are sheltering?"

Janina shrugged, then responded in German, "I have no idea who you are looking for."

"Then you, Mrs. Czarnek, will have the bad luck to come along with us." Only because she had spoken in flawless German had the officer addressed her as "Mrs. Czarnek." His voice nevertheless was abusive and threatening.

Standing in the hallway, Magda, Jaga, and Maria watched in horror as the Gestapo rushed their mother, still wearing her bathrobe, out the front door. As they left, the officer in charge turned to her daughters and said, "We don't need her. We need the people that you are sheltering here. Find them for us and we will release your mother." Moments later Janina and the Gestapo roared away in the car parked at the sidewalk.

By sheer luck the Gestapo had found no illegal residents. But for more than two years the Czarnek apartment had served as a safe house for the underground. The family continued to survive mainly by reselling food bought from Jaga at Mienl. Dr. Czarnek's disappearance, the brutal murder of his brother Witold, Staszek's treatment as a prisoner of war and his recent arrest, and finally the daily hardship of life under the German General Government made resistance seem their only recourse. Since early in the war, Janina had been involved in one of the underground's most dangerous day-to-day activities: distribution of its newspapers. Almost daily she would visit St. Mary's, the ancient Gothic church on Kraków's main square. She knelt there in the same pew beside a woman whose name she never knew and received a hundred or so illegal newspapers. With the bundle under her coat, she would deliver about twenty papers each to five carriers who were responsible for direct distribution. She always saved one for her family. Had she been caught, a brutal interrogation and a concentration-camp sentence would almost certainly have awaited her.

Harboring the underground was equally risky. But it represented a natural, even inconspicuous, extension of the Czarnek household's development early in the war. Because she was warm and open, visitors were always welcome in Janina's home. The German attack in September 1939 left many Poles homeless. Among them were a few friends and distant relatives who showed up on Janina's doorstep almost immediately. The strangers sent by the underground who soon followed added little to the usual commotion of the Czarnek household. In the unwritten code of the underground, Janina did not ask for information about these guests and received none. Occupation authorities required that such guests sign a registry. Janina maintained one, but she was well aware that many of the names in it were fictitious.

The day after Janina's arrest, Maria, her oldest daughter, returned from Lwów, where she was attending medical classes. Maria knew that unless quick action was taken, her mother would be sent to a concentration camp. After she heard the details, a daring idea occurred to her. She had recently learned that a high-ranking Gestapo officer had given up his quarters in a neighbor's home after being transferred away from Kraków. Maria had never seen the man in her life, but she decided to go immediately to Pomorska, Kraków's much-dreaded Gestapo headquarters, and ask for him.

Arriving there, she addressed her request to the guard using fluent German. Her brazen manner seemed to startle the man and make him wonder if perhaps she did know the high-ranking officer. Maria's appearance made her request more convincing. With her dark, flashing eyes and long, coal-black hair, she was luminously beautiful. The thought may well have occurred to the guard that she could be an important Gestapo contact or the officer's girlfriend. In any event, he asked if he could help her. She explained her mother's arrest, then said the Gestapo had also confiscated the family's food stamps, which meant they would have nothing to eat. Her contact would be willing to help her, she added. Her story sounded convincing enough to the dispatcher, so he passed Maria on to the officer in charge of the raid the previous evening, a man named Christiansen.

Despite his rough behavior the previous evening, Christiansen seemed almost cordial. He, too, seemed startled that Maria had managed to get inside Pomorska. It was not difficult at all, Maria coyly replied. When she told him about the food stamps, he agreed to give them back. "What I really want is my mother, not the cards," Maria blurted. Christiansen parried with more casual banter: How had Maria managed to get inside Pomorska? Finally, he came to the point: "We will hold your mother until you take us to the people you are sheltering." Maria knew Christiansen held the power of life and death over her mother. Yet she knew she could not betray those who had hidden in her home. A few days later she bumped into a man who had been the Czarneks' illegal guests and warned him about the Gestapo threat.

Meanwhile, Janina spent six weeks in prison in her bathrobe. Finally the Gestapo permitted her to receive a package of street clothes. That small concession suggested to Maria that Christiansen might relent, and she made another trip to Pomorska. Just prior to that visit, her mother was listed for transport to Auschwitz. When Maria saw Christiansen, she told him, "You must let Mama go or else she will be sent to Auschwitz." He stared back at Maria, a hint of bemusement on his face, then responded: "All right. Tomorrow at noon be out front and wait for me. I will bring you your mother." The next day shortly before noon he went to the cell where Janina was being held with thirty or more other women and called her name. "Take your things and come with me. Your little one is waiting for you." The officer then handed Janina her identification card, which Poles were required to carry.

Outside, Maria was waiting. After greeting her daughter Janina told the officer: "It's fine that you are releasing me, but my son in Auschwitz is who we really want." Wearily, with perhaps a hint of sadness, the Gestapo man shrugged and said, "That is outside of my authority."

After the war the Czarneks learned that the Gestapo officer was one of the most brutal assigned to Kraków in the entire war. Why had he agreed to Janina's release? Had Maria's courage and charm made him relent? The Czarneks were completely perplexed by these questions. But thousands of other young Poles who beseeched the Gestapo for the release of a mother or father were not nearly so fortunate.

CHAPTER 16

Wolf's Find

<<<<<<<<<<

The Katyń Forest massacre was discovered by chance at a timely moment for Germany. The revelation came quick on the heels of the Wehrmacht's greatest defeat of the war so far: Stalingrad. The battle had begun to turn in mid-October 1942. By then there was no chance that Germany's plan to split the Soviet Union along the mighty Volga River artery could succeed. With their advance stalled, the Germans were hit with a massive counterattack on November 19. Four days later, a German army group of 330,000 men under Field Marshal Friedrich von Paulus was surrounded. On February 2, 1943, after two months of desperate effort to save the encircled force, Von Paulus and ninety thousand men were taken prisoner by the Red Army.

The defeat was a disaster for Germany. The Wehrmacht's aura of invincibility was shattered. Allies began to waver, resistance stiffened in occupied Europe, and neutral states felt less threatened. The Red Army quickly followed its victory at Stalingrad with a general offensive along the entire front running from Leningrad to the Caucasus. These were indeed gloomy developments for the Reich, and the discoveries in Katyń Forest provided a welcome opportunity to rivet world attention on a sordid crime in the Allied camp. It was an opportunity that Nazi propaganda minister Joseph Goebbels vowed to exploit in "a grand style."

When the Germans occupied Katyń Forest in late summer 1941, the dacha in the former NKVD compound became the headquarters of the 537th Signal Regiment under Lieutenant Colonel Friedrich Ahrens. For the next eighteen months, Ahrens and his men went about their daily routine with no idea that the area around them was pockmarked with graves. They did sense an air of mystery about the place. From the local villagers they heard that for many years the forest was used by the Bolsheviks as an execution ground for political prisoners. Ahrens himself had one day noticed a birch cross not far from the dacha, but thought little of it since there had been heavy fighting in the vicinity.

203

After the war, at U.S. congressional hearings on the massacre, Ahrens testified that attention was first drawn to the graves by a wolf that dug bones from one of the pits. Ahrens said traces of the wolf were found in late January or early February 1943 by four Hiwis, Russian prisoners of war who worked for the Germans. He said the Hiwis saw no evidence of mass graves at the time, since snow and ice blanketed most of the area. In fact, the Hiwis did not tell Ahrens about their discovery until four weeks later, when the snow had melted, exposing the south slope of one of the mass graves. Ahrens testified that when he examined the area, "one could see that they were graves and that the wolf had been digging for bones."

Records of the German field police indicate that rumors of the wolf's discovery were circulating in February in Gniezdovo, a village at the edge of Katyń Forest. No doubt they fueled continuing rumors about Polish graves in the forest. The villagers had seen the Soviets unload hundreds of Polish officers from early April to mid-May 1940 at the Gniezdovo railway siding. The men had then been driven in special black vans into the forest, where the villagers assumed they were executed. An unusual coincidence occurred two years later when, in the spring of 1942, Polish workers in a German forced-labor battalion passed through the village, collecting scrap metal. Some of these workers spoke Russian and were told by the villagers about the unusual transports of Polish officers arriving in Gniezdovo two years earlier. A peasant named Ivan Kisselev later told the field police that he agreed to take ten of the Poles into the forest and show them where he thought their countrymen were buried. Kisselev said the Poles later told him that they found the bodies of Polish officers and marked the site with a birch cross. What the Poles had potentially discovered became clearer in January of 1943, when a Russian-language newspaper published by the Germans in Smolensk printed an article mentioning that several thousand Polish officers captured by the Soviets in 1939 were still missing. Someone in the village (police records did not make clear who) brought these matters to the attention of the German authorities near the end of February. At that time Kisselev again led a search party into the woods. The birch cross, apparently left by the Polish workers the previous year, was discovered and a test dig was made in that spot. The body of a Polish officer was found almost immediately. The field police then ordered the grave re-covered, postponing further excavation until a full report could be sent to the headquarters of the Central Army Group.

That report was made on March 1, and for the next six weeks, until mid-April 1943, the discovery was a tightly guarded secret. For most of March, the ground was too frozen to begin large-scale excavations. The Germans used this time to prepare for a comprehensive investigation and a massive propaganda blitz. Early in March, the OKW put Dr. Gerhard Buhtz, a professor of forensic medicine and criminology at Breslau (now Wrocław) University, in charge of preparations for exhumations. A large wooden house was brought to the site for post-mortem work and a field laboratory for forensic medicine in Smolensk was expanded to accommodate the large volume of forthcoming work. Detailed procedures were also developed for identifying and marking the bodies, as well as for preserving the articles found on them. At the same time preparations were made, under the direction of Lieutenant Ludwig Voss, head of the local field police, to comb the entire forest for more graves. Voss organized a labor gang of thirty-five local villagers to take care of the digging and recruited seven Russian civil guards as night watchmen to protect the bodies from looters.

By March 29 the ground had thawed sufficiently for digging to begin. By April 10 exploratory excavations had been made throughout the wooded area between the main road and the NKVD dacha that sat overlooking the Dnieper River marsh. The initial test digs yielded eleven mass graves, seven of which contained the bodies of Polish officers. These graves were all located in a clearing to the west side of the road leading into the dacha about three quarters of a mile from the Smolensk–Vitebsk main highway. All four graves on the east side contained the bodies of Russians who had been executed and buried there at least ten years earlier. Initially, most of the Polish graves were simply identified and marked off. The largest, grave number one, had been dug in an L shape, thirty-one yards long and eighteen yards wide on the "arm." In the center it was about eleven feet deep. It was excavated completely on one end and found to contain twelve layers of neatly stacked bodies. Since about 250 bodies were counted in the top row, the field police estimated that the largest of the graves held as many as three thousand bodies.

As the graves were excavated, the Germans found unexpected evidence of potentially acute embarrassment. The empty cartridge casings in and near the graves were German made. On the bottom of each shell, its trademark and caliber was clearly visible: Geco 7.65. The ammunition was produced by a Gustav Genschow factory in Durlach, Germany. The Wehrmacht immediately investigated Genschow records and found that prior to the war the firm exported 7.65-millimeter ammunition to a number of countries where it could have come into

NKVD possession. Estonia, Latvia, and Lithuania had purchased fifty thousand rounds each just before the war and their occupation by the Soviets. The Soviets themselves had made substantial purchases prior to 1928, but bought only two thousand to three thousand rounds subsequently. Sales had even been made to Poland, but were stopped several years before the war. Properly stored, such ammunition could be used for up to twenty years. The caliber, Geco 7.65 millimeter, did not fit the Tokarev or Nagan pistols generally carried by the NKVD. It did fit the Walther, a fine police pistol that had been exported to the Baltic states before the war. It is quite likely that the victims were shot with confiscated Walthers.

Documents on the first hundred bodies taken from this grave verified that all the men were officers. In this initial group were two generals, two colonels, and a number of other high-ranking Polish officers. Because these bodies had been stacked in an orderly fashion, those on top were removed without great difficulty. In other graves, however, most of the bodies had been thrown in at random. Limbs of corpses were often pinned beneath other bodies. Great care had to be exercised in order to remove such bodies intact. Exhumations were also complicated by water that had flooded some of the graves. Many of the bodies in the small graves were badly decomposed, but the bodies in the largest grave were preserved remarkably well. There was a logical explanation for this phenomenon. Most of the big grave had been dug in light sandy soil and on higher ground than the other graves. Tons of sand had been dumped on top of its neatly stacked bodies, pressing them even closer together. Because they were more exposed to bacteria, the bodies on top and at the outer edges leaked fluids first and, in effect, formed an airtight seal around the bodies in the core of the mass.

Once a body had been separated from the mass, it was taken on a stretcher and laid in the clearing. There it was given an identification number and an inspection was conducted to retrieve documents and personal objects. Each victim's pockets were slit open and searched. Because many victims had hidden objects in their knee-length cavalry boots, these too were slit open and searched. Any rings, medals, military identification cards, złoty, newspaper clippings, diaries, religious emblems, or other personal items were then placed in bags with markings that matched the victim's body-identification number. At this point many of the bodies were subjected to a detailed medical examination before being transferred to fresh communal graves for reburial. Because of the large number of bodies involved, postmortems were conducted only on special cases: bodies exhibiting multiple bullet or bayonet wounds, those that appeared to have sustained heavy blows from rifle butts, and those that had been tied up and gagged.

The personal possessions of the victims were then transferred to a laboratory in Smolensk for more detailed examination and treatment. Many of the printed documents had been soaked in cadaveric fluid and were thus illegible. To read such documents, they were often washed in xylol (xylene) or chloroform and, in some cases, treated with infrared rays. These detailed procedures were all developed with meticulous care before any public announcements and before the opening of the forest itself to visitors.

While the exploratory digging was under way and exhumation procedures were put in place, the field police interrogated villagers to determine what they knew about the NKVD compound and about the transports of Polish officers who had arrived in Gniezdovo in the spring of 1940. These interrogations had yielded a great deal of detail by mid-April, but the Central Army Group Command decided that the material lacked legal validity. Consequently, the same witnesses were summoned before a military court and examined again under oath.

The medical and criminal investigations set the stage for a massive propaganda program carried out in the forest itself under the direction of Lieutenant Gregor Sloventzik, a reserve officer from Vienna who had worked as a journalist before the war. Sloventzik's colleagues described him as a gregarious man, an exceptional speaker who was well connected with higher authorities. It was his job to guide numerous special foreign delegations through the site, explaining pertinent details of the grisly executions. He also coordinated procedures under which tens of thousands of visitors came to the forest between mid-April and June 1943. During this period, the site was visited by a constant stream of foreign delegations, including medical experts, journalists, authors, and even artists. Thousands of German soldiers and local citizens also came as gawkers.

The Germans recognized from the outset that their discovery presented a golden opportunity to split the Western Allies. They were keenly aware of the serious rift between the Soviets and the Polish government-in-exile over disputed territory in the western Ukraine and western Byelorussia. The Germans knew also that more than ten thousand Polish officers captured by the Soviets in 1939 were still missing when General Anders and his army-in-exile left the U.S.S.R. in 1942. In their determination to capitalize on these frictions, the Germans made one serious blunder: They assumed that the bodies of all the

missing Polish officers would be found in Katyń Forest. At first Voss
and Sloventzik seemed only vaguely aware that most of the Polish
officers had been kept in two camps, Kozelsk and Starobelsk. By mid-
April the exhumations had yet to yield the body of a single man from
Starobelsk, yet the Germans persisted in believing that, in time, all
the bodies would be found. This erroneous assumption would cause
the Germans a good bit of embarrassment later.

Once they had established their own procedures for handling the
exhumations, the Germans believed the findings would have more
credibility if the Poles took over much of the actual work at the site.
On April 10, 1943, a delegation of prominent Poles from Warsaw,
Kraków, and Lublin was flown to Smolensk and received with exaggerated courtesy as "representatives of the Polish people," according to
members of the group. Although the Polish Red Cross was invited,
its executive committee regarded the trip as a German propaganda-
trick and refused to be represented. The group was driven to Katyń
and examined two open pits from which about 250 corpses had
already been withdrawn. Among them were the bodies of General
M. Smorawiński and General Bronisław Bohatyrewicz, both in full uniform with their insignia intact. The delegation was then permitted to
examine documents taken from the bodies. Most members of the delegation carefully refrained from making any statements that could be
exploited by German propaganda. While their visit preceded the public
announcement of the mass graves, the Polish underground knew about
it and on April 13 sent a wireless report to the London government-
in-exile confirming that the bodies of Polish officers had, in fact, been
found. The underground also relayed the delegation's assessment that
the graves probably contained four thousand bodies, not twelve thousand as the Germans had estimated.

The report of this delegation convinced the Polish Red Cross that it
should cooperate with the investigation and on April 15, its representative, Kazimierz Skarzyński, arrived in Smolensk. He immediately informed Sloventzik that a Polish Red Cross technical commission would
assist at the scene, but that its role must be confined to identification
and reburial of bodies, and the return of the victims' possessions to
their families. Sloventzik told him that "German military authorities
will give the Red Cross every assistance." From late April to early
June, the technical commission of the Polish Red Cross had between
nine and ten representatives working at Katyń, including a forensic
specialist from the Jagiellonian University in Kraków and three laboratory assistants. The Germans never discovered that the group included

representatives of the Polish underground. One member of the commission later stated that "in the normal course of work done by us the Germans were in general not obstructive, leaving considerable freedom to the Technical [commission] and limiting themselves to the supervision of our heavy and extremely unpleasant work."

Members of the commission did have their differences with the Germans. On one occasion, Sloventzik told commission representatives that German authorities understood that some of the Polish officers were *Volksdeutsche*, or of German origin. He demanded that these victims be buried separately. He was told that it was impossible to ascertain the ethnic origins of the victims. A sharp clash came in the last week of May, when the war front began moving back toward Katyń Forest. During a night raid, Soviet planes had just destroyed a German supply dump between the forest and Gniezdovo. Fearing that they might fall into Soviet hands, members of the commission emphasized to Sloventzik that their work was nearing completion and they would soon be ready to return to Poland. Sloventzik bluntly pointed out that the number of exhumed bodies was far too small and told the commission that its report should list twelve thousand as the likely final total of bodies. One of the Polish doctors later reported that a strong disagreement ensued:

> When resisting this suggestion, I asked on what basis I could give such an untruthful figure[.] Lt. Sloventzik stressed that if the German authorities gave such a figure no one must be allowed to question it, as if they did, he might have to pay with his head. At that the conversation was interrupted but I personally realized what a dangerous situation I and the whole Technical Commission was [*sic*] in.

An unexpected development suddenly diverted attention from this controversy. Between 10 and 11 A.M. on June 1, members of the commission were completing work on grave five when word swept the compound that a new grave containing Polish officers had just been discovered. It was quite a distance from all the other graves—more than a hundred yards to the southwest and closer to the river. None of the ten bodies taken out immediately wore overcoats, long underwear, sweaters, or scarves. Their pockets contained newspaper clippings from early May, later than those on the other bodies. The grave's location far from the others initially convinced the Germans that the men from Starobelsk had finally been found. Sloventzik told members of the commission that Katyń Forest was one big cemetery. These theories, however, were quickly shattered by the discovery of identification cards and other personal records showing that the ten victims removed were all from Kozelsk.

Their disappointment about grave eight was apparently a decisive factor in the Germans' decision in early June to suspend the exhumations. New graves were not being found. The Soviet offensive was creeping closer. With warmer weather, swarms of flies had descended on the grounds, raising health risks considerably. Just over four thousand bodies had been exhumed when Sloventzik announced that the excavation of newly discovered grave eight and all remaining work at the site would be postponed until autumn. All members of the Polish Red Cross technical commission were on their way back to Poland by June 7.

The Germans withheld all public announcement of their discovery until the Wehrmacht's investigation under Dr. Buhtz was complete and until detailed procedures for handling the exhumations were in place. They also waited until the Poles themselves could be officially involved on the scene. Their propaganda offensive did not begin until these preparations were complete. Just prior to their announcement of the discovery, journalists from Sweden, Switzerland, Spain, Norway, Holland, Belgium, Hungary, and Serbia were taken on a tour of Katyń Forest by representatives of the Reich Chancellery press department and a senior official of the Foreign Office. Their reports apparently were filed just as the Germans made their official announcement.

Radio Berlin broke the sensational story at 9:15 A.M. New York time on April 13, 1943. German-controlled radio stations throughout Europe followed almost immediately with similar reports. The carefully orchestrated campaign identified the dead as "thousands of officers of the former Polish army, interned in the U.S.S.R. in 1939 and bestially murdered by the Bolsheviks." The German reports were generally accurate, but enough clumsy mistakes were made to cause much skepticism, especially in light of known Nazi atrocities. The first question everywhere was "Why now?" The Germans had captured Katyń Forest in the late summer of 1941. Why had they waited twenty months to announce their discovery? Nazi propaganda did not deal with this obvious question. The Germans botched other less significant points as well. They said the birch trees planted on top of the graves were three years old. A Swedish source pointed out that such trees are not usually planted until they are two years old. That meant that if the birches were three years old, the murders took place in April 1942, not April 1940 as the Germans claimed. There was also an inaccurate report about an emblem on the epaulettes of some of victims. The Germans said it carried the initials "J.P." which meant the men were members of the Józef Piłsudski Regiment. In fact, the initials were "S.P.," which stood for Szkoła Podchorążych, or Cadet Officers' School.

For a while the world reacted with stunned silence. Governments and news outlets in the West strongly suspected that the reports were fabricated by Nazi propaganda minister Joseph Goebbels. Neither the *New York Times* nor the London *Times* printed a word about the discovery for four days. TASS, *Pravda*, and *Izvestia* were also briefly silent.

For three years, the Soviets had equivocated and dissembled about the fate of the Polish officers. Stalin, Molotov, Vyshinsky, and numerous other high officials had repeatedly given vague, piecemeal, even conflicting answers to questions put forth by leaders of the Polish government-in-exile. But none of the Soviet leaders had ever given the slightest hint that they knew what happened to the Polish officers. That position was abruptly reversed at 7:15 A.M. Moscow time on April 15, 1943, when the Soviet Information Bureau unleashed a vitriolic counterattack to German statements about the massacre:

> In launching this monstrous invention the German-Fascist scoundrels did not hesitate at the most unscrupulous and base lies, in their attempts to cover up crimes which, as has now become evident, were perpetrated by themselves.
>
> The German-Fascist reports on this subject leave no doubt as to the tragic fate of the former Polish prisoners of war who in 1941 were engaged in construction work in areas west of Smolensk region, [and] fell into the hands of the German-Fascist hangmen in the summer of 1941, after the withdrawal of the Soviet troops from the Smolensk area.
>
> Beyond doubt Goebbels' slanderers are now trying by lies and calumnies to cover up the bloody crimes of the Hitlerite gangsters. In their clumsily concocted fabrication about the numerous graves which the Germans allegedly discovered near Smolensk, the Hitlerite liars mention the village of [Gniezdovo]. But, like the swindlers they are, they are silent about the fact that it was near the village of Gniezdovo that the archeological excavations of the historic "Gniezdovo burial place" were made. . . . These arrant German-Fascist murderers, whose hands are stained with the blood of hundreds of thousands of innocent victims, who methodically exterminate the population of countries they have occupied without sparing children, women or old people, who exterminated many thousands of Polish citizens in Poland itself, will deceive no one by their base lies and slander.
>
> The Hitlerite murders will not escape a just and inevitable retribution for their bloody crimes.

Almost twenty months after the Poles' official inquiries began, the Soviets had finally provided a specific explanation of the fate of the missing Polish officers. But their statement raised more questions than it answered. If the Soviets knew that the Polish officers had fallen into German hands in 1941, why had they withheld such vital information from the Poles for twenty months, especially when the Poles had desperately needed officers to command the new army they were organizing in the U.S.S.R.? The Soviets had adamantly maintained that they had released all the Polish officers. Was this a fabrication? The Soviet statement of April 15 strongly suggested to the Poles that it was. The statement's reference to "archeological excavations" also raised doubts. It said there was "no doubt" that the Germans had killed the Poles. If this was true, then why had the Soviets mentioned the historic "Gniezdovo burial place"? There were such excavations, but were the Soviets implying that the graves in Katyń Forest did not contain Polish officers? If this was the case, then why were the Soviets so certain that the Germans had, in fact, killed the Poles?

The Polish press in London also responded to the German accusations on April 15. The *Polish Daily* ventured, "This terrible accusation may be yet another lie of German propaganda, aimed at impairing Polish-Soviet relations. . . ." General Anders radioed a hasty report on this same day to the London government-in-exile. His troops and thousands of Polish citizens who had left the Soviet Union with his army were in shock from the German announcements. Anders's message reflected the deep concern of those with him in the Middle East:

> In spite of tremendous efforts on our side we have received absolutely no news of any of them. We have long held the deep conviction that none of them are alive but that they were deliberately murdered. . . .
> I consider it necessary for the Government to intervene in this affair with the object of obtaining official explanations from the Soviets, especially as our soldiers are convinced that the rest of our people in the U.S.S.R. will also be exterminated.

On April 17, the Polish Cabinet took several steps to deal with the crisis. In a statement on Polish radio, Defense Minister Marian Kukiel said that because of "the abundant and detailed German information" the crime should be investigated by a competent international body such as the International Red Cross. Kukiel said the Polish government was asking the Red Cross to send representatives to the scene. At the same time, the Germans were reprimanded for their "hypocritical" propaganda. The Cabinet then directed a request to the Soviets for "detailed information" concerning the fate of the missing Polish officers. The request was approved on April 17, but not passed on to the Soviet ambassador until April 20. The Poles would later say "technical reasons" caused this delay, but they used it to avoid a confrontation with the Soviets. The Poles knew that Moscow would blame the murders on the Germans. If they approached the Red Cross *after* receiving such an explanation, it would appear that they were undercutting an ally. But the strategy they followed would also leave them open to the charge that they had not gone through proper diplomatic channels. The Cabinet's note to the Soviets admonished them:

> Public opinion in Poland and throughout the world has rightly been so deeply shocked that only irrefutable facts can outweigh the numerous and detailed German statements concerning the discovery of the bodies of many thousands of Polish officers murdered near Smolensk in the spring of 1940.

Realizing that the controversy was getting out of hand, Churchill invited Sikorski to lunch at Number 10 Downing Street. After listening to what he later described as "a wealth of evidence" about possible Soviet guilt, Churchill told Sikorski, "If they are dead nothing you can do will bring them back." But by then it was too late. The Polish Cabinet's statement had already been issued.

Although the press gave scant attention to it, the Soviets also issued a statement on April 17. It was probably an attempt to strengthen their sketchy initial statement of April 15. In their second statement they blamed the murders on the Gestapo, claiming that some of the victims had been murdered immediately, while

> others were left alive for a special occasion. This occasion has now come. German Fascists have shot thousands of unarmed people, supplied the bodies with touched-up documents, which came from the German archives, and buried the victims on Soviet soil, using for this purpose the archaeological excavations of the [Gniezdovo] burial ground, the existence of which they are now ignoring. . . . This wholesale murder took place recently. That is why the bodies had not decomposed.

German authorities at the highest level were keenly observing reactions in the Allied camp, ready to fuel the controversy in any way possible. They were ecstatic at the initial results. On April 17, Goebbels wrote in his diary: "The Katyn incident is developing into a gigantic political affair which may have wide repercussions. We are exploiting it in every manner possible." A day earlier, at his instigation, the German Red Cross informally notified the International Red Cross in Geneva that the German government was prepared to cooperate fully with an independent investigation. Reuters news service carried a report that same day that the Polish government planned to ask the international body to investigate. Goebbels saw the Reuters report and told Hitler about it immediately. Hitler and Goebbels then decided to have a second, formal request sent to Geneva to create the appearance that action between the German and Polish governments had been coordinated. When the Poles delivered their request in Geneva at 4:30 P.M. on April 17, they were surprised to learn that a German request had arrived less than an hour earlier.

In considering these requests, the Red Cross emphasized that since 1939 its policy involving belligerent states required that all parties agree before it would investigate. Although the bodies had been found in German-held territory, the Red Cross emphasized that the Soviets must also concur before it would proceed. The concurrence of all parties seemed likely enough that a meeting of the Red Cross Executive Council was scheduled for April 20 to appoint a panel of neutral investigators.

It now appeared that a clever trap had been set by the Germans and baited, unintentionally, by the Poles: If the Soviets vetoed the investigation, their credibility would be damaged badly; if they concurred, they would face embarrassing questions in a neutral forum under the intense scrutiny of world opinion, already jolted by revelations about Katyń.

The Soviets quickly made clear their attitude toward the proposed investigation. On April 19 *Pravda* bitterly condemned the request in an article headlined "HITLER'S POLISH COLLABORATORS." Its concluding sentences contained a none-too-cryptic and ominous warning for the Poles:

> Slander spreads rapidly. Before the ink has dried on the pens of the German-Fascist scribblers, the vile inventions of Goebbels and Co. springing from the alleged mass shooting of Polish officers by the Soviet authorities in 1940, are taken up not only by faithful Hitlerite lackeys, but, Oh wonder, by General Sikorski's ministerial circles. . . . The Polish leaders have in an inexcusable manner fallen prey to the wily provocations of Goebbels and thus in reality are supporting the villainous tricks and slanderous inventions of the executioners of the Polish nation. After this it is hardly surprising that Hitler also has approached the International Red Cross with a proposal for an "investigation" of the scenery prepared by the hands of his masters of the science of crime. . . . Those

Poles who willingly take up and support Hitlerite falsehood, and are ready to co-operate with the Hitlerite executioners of the Polish nation, will go down in history as the helpmates of Cannibal Hitler. The Polish nation turns away from them, as from people who are giving aid to the sworn enemy of Poland, Hitler.

The *Pravda* article sent shock waves around the world. A *New York Times* headline the next day blared: "PRAVDA SEES POLES AS DUPED BY NAZIS—SIKORSKI REGIME, IN TAKING UP MASSACRE CHARGE, DECLARED AIDING HITLER'S HANGMEN." The *Times* article concluded that "this affair has led us to a critical turn in Polish Soviet relations, whose course has been so stormy since the beginning of the war." The charges caused genuine confusion. Until April 1943, the public in the West had heard nothing about the missing Polish officers. It admired Poland for its valiant underground resistance, for the fact that it had produced no quislings. But in terms of public awareness, the Poles' contributions paled in comparison to the heroic stand and recent successes of the Red Army. Now, suddenly, the Poles were accused of participating in a propaganda campaign against one of the "Big Allies." This was indeed a distraction—one that would have fatal consequences for the Polish government-in-exile.

In Lwów, Zbigniew and Anna Neuhoff and their four-year-old niece, Ewa, were still living in the family home at 69 Zadworzańska Street. They were surviving on Zbigniew's meager pay as a laboratory assistant and on the proceeds from the sale of family possessions. Zbigniew had heard nothing from his mother, Maria, or sister, Zofia, in Kazakhstan for almost two years. He had recently joined a group called the Citizens' Committee, formed by a prominent surgeon to help Polish prisoners in German hands. The committee provided food packages for prisoners, tracked their whereabouts, and bribed the Gestapo for their release when possible.

Zbigniew found the committee's work emotionally draining. But by early 1943, it had taken on a new dimension of heart-wrenching strain. When he and others arrived in the early morning to open the office, often a baby would be waiting by the door, left there in a bassinette or makeshift container by its Jewish mother. Occasionally, two or three babies would be waiting. Members of the committee saved these infants' lives by placing them with nuns in local convents. But their anonymous mothers were beyond help.

CHAPTER 17

The Rupture

For a few days the Soviets seemed trapped in a web of convincing details spun out by the Nazi propaganda machine. The victims in Katyń Forest *had* been captured by the Soviets, they *had* been interned in Soviet prisons, their bodies *had* been found on Soviet soil and they *had* disappeared in 1940, while they were *still* in Soviet custody. The Nazi message was suspect, but its images were spellbinding: a mysterious NKVD compound; seven graves, one an immense L-shaped pit said to contain three thousand neatly stacked victims; bodies in a mummified state; executions by Nackenschuss, or a bullet in the back of the head. What *had* happened? the world wondered as the Polish demand for clarification arrived in Moscow.

Any notion that the Soviets were trapped was strictly an illusion. The Poles had waited for twenty months for forthright answers from Moscow; none would come now. Ties between the two governments had deteriorated steadily since early December 1941, so much so that by April 1943 they were allies in name only. The relationship worsened as the Soviet military situation improved. The first difficulties had arisen shortly after the Soviets halted German Army Group Center on the outskirts of Moscow.

On December 4, Stalin and Sikorski seemed to patch up their differences. They signed a declaration promising "good neighborly collaboration, friendship, and reciprocal honest fulfillment of the obligations we have taken on ourselves." These words were proved meaningless by a series of unilateral Soviet actions over the next sixteen months that caused an ever-widening rift between the two governments. By the spring of 1942, the authorized size of the Polish Army had again been cut, further recruitment of deportees was prohibited, and all idea of having the Polish Army fight on the Eastern Front was abandoned. Relief programs for the deportees, the cause of soaring hopes during the first few months of the agreement, were squeezed and finally termi-

217

nated with tens of thousands of desperate Poles waiting for help. In July 1942, the embassy envoys charged with dispensing relief were summarily arrested and all their supplies were impounded. Then the exit door itself was slammed shut. On January 16, 1943, the Soviets declared that no more deportees, including ethnic Poles, would be permitted to leave. From that date forward, all the deportees, including ethnic Poles, became citizens of the U.S.S.R. in the eyes of the Soviet government. But the most telling action of all had come in March 1943, when the Soviets had organized a Polish "national committee"—precisely what they had first proposed when negotiating the pact of July 30, 1941. The committee was called the Union of Polish Patriots and its formation reflected the Soviets' clear intention to install a client regime in Poland once the Red Army had occupied the country. Having made that decision, the Soviets were secretly biding their time, waiting for the right moment to break with the government-in-exile. The Wehrmacht's dramatic discoveries near Smolensk provided just such an opportunity.

Accusations from the scene of the crime all came from the Germans. Not one shred of evidence pointed to collaboration between the Nazis and the Poles. But the facts could be conveniently twisted. Both the German and Polish press were treating the story like a sensation. A tenuous claim could be made that the news reports and the requests for an International Red Cross investigation by the German and Polish governments—arriving as they had within one hour of each other—had been coordinated. At a minimum, coordination *might* have occurred, and that was pretext enough for the Soviets. Thus, barely a week after the discovery of the graves, a monstrous trap was waiting. But it was the Poles, not the Soviets, who were about to be snared. It was they who were waiting, unwittingly, for a Soviet response that would deal their government a mortal blow.

On April 21, 1943, with the Polish Cabinet's demand for clarification yet to be delivered, Stalin sent identical secret cables to Churchill and Roosevelt claiming that

> The fact that the anti-Soviet campaign has been started simultaneously in the German and Polish press and follows identical lines is indubitable evidence of contact and collusion between Hitler—the Allies' enemy— and the Sikorski Government in this hostile campaign.
>
> At a time when the peoples of the Soviet Union are shedding their blood in a grim struggle against Hitler's Germany and bending their energies to defeat the common foe of the freedom-loving democratic

countries, the Sikorski Government is striking a treacherous blow at the
Soviet Union to help Hitler's tyranny.

These circumstances compel the Soviet Government to consider that
the present Polish Government, having descended to collusion with the
Hitler Government, has, in practice, severed its relations of alliance with
the U.S.S.R. and adopted a hostile attitude to the Soviet Union.

For these reasons the Soviet Government has decided to interrupt
relations with that Government.

Stalin also protested that the Polish government "has not found it
necessary even to address questions to the Soviet Government or to
request information on the matter." A calculated strategy accounted
for this diplomatic faux pas. Radio Moscow's April 15 broadcast had
already blamed the massacre on the Germans. The Polish leaders knew
that Moscow would respond to their inquiries with the same explanation. A subsequent appeal to the International Red Cross would then
seem an indirect rebuke to the Soviets. By requesting the Red Cross
investigation *before* seeking clarification from the Soviets, the Poles
hoped to avoid criticism that they lacked faith in the word of an ally.
Instead they left themselves vulnerable to the charge that they had
failed to consult an ally on a highly sensitive matter of deep mutual
concern. Either way the Polish leaders were in a terrible dilemma—a
position, at this point, that had become all too familiar to them.

Stalin's blunt cables touched off a frantic scramble at the Foreign
Office in London and the State Department in Washington. His message came as a shock to Churchill and Roosevelt. Both men were accus-
tomed to constant quarreling between the Poles and the Soviets, but
neither expected a rupture. Its timing was particularly disturbing. The
war had barely taken a favorable turn and dangerous distractions were
to be avoided at all cost. The Soviet break with the Poles was the first
such rift within the United Nations and had the potential to cause
great embarrassment. The war effort itself might suffer. Churchill and
Roosevelt also continued to worry about Stalin's remoteness, his enig-
matic leadership style. He had made one deal with Hitler and another
could not be ruled out entirely. These consensus concerns among the
Anglo-American leaders prompted a last-ditch effort over the next ten
days to prevent a complete rupture in relations between the Poles and
the Soviets.

Stalin's message was delivered to the Foreign Office and the State
Department on April 24. Churchill and Roosevelt both responded on
April 26. Churchill called the proposed Red Cross investigation "a

fraud" and promised to oppose it vigorously. "Mr. Eden is seeing Sikorski today," he added, "and will press him as strongly as possible to withdraw all countenance from any investigation under Nazi auspices." Churchill defended Sikorski strongly, saying: "He is in danger of being overthrown by the Poles who consider that he has not stood up sufficiently for his people against the Soviets. If he should go we should only get somebody worse." He urged Stalin to consider his decision as a "a final warning rather than . . . a break" and asked that no announcement be made "until every other plan has been tried."

Roosevelt, who was on a swing through several western U.S. states when Stalin's message arrived, tried much the same approach. "I fully understand your problem," Roosevelt conceded, urging Stalin to define his action as a "suspension of conversations" with the Poles, not a complete diplomatic break. He said he was "inclined to think that Churchill will find ways and means of getting the Polish Government in London to act with more common sense in the future." Both leaders concluded with tactfully worded references to the plight of Polish deportees, urging Stalin to facilitate their departure from the U.S.S.R.

Stalin cabled Churchill back the next day, April 25, saying the matter had "already been settled" and that his decision was that day being relayed to the Polish government by Molotov. He said it would be impossible to avoid announcing the decision. On April 25, he had not yet received Roosevelt's message. But Stalin sent the president essentially the same reply on April 29. By then it was too late to prevent the break. Stalin's actions on April 25 and April 26 leave no doubt that he was in no mood for compromise, that he had reached an irreversible decision to terminate relations with the Poles.

Shortly after midnight on Easter Sunday, on the Monday morning of April 26, the Polish ambassador, Tadeusz Romer, was summoned to the Soviet Ministry of Foreign Affairs, where Molotov read him a note denouncing the Polish government and severing relations. The Poles had received a similar message from the Soviets in the early-morning hours of September 17, 1939. Molotov's note reiterated the charges already lodged in Stalin's cables to Churchill and Roosevelt, but its tone was more strident. It claimed that "to please Hitler's tyranny," the Polish government had "dealt a treacherous blow to the Soviet Union." The Poles' purpose, according to the note, was to gain "territorial concessions at the expense of the interests of the Soviet Ukraine, Soviet Byelorussia and Soviet Lithuania."

After listening to the note, Romer said, "Mr. Molotov, that letter is couched in language which no ambassador can receive." He told

Molotov that he would never accept such a note and advised him to contact the Polish government in London through the Soviet ambassador there. Molotov's note confirmed a premonition Romer had related more than a month earlier, on March 22, to U.S. ambassador William H. Standley and British ambassador Sir Archibald Clark-Kerr. The three men met that day in Standley's office to discuss fears that Polish-Soviet relations were headed toward an impasse. Standley and Sir Archibald said they had updated their governments on the situation and were awaiting instructions. "I am in the same fix," Romer said. "Nothing to do but wait, wait, wait. And all the while, I feel something in the air—I feel it, I tell you. Something terrible is going to break, and soon."

Romer sounded out Standley again on April 26, after his unpleasant meeting with Molotov. "Do you know what he [Molotov] did? About two-thirty this morning, a Foreign Office messenger routed me out of bed and handed me a note." Romer said it was the identical message Molotov had read to him two hours earlier. "So, I came over to ask what you would do about it." Standley said he would take the note "back to the Kremlin gate" and tell them that "evidently it had been sent to me by mistake."

At 5:00 P.M. that same day, Standley himself was called to the Kremlin. As he entered Molotov's outer office, he met Sir Archibald leaving. As they passed each other, Sir Archibald said in a low voice, "I imagine you will be given the same information I just received— the Soviets have discontinued relations with the Polish Government." He said he had been trying for an hour to persuade Molotov to delay making the note public, but "I'm afraid I have failed."

Seated at a long table in Molotov's office, Standley also urged a delay in announcing the decision, to give the parties time to find a solution. Molotov slumped back wearily in his chair, shaking his head.

"Nyet, nyet!" he said. "It is no use. For two weeks, this slanderous campaign against the Soviet Union has dragged on. . . . We have shown a maximum of patience. Our people have become extremely indignant. We must make the break and publish the note."

Romer left Moscow on the afternoon of April 29. Standley, Sir Archibald, and a large contingent of foreign correspondents and news photographers saw him off at the Moscow train station. Standley later described it as a painful moment: "In the course of his few months in Moscow, Mr. Romer had become very popular with us all. It was a cold, rainy day, with an air of gloom over the assemblage. We gave Mr. Romer our little gifts and watched him waving from the window as the train pulled out of the station, feeling without quite knowing why that with him went some of our hope for a free and peaceful world."

The day before Romer left, Standley sent two secret messages to the president advising him of the situation. In one, he reported that his meeting with Molotov was futile because "the Kremlin policy was set before my interview. . . ." He said "hopes for reconciliation were apparently destroyed" by *Izvestia*'s publication that same day of an article by Wanda Wasilewska of the Union of Polish Patriots, condemning the Sikorski government for cowardice in "refusing to fight and withdrawing its forces from the Soviet Union." Standley pointed out that the article called on the Soviet government to form Polish units "which would proceed to the front to fight shoulder to shoulder with the Red Army rather than sitting for months in tents." Standley concluded by saying, "It is the consensus here that the article mentioned above has now closed the door definitely to any rapprochement between Moscow and the present Polish Government."

Standley amplified this conclusion in a second message that same day, reporting that in Moscow "many qualified observers" were predicting that the Soviets would soon recognize "an offspring" of the Union of Polish Patriots as "a satellite of the Soviet Government." Standley concluded the cable with a remarkable piece of prophecy: "We may, it seems to me, be faced with a reversal in European history. To protect itself from the influences of Bolshevism, Western Europe in 1918 attempted to set up a cordon sanitaire. The Kremlin, in order to protect itself from the influences of the west, might now envisage the formation of a belt of pro-Soviet states."

While these developments were taking place in Moscow, the Polish government was under intense pressure in London. The International Red Cross announced on April 23 that, because all interested parties had not agreed to an investigation, there would be none. The following day, British Foreign Secretary Eden called Sikorski to the Foreign Office and warned him that "it is highly dangerous for the Poles to get mixed up with the Germans." He urged Sikorski to declare that the massacre was an "invention" of the Nazis. Sikorski replied: "Our policy towards the Allies is honest. Force is on Russia's side, justice on ours. I do not advise the British people to cast their lot with brute force and to stampede justice before the eyes of all nations. For all these reasons I emphatically refuse to withdraw the Polish appeal to the International Red Cross."

But pressures on Sikorski were rapidly building to the point that some type of retraction was inevitable. The news on April 26 that Moscow had decided to sever relations brought the matter to a head. On April 27 and 28, Sikorski held several meetings with Churchill, Eden, and Drexel Biddle, the U.S. ambassador to the Polish government-in-exile. As a result, Sikorski and his cabinet formally withdrew their request for the investigation. That prompted Churchill to make one last appeal to Stalin on April 30. He expressed disappointment that Stalin had gone forward with his decision to sever relations with the Poles "without giving me time to inform you of the results of my approach to General Sikorski. . . . I am glad to tell you that they have accepted our view and that they want to work loyally with you." Churchill again urged Stalin to permit Poles in the U.S.S.R. who so wished to leave. He then noted that

> so far this business has been Goebbels' triumph. He is now busy suggesting that the U.S.S.R. will set up a Polish Government on Russian soil and deal only with them. We should not, of course, be able to recognise such a Government and would continue our relations with Sikorski who is far the most helpful man you or we are likely to find for the purposes of the common cause. I expect that this will also be the American view.
>
> My own feeling is that they [the Poles] have had a shock and that after whatever interval is thought convenient the relationship established on July 30, 1941, should be restored. No one will hate this more than Hitler and what he hates most is wise for us to do.

Stalin replied to this message on May 4, rehashing his earlier accusation that a "notorious anti-Soviet press campaign" had been launched by the Poles as early as April 15. He thanked Churchill for his efforts to clamp down on the Polish press in London, but said: "I doubt that it will be as easy as all that to impose discipline on the present Polish Government, its following of pro-Hitler boosters and its fanatical press." Then, he flatly denied suggestions that he might form a new Polish government in the U.S.S.R. "This does not rule out Great Britain, and the [U.S.S.R.] and the [U.S.A.] taking measures to improve the composition of the present Polish Government in terms of consolidating the Allied united front against Hitler. The sooner this is done, the better." He expressed the view that future prospects for the Sikorski government's return to Poland were poor. He concluded by saying, "As regards the Polish citizens in the [U.S.S.R.], whose number is not great . . . the Soviet Government has never raised any obstacles to their departure from the [U.S.S.R]."

The message was still blunt, his decision unchanged. It contained statements that Churchill knew to be untrue. But there was a note of conciliation. By now, Western opinion seemed anxious for some gesture of Soviet amity toward the Poles. Western media had prominently covered the Polish government's decision to withdraw its request for a Red Cross investigation, and seemed mollified by it. On April 29, London's evening press had also played up reports of exchanges "on the highest level" in London, Moscow, and Washington on the Russo-Polish difficulties. In responding to questions from the London *Times* and the *New York Times* on May 4, Stalin was even more conciliatory than in the cable he sent that same day to Churchill. He told the two newspapers that without question the Soviet Union desired a "strong and independent Poland" and hoped to base postwar relations "upon the fundamentals of solid good neighborly relations and mutual respect. . . ."

On the very day the Poles were being forced to make a face-saving gesture to Stalin, April 28, Goebbels wrote in his diary:

> The most important theme of all international discussion is naturally the break between Moscow and the Polish Émigré Government. . . . All enemy broadcasts and newspapers agree that this break represents a 100 per cent victory for German propaganda and especially for me personally. The commentators marvel at the extraordinary cleverness with which we have been able to convert the Katyn incident into a highly political question. There is grave apprehension in London about this success of German propaganda. Suddenly all sorts of rifts are noticed in the allied camp the existence of which nobody had hitherto admitted. . . . There is talk of a total victory by Goebbels! Even important American senators publish worried comments. . . . Alarm in London has reached its highest pitch. The Poles are given a perky talking to because of their precipitate action and are blamed for having played right into the hands of German propaganda. . . .
>
> One can speak of a complete triumph of German propaganda. Throughout this whole war we have seldom been able to register such a success.

The next day, Goebbels added:

> The Polish conflict still holds the center of the stage. Seldom since the beginning of the war has any affair stirred up so much public discussion as this. The Poles are given a brushoff by the English and the Americans as though they were enemies. It is admitted that I succeeded

in driving a deep wedge into the enemy, thereby provoking a much greater crisis than that between Darlan and de Gaulle some time ago.

Goebbels's diary entry for April 30 noted that his Katyń propaganda was being widely interpreted as a German effort to make a separate peace with either Great Britain or the Soviet Union. "That, of course, is not our intention," he wrote, "although such a possibility would naturally be very pleasing." His entry on the following day, May 1, astutely summarized the controversy.

> The conflict between the Polish Émigré Government and the Soviets still holds the world's interest. The Soviets at the moment are extremely insolent and arrogant. They are quite conscious of the security of their position. They have no consideration whatever for their Anglo-Saxon allies, nor need they have, as they are under no obligation to them for military achievements. The men in power in the Kremlin know exactly how far they can go. There is great bitterness in London and Washington about it which nobody seeks to disguise. The Anglo-Saxon camp is in a blue funk about the fact that our propaganda has succeeded in driving so deep a wedge into the enemy coalition.

Goebbels was right. Stalin and his inner circle understood their position. Because of the Red Army's heroic stand on the outskirts of Moscow in November 1941, because their nation had begun to reverse the course of the war in 1942 and had, in fact, reversed it only ninety days earlier at Stalingrad, the Soviet Union had paid a great price and expected great gains. From Stalin on down, Soviet authorities at every level constantly insisted to visiting correspondents, statesmen, and military advisers from the West that they were fighting alone. And often it seemed that they were. On October 3, 1942, Stalin had responded to a written question about the importance of a second front from Henry Cassidy, the Associated Press bureau chief in the Soviet capital. Among Soviet priorities, Stalin said the second front had "a very important, one might say, a prime place." In the same reply, he called for "full and prompt fulfillment by the Allies of their obligations" to provide aid to the Soviets. His perfunctory 149-word reply to Cassidy was emblazoned in headlines all over the world. The Allies made a series of amphibious landings in North Africa one month later. The action, called Operation Torch, represented the first joint invasion by the Allies. It was not considered a second front and did not result in any mitigation of Soviet demands in this area. Compared to the colossal life-and-death struggles on the Eastern Front, Operation Torch seemed like a skirmish.

The Germans used the Katyń revelations to sow discord in the Allied camp, but Goebbels relished them for another reason as well. The scope and importance of the Soviet victories had created a backwash of international approbation for Stalin, the Red Army, and the Russian people. The world press, particularly in the United States, was over-flowing with admiration, good feeling, even adulation for the miracles wrought by a nation that only one generation earlier had been the pariah of Europe. Goebbels hoped to poison what seemed, in the spring of 1943, an unending stream of praise for the Soviets.

The year had begun with a chiseled, demigodlike portrait of Stalin as "Man of the Year" on the cover of *Time* magazine. The caption beneath his flattering portrait read, "All that Hitler could give, he took for a second time." The text noted: "At banquets for such men as Winston Churchill, W. Averell Harriman and Wendell Willkie, host Stalin drank his vodka straight, talked the same way." Two weeks before the Katyń controversy erupted, a genial photograph of Stalin graced the cover of a special issue of *Life* magazine on the U.S.S.R. An editorial emphasized:

> So far as our intentions are concerned, they are warm and friendly. We respect the mighty Russian people and admire them. . . . They live under a system of tight state-controlled information. But probably the attitude to take toward this is not to get too excited about it. When we take account of what the [U.S.S.R.] has accomplished in the 20 years [*sic*] of its existence we can make allowances for certain shortcomings, however deplorable.

This same issue of *Life* likened the Soviet NKVD to "a national police similar to the FBI." It contained a lengthy interview with Joseph E. Davies, a U.S. ambassador to the U.S.S.R. from 1936 to 1938, who was well known for his pro-Soviet views. After returning to the United States, Davies had drawn on his diary as ambassador to produce a popular book called *Mission to Moscow*. A movie based on the book later reached a large and enthusiastic audience. In his interview with *Life*, Davies said, "If states adjacent to the Soviet Union should volun-tarily apply for admission to the [U.S.S.R.], I have no doubt that they would be admitted. If that were done, both countries being willing, it would be my opinion that it was none of our business; nor would our safety be necessarily imperiled thereby."

The flood of pro-Soviet sentiment reflected the profound appreciation of people everywhere in the West that Hitler had finally been forced to retreat. It put Poles in a completely untenable position. Their inevitable outcry over the discoveries at Katyń were discordant, even offensive to the public ear. And they were quickly squelched in the interest of harmony among the Big Allies. In his April 25 cable to Stalin, Churchill reported that he had succeeded in getting Sikorski to "restrain the Polish press from polemics. In this connection I am examining the possibility of silencing those Polish newspapers in this country which attacked the Soviet Government and at the same time attacked Sikorski for trying to work with the Soviet Government." In his April 30 message to Stalin, Churchill referred to the London-based Polish press as "miserable rags." Of their criticism, he said, "this must be stopped and it will be stopped."

Roosevelt was so concerned about the flap that he dispatched his old friend Davies to Moscow with a note to Stalin suggesting that they meet near the Bering Strait without Churchill present to discuss a number of matters. His appeal was so secret that Ambassador Standley was not told about the mission and was excluded from Davies's meeting with Stalin.

The handling of the Katyń controversy left little doubt about the standing of the Polish government-in-exile within the Allied camp. In a crisis, its fundamental interests were clearly secondary to the preservation of unity among the Big Allies. In negotiating the pact of July 30, 1941, the British had forced the Poles to swallow their pride and accept a distasteful agreement with the Soviets. Any doubts in Moscow that the Allies would or could still discipline the Poles were removed by the handling of the crisis over Katyń in late April and early May 1943. The crisis also dramatized how little the world knew about the plight of the Poles. The war had begun as a fight to preserve their independence. But by 1943 it had become a war to defeat Germany, and the initial objective was rapidly fading from view. Polish leaders were certainly powerless to prevent such a fundamental change and the Katyń crisis demonstrated how little political latitude they had in adapting to it. Relations between the Polish government-in-exile and the Soviet Union were never restored. The break initiated a long-term period of decline for the Polish government that resulted, by the end of the war, in the withdrawal of Allied recognition and the government's replacement by a provisional government in Poland, which quickly became a Soviet client regime. From events surrounding the diplomatic break in late April and early May 1943 forward, Katyń and the demise of the legitimate Polish government began to fuse into a powerful symbol of Stalin's subversion of the Poles.

*   *   *

With the scuttling of efforts for a Red Cross investigation, the Germans moved quickly to provide for an ostensibly neutral investigation of the Katyń murders. Medical analysis could be used with considerable precision to establish the date of the murders, the most crucial question of all. A finding that the men had been killed prior to July 16, 1941, when the Wehrmacht reached Smolensk, would be proof of Soviet guilt. The Germans knew that no one would believe their medical authorities, so they organized an international commission to conduct a neutral investigation. Twelve of Europe's leading experts in forensic medicine and criminology, none from Germany, were asked to visit the site and examine the victims. Members of this commission served voluntarily without compensation. They arrived on April 28, 1943, to conduct the third investigation, by far the most damaging to Soviet claims of innocence. The commission's members came from Belgium, Bulgaria, Czechoslovakia, Denmark, Finland, Italy, Holland, Hungary, Romania, and Switzerland. All these countries, with the exception of Switzerland, were either Nazi-occupied or allies of the Nazis.

Members of the commission were assisted by Dr. Buhtz, who had coordinated the Wehrmacht investigation and preparations at the site. The commission chose as its chairman Dr. Ferenc Orsos, director of the Institute for Judicial Medicine in Budapest—a man who, according to his own estimate, had conducted a great many autopsies, and had recently devised a way to analyze chemical formations inside the skull to determine how long a corpse had been interred. When they arrived at the gravesites, members of the commission were struck immediately by the terrible smell of decay from the 973 bodies, in long rows, that the German investigative team had already disinterred. The seven main graves had been opened in small clearings in the forest where they had been terraced into a long sloping hillside that ended at the marsh along the Dnieper River.

The experts quickly determined how the 2,500 to 2,800 bodies in grave number one had been mummified. Because they found the bodies preserved in such circumstances, the experts were convinced that the Germans could not possibly have tampered with the bodies in any way, as the Soviets alleged. Certainly it would have been impossible to remove the bodies, stuff incriminating items into the victims' pockets, and then return the bodies to such a tightly packed mass. For this reason, the commission's members concluded that the Germans were the first to exhume the bodies.

The commission spent its first day being briefed and reviewing work carried out by German investigators at the site. On the second morning, the commission began its own autopsies. Its members, who had complete freedom of movement, climbed inside the graves to select individual bodies for removal at random. Russian peasants then separated the designated bodies, often using picks and hooks to pry them loose. Separating a single body in some cases took almost an hour due to the great compression. Nine bodies were removed in this manner, then placed on wooden examination tables, where autopsies were performed to determine the victim's identity, cause of death, and length of interment.

In the pockets of the fully clothed victims, investigators from all three teams found a wealth of information—military passes, aluminum identification tags, letters, diaries, and medical records—that could be used to identify the victims. Death had been caused by what the Germans called a *Nackenschuss*, or shot at the top of the neck where it joins the base of the skull. Powder burns indicated that the shots had been fired from a distance of about six inches, striking the occipital bone before penetrating the medulla oblongata, or nerve center of respiration, and emerging above the root of the nose. Shots fired in this precise manner cause instantaneous death with minimal loss of blood. The fact that, with great uniformity, the shots struck within a one- to two-inch circumference at the base of the skull suggested the work of experienced executioners. The angle of the shots strongly indicated that most of the victims were kneeling when executed.

Finally, the autopsies provided two strong elements of evidence that the victims had been buried for at least three years. First, the bodies had begun to saponify, that is, to convert fats into a kind of soap; this sign can appear in the first year of interment. Closer examination, however, showed that saponification had penetrated into the musculature to an extent that generally did not occur in less than three years. Second, a claylike crust was found inside many of the victims' skulls. Dr. Orsos had pioneered pathological studies showing that it took three years for this crust to occur. He convinced his colleagues that his research and assessment were correct. The Soviet accusations that the men had been engaged in construction work when executed by the Germans in the summer of 1941 were at odds with several important circumstantial but valuable evidentiary findings:

1. Of the many newspapers, letters, and other documents recovered from victims' bodies, not one carried a date later than May 6, 1940.

2. Microscopic examination of bayonet thrusts into the victims' bodies revealed wounds from a four-cornered blade, the design of the Soviet, but not the German weapon.

3. The fact that no insects were found in the graves strongly indicated that the burials had occurred in cold weather, not late summer as claimed by the Soviets.

4. The victims all wore heavy winter clothing, including overcoats, most of it in excellent condition. Their clothing did not exhibit the wear a year of construction work would have caused. The stylish, high-topped, handmade military boots of the Polish officers showed little wear, even in the heels.

5. Some of the victims' hands were tied with cord manufactured in the Soviet Union. The knots were the same as those used to bind Russian victims buried nearby but executed many years earlier.

6. A microscopic examination of young trees growing on top of the graves showed that they had been transplanted three years earlier. (The Germans had left some of these trees on the edge of the graves to be examined by the commission.) It was clear that these trees were much younger than others nearby.

The international commission left Katyń on April 30, after its members had signed a unanimous report concluding that the executions had taken place in March and April of 1940.* Because they spent only three days at Katyń, the commission's members were forced to rely heavily on preparations and procedures established by Dr. Buhtz. However, members of the Polish Red Cross Commission were present, and closely observed the work of the international experts. The Poles were satisfied that the international experts focused entirely on technical issues within their competence and made no political statements. Subsequent revelations failed to discredit a single finding of the international commission.

During the first week of May, the Germans took several Allied prisoners of war, including Colonel John Van Vliet, Jr., and Captain Donald B. Stewart, both of the U.S. Army, to Katyń. Both men had been captured in North Africa and were being held at a prison camp for P.O.W. officers in Germany at the time. Van Vliet and Stewart both protested that they were being brought to Katyń for purposes that were blatantly propagandistic. The Germans ignored their protests, and took them by train to Berlin, flying them from there to Smolensk. Both men had heard about the Katyń discoveries, and arrived on the scene

---

*During its three-day visit, the international commission performed autopsies on only a few bodies and examined only a small percentage of the documents and memorabilia recovered from the victims' bodies. This may account for the discrepancy between the date given for the executions and the latest date the commission assigned to the documents that it found.

convinced that the Germans, having killed the Poles, were attempting to hide their guilt. As a result of their one-day stay, both Van Vliet and Stewart reversed their views and decided that in this case the Germans were telling the truth. Van Vliet filed a report on his visit to Katyń only a few days after the war in Europe ended. The disappearance of this report under circumstances that the War Department never fully explained caused considerable controversy when a select committee of the U.S. Congress investigated the massacre in 1951 and 1952.

The Germans closed their investigation embarrassed that less than half the number of bodies predicted in their April 13 announcement had been found. A total of 4,143 bodies had been found, but this total did not include those in grave eight, which might have pushed the total to 4,400. The last of the bodies were reburied in new common graves on June 7 as yet another pivotal battle began to take shape approximately 250 miles south of Smolensk in the Kursk Salient.

CHAPTER 18

Death Knell

<<<<<<<<<<

Strange incantations echoed from the loudspeakers, or "barkers" as the Poles called them, on Market Square in the center of Kraków in the last half of April 1943. In a slow, measured cadence, the names of the murdered men whose bodies had been pulled from the burial pits in Katyń Forest were being tolled lugubriously across the city by the German General Government.

The reverberations were eerie, unsettling, oppressive. Pedestrians within earshot moved briskly, as if hoping to outdistance the news. The pealing of a familiar-sounding name drew many up short. Cocking disbelieving ears toward the sound, they strained momentarily before moving on, grim-faced and shaken. Others shrugged off the funereal pronouncements as propaganda, more cynical this time than ever. But the booming monotony of the sound could not be blocked out. Even the skeptics agreed that, for once, the Germans *might* be telling the truth. The dead *had* been captured by the Soviets. Many familiar names, among them prominent sons of Poland, *were* being tolled. Their loss, if what the Germans said was true, *was* a staggering blow to the nation. Gloom enveloped the city as the maddening monotone continued:

"Body number 2129—Aleksander Marek Kowalski . . ."

Hardly an adult on the street failed to remember: "The great Kowalski! Now dead? Impossible!" In 1928 and again in 1932, his dazzling exploits at the Winter Olympics had electrified all of Poland. The nation's pride had ridden on his skates. The powerfully built, world-class hockey star was a symbol of modern Poland. Success as a banker had followed his Olympic laurels. Like so many reservists, he had been mobilized and rushed to the front early in September of 1939. He was captured by the Soviets near Równo (now Rovno, in the Ukraine). The dead lieutenant, thirty-eight, was survived by his wife, Janina, and two daughters, Hanna and Ewa, in Warsaw.

233

"Body number 2610—Tadeusz Zygmunt Hernes . . ."

A popular literary figure heard on Polish radio and read in popular newspapers, Hernes, thirty-four, had been president of Stratosfera, a literary and artistic club in Poznań, and a second lieutenant in the reserves.

"Body number 1539—Edward Giergielewicz . . ."

A judge and scholar from Lublin. He was quiet, calm, self-possessed—what one would expect in a legal theoretician. The study of Polish political and social thought during the Enlightenment occupied his spare time. He had many close friends at the theological seminary in Płock. The intellectual atmosphere there appealed to him greatly. He and others from the Ministry of Justice had been evacuated to the east following the German attack on September 1, 1939. In April 1940, he had managed to smuggle a note out to his brother. It said, "They are taking us away. Help us, for we are perishing." He was dead at thirty-seven.

"Body number 988—Stefan Pieńkowski . . ."

An eminent neurologist and psychiatrist, who had served in the Russian army during World War I. He had headed the neurological and psychiatric clinic at Jagiellonian University in Kraków. He was known there for his straightforward approach and the rigorous demands he placed on himself and his associates. A prolific author on medical subjects, he was a member of the Polish Academy of Sciences. He was executed at age fifty-five.

"Body number 2609—Stefan Lech Sokołowski . . ."

Once the Polish Army's youngest corporal, he had been wounded in the war of 1920. Afterward, he and his father designed and patented an automatic coupler for railroad cars. He then earned a doctorate in mathematics from the University of Warsaw. While working at the army's Center for Ballistic Research, he developed a quick way to calculate the position of an aircraft in flight. Shortly before his death he sent his mother, a well-known poet and novelist, a telegram asking if his wife, Celina, and his infant daughter, Krysia, were still alive. Krysia's birth certificate was found on his body. He was thirty-six when executed.

"Body number 2713—Szymon Fedoronko . . ."

The Polish Army's chief chaplain for the Orthodox creed. A highly decorated career army man who had served in the Polish Army during the Russo-Polish War. His wife, Wiera, and three sons survived. All three sons would later die fighting for Poland—two of them in the Warsaw Uprising and a third during a combat flight over Mannheim, Germany. He was murdered at forty-seven.

The tolling of these names continued for several days in the center of Kraków.

From Father Zdzisław Peszkowski of Orchard Lake, Michigan, I learned that not all the bodies had been correctly identified. The reader may recall an earlier description of Peszkowski's life as a cadet at Kozelsk. He had arrived there with his best friend, Julian Bakon. The two young men had grown up together, in Sanok on the San River, and were newly graduated from Dęblin Cavalry Academy when the war began. They had been captured together north of Lwów and remained inseparable companions at Kozelsk.

In an interview on October 2, 1989, Father Peszkowski told me that Julian was among those in the first transport that left Kozelsk for Katyń on April 3, 1940. "We had mixed emotions about being separated," he said. "In one sense we were glad because we thought he was going back to Poland. At the same time, we were very disappointed that we would no longer be together. It was still cold when he left and I remember that Julian's shoes were in bad shape. He did not have cavalry boots. He did not have an overcoat either. As he was leaving, I said, 'Here, take my blanket; you need something to wrap up in.' He took the blanket and he left the camp with it wrapped around his shoulders."

Young Zdzisław exchanged letters with his parents soon after he reached Camp Gryazovets with the remnant of four hundred men from Kozelsk, Starobelsk, and Ostashkov. "In their second letter to me, my parents wrote that Julian's parents were asking, in fact begging me to say something about their son. They were saying, 'Julian was with you at Kozelsk. He wrote us letters from there and now we have no news from him.' I remember that, for the first time, I began worrying about what had happened to Julian and the others."

Three years later, when the list of the dead rolled from the loud-speakers in Kraków, the name "Zdzisław Peszkowski" was called. His name also appeared almost simultaneously on a list of the Katyń dead published by the German propaganda press. These announcements quickly reached the Peszkowski family in Sanok, plunging them into confusion and despair. Having heard several times from their son, they assumed he was safe. They could not understand how his body had been found in Katyń Forest.

Two weeks later, their grief was lifted. The Germans revised the list of the dead from Katyń. They said the name Zdzisław Peszkowski had been mistakenly recorded. The body identified as his had, in fact, been that of Julian Bakon, whose name appeared on a revised list. There was a simple explanation for the mistake. When Julian's body was taken from the grave, it was still wrapped in the blanket his friend Zdzisław had given him. A laundry tag on that blanket, marked "Property of Zdzisław Peszkowski," had been used initially to identify the body.

Riding through the center of Kraków on her bicycle, Magda Czarnek felt bombarded from all directions with news of the Katyń discoveries. German radio relentlessly blared the sickening details. Newspaper-plastered kiosks everywhere featured the grisly scene of the crime. Worst of all were the loudspeakers and their constant assault on the ears. To escape the drumbeat of propaganda was impossible.

Magda's duties as a courier for a German school of welding kept her on the street often during April of 1943. The school provided on-the-job training for about 30 Polish students. Its records and correspondence were ferried about the city for several hours each day by Magda. The work was easy and offered one exceptional benefit: she could keep her own bicycle. Technically, because Poles could not own bicycles, Magda's bike had become the property of the welding school. But the director, a Dr. Sippel, permitted Magda to ride the bike home after work. Unwittingly, by this concession he facilitated Magda's work in delivering the underground press, in contacting families of prisoners, and in attending clandestine classes in Polish literature and other prohibited subjects.

Dr. Sippel was a loyal Nazi from the heart of Germany, but did not entirely fit the image of the coarse, overbearing *gauleiter*. He treated Magda with studied politeness, never raising his voice or harming her in any way. He was fairly well educated, immaculate in appearance, and pretended to refinement. Occasionally in Magda's presence he would shift from German to a clipped English. Magda had studied English illegally at that point for two years, but she could understand little of what he said. Gradually, however, she began to believe that should the occasion arise, Dr. Sippel might be useful.

From the outset, Magda had refused to believe that the Germans were telling the truth about Katyń. "This is just a German trick to break us down," she thought. Even the pictures did not convince her. "The Germans have enough bodies at their disposal to produce any false evidence they want," she told herself.

The situation was not entirely bleak. Several days after the first names were announced, Dr. Czarnek's name had not once been mentioned. Hundreds of names were being published daily in the propaganda press and posted at the kiosks. Magda, Jaga, Maria, and their mother approached each new list engulfed in anxiety. A quick scan of the C's, then a slow, careful perusal brought a brief respite from fear.

Then came a fresh rush of doubt: Perhaps he would yet be listed; perhaps he had not yet been found. Why, after more than three years, had there been no word from him at all? Such thoughts swirled with the posting and scanning of each new list.

By early June, news from Katyń had been muted by the German propaganda service. By tacit agreement, the subject was not discussed in the Czarnek family. Maria and Jaga had given up all hope that their father would ever return; such convincing evidence could not be fabricated, they felt, even by the Germans. But Magda and her mother refused to give up hope. They based all their faith on the fact that Dr. Czarnek had not been listed among the victims. Official confirmation of his death would not reach the Czarnek family for forty-seven years. An order to the NKVD in Smolensk to carry out his execution was found in the files released to the Polish government by Soviet president Gorbachev on April 13, 1990. Sometime between the seventh and the tenth of April, a special transport made up of many of the oldest and highest-ranking officers at Kozelsk was sent to Katyń Forest. Prisoner number 1193, Lieutenant Colonel Zbigniew Czarnek, was included in that transport.

Magda's self-consoling thought that the Nazis had "enough bodies to find anybody they want" at Katyń proved prophetic. On July 4, 1943, the Germans made yet another shocking announcement. A plane carrying Polish prime minister and commander in chief Władysław Sikorski had crashed on takeoff at Gibraltar. The German propaganda service called him "the last victim of Katyń." The general was en route back to London after inspecting Polish troops in the Middle East. After lifting off the runway, his plane had flown a few hundred yards before falling, mysteriously, into the Mediterranean. Several others had been killed, including Sikorski's daughter, Zofia, a high-ranking member of the Polish Women's Auxiliary, and Lieutenant Colonel Victor A. Cazalet, a member of the British Parliament and British liaison to General Sikorski. Only the Czech pilot, Edward Prchal, who was found floating in the sea, survived.

The blow to Poles everywhere was staggering, but particularly so in German-occupied Poland, where Sikorski was embraced as a father figure by millions of his beleaguered countrymen. For a majority of these Poles, he personified an embattled Polish state struggling valiantly and against great odds for the nation's independence. Time and time again he had spoken to them by radio from London, appealing to their patience, their perseverance, their courage, even asking them to lay down their lives to achieve the ultimate victory.

Was it possible that the Poles' own allies had victimized Sikorski through sabotage? Barely two hours after his death, German radio was broadcasting that claim. The following day the same report was trumpeted by the loudspeakers on Market Square to the Czarneks and other citizens of Kraków. Heavy-handed as the allegations were, they struck a raw nerve. They contained at least the remote possibility of truth. Before Sikorski left London, fears that he might be assassinated were widespread in his own government. In a cruel twist, Sikorski himself, as he left Cairo on the journey home, had dismissed these fears as inconsequential. Then came the crash at Gibraltar. Could chance alone explain such a tragedy? Had not Sikorski been a thorn in the side of Allied unity? Had he not weathered many stinging reproaches for his embarrassing questions about the Katyń murders? Would the transparency of Russian excuses otherwise have been exposed? These agonizing questions left many Poles convinced that, to their allies, Sikorski was expendable; that, in fact, he might have been the last victim of Katyń. German propaganda played skillfully on such suspicions. Shortly after the crash, a cartoon in the magazine *Das Reich* depicted Sikorski being entertained by a seductress. The caption read: "I'll put my cards on the table, General. I am from the British Secret Service. You don't fit in with Britain's plans any more. Will you take the tea, or do you prefer the aeroplane. . . . ?"

The suggestion that the British were responsible for Sikorski's death was a farfetched attempt to capitalize on recent strains in the alliance. It conveniently overlooked the fact that Britain had gone to war to save Poland. In Sikorski, Churchill saw the one man who could unite the factions of prewar Poland. Only Sikorski commanded the stature to bridge the deep animosities toward the U.S.S.R. that were left in his country after the Red Army's September 17, 1939, "stab in the back." Churchill had stressed these points to Stalin and others on many occasions. During the dark days when their governments alone had opposed the Nazi menace, Churchill and Sikorski had collaborated closely. "I loved that man," Churchill told Sikorski's successor, Stanisław Mikołajczyk, during their first meeting after the crash. "He was one of the truly great statesmen of this war."

More than the strong ties between the two men and their governments, a thorough investigation absolved the British from blame. As a part of its inquiry, the British Air Ministry retrieved the plane's broken fuselage from the Mediterranean and determined that it had been fractured on impact. The ministry's conclusion, announced on September 21, 1943, was that a defect in the rudders of the plane had caused the crash. The Air Ministry said it was impossible to say what caused this defect: "It has been established however, that this was not an act of sabotage. It is also clear that the pilot, an aviator of great experience and unusual abilities, was not to blame. An officer of the Polish Air Force was present throughout the whole investigation."

Yet doubts persisted. Stalin was disloyal enough to blame his own ally, telling the Yugoslavs in 1944 that the British had killed Sikorski. He claimed that the RAF had shot down the Liberator that bore the Polish leader. That such evidence might have been overlooked by Poles involved in the investigation was, of course, absurd. A more likely explanation was that Stalin himself had issued Sikorski's death warrant. At the time of the crash, Soviet superspy Kim Philby was in charge of British security for North Africa. Philby's knowledge of Sikorski's route and schedule, as well as his contacts along the way, could have greatly aided any Soviet plot to engineer the crash. No evidence has ever been found to link Philby to Sikorski's death. He did not become a target of suspicion until twenty years after the crash when, in 1963, he defected to Russia as one of the most successful Soviet spies of the Cold War period. A case against the Soviets could hardly be based on Philby's position alone. It is tempting to speculate that Stalin may have had the means to cause the crash. His motive seems much clearer. Even better than Churchill, Stalin knew Sikorski's position among the Poles. He knew also that Sikorski commanded great respect among the Allied leaders. In their personal relations, Sikorski had been firm with Stalin and had shown that he intended to fight at all costs to preserve Polish independence. When Sikorski's plane went down, the Soviet effort to groom a puppet regime for Poland was already several months old. Sikorski represented a formidable obstacle to any plan to impose such a regime on the Poles. Whether by accident or sabotage, his death greatly simplified the subversion of Poland.

The Germans blamed the crash on the British, but they could hardly be excluded as suspects. Early in the war, their agents had conducted numerous sabotage operations, aimed at Gibraltar, from an office in Spain. The power station, fuel dumps, parked aircraft, and food stores had all been hit by the Abwehr. These operations were suspended in mid-1941. Then, about a month before Sikorski's plane went down, a decision was reached to resume them. But again no evidence was found to link the Germans to the crash.

Coming when it did, only weeks after the discoveries at Katyń, Sikorski's death seemed too convenient. Evidence of sabotage was not found, but conclusive proof of an accident was not found either. Continuing doubts persisted. On November 12, 1952, Sumner Welles, who was U.S. under secretary of state at the time of the crash, told a House committee investigating the Katyń murders, "I have always believed that there was sabotage." Welles noted that Sikorski had narrowly escaped death in a similar incident the year before in Montreal. "To put it mildly, it would seem to be an odd coincidence," Welles concluded. Welles gave no indication who might have been responsible. Many Poles shared his view and still do today.

If sabotage did occur, even the Poles themselves could not be ruled out as suspects. The widespread fears in their London government on the eve of Sikorski's departure for the Middle East centered on threats from within, not without. The attitude of Anders's army and of Polish civilians in the Middle East presented a serious problem for Sikorski. Many were contemptuous of their government's conciliatory attitude and policies toward the Soviets. These efforts had involved untold pain and sacrifice, but what was there to show for them? Many of Anders's men had left families in the U.S.S.R. and despaired of ever seeing them again. Thousands of his men came from the eastern provinces now claimed by the Soviets. To these men, it appeared that they were being asked to fight and die for an alliance that would deny them the right to return to their homes in Tarnopol, Wilno, Lwów, and hundreds of other cities, towns, and villages in eastern Poland. Such despair kindled desperation, and the fear that a half-crazed Pole in the Middle East might make an attempt on Sikorski's life was not to be taken lightly.

By the spring of 1943, the rumblings of deep discontent in the army-in-exile and among dispossessed civilians in the Middle East were reverberating loudly in the government-in-exile. They would erupt openly in the aftermath of the Polish prime minister's death. Paweł Zaleski, who later became Mikołajczyk's aide and confidant, told me that "Mikołajczyk regretted deeply that General Sikorski did not follow the advice of those closest to him in London and cancel his trip to the Middle East. He blamed General Anders's opposition to policies of the government-in-exile for forcing Sikorski to go. Had Anders not instigated this campaign, he believed, Sikorski would be alive."

Who had opposed Sikorski so bitterly? Was there no cohesion at all among the London Poles? At times it did appear that Sikorski held his squabbling colleagues together by sheer force of personality. It had been evident for some time that the London government had never fully bridged the deep divisions of interwar Poland. It had been organized as a coalition in the aftermath of the September 1939 collapse, when the Poles' confident assumptions about Beck's policies had proven so disastrous. The powerful Piłsudski faction, which had run Poland for almost a generation, had been completely discredited by the defeat. The pieces had been picked up in France in the fall of 1940 by four major opposition groups—the National, Peasant, Socialist, and Christian Labor parties. These parties united behind Sikorski as prime minister and commander in chief of the armed forces. But a Piłsudski loyalist, Władysław Raczkiewicz, had administered the oath of office as president. Because of his pro-French orientation, August Zaleski, another Piłsudski loyalist, was made foreign minister. The diplomatic service under Zaleski came almost entirely from the Piłsudski faction. Later, because Sikorski admired his war record and military expertise, General Kazimierz Sosnkowski was made a member of the cabinet. He, too, was an ardent Piłsudski loyalist. Until the collapse of France, the Piłsudski loyalists were content to lick their wounds and bide their time. But the debacle that ended at Dunkirk caused a sharp change in their attitude. Poland's performance the previous fall, many of them began to claim, had not been that bad. In hindsight, the Wehrmacht's victory seemed inevitable; at least, the Piłsudski loyalists were emboldened to begin making that claim. And gradually they began to exert more influence in the new government. This was true not only in London, but also within the hierarchy of the secret state within Poland. General Sosnkowski himself recruited many of the leaders of the Home Army, and many of those chosen by him had been loyal to the government before the war.

Internal dissension had first flared into the open with the signing of the Polish-Soviet Agreement of July 30, 1941. Three members of the Polish Cabinet, including Sosnkowski and Zaleski, had resigned in protest. Over the next two years, relations between the two countries continued to deteriorate and the Polish government became irreconcilably divided over policy toward the Soviets. For the Piłsudski loyalists compromise was not possible. The Red Army's great victories made no difference. Attempts by Western politicians to placate Stalin left the Piłsudski faction increasingly embittered and isolated on an international level. But their hard-line anti-Soviet stand tapped a deep wellspring of support in the army-in-exile and in Poland itself. Moderates like Sikorski felt that, unfortunately, the British and Americans were right: The Soviets were certain to emerge from the war in a powerful position; Poland was unlikely to survive as an independent state unless some accommodation was reached with the Soviets.

As long as Sikorski lived, the government-in-exile wore a veneer of unity. With his death, it collapsed overnight. His responsibilities were immediately split between Mikołajczyk, a moderate and Sikorski's choice to follow him as prime minister, and Sosnkowski, an inveterate anti-Soviet who became commander in chief of the armed forces. Two more different men could not have been placed at the helm of the Polish government. Sosnkowski was conservative, outspoken, and impetuous. Although he fought with Piłsudski's Legions in World War I, he had opposed the 1926 coup. That upheaval had shocked Sosnkowski and left him deeply disillusioned. He had attempted suicide as a result of it. Fourteen years later, his reaction to the coup was one factor that had made him acceptable to Sikorski as a leader of the new government. A second factor was his legendary courage. Sosnkowski had fought valiantly to the bitter end during the 1939 September campaign. He and his troops were among the last to make their way across the border into Hungary.

In contrast, Mikołajczyk was quiet and unassuming. Born in 1901, he had grown up on a farm near Poznań. He fought and was wounded in the Russo-Polish War of 1920. His political baptism had come as an organizer for the Peasant Party, the largest political party in Poland. Later, he had been elected on its ticket as the youngest member of the Sejm, or Polish parliament. In 1939, he had been mobilized to fight the Germans and had escaped with his regiment into Hungary at the end of the campaign. Once he reached France, Sikorski had asked him, because of his prominence in the Peasant Party, to replace the aging pianist, Ignacy Jan Paderewski, as speaker of the parliament-in-exile. Although he was largely self-taught, Mikołajczyk was a voracious reader, and by the time he became prime minister had developed an encyclopedic knowledge of world affairs.

In the months that followed the crash at Gibraltar, Mikołajczyk struggled to carry forward Sikorski's policies, in particular to bring about the reestablishment of diplomatic relations with the Soviet Union. He knew that Poland faced an uncertain future unless cooperation with the Soviets could be achieved. Like Sikorski, he believed that solutions could only be found by cooperating closely with Poland's British and American allies. What Mikołajczyk did not know, as 1943 came to an end, was that Churchill, Roosevelt, and Stalin were about to reach an agreement in principle on the future of Poland. They would make that decision in Tehran, at the first face-to-face meeting of the Big Three, without consulting Mikołajczyk. In fact, the new Polish prime minister would not be told of the agreement until October of the following year. By then there was little chance that he, or anyone else, could save the government-in-exile.

* * *

A few of the wheelchair patients began arriving well in advance of the service. The ambulatory patients came last, and by the time Maria Pawulska arrived, people packed the vestibule and corridor of the Tehran hospital. They suffered from many individual ailments—typhus, malaria, and dysentery, among others, caused by two harsh years in the Soviet Union—and one collective malady, an aching soul-sickness brought on by the death of General Sikorski. Dusk was gathering as the memorial service began. Candles lit by a priest cast long shadows across the room. A soft half light mingled with tears on many faces. Contained sobs punctuated the words of the priest. An official from the Polish consulate rose to speak. The Poles must carry on, he said, in the face of an irreparable loss.

"We had the feeling that we were pulling ourselves out of a dark hole, but had begun sliding back," Maria told me. "I'm sure this related to the news about Katyń just before [Sikorski's death]. Somehow, I can't remember that—just this feeling that we were recovering. Then came this great shock. I couldn't believe it. We felt it was the worst thing that could have happened. All our hopes rested with Sikorski. We felt that he held our future in his hands, that he was leading us back to Poland. . . . It was a feeling of total despair: What now? What now? Everything is lost."

The July 11, 1943, edition of a weekly called *The Pole in Iran* reflected the Poles' universal sense of loss. A thick black border framed the entire front page. A banner headline proclaimed "FUNERAL DRUMS." Below that was the first line of the Polish national anthem: "Poland is not yet dead, as long as we live!" The heading over the main story read "IMMEASURABLY TRAGIC NEWS." That story began: "He trusted the people of his nation. Now it is time that we prove that his faith was well founded."

After two years of barely surviving in the Soviet Union, the Pawulski family found little relief in Iran. While living on the beach at Pahlevi, Mrs. Pawulska became seriously ill after eating a greasy lamb stew. The family's diet in the U.S.S.R. had been practically devoid of fat. Almost immediately she suffered an attack of bleeding dysentery. During a frightening ride by truck convoy through the spectacular mountains that separated the Caspian coast from the capital, her condition had worsened, causing her to hallucinate frequently. On arrival in Tehran, she was taken straight from the truck to a clinic and from there to a hospital, where she stayed until early December. In addition to dysentery, she was also diagnosed as having typhoid fever. During the long period while her mother was in the hospital, Maria assumed responsibility as the head of household. She found Tadeusz in a nearby school for young boys being groomed for cadet school and visited him frequently. During these visits, it seemed to her that the noncommissioned officers in charge were excessively abusive. Tadeusz was being trained, she felt, to be an orderly, to polish shoes and run errands for the noncoms. As a result, she wrote a short note in behalf of her mother, asking Polish authorities to permit Tadeusz to rejoin his family. Maria knew her mother was too sick to sign the letter, but took it to her anyway. At the hospital, she put a pen in Mrs. Pawulska's hand and guided both across the bottom of the page. The signature that emerged was barely more than a straight line, but the authorities accepted it and Tadeusz was released.

Mrs. Pawulska had barely recovered when Maria suffered the first of two life-threatening bouts with pleuropneumonia. She had first suffered chills in late winter while standing in line for food. The chill kept getting worse and finally turned into pneumonia. Her temperature began to rise and she began experiencing acute pains in her side. When she mentioned the pain, pointing to her side, the nurse at the clinic had told her, "That's something for old people." Later, a female physician examined Maria and became quite irritated. "No wonder this girl is in pain!" she said. "She has pleurisy." Immediately Maria was taken by special bus to a large civilian hospital. Every bump over the stones caused her excruciating pain. Her recovery took several months and she had been out of the hospital for only two weeks when she suffered a relapse. This was too much. Toughened by all the perils of the past two years, the Pawulskis were not prone to tears. During all that time, Maria could remember crying only once, that being at the memorial service for Sikorski. Her mother was similarly stoic. But she too had been overcome after one visit to the hospital during Maria's second illness. Her daughter was noticeably worse and had told her on that occasion, "Mommy, I don't want to die."

Though she was still in the hospital, Maria's full recovery was at last under way when the world's three most powerful leaders came to Teheran. Elaborate security precautions cloaked their visit in the utmost secrecy, but word of it crept out to the hospital ward where Maria was recovering and to thousands of others in the Polish refugee camps that still rimmed the city.

"Our feeling was that they had come to set matters straight," Maria said. "We had the feeling that something good was finally being done to correct the injustices suffered by the Polish people. We felt that finally there was light at the end of the tunnel, that bright and sunny days were ahead. Obviously we had the wrong idea. It may have been based on nothing more than a childlike perception or naïveté, but that was how we felt."

The Second Republic of Poland would not recover from the blow about to be imparted. The first of World War II's Big Three conferences got under way in Tehran on November 28, 1943. That evening, Stalin and Churchill met over cigars and coffee after dinner for a heart-to-heart talk about Poland, with Molotov and Eden present. The exploratory conversation took place without Roosevelt, whose absence was probably prompted by concern about potential domestic political repercussions. With the 1944 presidential election less than a year away, Roosevelt was anxious not to antagonize his strong base of support among the six to seven million Americans of Polish descent. His most trusted adviser, Harry Hopkins, felt the Polish problem was "political dynamite." For this reason, as he would later make clear, Roosevelt was anxious to avoid a formal commitment on Poland's frontiers that might be leaked. Besides, the broad outlines of an agreement on Poland had already begun to take a definite shape before the Big Three arrived in Tehran. There was no doubt how Stalin stood on the western Ukraine and western Byelorussia: He had annexed both areas two years earlier. In months of discussion in Washington, London, and Moscow, Britain and the United States had already indicated their willingness to back Stalin's demands.

By the time they met in Tehran, Churchill and Roosevelt had little bargaining power with Stalin. The Red Army's smashing victories earlier in the year at Stalingrad and in the Kursk Salient had broken the back of the Wehrmacht. It seemed likely that his armies would liberate Poland and the rest of Eastern Europe. During the same period, the Allies had decisively defeated Rommel's Afrika Korps, but it was hardly a comparable victory. The Italian campaign was just getting under way, but it was not represented as a second front. Meanwhile, Stalin continued to wait, impatiently, for the British and the Americans to launch their long-promised assault on the main part of the European continent.

In the course of their chat, Churchill hinted to Stalin that he and Roosevelt were prepared to make major concessions on the question of Poland's postwar frontiers. Churchill emphasized to Stalin that the security of the Soviet Union's western frontier was of paramount importance. Stalin cautiously asked if such an agreement could be worked out without the Poles present. When Churchill assured him that it could, Stalin responded by saying he favored a German-Polish frontier as far west as the Oder River. Churchill agreed that the entire Polish nation could be moved 150 miles west, "like soldiers taking two steps left close." At one point, he used three matches to illustrate how the Polish frontiers could be moved to the west in lockstep. Such a solution, of course, would permit the Soviets to keep the western Ukraine and western Byelorussia. Poland, in turn, would be compensated with German territory, East Prussia and land to the east of the Oder River. Churchill emphasized that he and Roosevelt did not have the legislative authority to commit formally to such a decision. Instead, he said, the Big Three should come to an agreement, which the Poles could then be pressed into accepting.

Formal discussions on Poland were not scheduled until the final day of the conference, December 1. The major matter to be settled was where and when to launch the second front. Churchill's cherished plan for an attack on Europe's "soft underbelly" through the Balkans was rejected by Stalin and Roosevelt. That decision ended any prospect that the Western Allies would liberate Poland and other parts of Eastern Europe. Instead, a cross-Channel invasion of France, Operation Overlord, was approved for the following spring. Stalin agreed that the Red Army would time a major offensive in concert with Operation Overlord to pin down as many Wehrmacht divisions as possible. Both Churchill and Roosevelt knew how essential it would be to have the support of the Red Army during the crucial period when an Allied amphibious force was establishing a toehold in Europe. That knowledge would make it even more difficult for either of them to oppose the Soviet dictator on the matter of Poland.

But why should they disagree? Roosevelt's position in preparing for the conference was that most of the problems that separated Russia and her Western allies could be solved if he and Stalin had closer personal rapport. Before leaving for Tehran, he had told his advisers that he planned to talk man-to-man with Stalin and appeal to him "on grounds of high morality." His chance came on the last day of the conference. Shortly after 3:00 P.M., he, Stalin, Harriman, Molotov, and their interpreters gathered for a private session. Roosevelt told Stalin that the upcoming presidential campaign put him in an awkward position. Because of it, he could not be publicly associated with any decision to change Poland's frontiers, even though he personally agreed that they should be shifted to the Curzon Line in the east and the Oder River in the west. He said he was not sure he would run again, but might be forced to if the war continued. If he did run, he said he did not want to risk losing the six to seven million Polish-American votes.

In his separate conversations with Churchill and Roosevelt, Stalin had learned a great deal: The Big Three would decide the future of Poland's frontiers *without* the Poles; that decision would then be forced on the Poles whether they liked it or not. It was also evident that neither Churchill nor Roosevelt would put up much of a fight in behalf of the Poles. The final political session of the conference began at 6:00 P.M. on December 1. Roosevelt emphasized at the outset that he hoped relations between the Polish government-in-exile and the Soviets would be resumed. Stalin immediately interjected the absurd complaint that the London Poles were cooperating with the Nazis. It was the excuse he had manufactured during the Katyń controversy to break relations with the London Poles seven months earlier, one he would repeat at every opportunity until the end of the war. Churchill offered the reminder that Britain had gone to war over Poland, then assured Stalin that his allies were determined "to achieve the security of the Soviet western frontier and so prevent an attack by Germany in the future."

But the mere mention of negotiations with the Polish government-in-exile apparently set Stalin off. "Yesterday there was no mention of negotiations with the Polish government. Yesterday it was said that the Polish government must be directed to do this and that." He continued by drawing a sharp distinction between the Polish people and the government in London. "We broke off relations with that government not out of any whim on our part, but because the Polish government joined Hitler in slandering the Soviet Union." Stalin concluded his diatribe by claiming that agents of the Polish government-in-exile were collaborating with the Germans, in fact fighting the Communist partisans in Poland. His charges were based on a growing number of incidents in which Communist partisans, parachuted into Poland by the Red Air Force, had provoked reprisals on the part of the Germans. Such incidents had been reported to the Polish government in London, which had become alarmed enough to report the problem to the British. No one challenged Stalin's groundless charges and the discussion shifted to the fine points of the Curzon Line.

Eden did interrupt Stalin at one point to ask if by the Curzon Line he meant the "Ribbentrop-Molotov Line." Stalin's reply was "Call it whatever you like." Molotov quickly attempted to explain that the two lines were really the same. Eden pointed out there were important differences. The group then gathered around two large maps, one

British and one American, to discuss the specific changes to be made in Poland's frontier. Stalin noted that the maps incorrectly placed Lwów on the western side of the frontier and asked Molotov to fetch a map showing the Soviet version of the Curzon Line. Churchill pointed out that the land the Poles would receive along the Oder and in East Prussia was more valuable than the Pripet Marshes, a huge swampy area in the east, which they would lose. The reconstructed Poland would also have a stronger industrial base, Stalin pointed out. By then, Molotov had produced the Soviet map and a telegram from Lord Curzon listing place names. Peering at Stalin's proof, Churchill proclaimed that he was "not prepared to make a great squawk about Lwów." He said the Poles "would be wise" to take the advice of the Big Three. At several points during the discussion, Churchill had emphasized his intention to present the decision to the Poles once it had been agreed to in principle. Furthermore, he said he would tell the Poles that the terms were not only fair, but also the best they were likely to get. Roosevelt hardly said a word during the entire discussion.

Stalin had made a clever choice in pushing the Curzon Line as Poland's eastern frontier. Its variations from the Ribbentrop-Molotov Line were slight, but its British origins made it much more palatable. When first proposed in 1920, it required concessions unsatisfactory to both the Poles and the Soviets. Not once did Stalin or anyone else mention highly questionable circumstances that clouded the Line's validity. At one point in 1920, either through clerical error or through intentional falsification, Lwów had been placed on the Soviet side, disregarding the city's identity as an ancient wellspring of Polish culture. In the December 1 session, Molotov had produced a version of the map that put Lwów on the east side of the line. This map had been tacitly accepted. All this was a façade to capitalize on the fact that twenty-four years earlier the British foreign secretary, Lord Curzon, had lent his name to the Line and the mediation process. Beyond the façade, there was a certain substance to Stalin's claim. The Poles had, in fact, forced a humiliating territorial settlement on the Soviets in the 1921 Treaty of Riga. Their unexpected and total victory the previous year at the Battle of Warsaw had permitted the Poles to drive the Soviets far to the west of the Curzon Line. The territory they acquired as a result was neither Polish nor Russian. Instead, it contained large numbers of Ukrainians, Byelorussians, and Jews, who had chafed under Polish rule. It was a no-man's-land and Stalin's claim to it was as good as that of the Poles. For Allies who felt beholden to Stalin, it, too, was not a matter to squawk about.

But the Polish government-in-exile was now on the road to ruin. Its leaders would not learn until late in the following year about the fateful decisions taken in Tehran. Churchill would spend much of that time attempting to convince them that they should willingly accept the decisions already agreed to. But how could they? The Big Three's secret agreement meant that Poland would lose more than half of her prewar territory, and a third of her population. Many men who were fighting and dying in the Polish army-in-exile came from the provinces to be relinquished. So did many in the government-in-exile. There was hardly a Pole alive who could not count friends and relatives among those from cities like Wilno, Tarnopol, and Lwów. To sign such an agreement meant that Poles from the east could never return to their homeland. The Soviet occupation between late 1939 and mid-1941 had already shown what such an agreement would mean to the unfortunate Poles still there.

Had the decision been presented as a fait accompli, the Poles, no doubt, would have mobilized to oppose it. It seems likely that they could have aroused considerable sympathy in the West, enough to complicate matters at Yalta where, fifteen months later, the Tehran agreement-in-principle would be implemented. Because the Poles did not know that the Big Three had already decided, they were put in an impossible position. In the months that followed the Tehran Conference, they would seem ungrateful, implacable, even irresponsible as Churchill and Eden pressed them to accept the Big Three solution. The British leaders became increasingly impatient as the Red Army rolled the Eastern Front inexorably west into Poland. Churchill and Eden knew that unless the Poles accepted Stalin's terms, relations between the Soviets and the Poles would not be restored. That might not have been such a pressing problem in 1944 if Churchill and Roosevelt had gotten any concessions from Stalin at Tehran. They did suggest that he restore diplomatic relations with the legitimate government of Poland. After Stalin's outburst, the matter was dropped. It would have been a small concession for Stalin after the Poles, in absentia, had given up more than half of their country's prewar territory. But there is no indication that the Soviet ruler was willing to make even the slightest concession to them.

More than eighteen months earlier, during the long trek southwest from Buzuluk to the port of Krasnovodsk, all contact between Zofia Hoffman and her mother, and their family in Poland had been severed. After joining the army-in-exile in Buzuluk, the two women were among those evacuated from the Soviet Union in late March and early April 1942. About forty thousand army personnel and civilians had crossed the Caspian Sea to Iran in that group. After landing on the beach at Pahlevi, Zofia and her mother spent a brief time recuperating before going on to Tehran, where they lived briefly at 15 Sepaselar Street in the home of an elderly, well-to-do Iranian who held a high post in the government. Spare rooms all over the city were being requisitioned for Polish soldiers. The elderly Iranian had pleaded with authorities not to billet men in his home. His reason soon became apparent to Zofia and her mother. Shortly after they arrived, their host invited them to join the rest of his family for coffee in the main sitting room. He was a highly cultured man with polished manners who spoke fluent French. Zofia and her mother had barely seated themselves when a young woman of stunning beauty, a fresh rose pinned to her Western-style dress, glided into the room. The household's newest wife had arrived. There were other women in the house, but clearly none of them commanded such an exalted position. Were they older wives? This question was never answered for Zofia and her mother. These coffees, which became a daily ritual, were as close as the young wife came to venturing out in public. It was evident that her beauty would remain a closely guarded family secret.

Zofia and her mother went from Tehran to Iraq, Syria, Palestine, and finally Egypt with the main force of the army-in-exile. Maria Neuhoff, Zofia's mother, remained a "senior private" during this period, but Zofia began a rapid rise in rank. Both women had begun their military careers as privates peeling rotten carrots in Buzuluk. Because of her organizational ability and background as an attorney, Zofia had risen rapidly and was serving as an inspector in the Women's Auxiliary by the time she reached Cairo. A major step up in responsibility came in early fall 1943, when she was summoned to London as deputy commander to Colonel Maria Leśniak, who was commander in chief of all Polish women's forces. She accepted on condition that her mother be transferred to London as quickly as possible.

Zofia left Cairo on October 8, 1943, in a small plane with two other passengers and an RAF pilot who took them hopscotching south across the African desert and then over the jungles of the Belgian Congo (now Zaire). One of the passengers was a close friend, Mrs. Bronisława Wysłouchowa, the chief inspector of the Women's Auxiliary Forces. During the Nazi-Soviet honeymoon, Mrs. Wysłouchowa had been beaten and tortured by the NKVD in Moscow's Lubyanka prison. General Anders had personally demanded and secured her release shortly after his own release on August 4, 1941. In the Belgian Congo the women stayed overnight in a convent. After mass and breakfast the next morning, the mother superior prayed for their continued safety and gave each a small figurine of the Mother of Christ exquisitely carved in ivory. It was the only likeness of the Virgin Mary with Negroid features Zofia had ever seen.

The small party reached Nigeria on October 13, then flew north up the Atlantic coast, reaching Lisbon two days later. Because of Portugal's neutrality, Zofia and the others had changed from their military uniforms into civilian clothes at the previous stop. The brief stop in a neutral country where the International Red Cross was prominently represented afforded Zofia her first chance to get specific information about her family in Poland. As soon as the plane landed, she went straight to Red Cross authorities to request that a search be made. A brief message came back the next day, October 16. It confirmed that Ewa, her uncle Zbigniew, and her aunt Anna were alive and still living at 69 Zadworzańska Street in Lwów. Zofia and her small party flew on to Ireland and London that same day.

CHAPTER 19

The Whitewash

<><><><><><><><

While Stalin was in Tehran, his personal physician, N. N. Burdenko, who was also the chief surgeon of the Red Army, was organizing a Soviet investigation of the murders in Katyń Forest. The Red Army had liberated the woods west of Smolensk on September 25, 1943, and Burdenko had arrived there the next day to take a preliminary look. Over the next four months, he coordinated the work of a "Special Commission for Ascertaining and Investigating the Circumstances of the Shooting of Polish Officer Prisoners by the German-Fascist Invaders in Katyń Forest." The commission's ponderous name, spurning even the pretense of impartiality, was attached to a process and findings that verged on the farcical.

The commission had no members from countries other than the Soviet Union. Even the Poles, including pro-Soviet Poles in Russia, were not privy to its work, which was carried out in utmost secrecy. Its important findings were completely at odds with those of the Wehrmacht, the technical commission of the Polish Red Cross, and the international commission.

In a few respects, the Soviet commission did concur with the earlier investigations. It agreed that the men had all been shot from behind at point-blank range with their heads bent forward, and that the caliber of ammunition used was 7.65 millimeters. It, too, held that "as a rule" the bullets struck in the area of the occipital bone and had been fired from pistols. These same methods had been used by the Germans to execute many Russians in Orël, Voronezh, Krasnodar, and Smolensk, according to the Soviet report.

But the question that mattered most was: When were the men killed? Here the Soviet commission split sharply with the German-sponsored investigations. The Soviet report claimed that the Polish officers spent their last days in three camps in the vicinity of Smolensk and were engaged in road repair and construction. Between mid-July and early August, the Germans had overrun the camps before the men could be evacuated, according to the Soviets. When the guards fled, many of the men had tried to escape but were quickly rounded up by the Germans. Some were shot and hauled by truck to Katyń Forest. Others were taken alive to the forest, said the Soviets, and then executed.

When the Eastern Front began collapsing, the Soviets claimed that the Germans decided to hide their ugly deed by exhuming the bodies and removing incriminating evidence (i.e., papers dated after 1940) from the pockets of the dead Poles. The Soviets said these operations had been carried out with the help of five hundred Soviet prisoners of war who were later shot by the Germans as potentially incriminating witnesses. The Germans had then staged their April propaganda show to sow discord among the Allies, according to the Soviets.

In contrast to a voluminous report of more than three hundred pages prepared by the Germans on their investigation, the Soviet commission's findings and conclusions took up only thirty-eight pages. Thirty of these pages dealt with statements from local citizens who allegedly saw Polish officers in the Smolensk-Katyń area in 1941. Many of these witnesses said they saw the men being transported to Katyń. Some said they heard shots being fired. Several of the Soviet witnesses recanted testimony already given in the German-sponsored investigations. One witness cited in the Soviet report, Alexandra M. Moskovskaya, said that in March 1943 she found a man in her woodshed who claimed to have escaped from the group of five hundred Russian POWs forced by the Germans to dig up the Polish officers. She testified that the man told her that he escaped in April 1943. Clearly the man could not have told the woman about his escape *before* it occurred. A misprint, perhaps? Lapses and inconsistencies permeated the Soviet report. The document's errors, coupled with its glaring omissions, raised more questions than it answered.

Only a few paragraphs of medical analysis were presented to support the report's most important conclusion—that the Poles had been executed "about two years ago, i.e., between September and December of 1941." This conclusion was based entirely on the appearance of the bodies and the general state of the men's clothing. The report quoted a Soviet pathologist, Dr. K. P. Zubkov, who found that "the metal parts of the clothing—belt buckles, button hooks, and spikes on shoe soles, etc.—were not heavily rusted, and in some cases the metal still retained its polish." Dr. Zubkov also testified that "there was no complete disintegration of the tissues. . . ." and that while observing bodies being removed from the graves "I did not see a single case of bodies falling apart or any member being torn off." In contrast, the international commission had cited the expert opinion of Dr. Orsos of Hungary, who observed calcification inside many victims' skulls. He had published detailed studies demonstrating that calcification would not begin to appear until a body had been interred for about three years.

In its conclusions, the report held that parts of the bodies were of "almost normal color." In addition to making these macroscopic observations, the report said, "medico-legal experts removed the necessary material for subsequent microscopic and chemical studies in laboratory conditions." No results of laboratory studies were presented in the report.

The Soviet commission's report simply ignored many obvious questions raised by its own findings:

1. What evidence did it have that the graves in Katyń Forest did, in fact, contain eleven thousand bodies, the number cited in the first Soviet reactions to Goebbels's announcement and in the commission's own report? No such evidence was offered. The commission's report simply noted that 925 bodies had been exhumed. The total of eleven thousand was close to that cited by German propaganda when the massacre was announced. The number closely approximated the number of Polish officers captured by the Soviets in 1939. A number substantially lower would still leave officers unaccounted for. In using the number 11,000, did the Soviets hope to deflect further questions from the Poles?

2. The Soviet report said that the Germans killed the Poles sometime between August and December of 1941. How could the Germans have concealed such information for almost two years without the highly efficient Polish underground finding out? Was it possible that the Germans captured *all* eleven thousand of the men ostensibly held in the three camps near Smolensk? The Soviets admitted that some of the men dispersed when the guards left. Surely not all were caught by the Germans. The testimony of anyone who had escaped would certainly have greatly buttressed the Soviet case.

3. If the Polish officers were captured and killed by the Germans between September and December of 1941, why was this information withheld from the Poles? Sikorski, Anders, Kot, and others all met with Stalin and other senior Soviet leaders during this period. The Poles were told over and over again that their men had been released, that the Soviets had no idea where they were. Furthermore, the

Soviets had every reason to tell the Poles if they knew that the Germans had captured and killed their men. Such information would have further inflamed the Poles against Germany and greatly eased tensions about Soviet treatment of Polish prisoners.

4. Did the Soviet commission have any evidence to support its claim that five hundred Soviet POWs had been shot by the Germans after digging the graves of the Polish officers? The report simply leveled this charge, but offered nothing to substantiate it. Presumably the Germans would have buried these men with the Poles. Any evidence that such liquidations actually occurred would have been extremely damaging to the German account of the crime.

5. The Soviets claimed that the men may have been killed in August 1941. If this was true, why would they have been wearing overcoats and heavy winter clothes?

These were all obvious questions of paramount importance, which the Soviet report failed to address. But other important questions had been overlooked as well. What caused the puncture wounds on some of the bodies? The German, Red Cross, and independent commissions all cited the four-cornered Soviet bayonet blade, but these wounds were not mentioned in the Soviet report. Where did the cord used to tie some victims' hands come from? The Soviet report did not mention this issue.

In addition to all these points, many practical questions surrounded the documents found on the bodies of the murdered Poles. If the men had been killed in 1941, the Germans had taken a colossal risk in dating the murders a year earlier. Public verification that a single card or letter had been written by one of the Poles *after* the spring of 1940 would destroy the entire German case. The Soviet commission claimed that several documents dated between November 12, 1940, and June 6, 1941, had been found in the graves. Among them were one letter, two postcards (only one postmarked), five receipts, and a paper icon with a signature on the back. None of these documents was removed from the graves in the presence of neutral observers. No evidence was offered to authenticate the signatures on any of these documents. In contrast, the Germans had removed many documents in the presence of neutral, even hostile observers. They also saved thousands of letters, cards, photographs, and other personal possessions found in the graves.

The Soviet commission carried out its preliminary investigation between late September 1943 and early January 1944. It claimed to have exhumed 925 bodies during the week of January 16–23 to identify them and to determine causes of death and time of burial. Its members interviewed a number of witnesses during this period, and at the end of that week they staged an extravaganza for Western newsmen. Seventeen foreign correspondents, including representatives of the Associated Press, the *New York Times*, Reuters, and the British Broadcasting Corporation were taken to the forest for a press briefing and to witness a formal session of the commision. Kathleen Harriman, the twenty-five-year-old daughter of U.S. ambassador Averell Harriman, went along, chaperoned by John Melby, the Third Secretary in the embassy. At the time, she was the only American woman in Moscow. She had come there after working in London as a correspondent for *Newsweek* and was filling in unofficially for the Office of War Information. Her father later said he had wanted an embassy observer present and felt the Soviets would be less likely to turn down a request involving a member of his own family.

The Soviets had first planned to take the correspondents to Smolensk by car. But when Miss Harriman was added to the group, they rolled out a special train belonging to the Soviet Foreign Office. W. H. Lawrence of the *New York Times* described the trip as "probably the most unusual press junket in the history of the world—and certainly of the Soviet Union." He wrote that the train came "complete with well-heated, lighted, plush-carpeted compartment cars and a bright cheery dining car whose windows were curtained in pastel green."

The newsmen were the first foreigners to visit Smolensk since its liberation. Presumably because the route was crowded with higher-priority military traffic, the 125-mile trip took eighteen hours. After being fed two breakfasts, the entourage left the train about 10:00 A.M. for a brief tour of war-ravaged Smolensk. They found most of its buildings in ruins, its bridges over the Dnieper River all destroyed. One temporary span had been put back across the waterway and the group crossed it en route to Katyń Forest about ten miles west of the city. There, the commission chairman, Burdenko; a battery of movie cameras; and long rows of corpses were waiting. The group was taken inside a large heated tent to watch an autopsy. The stench was almost overpowering. The *Time* correspondent wrote that a Soviet physician "sliced chunks off the brain like cold meat, knifed through the chest and pulled out an atrophied organ. 'Heart,' he said, holding it out to Kathy. Then he slit a leg muscle. 'Look how well preserved the meat is,' he said." Apparently Miss Harriman did not flinch from these gruesome sights.

What the press entourage saw and did was carefully controlled at all times. No bodies were selected at random by the group for examination by medical experts. No one saw any documents removed from any of the bodies. In the afternoon, the commission held a press conference at which one member, V. P. Potemkin, read a prepared statement outlining its principal conclusions. The press had an opportunity to ask a few questions and was permitted to examine items taken from the pockets of the murdered men. They were displayed in a museumlike atmosphere under heavy glass. The collection included letters, newspapers, and money, among other things. One letter bore a Moscow postmark as late as June 1941.

That night the commission examined five witnesses whose testimony had been summarized earlier in the day by Potemkin. Its members were seated at a long table covered in red baize. The press was strung out along a similar table to one side. The witnesses, under the glare of klieg lights and movie cameras, sat facing the commission.

In her report on the visit, Miss Harriman wrote that the witnesses "were very well rehearsed, and they appeared subdued rather than nervous, their pieces having been learned by heart." In his report, Melby said: "All the statements were glibly given, as though by rote. Under questioning the witnesses became hestitant and stumbled, until they were dismissed by the Commission." Melby pointed out that "the atmosphere at the session grew progressively tense as the correspondents asked one pointed and usually rude question after another." About midnight, sensing that the session was heading downhill, the Soviets abruptly announced that the correspondents' train would leave in one hour.

A reporter for the pro-Soviet Union of Polish Patriots had accompanied the group to Katyń. Melby said the man "slept noisily" through most of the press conference and later told him that the investigation "has no interest for the Poles in Russia since it is obvious that the Germans committed the crimes. . . ."

Melby reported that officials of the Soviet Foreign Office "were almost unduly anxious on the return trip to be assured that we were convinced." Several in the group, including the chief correspondent for the Associated Press, Henry C. Cassidy, ribbed Soviet press officials that there was only one convincing item of evidence to support their case: The murdered men still had their boots on. On the Russian side of the battlefield, Cassidy pointed out, "you lose your boots when you lose your life." Cassidy later said the newsmen "were not convinced by what the Russians showed us that the Germans had done it." Their reports, for the most part straightforward accounts of what they had seen and heard, were not cleared by Soviet censors for several days.

Both Miss Harriman and Melby wrote highly skeptical reports of what they saw, but their conclusions were sharply at variance with their own observations. Miss Harriman concluded:

> The testimonial evidence provided by the Commission and witnesses was minute in detail and by American standards petty. We were expected to accept the statements of the high ranking Soviet officials as true, because they said it was true.
>
> Despite this it is my opinion that the Poles were murdered by the Germans. The most convincing evidence to uphold this was the methodical manner in which the job was done, something the Commission thought not sufficiently important to stress.

And Melby concluded:

> It is apparent that the evidence in the Russian case is incomplete in several respects, that it is badly put together, and that the show was put on for the benefit of the correspondents without opportunity for independent investigation or verification. On balance, however, and despite the loopholes the Russian case is convincing.

Ambassador Harriman conferred with his daughter and Melby after they returned to Moscow. On January 25, he cabled the secretary of state: "The general evidence and testimony are inconclusive, but Kathleen and Embassy staff member believe probability massacre perpetrated by Germans."

Eight years later, Miss Harriman and Melby both reversed their conclusions. On November 12, 1952, they told a select committee of the U.S. House of Representatives then investigating the crime that subsequent revelations had convinced them that the Russians, not the Germans, were guilty.

The select congressional committee also heard evidence that Stalin personally ordered Burdenko to prepare a report showing that the Germans had committed the crime. On June 4, 1952, Boris Olshansky, a former mathematics professor at Voronezh State University who defected to the West in 1948, voluntarily testified about a private conversation in which Burdenko told him of Stalin's order. He said Burdenko and his (Olshansky's) father, also a physician, had been close friends in Voronezh; that following his father's death in 1929, Burdenko helped Olshansky financially to finish his education; and that in 1946 they visited in Burdenko's Moscow apartment for the last time. Olshansky testified that Burdenko told him on that occasion:

Katyns existed and are existing and will be existing. Anyone who will go and dig up things in our country, Russia, would find a lot of things. . . . I was appointed by Stalin personally to go to the Katyn place. All the corpses were four [sic] years old. . . . For me, as a medical man, this problem was quite clear. Our NKVD friends made a mistake.

Burdenko's words as quoted by Olshansky bore a remarkable similarity to the answer given to Colonel Berling (in 1943 a general in the Red Army) and other pro-Soviet Poles in the fall of 1940 when they asked about using the officers at Kozelsk and Starobelsk to form special units of the Red Army. "We made a blunder—we *did* make a blunder" was the reply they received from Beria and Merkulov, the top two men in the NKVD. Burdenko's comments and those of Beria and Merkulov suggest that in the wake of the Wehrmacht's quick and easy victories in Western Europe, which seemed to spur Soviet efforts to form Polish units in the Red Army, Soviet leaders may have regretted that the murdered Polish officers had not been kept for that purpose.

Burdenko's words also suggested something less than full enthusiasm for the investigation. That may explain why such an inept report was published by the Soviet special commission. The document was unanimously approved by Burdenko and the other members of the commission on January 24, 1944.

Six days after the report was published, on January 30, 1944, Polish troops in the Red Army paraded in Katyń Forest. An eyewitness quoted their commander, Colonel Berling, speaking in a ceremony at the gravesite:

Our inexorable foe, the German, wishes to destroy our whole nation because he desires to seize our land. The earth on which we Poles have, for centuries, lived. That is why the Germans destroy and murder our brothers in Poland. . . . That is why they murdered here in Katyn Forest the Polish officers and men. The blood of our brothers which was spilled in this forest, cries out for revenge.

Now we have arms in our hands, arms given to us by a friendly neighbor ally, by the Soviet Union. We must use these arms to liberate our oppressed Fatherland and to revenge the unheard of crime committed here by the Germans. Remember men and officers, remember the voices of our murdered brothers which call to us. We must answer this call.

The ringing cry for revenge was taken up at meetings all over the Soviet Union. It was directed not only at deported Poles, but also at ordinary Soviet citizens. A campaign was even organized to collect money to purchase a column of tanks to be called Avenger of Katyń.

The liberation of Poland was now under way. The first units of the Red Army had crossed the prewar frontier on January 4. Their arrival was preceded by a rash of incidents designed to discredit the Polish government-in-exile and its Home Army with the local citizenry. In an all-too-familiar pattern, Soviet agents were parachuted into Poland to carry out clumsy or ill-conceived attacks on German forces. None of these were coordinated with the Home Army. Predictably, the Germans responded with harsh reprisals. In several instances, the inhabitants of entire villages were liquidated as a result. Not understanding who was responsible for the provocations, local citizens increasingly blamed the Home Army. Compounding the confusion was a vituperative stream of Soviet propaganda designed to establish the claim that members of the Home Army were collaborating with the Nazis.

Despite these alarming incidents, the London government-in-exile decided to proceed with its long-planned Operation Burza, or Tempest. Local commanders of the Home Army were ordered to delay attacks against the retreating Wehrmacht until maximum support could be given the Red Army. The policy quickly proved disastrous as officer after officer of the Home Army was arrested and executed after coming to the Red Army's assistance against the Germans. Large numbers of partisans in the Home Army were also arrested and given the choice of joining the Red Army's Kościuszko Division under Colonel Berling or facing imprisonment and deportation. During this period, the Soviet attitude toward the Polish government-in-exile hardened considerably. Increasingly it became evident that relations between the two governments would not be restored unless the Poles accepted the Curzon Line as their eastern frontier and removed conservative, anti-Soviet elements from their government. Still unaware of the Tehran agreement-in-principle, the Poles appealed to the British and American governments for mediation. They, in turn, stepped up the pressure on the Polish government to accept the Soviet terms. On January 20, 1944, Churchill told Mikołajczyk: "If you do not act quickly, I cannot be responsible for anything that might take place."

The Pawulskis, minus Tadeusz, were among eight hundred Poles who boarded a British troop transport, the *Nevasa*, at Basra in Iraq near the border of Iran, toward the end of March 1944. They were among thousands of Polish refugees evacuated from the Soviet Union in 1942 who were being sent to more permanent settlements in the British Empire, principally in India and Africa. The family had left Tehran early in 1944 and moved briefly to another temporary camp at Ahwāz, Iran, one of the world's hottest cities. While there, Tadeusz, then fourteen, had enrolled in the *junak* precadet training program, and had been sent to Palestine. The family left for Basra soon after his departure.

The *Nevasa* was expected to sail in a convoy through the Persian Gulf, on through the Gulf of Oman, and to the port of Karachi on the Arabian Sea. A large number of Poles had already been sent in this direction. Among them was Zdzisław Peszkowski, who had gone on to Bombay where he was organizing an orphanage for Polish evacuees. Reports filtering back from those who had gone ahead were quite encouraging. India in particular was said to be a most hospitable environment. It was widely rumored on the *Nevasa* that one generous maharaja had made his palace and personal fortune available to Polish orphans.

The ship had just reached the Gulf of Oman when the captain received a disturbing report. The waters to the southeast, in the direction of Karachi, were filled with Japanese submarines. For the convoy to continue in that direction invited grave risk. Instead, the ships turned west toward the Arabian Peninsula and hugged the shoreline until reaching the heavily fortified port of Aden. The *Nevasa* and her sister ships anchored several hundred yards out in the harbor, waiting for the threat to pass. They bided their time for several days, waiting to make a quick dash across the open sea from Aden to Karachi. But the Japanese subs did not leave. Finally, the passengers were told that they would be taken south to camps set up by the British along the coast of East Africa.

The *Nevasa* first called at Mombasa and then at Dar es Salaam, but was turned away in both places. Local authorities said nearby refugee camps were already overflowing, that the ship's passengers could not be accommodated. The convoy was ordered to proceed further south to the port of Beira in Mozambique, where its passengers could disembark and proceed by train to camps with adequate space near Salisbury (now Harare) in Southern Rhodesia (Zimbabwe).

During the long trip down the east coast of Africa, Maria's first romance blossomed. During the endless hours with nothing to do, she began playing classical music over the ship's public-address system each day for the other passengers. Often she gave brief descriptions of composers and individual selections. The records and many interesting tidbits for her commentaries came from Fred Anscombe, one of the ship's engineers, who had the largest collection of albums on the *Nevasa*. Their daily discussions of music soon led to a close friendship between Fred and Maria. Gradually, they began spending more and more time together. Although Maria was only sixteen, girls her age soon began ooh-ing and aah-ing about how fortunate she was to attract Fred's attention. Her lame protests did nothing to deter them. Secretly she agreed: Fred *was* handsome. His face was sharply chiseled, yet his features seemed refined, faintly effeminate. His eyes, an unusual violet color, added softness and geniality, to his face. His sinewy six-foot frame, clear complexion, and sandy blond hair fused into an image of vigor and confidence. At twenty-five, he had traveled widely and was well educated. His father was a well-to-do Glasgow banker. His worldly aspect made his attention even more flattering to Maria.

Fred's rapidly budding romantic interest was soon evident to Mrs. Pawulska, who did not disapprove but did worry about the potential for miscommunication. She knew that Maria's knowledge of English was limited and feared that her daughter might encourage amorous intentions by using the wrong word. Her friends, like Maria's, took considerable interest in the relationship and strongly agreed that nothing should be done to discourage it. Maria appeared to be the only one surprised when Fred proposed marriage after several weeks at sea. "I thought of him as a very close friend," Maria told me. "I think emotionally I was still twelve. The idea of marriage had never occurred to me." Confused about how to respond, Maria gave Fred a noncommittal answer. Her own and her mother's friends were agape with amazement.

En route to Beira, the *Nevasa* was hit by a big storm that drove the ship outside the Mozambique Channel and down the east coast of Madagascar. Maria was among the few passengers who did not become violently ill from the prolonged pitching and tossing. Fred had spared her that ordeal with some simple advice. He told her never to look at the horizon and always to walk in a straight line, looking down at and carefully following the deck planks. His directions worked amazingly well. Once the storm cleared, the *Nevasa* proceeded to Durban, arriving there the last week of April. After about five weeks aboard ship, the Poles were finally permitted to disembark with the understanding that none could stay in the South African port city. British authorities had arranged for a special train, which took them north immediately to the camps near Salisbury.

The Pawulskis arrived there the first week of May and were first settled about an hour away in verdant countryside at a camp called Marandellas. Within a few weeks, Maria moved to Digglefold Plantation, where a high school for Polish girls had been established despite an acute shortage of books. A short time later, her mother also moved to Digglefold, accepting an offer to become one of several housemothers there. The Marandellas camp operated a fine school for boys, so she decided to leave Jerzy there with friends. Maria's classes were in the main house at Digglefold, which featured a large atrium surrounded by several rooms. The plantation had been developed by a British couple who had suffered a traumatic loss shortly before the war. Their only child had been bitten by a snake while playing in the yard and had died soon afterward. To remain at Digglefold became more than the couple could bear. They decided to give the plantation to the colonial government in Salisbury and return to Great Britain. With the influx of refugees, authorities decided that the plantation provided an ideal setting for a small school. There were plenty of teachers among the refugees, and the school was able to open after the importation of a limited number of textbooks from Polish Jews in Palestine. In its oasislike setting, under a canopy of pines and cedars, Maria and her classmates began an intense program of study designed to make up for years lost in the Soviet Union.

Fred wrote often during this period, pressing Maria for an answer to his proposal. Her initial confusion continued. She wrote back saying "maybe" but then "maybe not." Word of her ambiguous replies caused considerable surprise among friends and acquaintances. Several of Mrs. Pawulska's friends were sharply critical of Maria's hesitation. How could she be so selfish? they asked. If she married Fred, she could go to Glasgow, then have her mother and Jerzy join her. They could all then lead normal lives.

Finally, a comment in one of Fred's last letters helped clarify Maria's thinking. She was worrying too much, he said, about the future of Poland. The situation was not her personal responsibility. "After all," he wrote, "it is not up to you to save Poland." These comments startled Maria. Had her letters been *that* preoccupied with Poland? Perhaps so. But why was he unable to understand? It occurred to her that he might never understand how she felt about her country. She wrote back telling Fred that, for the time being, they should continue as friends. His letters stopped coming almost immediately.

Sometime later, Maria learned through a friend who corresponded with another member of the *Nevasa* crew that the ship had been badly damaged in a torpedo attack. Fred had been severely wounded and afterward spent almost a year convalescing.

*   *   *

The raid, on the big Soviet holiday of May 1, 1944, was not expected
and the Germans in Lwów were caught completely by surprise. Many
of their antiaircraft batteries were not even manned when the sirens
at the factories began screaming about 9:30 P.M. Moments before, several Soviet fighters had swooped down, dropping parachute flares in a
trim rectangle over the villa district. Every house and street in the
marked area suddenly seemed ablaze in light. A brief but agonizing
lull preceded the drone of big planes in the distance.

About fifty yards outside the rectangle, the residents of 69
Zadworzańska Street were scrambling for safety. Zbigniew Neuhoff
slammed the cellar door shut behind his wife, Anna, their five-year-
old niece, Ewa, and a few renters who now lived with them in the
three-story house. They all crouched in darkness as the bombs began
crashing to earth. From the sound of it, the Soviets were inflicting a
severe pounding on the German brass, who had requisitioned most of
the homes in the villa district.

Then came a jarring thud that caused every timber in the house to
shudder. Ewa told me that the lingering vibrations made her uncle
and aunt think that something nearby, possibly the house next door,
had been hit and damaged heavily. It was their decision, she said, that
no one should venture outside until morning. Anna opened the cellar
doors about daylight and was greeted by a shocking sight. The bomb
had struck their house, not their neighbor's, and large chunks of it had
been blown apart. Some of the first floor was still intact, but the second
was nearly all destroyed, the third gone completely. The balcony at
the top of a winding staircase had vanished. Twisted stairs now led
grotesquely into empty space. What was left of the Neuhoff family
home was little more than a shell. Out back, Zbigniew's baby grand
piano sat upside down, all four legs pointing skyward. It had landed
in the middle of a small garden planted the previous day by Ewa.

Fires still smoldered across the villa district. Many of the houses
occupied by senior German officers had been flattened. The
Wehrmacht had offered little resistance and was unlikely to hold Lwów
much longer. "My uncle and aunt knew that it was only a matter of
time before the Soviets returned," Ewa told me. "They shuddered to
think of a second occupation and began packing immediately."

Throughout the German occupation, Zbigniew had been deeply
involved in the Citizens' Committee, a group organized by a prominent
Polish surgeon in Lwów to provide food and clothing for prisoners in
concentration camps. The committee owned a truck, which Zbigniew
borrowed a few days after the bombing raid and loaded with all that

could be saved from the wreckage of the Neuhoff home. Among these items were seventy-five pounds of his mother's silver. Then, with Anna and Ewa, he drove about fifty miles west to the small town of Jarosław, where they managed to find a cramped apartment. After getting Anna and Ewa settled, Zbigniew took the truck back to Lwów and briefly continued his work with the Citizens' Committee. He left just before the Soviets occupied Lwów a few weeks later. His departure was none too soon. Once in Jarosław, he learned that in absentia the Soviets had imposed a sentence of twenty-five years at hard labor on Zbigniew Jan Neuhoff for his work with the Citizens' Committee. A short time later, his uncle Jan Neuhoff was arrested and executed in prison. It was a case of mistaken identity.

The blunder appalled Janina Czarnek. Not attending to such a thing was foolish and careless. On her kitchen table lay five green sheets, food stamps minted by the German General Government and illegally purchased weeks earlier by Magda from a German soldier. Her concern centered on the stamps' expiration date: April 30, 1944. In a single day, all five sheets would be worthless.

Her daughters, too, were concerned about the slipup. No one had an explanation, but the difficulty was clear: to use so many stamps at once invited trouble needlessly. Since 1940, the family had supplemented its income by buying food from Mienl, the large German food chain where Jaga worked. The Czarneks, like other Poles, got a small allotment of stamps to buy bread, marmalade, and a few other items. On occasion they were able to buy extra stamps from German soldiers or officials who were leaving Poland.

Using these stamps in quantity was fraught with risk and opportunity. The rationing system was set up to ensure that Germans in the General Government could buy staples and other hard-to-get items at reasonable prices. Germans received the stamps in a monthly allotment and could not get by without them. Poles caught using stamps illegally risked harsh punishment. The system was closely monitored by the police, particularly at the point of purchase. But leaks sprang quickly. Poles often made purchases for German employers. Germans who no longer needed the stamps—soldiers en route to the front, or civilians returning to Germany—often gave or sold stamps to Poles. Some Poles got stamps from the underground, which pilfered them in the minting process. There were even counterfeit coupons, but these were especially dangerous. A Pole caught with fake stamps faced a concentration-camp sentence or even execution. Still, stamps filtered into Polish hands from so many directions that the police could not possibly stop the flow. Usually they watched for large purchases. The Poles all knew that large transactions were a certain tipoff and magnified the risk considerably.

The day before the April sheets expired, Janina and a former maid named Salka, who had recently returned to live in the Czarnek household, began shopping in several stores to use up the stamps. Late that afternoon, a policeman stopped Salka in a food store and found that she had a sizable number of stamps. He insisted on knowing where they had come from. Salka, who did not speak German, panicked and refused to say anything. She was then taken to police headquarters for interrogation. Smashing her head against the wall, the police punctured one of her eardrums. Finally, she confessed: The stamps had come from Janina Czarnek.

Coming home that evening, almost at dark, Magda realized a block or more from her door that something was wrong. From that distance she could see a car at the sidewalk, a certain sign of trouble. She knew that only the police were likely to come in a car. A chilling fear reduced her brisk pace to a faltering creep. At that moment, the front door opened and her mother and her sister Maria emerged flanked by two Germans in plain clothes. Magda made a darting turn into the shadows of the garden next door and watched as her mother climbed into the back seat of the waiting car. Maria watched helplessly as her mother was driven away.

Seconds later, Magda followed Maria into the apartment, where she learned that her mother had just been arrested and would be kept in custody until someone in the family could prove that the stamps had not been illegally obtained.

Instantly Magda knew she would have to get Dr. Sippel's help. She raced immediately to the welding school on her bicycle, hoping that he would still be there, and found him seated behind the desk in his office.

"He was sitting there like he always sat there—puffing on a large cigar," Magda told me. "I blurted out what had happened. Told him that Mama had been arrested without going into the full story. I finished by saying, 'Would you help me by testifying that I got the food stamps from you?'

"He had listened patiently to my story, but said nothing. He blew a long thin cloud of smoke and finally he said, 'Now suppose I go with you and testify that I gave you five sheets of stamps—a whole month's supply. They are going to ask me, "How did you live? How did you eat all month? You are not alone. You have a wife." How can I answer these questions? I would like to help you, but these questions cannot be answered.'

"He was right and I knew it," Magda said. "Then he said, 'I guess I could go and testify that you are a good person; that your work is important to me: and that I need you here.'

"So then I told him that a German soldier offered to sell me his food stamps, that I took my watch off and gave it to him for the stamps. He thought for a while and kept blowing his smoke.

"Then he said, 'All right, let's go.'

"We went immediately to the main police station and I explained where I had gotten the stamps. He vouched for me, which was a very crucial thing."

Magda was charged with a crime against the German economic system and her mother was released immediately.

Two or three months later, Magda appeared before a judge in a trial that lasted less than thirty minutes. She received a two-month term at St. Michael's, a prison near Wawel Castle. Her family drew a deep sigh of relief that she had not been sent to Montelupich, where political offenders were held. Before beginning her sentence, Magda was permitted to go home and collect things to take with her.

"I was not mistreated," she said. "I was scared because I was afraid the sentence would be extended or changed to forced labor in Germany. We all knew what that meant." At the end of her sentence, Dr. Sippel certified that Magda was needed in her old job.

Had Janina Czarnek been convicted of the same offense, a sentence to a concentration camp almost certainly would have awaited her.

"My mother was bitter that I had to go," Magda said. "I felt that it was my part of a common effort to keep the family together."

Shortly after she arrived at St. Michael's, Magda received a letter from Jaga. The postscript said, "Always keep your face away from the bars. Otherwise you will get bar burns on your face." After mailing this admonishment, Jaga had second thoughts. She quickly wrote again saying that her comments about bar burns were meant to cheer Magda up. "I hope I didn't hurt your feelings," she added.

CHAPTER 20

Clandestine Designs

Documents found in the Katyń victims' boots and pockets during the German-sponsored investigations could be used to prove beyond a reasonable doubt who was guilty of the murders in Katyń Forest. With the tide of battle turning against them, the Germans moved these documents, the material evidence collected during the exhumation, to Poland for further analysis and safekeeping. They were determined that the documents would never fall into the hands of the NKVD. Should that happen, the Germans had no doubt that the evidence would be cleverly altered and cited as proof of Soviet innocence. Their fears were well founded. NKVD agents were soon on the trail of the documents and tracked them, eventually, all the way across Poland. So did the Polish underground, which was also determined to capture the material evidence from Katyń. The documents thus became the focal point of a high-stakes intrigue that would not end until the final days of the war.

Near the end of January 1944, the Polish officers were buried for the third and last time with all personal effects stripped from their bodies. A few days earlier, on January 22, the Soviet commission had shown Kathleen Harriman and seventeen Western newsmen nine glass-encased documents that it considered the most decisive and convincing proof of German guilt. This collection included one letter, two postcards, five receipts, and one religious icon, all dated *after* the spring of 1940. No neutral witness saw any of these documents removed from the victims' bodies. Each document was issued or processed by Soviet officials. That any of those who sent or received these documents were ever prisoners at Kozelsk was not documented. "There were very few [documents]," Henry Cassidy later noted. "That was one of the points we made to them [the Soviet commission] in saying we had not been convinced." But nine documents of dubious authenticity were all the Soviet commission could muster. The rest had been taken by the Germans many months earlier.

From the day the Germans announced their discovery, the documents found on the officers' bodies had caused the Soviets deep concern. In their April 15 response to Goebbels's first statement, they accused the Germans of "the clumsiest forgeries." Two days later, the Soviets charged that the Germans had "the foresight to put into the pockets of the bestially tortured officers" evidence to support their claim that the men had been murdered in 1940. The Soviets said these actions were taken shortly before the German propaganda offensive began, at a time when the Germans knew that the Katyń area might be lost and their crime discovered. That prospect, according to the Soviets, had prompted the Germans to dig up the bodies and replace recent incriminating documents with older documents taken from Gestapo archives. Clearly the Soviets were anxious to explain why material evidence damaging to their version of the crime might be found in the graves. Their determination to discredit documents being unearthed by the Germans was obvious. While the Soviet explanation would not bear up under close scrutiny, it did serve to raise doubts about the authenticity of the documents being found by the Germans.

At the outset of the German investigation, its coordinator, Dr. Buhtz, had established painstaking procedures for the removal and cataloging of material evidence. He had then put the technical commission formed by the Polish Red Cross in charge of the day-to-day process in which evidence was collected from individual bodies. Members of this commission came to Katyń highly skeptical of German motives and procedures. Unknown to Dr. Buhtz, or to other German authorities, its ranks had been infiltrated by the Polish underground. Numerous coded messages providing assessments from the scene were sent back to Poland by the underground and then on to the London government-in-exile by radiogram. Under the watchful eye of the Poles, it was virtually impossible that documents faked, as the Soviets alleged, could have gone undetected.

From late April through the first week of June 1943, the Polish commission identified the bodies of 4,243 of their countrymen using Buhtz's procedures. From six to ten Russian peasants assisted members of the Polish commission throughout this period. Two peasants and one commission member generally worked as a team. In a routine repeated many times each day, the commission member designated an individual body for removal from one of the seven main graves. The peasants, often using picks and other sharp instruments, then pried the designated body from the mass of bodies around it. This process was particularly arduous in grave one, where most of the bodies had sealed tightly together in one huge mass that could only have formed over a considerable time. Those at the scene had no doubt about the absurdity of the Soviet contention that the Germans had exhumed individual bodies, changed documents on them, and then returned them to the sealed mass in which they were found.

Once removed, individual bodies were placed on a stretcher and carried by the Russian peasants to an examining table outside the graves. There, under the direction of the Polish commission member and with German authorities circulating about, the peasants slit the pockets and boots of the victims and removed all the contents. The material evidence found included notebooks, diaries, newspaper articles, snapshots, passports and other identity papers, letters, wallets, rings, bracelets, watches, and several denominations of currency such as Polish złotys, Russian rubles, and U.S. dollars. Such articles were then placed in a large yellow envelope marked with a serial number. A metal disk stamped with a number matching that on the envelope was then placed on the front of the victim's uniform. From bodies on which no identity documents were found, one shoulder strap was removed and placed in an envelope to establish the victim's rank. The bodies were then reburied nearby in fresh common graves. The envelopes were collected at noon and at five P.M. each day and taken to a house behind the Gniezdovo railway station about three miles away. There other members of the Polish commission added the names from each envelope to the list of identified bodies. An inventory of documents and articles found on each body was also prepared.

Proof of Soviet guilt beyond any reasonable doubt evolved from this process. The evidence collected included twenty-two diaries. Several of these listed the names and dates on which prisoners left Kozelsk in the daily transports during April and May of 1940. Most of these entries expressed joy at the apparent good fortune of friends who—so the authors thought—were finally being sent back home. Information in these diaries enabled investigators to identify a few names on each of the daily transport lists. When these partially reconstructed lists were compared to the serial numbers assigned to individual bodies a dramatic fact became clear: The victims had been removed from the graves in Katyń Forest in approximately the reverse order in which they left Kozelsk. Once this connection was established, the Soviet version of the crime became impossible to believe. The Soviets had claimed that the men had been moved from Kozelsk to three camps in the Smolensk area and then worked in road construction and repair for more than a year before being captured by the Germans. According to the Soviets, many of the men left these camps just as the Red Army yielded the Smolensk area. That the Germans could have rounded the men up, executed them, and then buried them in the same order in which they left Kozelsk a year and a half earlier was, of course, preposterous.

There was no doubt either about the authenticity of the diaries. They were full of convincing details about life at Kozelsk—"In the morning we decided to buy stamps and send a letter. . . ." The author, Major Adam Solski, continued with a detailed explanation of whom the letter was mailed to and why. Through the underground, the Polish commission checked with survivors of Kozelsk to confirm details from the diaries, and concluded that these documents could not possibly have been faked.

Many facts uncovered early in the investigation pointed toward Soviet guilt. But for the Poles at the scene, any remaining doubts were removed by the matching of the transport lists and the serial numbers reflecting the order in which bodies had been removed from the graves. The Poles themselves had collected the evidence that made this conclusion possible in a lengthy and carefully organized exhumation process that ended on June 7, 1943. At that point the investigation had been suspended by the Germans, who were embarrassed at finding fewer than half the ten thousand victims initially predicted. The Poles then turned their attention, still under the watchful eye of German authorities, to documenting the case against the Soviets as fully and convincingly as possible.

Concern that Katyń Forest might soon be recaptured by the Soviets was already mounting when the investigation was suspended. Forces were then concentrating about 250 miles south of Smolensk in the Kursk Salient for what would become the largest tank battle in history. The last great German offensive on the Eastern Front, it resulted in a stunning defeat that forced the Wehrmacht on the long road back to Berlin. The Germans attacked on July 5. A week later they were thrown on the defensive. By July 23, they had been driven out of the Kursk Salient and the entire front was about to undergo a dramatic shift. By then it was clear that the Wehrmacht could not hold the Smolensk area much longer.

While this threat unfolded, all the envelopes containing the material evidence collected in Katyń Forest were packed, locked in fourteen boxes, and shipped seven hundred miles southwest to the Institute of Forensic Medicine in Kraków, where a new, even more laborious phase of the investigation began. There, the contents of each individual envelope were subjected to detailed analysis. Documents of a potentially incriminating nature were singled out for special attention. Many were covered in adipocere, a wax that forms in the decomposition process, and required delicate handling. After papers were cleaned, chemical treatment was necessary in many cases to make handwriting legible. Anything written in pen was often undecipherable with the naked eye due to the bleaching of the ink. Once these documents had been cleaned and chemically treated to make them as legible as possible, they were all photostated.

The purpose of these painstaking procedures was to document the case against the Soviets as specifically and as fully as possible. Results also were used to issue death certificates to the victims' next of kin and to establish a basis for legal claims in the event that civil actions could later be brought against the murderers. Once the experts had completed their analysis, the victims' personal possessions could be examined and claimed by their families. Families of unidentified victims often examined personal possessions and handwriting specimens to help confirm the names of the dead. In all these matters, the Poles again were in charge of the day-to-day details. A team of ten Polish forensic specialists under Dr. Jan Zygmunt Robel, the chairman of the institute's chemical department, spent many months analyzing and restoring the documents.

Throughout this period, the Poles were closely supervised by Dr. Werner Beck, a native of Hamburg and a former assistant to Dr. Buhtz at the University of Breslau. Beck had been put in charge of the Institute of Forensic Medicine in 1940, only a few months after the German General Government established itself in Kraków. The faculty and facilities of the Jagiellonian University, which was closed by the Germans, were put at his disposal. Beck apparently developed a close rapport with the Polish physicians and technicians who worked under him. It seems likely, also, that the continuing visits of bereaved families coming to claim or identify the victims' possessions had a pronounced impact on Beck. In any event, he developed a strong compassion for the Poles and a determination to assist them in making the maximum use possible of the evidence sent to his institute.

In the last year of the war, Beck became the central figure in a tense behind-the-scenes struggle to keep the material evidence sent to his institute from falling into Soviet hands. The dramatic story can be pieced together from testimony provided seven years after the war to the select committee of the U.S. Congress that investigated the crime. Beck himself testified at those hearings, as did Kazimierz Skarzyński, the wartime head of the Polish Red Cross, and Karl Herrmann, a member of the German security police. The following account is drawn directly from the testimony of these three men.

The fourteen boxes containing the evidence from Katyń were each fitted with built-in locks. They were taken on arrival to the laboratory of the institute and the keys were given to Beck, who in turn handed them over to Robel. As the investigation commenced, Beck developed a routine of checking daily on the work of the Polish team, but delegated most of the administrative responsibility for the investigations to Robel. The work proceeded for several months without incident. Throughout this period, the German position on the Eastern Front continued to deteriorate. Sometime early in 1944, the Polish underground decided that action must be taken to prevent the documents from being captured by the Soviets. A plan was developed to steal the evidence from Beck's laboratory and hide it until the end of the war, when, presumably, it could be presented in a trial on Polish soil. When the decision was made is unclear, but more than likely it came soon after the Red Army crossed the prewar boundary of Poland on January 4.

The heist centered on a daring idea: Replicas of the fourteen boxes that contained the material evidence would be built and smuggled into Beck's laboratory, which was surrounded by SS barracks. Each box would be lined with tin and fitted with lids that could be hermetically sealed. The documents would then be transferred from the German boxes to the airtight boxes built by the Home Army. Once the switch had been made, the tin-lined boxes containing the materials would then be taken to a lake and sunk for safekeeping. The plot was designed, according to Skarzyński, by "our chief officer of the Red Cross in Kraków, who was a man of the intelligence service and a very capable man." The boxes—about five feet long, two and a half feet high, and two feet wide—were then built. Shortly afterward the underground smuggled the boxes inside Beck's laboratory and began the transfer.

Exactly what happened next is unclear. A janitor may have stumbled on the operation and reported a disturbance in the laboratory. Skarzyński's testimony notes only that "through the indiscretion of a physical worker, absolutely incidental," the SS got wind of the plot and a special detachment of its troops quickly arrived on the scene while the underground team was still inside. Caught in the act, the Home Army members could not escape. They might well have been executed on the spot. But the Germans, apparently preoccupied with the Red Army's menacing advance from the east, decided to let them go without punishment.

The foiling of the underground plot apparently prompted the German General Government to reassess the safety of the evidence from Katyń. Later—probably sometime in the summer of 1944—the head of the Gestapo gave Beck a written order to burn all the boxes immediately to eliminate the risk that they might be captured by the Red Army, then about two hundred miles east of Kraków. Feeling strongly that the documents "should be kept for the benefit of the Polish nation," Beck refused to obey the order. Instead, he and Robel decided "to distribute those documents amongst the reliable Poles and subsequently report to the security police that the destruction of the documents had been concluded. This plan, however, could not be effected, because such a stench emanated from these documents that they could not be kept in private homes."

Beck then took the matter up personally with the Gestapo and other agencies of the German General Government. After considerable negotiation, he wrangled a permit to transfer the documents about 150 miles northwest to Breslau. Through his connections at the University of Breslau, Beck had already arranged for storage space in his old department. The fourteen boxes, each bearing in large black letters the inscription "INSTITUTE KRAKÓW LIBRARY," were then trucked to Breslau—probably in early fall of 1944—and stored in the Anatomical Institute. During the trip, Beck broke his leg and came back to a hospital in Kraków to recover. While he recovered, or soon afterward, Beck resumed his duties at the Institute of Forensic Medicine. The underground immediately began pumping him for information about the fate of the evidence. In the meantime, Beck sent Robel on the first of several trips to Breslau (the city was renamed Wrocław and became a part of Poland after the war) during the last part of 1944 to continue work on the documents. From either Beck or Robel, the underground found out where the documents were and probably began planning a second attempt to steal them. But time would run out before any such plan could be put into operation.

The Wehrmacht was now collapsing between two walls of steel. Beck closed his institute and left Kraków shortly before the city fell to the Soviets in mid-January 1945. He moved his staff to Breslau, knowing that that city, too, might be captured within a matter of weeks, perhaps sooner. Beck knew the war was lost, and shortly after his return to Breslau began looking for a way to move the fourteen boxes farther west. He barely succeeded. Sometime early in February, he was able to secure a postal truck and had the documents driven by Karl Herrmann to the platform of the Breslau railroad station. Herrmann testified that, when he arrived, officials of the Breslau city administration were at the station waiting to be evacuated. The train was the last one scheduled to leave Breslau, according to Herrmann. Somehow, Beck had persuaded authorities to allocate one of the few available coaches for the boxes from Katyń, and they were loaded aboard.

The evidence was then taken from Breslau to Dresden, where "Gestapo headquarters were notified to send us a truck," according to Herrmann. "Originally, as far as I heard, the boxes were supposed to proceed straight to Berlin. In the meantime, however, the Russians had made a forced advance, so it was no longer feasible to take the boxes, as originally intended, to Berlin. The boxes were laden on a truck and taken to Radebeul" (a suburb of Dresden).

NKVD agents were now in hot pursuit. Apparently they were well aware through their own intelligence sources that the evidence they coveted had been housed at the Institute of Forensic Medicine in Kraków. As soon as the city was captured, they began combing the premises, looking for the evidence. They apparently found and arrested Robel, but otherwise had no success. A short time later, when the Red Army occupied Breslau, the NKVD hurried to the Anatomical Institute at the university, but again found nothing. Before the NKVD arrived in Breslau, the Polish underground had already confirmed—probably as a result of a second effort to capture the evidence—that the boxes were gone.

Once he got the boxes to Radebeul, Beck stored them in a private home. But because the odor was overpowering, they were soon moved to the freight depot of the railway station. Beck planned to leave them in this location only until he could get the German government to turn them over to the International Red Cross in Prague. But after several weeks, he had failed to get any agency of the government to undertake this responsibility. Beck knew that time was now almost gone. The two war fronts were converging. No one knew which army would reach Radebeul first. To keep the Soviets from capturing the documents, he was forced to try something else. Only a few days before the war ended, Beck decided to go personally to Prague. He hoped to convince the Red Cross to send a truck to Radebeul to pick up the documents.

Before leaving Radebeul, Beck issued a fateful order. "We still antici- pated and hoped that the Americans would occupy Dresden," Beck testified. "However, in order to cover all possibilities, I had given an order that should the Russians come and occupy Dresden, the boxes should be burned."

Beck then left for Prague, but made it only part of the way when fighting blocked his path. He went instead to Plzeň (Pilsen), which had already been occupied by the Americans. There, a U.S. Army officer listened to his story and gave him a pass to return to Dresden. On his way back, Beck learned that Dresden had just been occupied by the Soviets, not the Americans. Knowing that he could not return to Dresden under these circumstances, Beck made his way instead to the American zone of occupation in Bavaria. But he did confirm that the instructions he gave on his departure from Dresden had been carried out; the forwarding agent had burned all fourteen boxes. Ironically, the spearhead for the liberation of Dresden and its suburbs was the Polish Second Army, under Soviet command. This army was responsible for the greatest victory fought by Poles in World War II, smashing the larger forces of German Army Group Center in late April 1945. It was commanded by General Karol Świerczewski, the famous "General Golz" of Ernest Hemingway's *For Whom the Bell Tolls.*

During his appearance before the investigating committee at a hearing in Frankfurt, West Germany, in 1952, Representative Daniel J. Flood of Pennslyvania asked Beck, "Did you ever receive any information from anybody in Dresden after the Russian occupation that your orders had been carried out?"

"Yes, I did," Beck replied.

"Now, the committee has been advised of the name of the person who gave you that [information], and of the repute and standing of that informant. We can understand why you may not want to tell us, but, if you wish to, we would be glad to have the name of the person for the record, although the committee is aware of it anyhow. That is up you."

"For security reasons, and in the best interests of persons residing in the Russian zone who are connected with this business, I take it that it would be advisable not to mention or divulge the name here in an open session," Beck replied.

Beck's anonymous informant was his own father, Oscar Beck, a retired Evangelical Lutheran minister, who confirmed that the documents were doused in gasoline and set ablaze. Congress did not open the records of this investigating committee to the public until 1989. Part of the Beck file remains classified. But I learned who his informant was while reviewing the records thirty-seven years after his appearance before the committee.

The physician's anxiety about his father's safety was more than justified. The NKVD had not given up. It had trailed Beck at every stop along the way from Kraków to Radebeul. It learned that Beck's parents lived near Dresden and that the documents had been stored briefly in their house. The premises were searched several times. His mother, then sixty-two, was immediately arrested and thrown into prison in Dresden. The NKVD told her she would not be released until she revealed her son's whereabouts. Finally, six months later, she was released.

"The Russians also traced the exact route of my flight up to the border of the Russian zone," Beck testified. "The Russians searched the homes of all persons who sheltered me at that time, particularly so the houses of friends of mine. They lost track of me only at the zonal border."

The forwarding agent who burned the documents was arrested by the NKVD and disappeared. Beck testified in 1952 that the man's family never heard from him again.

The blaze on the freight-forwarding dock at Radebeul station by no means settled the question of what happened to the documents. After the war, rumors began circulating in Poland—and continue circulating to this day—that the underground succeeded in stealing the evidence and that someday the documents will be found. These hopes are not as farfetched as they might seem. One phrase in Beck's testimony explains why. When he closed the institute in Kraków and moved to Breslau early in 1945, Beck said, "the first thing I took care of were the documents, these original documents, from Katyn." The phrase "original documents" provides a striking reminder that hundreds of documents were photostated for safekeeping. Copies of the twenty-two diaries were obtained by the underground and sent to the London government-in-exile. Where are the remaining photostats? Perhaps they are still moldering in some long-forgotten hiding place in Kraków or Wrocław. Even if their whereabouts are known, many persons might be reluctant, even now, to reveal such information.

One fleeting encounter in Kraków on the evening of November 1, 1989, dramatized for me why persons with information about the documents might be unwilling to come forward. Earlier in the day, I had met with Władysław Klimczak, the director of the city's Museum of History and Photography, who told me about a man named Didur who "might have known a lot about these documents." During the war K. Didur had walked an unusual tightrope: He was a member of the underground serving as personal photographer to Hans Frank, the notorious head of the German General Government. According to Klimczak, Didur had taken many photographs for the Germans at Katyń, which were subsequently used to publicize the massacre in Poland. Many of his photographs had later been smuggled from Kraków to London. "Unfortunately he died just a few months ago," Klimczak told me, "but his wife is still alive and she might be able to tell you something about this whole episode." Klimczak then tried to phone her to arrange a meeting, but got no answer. He gave me her number and address and suggested that I try later.

Leaving the museum, my translator, Martin Zaczek, a young physician who is one of Dr. Czarnek's grandsons, suggested that we drive by Mrs. Didur's apartment. "I know the address," he said. "Maybe she will be back when we get there." Dusk was covering the city when we arrived. Her door was up several flights of stairs. Martin knocked boldly several times, but there was no response. "She must be out of town," he shrugged. Just then the door cracked open slightly. An elderly woman peered out, her eyes filled with fear. It was clear that we had frightened her and Martin tried awkwardly to explain why we had knocked. She listened, but the fear never left her eyes. Finally, she murmured a short phrase in Polish, repeating it several times as she shook her head adamantly. Martin turned to me, "All she will say is, 'I know nothing about this.' " Walking back to the car, Martin said regretfully, "I think she thought we were the police. They have knocked on her door too many times."*

*In May 1991, while this book was in the final stages of production, copies of some of the original documents taken from the graves in Katyń Forest were found in the attic area of the building that had housed Dr. Beck's Institute for Forensic Medicine in Kraków. Workmen were removing cracked supports near the roof of the building when they found a box wrapped in heavy construction paper. It contained copies of many of the documents saved by Dr. Robel and others working under the direction of Dr. Beck.

CHAPTER 21

Moments of Truth

‹‹‹‹‹‹‹‹‹‹

Right made no difference. What was possible was all that mattered. But anti-Soviet émigré Poles rejected that harsh reality as the Red Army advanced into Poland. Their position was visceral, foolish, and impetuous. It was also predictable, credible, and compelling. And its appeal galvanized conservative, hard-line strength among the Poles abroad in the year following General Sikorski's death. The result was a paralysis that gripped the government-in-exile at a time when flexibility alone might have saved it.

The hard-liners summoned powerful arguments based on a large and irrefutable body of fact to support their anti-Soviet stance. In the year following the diplomatic break over Katyń, all effort to mollify Stalin— what the hard-liners regarded as a series of dangerous, disgusting, and spineless concessions forced by their government's Anglo-American allies—had come to nothing. Increasingly, it was clear that Stalin demanded not compromise, but capitulation, from the émigré Poles. They viewed his intention to impose a pro-Soviet, Moscow-oriented government on Poland as clear beyond a doubt. Conciliatory gestures could only have whetted his appetite, or so they contended. Were the Poles that bereft of options? Not if their Anglo-American allies would fulfill their obligations, according to the hard-liners. Stalin could be put in his place, or so they believed, if the Allies would only meet their responsibilities. Fundamental justice demanded no less. Had not the British, after all, guaranteed Polish independence? Had not the war erupted as a conflict over Poland's territorial integrity? Who had been first to stand against Hitler? What people had paid a more terrible price for opposing the Nazi dictator? Whose army had fought longer and harder? And who, from the beginning, had proven less deserving of trust and reliance than Stalin? Why shouldn't the allies confront him? After all, Stalin was Hitler's accomplice. . . .

The litany of outrages was endless: the phony plebiscite in 1939; the subsequent annexations; the mass deportations; the refusal to renounce ill-gotten gains; the treaty of July 30, 1941, with its shameful amnesty clause; the inhuman treatment of deported women and children; the starving of the army-in-exile; and the stream of lies about thousands of captured officers who had been ruthlessly murdered in the spring of 1940. These outrages proved, to the hard-liners, how right Piłsudski had been: Russia was the historic enemy. A blind man could see it. And Poland would again be swallowed up unless her Anglo-American allies met their obligations, unless they came decisively to her rescue.

Increasingly these claims were made by the large percentage of Poles abroad with ties to, or at least a nostalgia for, the Piłsudski regime. Among them were many with positions of considerable influence. Most of the diplomatic corps had been appointed by the old regime. So had many mid-level officials serving in the government-in-exile. Many of the Polish journalists abroad had been beholden, in an era of censorship, to the old authorities. Anti-Sovietism was especially rampant in the army in the Middle East. Painful memories of their years in the U.S.S.R. were etched deeply into the minds of General Anders's men. They were bitterly outspoken. A chorus of demands, many of them irrational, thus came from the émigré Poles. Calls for a firmer hand, for Allied intervention, for armed struggle in Poland against the Nazis *and* the Soviets welled louder all through 1943 and 1944.

But a rescue was *not* in the making, was *not* contemplated, would *not* materialize. Sikorski had known that. So did his successor. They had seen the line between what was right and what was possible blurring among the hard-liners. Sikorski could and did use his stature, connections, and authority to keep that line from blurring completely. In his fateful meeting on April 24, 1943, at the height of the Katyń crisis, Sikorski had told Eden, "Force is on Russia's side, justice on ours. I do not advise the British people to cast their lot with brute force and to stampede justice before the eyes of all nations. For these reasons I emphatically refuse to withdraw the Polish appeal to the International Red Cross." But Sikorski had also known that a middle ground must be found. In the same meeting he had agreed that the Poles would press the Katyń issue no further. Sikorski realized that Poland's future hinged on the willingness of her Anglo-American allies to coax concessions from Stalin. He knew that without a second front, with the heavy toll in human life being sustained by the Soviets, with the Red Army beating the Wehrmacht, Churchill and Roosevelt could not push Stalin, and he knew that Poland's future, under these circumstances, was not one of their primary concerns.

Later, Sikorski had heard the murmuring undertone, the bitter recriminations among his own people about his so-called policy of Soviet appeasement. There had even been talk in the army of a coup. In his inner circle there were growing fears that an attempt would be made on his life, especially as he left on his last journey to the Middle East. Not for a moment had the rumors deterred him. Despite the break over Katyń, Sikorski entertained no doubt that the breach with Stalin could, in fact must, be bridged. Then came the tragic crash, and in his footsteps a successor who lacked Sikorski's stature, who did not command the unquestioning loyalty of the Poles in exile, a man of the center who was attacked immediately by the powerful Piłsudski faction as a "collaborationist," and an "appeaser."

No wartime leader stepped into a hotter caldron than did Stanisław Mikołajczyk. His public image as a farmer from Poznań and the spokesman for peasant interests was reinforced by a quiet, reserved, almost self-effacing manner. He lacked Sikorski's good looks, patrician manner, and Establishment ties. But he brought fundamental strengths to the exile government, strengths that Sikorski had increasingly come to value and rely on as the war continued.

First among them was a powerful constituency, the Peasant Party of Poland. It was the largest of all the prewar political parties and a force that even the dominant Piłsudski faction could not ignore. With the Soviets marching on Warsaw in 1920, its legendary leader, Wincenty Witos, had been asked to leave his farm to serve as prime minister in a government of national defense. Witos had mobilized the peasants to fight Tukhachevsky's advancing army, warning them that they would be enslaved if the Bolsheviks won. Throughout the years of benign dictatorship, the peasants had agitated strongly for democratic reforms. In the wake of the collapse of the pro-Piłsudski government, it was clear that the peasants would play a powerful role in any postwar reconstruction effort. Early in the war it also seemed clear that the Peasant Battalions, the core of the Home Army's rural support, would play a key role in winning the peace. Because Mikołajczyk enjoyed strong recognition and a high level of popularity among Poland's huge peasant population, he represented a crucial constituency in the coalition government formed under Sikorski.

During the exile years, he and Sikorski developed a close rapport and a genuine fondness for each other. Sikorski, the soldier-statesman, discovered that the peasant leader was an able organizer and had keen intellectual gifts, including an uncanny ability to synthesize vast amounts of information. As interior minister, Mikołajczyk pored daily

over news reported by Poland's prolific underground press and kept
attuned to all shades of opinion on the political spectrum. His position
kept him in constant contact with the county's underground leaders.
Intelligence reports, embassy dispatches, and British and American
news coverage were all carefully monitored by Mikołajczyk. Increasingly Sikorski came to rely on Mikołajczyk's analysis of developments
in Poland and abroad. As time went on, both men shared a deepening
conviction that a free and independent Poland could not be established
without the close cooperation of the Anglo-American allies, and that
such cooperation could entail unpleasant compromises. Their compati-
bility on that issue, more than any other, had prompted Sikorski to
name Mikołajczyk as acting prime minister during many of his prolonged absences from London.

In the aftermath of Sikorski's death, Mikołajczyk left no doubt that
he fully intended to carry forward with the fallen general's foreign
policy, which put complete faith and trust in the Anglo-American allies
to help establish an acceptable level of Polish-Soviet cooperation. That
trust was at one and the same time the Poles' only hope and a prime
cause of their downfall. Defense Minister Sosnkowski, who assumed
Sikorski's powers as commander in chief of the armed forces, deeply
suspected that the West could not be relied on and quickly emerged
as the rallying point of the Piłsudski faction. He and Mikołajczyk had
never been close, but in the aftermath of Sikorski's crash they became
bitterly estranged. Long periods passed in which the two men refused
to speak to each other.

Rapidly unfolding events put the new prime minister on the defensive with his own cabinet and with the Anglo-American leadership.
Stalin spurned all of Mikołajczyk's overtures for a resumption of diplomatic relations in the aftermath of Sikorski's death. Operation Tempest,
the government's October 27, 1943, order to underground leaders calling for maximum cooperation with the advancing Red Army, had
proven to be a disaster. Stalin had not only refused to coordinate action
against the retreating Germans, he continued openly to accuse the
underground of pro-Nazi collaboration. His agents provoked incident
after incident in which Nazi reprisals against the Polish population were
blamed on the Home Army. Several Home Army commanders had
been executed in the wake of Soviet victories and the many Polish
partisans who had cooperated with the advancing Red Army were confronted with the choice of joining Berling's pro-Soviet army or being
deported. More and more it was clear that the absence of an agreement
between Moscow and the exile government could cost the Poles their

country. Churchill and Eden had feared as much, and bluntly told Mikołajczyk so. On January 11, 1944, the Soviets issued a statement saying that their territorial acquisitions in 1939 were nonnegotiable and again chastised the government-in-exile for failing to fight the Nazis. The statement warmly praised the Union of Polish Patriots for their efforts in this regard. Because the statement did not close the door entirely on future relations with the government-in-exile, it was warmly received by the British press, which advised the Poles to secure Stalin's friendship by accepting his terms.

The disaster at Tehran remained undetected, but reports filtering out all through the first half of 1944 strongly indicated that Polish interests might have been compromised at the Big Three conference in the Iranian capital. What Mikołajczyk and the members of his cabinet did not know was that Churchill had taken responsibility for convincing the Poles that they should accept a massive westward shift in their frontiers. In the months that followed Tehran, the Poles felt badgered and coerced by Churchill's insistence on a sweeping territorial change that, unknown to them, Churchill, Roosevelt, and Stalin had already agreed to in principle. The lofty commitments made in the Atlantic Charter more than three years earlier had been abandoned, but the Poles did not know it. And their leaders constantly cited the document as a guarantee that they expected Great Britain, the United States, and the Soviet Union to live up to. The Poles' resistance to the proposed changes caused Churchill and Eden much irritation; "the Polish problem" was seen as an unwarranted and unwelcome distraction from more pressing war matters. Meanwhile, the Red Army's continuing advance, earned at great sacrifice in human life, was hailed with genuine admiration in Western newspapers and magazines. That same army's continuing harsh treatment of the Polish underground was overshadowed by this outpouring of praise. In his excellent study of the period, *The Great Powers & Poland, 1919–1945*, Jan Karski writes that

> most newspapers and magazines either denied publicity to the Poles or refused to believe what was happening. When the information did appear in print, it usually brought severe criticism as "insulting" to Russia or "damaging" to Allied unity. . . . As a result of the continuous and unrestrained propaganda on behalf of the Soviet policies, and the inability of the Poles in London to present their case, the public opinion in the West increasingly considered the "Polish Exiles" obstinate, reactionary or unrealistic.

Throughout the early part of 1944, Churchill pressed hard to gain the concurrence of Mikołajczyk and his government for the Tehran agreement-in-principle on Poland's frontiers. The Poles still were unaware that they were being presented with a fait accompli. During this period, Churchill assumed the role of a broker between Stalin and the Poles in attempting to hammer out the substance of an agreement. On February 4, Stalin sent Churchill his terms: Not only, he said, must the Poles accept the Curzon Line unconditionally, but also the government-in-exile itself must be thoroughly reorganized. When Churchill presented that news to Mikołajczyk two days later, the Polish prime minister emphasized that even if he were to accept such terms, they would be repudiated by his countrymen. At a meeting on February 16, Mikołajczyk told Churchill that his Cabinet had authorized him to propose a compromise—a line between Poland's prewar frontier and the Curzon Line that left Wilno and Lwów in Poland. Churchill said that Stalin would not accept it and that unless the Poles quickly agreed to the Curzon Line they could expect Stalin to set up a government subservient to Moscow. He told the Poles that Stalin's territorial demands were not unreasonable and that Britain and the United States certainly would not force him to revise them.

Mikołajczyk realized that further opposition to Churchill was useless, that a bad agreement with Moscow was better than no agreement at all. The next day he and his foreign minister, Tadeusz Romer, told Churchill that they would accept the Curzon Line even though the rest of the Cabinet would not. With Mikołajczyk's personal pledge in hand, Churchill informed Stalin that he believed his conditions could be met. He assured Stalin that with the reestablishment of diplomatic relations, an effective reorganization of the Polish government would be carried out to ensure cooperation with Moscow.

On February 22, Churchill informed the House of Commons that major changes on Polish policy were in the wind. He admitted that Poland's future had been discussed in Tehran, emphasizing that Stalin favored "a strong, integral, independent Poland as one of the leading powers in Europe." He reminded his colleagues that Great Britain had supported the Curzon Line in 1919 and emphasized that Stalin believed that Poland should be compensated for any losses in the east with "compensation at the expense of Germany" in Prussia, in Silesia, and in Pomerania. For the first time, Churchill's speech clearly revealed to Polish public opinion, both at home and abroad, how far the Anglo-American allies were prepared to go to satisfy Stalin in securing the western frontier of the Soviet Union. The Poles and many of their supporters in the British Parliament were shocked by the concessions.

Churchill, in turn, was shocked by the response that came back from Stalin on March 3. Taking note of their internal disagreement, the Soviet dictator said émigré Poles were "incapable of establishing normal relations" with the Soviet Union. It was clear, he said, that the Poles still wanted Wilno and Lwów and that they were not serious about removing anti-Soviet elements from their ranks. He closed by saying he would not resume relations with the London government-in-exile. Gradually, over the next few weeks, Churchill let the proposed agreement slide. The Allied invasion of France was fast approaching. The Soviets had been committed since Tehran to time an offensive on the Eastern Front to coincide with D-Day in Normandy. The British prime minister was in no position during that tense period to risk Stalin's ire any further.

Two and a half weeks before the Normandy invasion, at 10:20 A.M. on May 18, a patrol of General Anders's Second Corps had hoisted the white-and-red flag of Poland over the ruins of Monte Cassino. The Poles had stormed the slopes below the ancient abbey and had succeeded, at the cost of 3,784 casualties, where others had failed. After five months of stalemate, the victory had opened the road to Rome. The Eternal City itself had fallen on June 4. The next day, the eve of Operation Overlord, Mikołajczyk arrived in Washington on a state visit while Polish troops under General Stanisław Maczek waited to wade into the Normandy surf. Polish arms were making an important contribution to the Allied war effort and, in an election year, the president was anxious to pay proper tribute. Accordingly, he turned on the charm and rolled out the red carpet. Despite the tense struggle under way at that moment to establish a toehold on the coast of France, Roosevelt visited with the Polish prime minister on four occasions.

After the war, Mikołajczyk gave a precise account of the discussions. In one of these meetings, he said, he asked Roosevelt what had been decided at Tehran about Polish frontiers. "Stalin wasn't eager to talk about it," the president replied. "I want you to know that I am still opposed to dividing Poland with this line [the Curzon Line] and that eventually I will act as a moderator in this problem and effect a settlement."

"I understand, Mr. President," Mikołajczyk replied. "But in the case of domestic problems you are dealing with your own citizens. You can settle matters by a bill or decree. But this would hardly apply to the current Polish problem."

Roosevelt then told Mikołajczyk, "I haven't acted on the Polish question because this is an election year. You as a democrat understand such things." The president said he had mentioned the forthcoming U.S. elections to Stalin and "he just couldn't comprehend what I was talking about." That aspect of Stalin's outlook bothered him, Mikołajczyk replied.

"Don't worry," Roosevelt continued. "Stalin doesn't intend to take freedom from Poland. He wouldn't dare do that because he knows that the United States government stands solidly behind you. I will see to it that Poland does not come out of this war injured."

On the evening of June 7, a state dinner was held in Mikołajczyk's honor. Jan Ciechanowski, the Polish government-in-exile's ambassador to the United States and an astute observer of the Washington scene, later wrote that following the dinner the president gave a brilliant speech full of references to Poland's "long history, to her precarious geographical situation, to her great mission as the bulwark of Christianity and Western civilization. He spoke of the partitions of Poland in the eighteenth century, of 'the injustice of these shameful acts of imperialism. . . .' " Ciechanowski said he and Mikołajczyk "left the president at midnight, definitely under his spell."

Mikołajczyk left Washington under the impression that Roosevelt was determined to keep Lwów in Poland. The president had also held out hopes that Wilno might remain in Poland. These were serious misrepresentations, to say the least. Both these matters had been settled months earlier at Tehran. Mikołajczyk's plane was barely off the ground when Roosevelt cabled Stalin, saying that the visit was not an attempt "to inject myself into the merits of the differences" between the Soviets and the Poles. He added that "no specific plan or proposal in any way affecting Polish-Soviet relations was drawn up."

Any doubt about Stalin's plans for Poland was removed in July 1944, shortly after the Red Army crossed the Curzon Line and began occupying territory that ostensibly the Soviet dictator laid no claim to. Lublin, the first important city west of the Line, was liberated on July 22 and a pro-Soviet Polish Committee of National Liberation was announced that same day. Denouncing the government-in-exile, the group, later known as the Lublin committee, claimed "legal and provisional executive authority" over all Polish territory liberated. Most of its self-proclaimed leaders were Moscow-trained professional Communists whose names were completely unfamiliar to their countrymen. They came from the Union of Polish Patriots, which Stalin had organized in Moscow in March of 1943, only a short time before he severed diplomatic relations with the London government-in-exile. On July 26, the Soviet government officially recognized the Lublin committee as politically sovereign in the newly liberated areas. The Red Army, in turn, was granted broad powers in these areas for the establishment of public safety and order.

These grim developments left the government-in-exile and its Home Army in an increasingly desperate position. Operation Tempest had failed completely. The advancing Red Army was still arresting and executing underground leaders; thousands of rank-and-file members of the Home Army were being shipped to Siberia. Soviet propaganda was spewing out blatant falsehoods designed to erode Home Army strength: The underground, according to the Soviets, refused to fight the Wehrmacht. Soviet propaganda still alleged that the Home Army was collaborating with the Germans. These charges left the underground with a difficult choice: It could either bide its time while the Red Army swept across Poland, or stage an uprising against the Germans and attempt to achieve a military contribution of undeniable importance. It chose the latter option, hoping to liberate Warsaw because of its importance as a center of German communications and transportation. In late July, a determined force of thirty-five thousand frontline fighters and seven thousand auxiliary troops waited anxiously in the Polish capital for the signal to attack.

With the Red Army approaching the banks of the Vistula River, Soviet radio broadcast an appeal on July 29, calling on the Poles to revolt and claiming, "There is not a moment to lose." At 5:00 P.M. on August 1, the uprising began. It appeared to be perfectly timed with units of the Red Army advancing into Warsaw's eastern suburbs. Initial results were encouraging. Within hours, the underground had seized the Old Town and other parts of central Warsaw. Underground control soon covered most of the Polish capital. But the Red Army suddenly stopped and its units east of Warsaw began withdrawing. Meanwhile, eight German divisions attacked the city and over a sixty-three-day period proceeded to reduce it to rubble. Both Roosevelt and Churchill implored Stalin, to no avail, to come to the aid of the beleaguered city. Polish pilots in British and American planes tried to fly relief supplies to the resistance, but the effort was futile unless refueling could be arranged on Soviet bases. Stalin denied his allies access to them. Allied planes attempted the run anyway, flying 1,750 miles round-trip from Brindisi, Italy, and experiencing heavy losses. Stalin finally relented on September 9, but by this time the Wehrmacht had the resistance well in hand. By the time the Home Army commander, General

Tadeusz Bór-Komorowski, surrendered on October 2, one quarter of Warsaw's population was dead, wounded, or missing.

Roosevelt's cheery optimism had been a welcome relief for Mikołajczyk after Churchill's blunt insistence that he accept Stalin's demands. The Polish prime minister was determined to follow the president's advice and see Stalin as soon as possible. He left London on July 26, and in Cairo and Tehran received reports that the Soviets had just granted recognition to the Lublin committee. He considered turning back, but in Tehran, where copies of wires sent by Churchill and Roosevelt to Stalin had awaited him, decided to go on. These messages had urged the Soviet dictator to welcome Mikołajczyk and cooperate with his government.

Mikołajczyk arrived in Moscow on the eve of the Warsaw Uprising. He met with Stalin at 9:30 P.M. on August 3 and appealed immediately for help for the resistance under way in the Polish capital. Stalin gave him a noncommittal response. "I cannot trust the Poles," he said. "They suspect me of wanting to occupy Poland again. They're making a lot of trouble for me." Then he bluntly informed Mikołajczyk that he had no intention of dealing with two Polish governments, that Mikołajczyk should meet with the Lublin committee to work out an agreement. In meetings over the next few days, it was clear to Mikołajczyk how subservient to Stalin the committee's members were. They contended that there was no rebellion in Warsaw and that the Curzon Line was a just line of demarcation between Poland and the Soviet Union. The committee's terms were harsh. They agreed to make Mikołajczyk prime minister of a new coalition government, but only four of eighteen places in the Cabinet would go to the exile government. Mikołajczyk left Moscow on August 9, deeply pessimistic that cooperation on any level could be established with the Soviets.

After returning to London he organized one last initiative to save his government. In the last half of August, he engaged his Cabinet and the underground in drafting a new plan designed to break the stalemate. The process provoked sharp and painful debate, but finally resulted in an agreement, which was submitted to Soviet, British, and American authorities on August 30, 1944. The plan proposed equal representation in a coalition government among four major prewar parties—the Peasant, the National, the Socialist, and the Christian Labor—and a fifth—the Communist, or Polish Workers', party. The plan stipulated that the Piłsudski faction would be excluded from the coalition and implied acceptance of frontier adjustments demanded by the Soviet Union.

The British and Americans indicated their support of the new plan and promised to lobby Stalin in behalf of it. The Soviet government offered no response. Early in October, Churchill and Eden went to Moscow; believing that Germany might collapse before the end of the year, they hoped to reach agreement with Stalin on spheres of influence in Eastern Europe. Control of Polish territory newly liberated by the Red Army was being handed over to the Lublin committee. It was an ominous sign to Churchill, who knew that the impasse between Stalin and the Polish government-in-exile must be broken immediately, or all opportunity to establish an independent Poland would vanish. The underground had just capitulated in Warsaw when Churchill sent Mikołajczyk a message urging him "to fly at once to join us in Moscow. I am sure that this is the only way in which we can break the present deadlock. . . ." Mikołajczyk left almost immediately and arrived in Moscow on October 12.

The following day he met with Stalin, Churchill, Eden, and Molotov. Ambassador Harriman sat in as an observer. Mikołajczyk's memoirs provide a detailed account of the discussion. The Polish prime minister emphasized at the outset the fairness of his plan "to bring about an agreement between Poland and Russia, not between Russia and a handful of Poles—arbitrarily and unilaterally chosen by a foreign power."

Churchill asked if the advice of the Lublin committee had been considered. Mikołajczyk replied that he had gone "much deeper than the Lublin Poles. I went to the Polish people." He emphasized that his solution would include all parties, including the Communists.

"The Lublin government should have a bigger share in the postwar Polish government," Churchill interjected.

"Your plan has two big defects," Stalin commented. "It ignores the Lublin Poles who have done such a good job in that part of Poland which the Soviet Army has liberated. And, secondly, if any Polish government wants relations with the Soviet Union, it must recognize the Curzon Line as an actuality." Stalin paused, then continued: "Perhaps the rest of your plan is acceptable. But these two flaws must be corrected."

Churchill brightened with enthusiasm. "I see now a new hope for agreement." He said his government agreed that in view of the Red Army losses and its role in Poland's liberation "the Curzon Line must be your eastern frontier."

"Don't worry," Churchill told Mikołajczyk. "We will see to it that for the land you lose in the east there will be compensations in Germany. . . . You'll have a nice big country. Not the one created at

Versailles, certainly, but a real, solid, new home in which the Polish nation can live and develop in security, freedom, and prosperity."

Mikołajczyk then told Stalin, "You accuse me of ignoring the Lublin Committee. You're ignoring the Polish government, which has fought the Germans, our common foe, for five years. . . ."

"I recognize this," Stalin answered. "I have given the proper credit."

"But you haven't," Mikołajczyk persisted. "Other governments have been reinstated in liberated areas, but not the Polish government."

"I want no argument," Stalin warned.

"Neither do I," Mikołajczyk shot back. He then pointed out that the Lublin committee had permitted Soviet agents to arrest and deport members of the Home Army who had assisted the Red Army in liberating Poland.

"Things are bad everywhere," Stalin said laughingly.

"Anyway, I cannot accept the Curzon Line," Mikołajczyk pointed out. "I have no authority to yield 48 per cent of our country, no authority to forsake millions of my countrymen and leave them to their fate. If I agreed, everyone would have the right to say, 'It was for this that the Polish soldiers fought—a politician's sellout.' "

"You're an imperialist," Stalin told him, and then offered a lengthy explanation of the Soviet position. Mikołajczyk pointed out that even if the area were yielded the Poles still would have no guarantee on the future independence of what was left of their country.

"Who is threatening the independence of Poland?" Stalin barked.

Suddenly Molotov interrupted. "But all this was settled at Teheran!" he said in an irritated voice, looking directly at Churchill and Harriman, who remained silent.

"If your memories fail you, let me recall the facts to you," Molotov intoned. "We all agreed at Teheran that the Curzon Line must divide Poland. You will recall that President Roosevelt agreed to this solution and strongly endorsed the line. And then we agreed that it would be best not to issue any public declaration about our agreement."

Recalling all the assurances to the contrary, Mikołajczyk looked first at Churchill, then at Harriman. There was silence as he waited for an explanation. Finally, Churchill looked him in the eye and softly said, "I confirm this." The decision, made almost a year earlier in Tehran, had finally been acknowledged to the Polish leader.

The meeting quickly degenerated into an acrimonious debate between Churchill and Mikołajczyk. Stalin excused himself gruffly. Later, Churchill accused Mikołajczyk of failing to compromise earlier in the year when the organization of a rival government might have been avoided. That session degenerated further, into a shouting match between two leaders who had developed a genuine fondness for each other during the wartime struggles. At one point, Mikołajczyk later noted, "we were both on the point of tears."

"You're no government," Churchill said at one point. "You're a callous people who want to wreck Europe. I shall leave you to your own troubles. . . . You have only your miserable, petty, selfish interests in mind." He threatened to withdraw recognition and told Mikołajczyk that he should be in a lunatic asylum. Choked with fury, Mikołajczyk said he would prefer to parachute into Poland to join the underground struggle rather than "to be hanged later by the Russians in full view of your British Ambassador!" The comment cut Churchill to the quick and he abruptly left the room. A few minutes later, he returned and put his arm around Mikołajczyk's shoulders, but both men knew that all real remedies were exhausted. Mikołajczyk made one last attempt to compromise with Stalin, offering to give up Wilno in return for Lwów. Stalin refused.

Mikołajczyk knew further opposition was futile. He flew back to London and informed his Cabinet of the ugly truth: Further negotiation was impossible. To have any role in any new Polish government, acceptance of the Soviet terms was imperative. His deeply divided cabinet could not swallow such repugnant terms. Its conservative members were convinced that Mikołajczyk had gone too far, and rejected his recommendation that the Curzon Line be accepted as Poland's eastern frontier. To the hardliners, Mikołajczyk had shown his true colors. He was worse than an "appeaser" and a "collaborationist." His performance in Moscow had earned him a new, more scathing epithet: that of "traitor to the Polish nation." In the end his opponents had won a Pyrrhic victory. Mikołajczyk resigned as prime minister on November 24, 1944. But the government-in-exile, the legitimate government of Poland, quickly sank into oblivion.

Late in 1944, underground authorities in Kraków agreed to send an unusual mission south to a partisan base camp deep in a Tatra mountain forest near the town of Tymbark. Operating there were members of the Home Army who had not been home in years, men who faced the prospect of yet another lonely holiday away from family and friends. What better way to boost their spirits, the underground decided, than to have several young women from Kraków pay a visit to their hideout.

The young women—Magda, Jaga, and three friends—represented a typical cell in an arm of the Home Army known as Pomoc Żołnierzom,

Aid for the Soldiers. PZ's structure resembled that of other parts of the underground, in theory if not in practice. Each cell consisted of five or six members who, ostensibly, knew each other only by pseudonyms. Magda called herself "Malinka" and Jaga chose "Mija," but the names were superfluous because the group's members were all close friends from the same neighborhood.

"How we were organized seemed a bit mysterious, but actually some of the procedures were fairly ridiculous," Magda told me. "We all had known each other for some time. The main point, I think, was that these organized activities were a help to us. They gave us a reason to survive."

The cell met at least once a week. Adults with specialized knowledge frequently came to teach practical subjects like nutrition, the use of small firearms, and how to avoid the łapanki, or street sweeps, in which the Germans shut off both ends of a thoroughfare and arrested everyone in between. To avoid these traps, PZ cells studied maps of the center of Kraków, showing alley ways and escape passages to be used in an emergency. Magda's sister Maria was trapped in one such sweep in the fall of 1944 and taken to Montelupich prison for interrogation. The Gestapo agent who examined her papers said immediately: "Oh, you were born in Vienna. You are free to go."

The PZ cell's most important responsibility was to prepare small packages of food for prisoners in concentration camps. Any organized public effort to provide such assistance had been banned by the Germans. But individuals could send packages, so the underground used PZ cells to prepare for such shipments on a large scale. One grim aspect of the work was the monthly task of verifying whether individual prisoners were still alive. Armed with a list of ten or more names, members of the cell generally went to the prisoners' homes to obtain this information.

Packages for the camps were packed by Magda's group in a business office in the center of Kraków under the supervision of a woman named Agata who held a fairly high rank in the underground. Agata arranged to have the contents of the packages—generally słonina (pork fat) mixed with bacon and onions; bread; artificial honey; and, occasionally, apples—delivered for assembly. Once individual paper cartons were filled, wrapped, and addressed, Agata coordinated their shipment.

All these arrangements made a clerk in the office, a man of about sixty named Fredzio, extremely nervous. Although he had nothing to do with the project, he kept a constant lookout for the police and issued a steady stream of complaints that the operation's messiness and clutter could only lead to trouble. The young women resented his fussiness, but Fredzio was right. In the summer of 1944, the police came to arrest Agata one day while the boxes were being packed. They took her and, as an afterthought, arrested Fredzio because he happened to be on the scene. Agata was sent to a concentration camp, but Fredzio was executed a short time after his arrest. "This made a great impression on us," Magda said. "They had taken him just because he was there. We said to ourselves, 'Look at Fredzio. He was always so careful. He took no chances. He didn't want to get involved, but he was arrested anyway.' "

The Warsaw Uprising had a powerful effect on attitudes in Magda's PZ cell. The uprising was still under way in September, when she was released from St. Michael's prison. At her first PZ meeting, she found the atmosphere changed completely. Cell members were working feverishly to prepare and store as much food as possible for the expected uprising in Kraków. Large supplies of homemade noodles and other dishes were being prepared and hidden in individual homes to be used once the Home Army began its armed resistance.

But the uprising never came. "We felt ashamed because we knew the people in Warsaw were sacrificing their lives and we were doing nothing," Magda said. "When it ended we felt that all these preparations were a waste." Soon afterward the idea of paying a visit to the partisans first surfaced. It was prompted by a request that the PZ cell prepare and present a puppet show at a home for the elderly. The idea appealed to no one.

"Then someone suggested, 'Why not do it for the partisans instead?' " Magda told me. "We all agreed that this was a terrific idea. It would help boost morale and show how much we all supported the Home Army. At first our supervisor discouraged us, but finally she agreed to take it up with her superiors." With the holidays approaching, the answer came back from underground authorities. The trip would be approved and arrangements would be made if each member of the cell obtained approval from her family. Reluctantly Janina agreed for Magda and Jaga to go. The others in the group gained permission from their families, and on Christmas night they all began their journey to an unknown destination where several companies of partisans were hiding.

Shortly before eight P.M. curfew, the young women met, as directed, a railroad man and Home Army member who led them to the watchman's tower in the Kraków switching yard. They climbed into the tower and waited in the stifling heat generated by a large coal stove until the watchman returned for them about ten P.M. He gave them tickets on a train leaving shortly for the south and led them along the track to board it just moments before its departure. As they climbed aboard they were told to disembark at Rabka, a resort station not far from Zakopane, where someone would be waiting to meet them.

During the three-hour trip south, Magda and Jaga speculated about how near they would come to Skawa, the small village where their family had been on vacation in August 1939. They knew that near Skawa there were large forests where a partisan base camp might well be located. The women also laughed about how they would describe the purpose of their trip if stopped by German authorities. "To see our boyfriends," someone suggested. "No, our grandfather," someone else opted. Discussion had then centered for some time on the identification of names of ficticious people they could say they were visiting.

At Rabka, they stepped off the train and were approached immediately by an underground guide who took the group to a nearby house, where they were told to wait for another guide who would take them on the final leg of the journey. Here they learned that their destination was a partisan sanctuary in Tymbark Forest several kilometers away. They left a few hours before dawn under a full moon and bright stars and tramped for about two hours along a path that wound its way through heavy snow in rugged countryside. A bulky satchel containing the marionettes and other props for the puppet show was heavy and difficult to manage. It changed hands frequently during the journey.

Suddenly a voice up the path barked, "Stop! Who goes there?"

A tall, young, blond-headed guard with a rifle stepped out of the shadows. The guide quickly spoke a password and the group moved through. Only a few paces farther on, the path curled toward a clearing. Open ground and a few houses could be seen in the distance. At the edge of the clearing a large banner had been draped high above the path from two trees. It proclaimed simply, "RZECZPOSPOLITA POLSKA"—Republic of Poland.

It was the first time in five years that Magda and the others had seen the words so boldly displayed. "It gave me such a feeling of pride to see that banner," Magda said. "Its impact was very dramatic. It gave us such a feeling of elation."

The small village in the clearing was the center of the base camp. About twenty partisans lived there in the villagers' houses. Other members of the underground were scattered a short distance away in other small villages. From these communities, the partisans roamed freely over the huge wooded area south of Zakopane, venturing out to raid German supply trains, ammunition dumps, and other military targets.

The young women were housed in one of the huts at the base camp. Their arrival had been eagerly awaited and caused a great sensation among the two hundred or so men based in Tymbark Forest. A full evening of fun was planned each night for a week. Dinner each evening was to be followed by a performance of the puppet show and then singing and dancing. The dances were a late addition made possible when someone produced a record player just before the young women arrived. Rollicking howls and cheers greeted the first night's puppet show. Several of the marionettes were pompous German officials, the objects of relentless satire. Their predictable demise at the end of the show brought the house down.

One night soon after the PZ cell arrived an important airdrop was scheduled. For some time supplies had been parachuted periodically to the partisans in Tymbark from Allied planes. Several boxes of food and ammunition were delivered that evening and brought back to the base camp. The returning men gave the parachute to Magda and her friends, insisting that they take the nylon material home and use it to make blouses.

A farewell dinner and a big New Year's Eve party were planned for the last evening the young women would be in Tymbark. At dinner, Magda sat with a young officer whose pseudonym was Lieutenant Olcha. She had spoken with him several times during her week in the forest and had learned much about his unusual war record. The lieutenant had been captured by the Soviets in late September, 1939, and taken to Kozelshchina, the same transition camp where her father and her uncle Staszek Niewiadomski had been held. He had even met Colonel Marian Bolesławicz, the father of Magda's close friend Iwa. Later, for reasons never explained to Olcha, the Soviets transferred him to Butyrki Prison in Moscow. He had suffered greatly at Butyrki because of an acute lack of water. At the same time he had become fluent in Russian and had learned a great deal about his captors. Shortly after the signing of the Polish-Soviet agreement of July 30, 1941, the Russians released Olcha and he immediately joined General Anders's army-in-exile. He had left the Soviet Union with the army, trained in the Middle East, fought at Monte Cassino, and had then been sent to England. In the fall of 1944, he had parachuted into Tymbark Forest to help with the resistance.

He was the first man Magda had met who had been a prisoner of the Soviets. She regarded him as a hero, who obviously knew a great deal about the Soviet Union. Several times during the week she had wanted to ask him his opinion about the German propaganda campaign the previous year concerning the bodies in Katyń Forest. Dining with him on New Year's Eve over broth, macaroni, and oat flakes, she abruptly raised the question. "Lieutenant Olcha, what do you think the Russians have done with our officers who were captured in 1939? Were the Germans playing a propaganda trick on us last year?" She added that her own father was among the captured men.

A change came over the lieutenant's face with this question. It seemed drained of color and life. A long pause followed in which he merely stared in her direction. Then he said, "I do not know for a fact what happened. But based on my own experiences, based on how I was treated and how other Poles there were treated, I do not have the slightest doubt in my mind that the Russians have murdered every one of our men."

His words struck Magda with all the force of a heavy blow. She had hoped that he would say the Germans had trumped up the whole affair.

Confused, stammering, she excused herself from the table and hurried out into the night air. "Tata is dead. Tata is dead." The words echoed in her mind over and over.

"From that moment I knew he was not coming home," Magda continued. "I did not pray for his return any more."

On the long trip back to Kraków, Magda said almost nothing to her companions. Lieutenant Olcha's words depressed her deeply. "He was there. He knows the Russians," she kept thinking over and over. Finally, she confided to Jaga what was wrong.

How had she managed to come so late to her conclusion? Jaga asked. "I knew he was dead last year," she said. "There was never a doubt in my mind."

A postcard from Staszek arrived a few days after Magda and Jaga returned to Kraków. It was written in Polish, not German as required by concentration-camp censors. Somehow he had managed to smuggle the card outside the camp and have it sent to Kraków by regular mail. It carried no return address, and, to further conceal his identity, Staszek had addressed the card to Maria, using her married name, Zaczek. The card, dated January 1, 1945, said:

Last night at midnight, I tipped the cup in your honor. May this year be for you a year of happiness and joy that makes all your dreams and wishes come true. And above all, may it keep you smiling and joyful. May I be able to see you, Mama, healthy and happy. Even though these holidays find me in high spirits, they give me the most acute feeling of missing home and all of you. Perhaps that is because I am doing quite all right. You have not the least reason to worry about me. . . .

These were the last words Staszek's mother and sisters would hear from him. Sometime near the end of April 1945, the U.S. Army liberated the camp where he was held. He was found in an emaciated state, suffering from acute pneumonia, and was hospitalized immediately at Dora. In the last few days of the war, the hospital was bombed accidentally by American planes. During the attack, Staszek and an elderly Jewish patient in the next bed were too weak to take refuge in the basement with the other patients and the staff. The two men covered their heads with blankets instead. Staszek's fellow patient recovered. He returned to Kraków two months later and at that time wrote the Czarneks a brief note saying that an accumulation of illnesses had taken Staszek's life on May 6, the last day of the war in Europe.

CHAPTER 22

The Allies' Blind Eye

<<<<<<<<<<<<

The rubble in Warsaw and the rubble in Radebeul symbolized the recurring Polish tragedy. The failed uprising denied the government-in-exile a physical presence in Poland and presaged yet another era of foreign domination. The fire at the freight-forwarding depot in the Dresden suburb consumed material evidence that presumably could have been used abroad to bring the Soviets to account for the murders in Katyń Forest. Poland's allies in the West had been powerless to assist her in either instance.

On the face of it, the burning of Dr. Beck's boxes was fate's last cruel twist. Polish specialists had been working for more than two years on the tedious task of restoring and cataloging evidence found on the bodies of the murdered men. That effort was undertaken primarily to prove to the West that the Soviets were guilty. But there is clear evidence that by mid-1943 Anglo-American leaders needed no convincing. Results from the graveside investigations, spirited to London through the underground, had already accomplished that task. It is also clear that that evidence would not be used to call the Soviets to account for the crime. To the contrary, all traces of Soviet guilt were being concealed and their concealment would continue over the last two years of the war.

That being the case, the burning of the boxes was not the cruel twist that it seemed. The Allies already knew, essentially, what the material inside could prove. They were determined to do nothing about it. A small but poignant aspect of the Polish tragedy was the futility of the chase across Poland to Germany in the closing months of the war. Dr. Beck's mission was doomed because no authorities in the West would draw up an indictment, no jurisdiction there could render a verdict, and—even if guilt was found—no sentence could be imposed. To compound the tragedy, the Poles' allies would not dare to raise the issue with the Soviets, let alone bring accusations for the murders at Katyń.

301

Churchill hinted as much when he told Sikorski over lunch at No. 10 Downing Street in April 1943: "If they [the officers] are dead, nothing you can do will bring them back."

But the Poles were hardly betrayed. Circumstances had once again laid bare their historic predicament: They were trapped by their own geography and the present political realities. Allies who understood their dilemma could help no more at the end than at the beginning of the war. A war that had begun to save Poland had, by the time of these events, become a war to destroy Hitler and create a new and safer world order. Polish independence was a small piece in that large puzzle. Mikołajczyk and a few other members of the government-in-exile understood that point all too well. For others, the actions of the Allies represented the worst kind of treachery and betrayal. And efforts to conceal evidence of Soviet guilt at Katyń gave some foundation to their claims. In the last two years of the war secret reports did vanish, men were muzzled, broadcasts were censored, and careers were ruined to keep a tight lid on evidence of an ugly crime in the Allied camp. But none of these actions was designed to help Stalin. All were undertaken only because war strategy required it. Throughout this period Allied statesmen sympathized deeply with the Poles. And many of them detested the silence they were obliged to observe in the interest of Big Three harmony. The result for some was a deeply troubling moral conflict.

In mid-June 1943, the king and the War Cabinet of Great Britain received a top-secret memorandum written by Sir Owen O'Malley, the British ambassador to the Polish government-in-exile. In it, O'Malley, a career diplomat, presented detailed evidence of how and why the Soviets had "broken apart the heads of [several] thousand Polish officers with the insouciance of a monkey cracking walnuts." O'Malley's memorandum stirred the consciences of senior statesmen deeply for two reasons. First, his evidence against the Soviets was overwhelming. And second, he developed a persuasive argument that the crime could cause the British enduring "moral repercussions." O'Malley's arguments were so moving, in fact, that on June 18, 1943, Sir Alexander Cadogan, Britain's permanent under secretary of state, attached to the memorandum a lengthy handwritten note, which read as follows:

> This is very disturbing. I confess that in cowardly fashion, I had rather turned my head away from the scene at Katyn—for fear of what I should find there. There may be evidence, that we do not know of, that may point in another direction. But on the evidence that we have, it is difficult to escape from a presumption of Russian guilt.

This of course raises terrible problems, but I think no one has pointed out that, on the purely moral plane, these are not new. How many thousands of its own citizens has the Soviet regime butchered? And I don't know that the blood of a Pole cries louder to heaven that that of a Russian. But we have perforce welcomed the Russians as allies and have set ourselves to work with them in war and peace.

The ominous thing about this incident is the ultimate political repercussions. How, if Russian guilt is established, can we expect Poles to live amicably side by side with Russians for generations to come? I fear there is no answer to that question.

And one other disturbing thought is that we may eventually, by agreement and in collaboration with the Russians, proceed to the trial and perhaps execution of Axis "war criminals" while condoning this atrocity. I confess that I shall find that extremely difficult to swallow.

However, quite clearly for the moment, there is nothing to be done. As to what circulation we give to this explosive material, I find it difficult to make up my mind. Of course it would be only honest to circulate it. But as we know (all admit) that the knowledge of this evidence cannot affect the course of action, or policy, is there any advantage in exposing more individuals than necessary to the spiritual conflict that a reading of this dispatch excites?

Cadogan's comments settled an argument within the Foreign Office about whether O'Malley's memorandum should be circulated to the War Cabinet. Cover comments attached to the memorandum include those of one official who told Cadogan, "This is a brilliant, unorthodox and disquieting despatch. . . . In effect Mr. O'Malley urges that we should follow the example which the Poles themselves are unhappily so prone to offer us and in our diplomacy allow our heads to be governed by our hearts." Another wrote, "It is obviously a very awkward matter when we are fighting for a moral cause and when we intend to deal adequately with war criminals, that our Allies should be open to accusations of this kind. . . ." Cadogan and Eden decided to circulate the memorandum.

How had O'Malley managed to "excite," as Cadogan put it, such spiritual conflict? The first few pages of his lengthy memorandum described most of the evidence accumulated at the grave site and transmitted to London by the Polish underground, and other information provided by the remnant of 448 men sent to Gryazovets. It described the circumstances in which the officers were captured, the camps they were kept in, their scribblings on the walls of train carriages, how letters to relatives suddenly stopped at the end of March 1940, the

Poles' futile inquiries to the Soviets for information about the men, and the findings at Katyń by the technical commission of the Polish Red Cross. O'Malley concluded that the Soviets' confused response to the German announcement of the discovery of the graves could only mean "that the Russian Government had something to hide." The ambassador's report even provided a graphic account of the victims' last moments:

> If a man struggled, it seems that the executioner threw his coat over his head, tying it round his neck and leading him hooded to the pit's edge, for in many cases a body was found to be thus hooded and the coat to have been pierced by a bullet where it covered the base of the skull. But those who went quietly to their death must have seen a monstrous sight. In the broad deep pit their comrades lay, packed closely round the edge, head to feet, like sardines in a tin. . . . Up and down on the bodies the executioners tramped, hauling the dead bodies about and treading in the blood like butchers in a stockyard.

O'Malley drew attention to the trees planted on the graves, suggesting that a competent botanist could prove whether they have been transplanted in May 1940 or sometime after July 1941. This part of the report would prompt Churchill to write Eden, five days after the Soviet commission published its report:

> I think Sir Owen O'Malley should have been asked very secretly to express his opinion on the K.W. [Katyń Woods] inquiry. How does the argument about the length of time the birch [sic] trees had grown over the grave fit in with this new tale? Did anybody look at the birch trees? All this is merely to ascertain the facts because we should none of us ever speak a word about it.

The final part of the report dealt with the moral implications of the crime from a British perspective. It provides a view from inside the Foreign Office that explains what set the Katyń case apart. The excerpts below present the essence of O'Malley's arguments:

> In handling the publicity side of the Katyn affair we have been constrained by the urgent need for cordial relations with the Soviet Government to appear to appraise the evidence with more hesitation and lenience than we should do in forming a commonsense judgement on events occurring in normal times or in the ordinary course of our private lives; we have been obliged to appear to distort the normal and healthy operation of our intellectual and moral judgments; we have been

obliged to give undue prominence to the tactlessness or impulsiveness of Poles, to restrain the Poles from putting their case clearly before the public, to discourage any attempt by the public and the press to probe the ugly story to the bottom. In general we have been obliged to deflect attention from possibilities which in the ordinary affairs of life would cry to high heaven for elucidation, and to withhold the full measure of solicitude which, in other circumstances, would be shown to acquaintances situated as a large number of Poles now are. We have in fact perforce used the good name of England like the murderers used the little conifers to cover up a massacre; and in view of the immense importance of an appearance of Allied unity and of the heroic resistance of Russia to Germany, few will think that any other course would have been wise or right.

This dislocation between our public attitude and our private feelings we may know to be deliberate and inevitable; but at the same time we may perhaps wonder whether, by representing to others something less than the whole truth so far as we know it, and something less than the probabilities so far as they seem to us probable, we are not incurring a risk of what—not to put a fine point on it—might darken our vision and take the edge off our moral sensibility. If so, how is this risk to be avoided?

. . .

Nobody doubts that morals now enter into the domestic politics of the United Kingdom, but it was not always so. There was a time when the acts of the Government in London were less often the fruit of consultation and compromise in the general interests of all than of the ascendancy of one class or group of citizens who had been temporarily successful in the domestic arena. It was realisation of the interdependence of all classes and groups of the population of England, Scotland and Wales which discouraged the play of internecine power-politics and set the welfare of all above the advantage of the strong. Similar causes are producing similar results in the relations of states to each other. . . . [The] conception of the nation state as the largest group in which human beings are organically associated with each other is being superseded by the conception of a larger, it may be of a European, or indeed of a worldwide unity. . . . Europe, and indeed the world, are in process of integrating themselves. . . . This being so, it would be strange if the same movement towards the coalescence of smaller into larger groups which brought about the infiltration of morals into domestic politics were not also now bringing about the infiltration of morals into international politics. This, in fact, it seems to many of us is exactly what is happening, and is why, as the late Mr. Headlam Morley said, "what in the international sphere is morally indefensible generally turns out in the long run to have been politically inept." It is surely the case that many of the political troubles of neighboring countries and some of our own have in the past arisen because they and we were incapable of seeing this or unwilling to admit it.

If, then, morals have become involved with international politics, if it be the case that a monstrous crime has been committed by a foreign government—albeit a friendly one—and that we, for however valid reasons, have been obliged to behave as if the deed was not theirs, may it not be that we now stand in danger of bemusing not only others but ourselves; of falling, as Mr. Winant said recently at Birmingham, under St. Paul's curse on those who can see cruelty "and burn not"? If so, and since no remedy can be found in an early alteration of our public attitude towards the Katyn affair, we ought, maybe, to ask ourselves how, consistently with the necessities of our relations with the Soviet Government, the voice of our political conscience is to be kept up to concert pitch. It may be that the answer lies, for the moment, only in something to be done inside our own hearts and minds where we are masters. Here at any rate we can make a compensatory contribution—a reaffirmation of our allegiance to truth and justice and compassion. If we do this we shall at least be predisposing ourselves to the exercise of a right judgement on all those half political, half moral, questions (such as the fate of Polish deportees now in Russia) which will confront us both here and elsewhere and more particularly in respect to Polish-Russian relations as the war pursues its course and draws to its end; and so, if the facts about the Katyn massacre turn out to be as most of us incline to think, shall we vindicate the spirit of these brave unlucky men and justify the living to the dead.

About a month after O'Malley's memorandum was circulated to the War Cabinet, Churchill apparently suggested sending it to Roosevelt. On July 16, Eden advised against it, noting that "the document is pretty explosive, and in some respects, prejudicial. I thought that my colleagues should see it, but if it was to find its way into unauthorized hands, the reaction on our relations with Russia would be serious." Churchill ignored the advice and wrote Roosevelt on August 13 suggesting that he read the O'Malley memorandum carefully. Ten days later Churchill asked Harry Hopkins if Roosevelt had read the document, and asked to have it returned once he was finished with it. On September 4, he reminded the White House staff that he wanted the

O'Malley report back when the president was finished with it. One week later, the White House staff confirmed that the document had been handed to Roosevelt.

It is unlikely that O'Malley's findings caused shock or surprise at the White House. Six weeks after Goebbels's announcement of the crime, Lieutenant Colonel Henry I. Szymanski, the U.S. Army liaison officer to the Polish army-in-exile, sent a comprehensive background report on the situation to Major General George V. Strong, the head of G-2 (intelligence) at the War Department. In a cover note, he said the material was being carried by hand from Cairo to Washington because it "contains too much dynamite to be forwarded through regular channels. . . ." Included among the documents relayed was a dramatic statement by Captain Józef Czapski, who had been ordered by General Anders in the fall of 1941 to investigate the whereabouts of the missing officers. Czapski, the reader will recall, was himself a prisoner at Starobelsk. These experiences gave him insights that few others had. Czapski concluded that the Soviets had murdered his fellow officers at a time when they were "certain that Poland would never rise again." The materials sent by Szymanski also included an account of the circumstances in which Beria made his chilling comment in 1940—"We made a blunder, we *did* make a blunder"—concerning the officers at Kozelsk and Starobelsk. His report also contained extensive background material on inquiries about the missing men addressed to Stalin personally by Generals Sikorski and Anders.

Szymanski's report after the discovery of the crime was in addition to a thorough investigation and report he had prepared for the War Department on November 23, 1942. It included a large number of case histories of deported Poles who were then in Iran. Szymanski was a West Point graduate and a career army officer, but his background as a Polish-American from Milwaukee led him to take great personal interest in the plight of the women and children, including thousands of orphans, on the beaches of Pahlevi and in the camps that ringed Tehran. He supplied the War Department with a great many photographs of emaciated, half-dead Poles who had managed to escape the U.S.S.R. with the army-in-exile. In that report, written six months before the crime was discovered, Szymanski observed that "there are still some 900,000 Polish citizens, deportees, in Russia slowly being exterminated through overwork and undernourishment. . . . Thousands of families broken up, deported, tortured and starved cannot so easily forget the immediate past. . . ."

The Szymanski reports were filed, as one investigating congressman would complain several years later, "in a warehouse somewhere and not found until we finally made a little noise about it." In 1944, during the Warsaw Uprising, nine members of Congress who were of Polish descent pressed for the release of the Szymanski reports. Six years later, one of them, Rep. Alvin E. O'Konski of Wisconsin, told his colleagues:

> After we saw that we were not getting anywhere, I believe that just about every one of us had tears in our eyes. So we said, "In the name of mercy and in the name of God, Mr. Secretary of State, will you please convey our message to the President of the United States to intervene at least so that the Russians will show a little bit of mercy on the Poles in this great crisis?"

The case of Szymanski's reports was not the only one in which incriminating evidence against the Soviets was turned over to G-2 at the War Department and then disappeared. The most controversial case involved an American prisoner of war who was liberated when the Red Army overran his POW camp at Luckenwalde, south of Berlin, in late April 1945. Lieutenant Colonel John Van Vliet, Jr., a career U.S. Army officer, had been waiting for two years to tell what he knew about the murders in Katyń Forest. His story, too, was politically explosive, so sensitive that he was anxious to find someone at a high enough level who could decide how to handle the matter. That was no easy task. The same web of confusion that trapped Dr. Beck, resulting in the burning of the material evidence from Katyń, also stood in Van Vliet's way. The entire area south of Berlin was in chaos. A mélange of troops, equipment, and refugees choked roads in every direction. In the last days of the war, three armies had converged there, making movement in any direction difficult, at times impossible. Finally, on May 5, Van Vliet reached the American lines near Duben and found G-2 for the 144th Division of the U.S. First Army. Revealing only the bare outlines of his story, he stressed that he probably should "have words with somebody in either the War Department or the State Department and no one else." Someone at an appropriate level, he said, should make that decision. Van Vliet's request for an audience with senior brass was granted. That very day he was whisked to Leipzig and the next morning he was ushered into the office of General "Lightning Joe" Collins, the commanding officer of the United States Army's 7th Corps.

Van Vliet laid the whole story out for the general. It began with his capture in Tunisia in February 1943 when his battalion had suddenly been overrun by the Germans. Van Vliet said he and a few others were flown a short time later to Naples and then taken by train to Oflag IX A/Z at Rotenburg, Germany, where about 350 British and 125 American POWs were being held. As it turned out, he was the senior American officer in camp. In the last half of April, about two months after his arrival in camp, the officers at Oflag IX A/Z became aware of an apparent atrocity near Smolensk that was receiving sensational coverage in the German press. Lurid photographs purported to show the bodies of some of the ten thousand Polish officers murdered by the Soviets in a place called Katyń Forest. Van Vliet and his companions paid only passing attention to the story, assuming that the coverage was part of a carefully contrived German propaganda campaign. Then, a few days later, without warning, Van Vliet received a disturbing notice: He and several other prisoners were to be taken to Katyń Forest to witness the exhumations. Van Vliet was told that he and the senior British officer in the camp, a Brigadier Nicholson, would lead the delegation. Both would be required to choose fellow officers to round out the group. When the German security officer, a Hauptmann Heyl, delivered this news, Van Vliet angrily protested the decision as a blatant violation of the Geneva Convention on the treatment of war prisoners. He had put his objections in writing, but Heyl had shrugged off the protest, saying Van Vliet would be forced to go whether he liked it or not.

On May 10, the prisoners had been taken by train from Rotenburg to Berlin. The group included Van Vliet, six Britishers, and the second American, Captain Donald B. Stewart, selected by Van Vliet as the Germans had ordered. Van Vliet later said he chose Stewart because he was a West Point graduate and a career army man and had a reputation "of unquestioned integrity." In Berlin the group boarded a German trimotor passenger plane at Tempelhof airport and was flown east to Smolensk. En route, the men had carefully discussed the mission, agreeing that they would resist being drawn into any statements or actions that might be used in German propaganda.

On May 13, the morning after they reached Smolensk, they were driven in bright, cool weather to Katyń Forest, arriving about ten A.M. At the edge of the forest, a Polish honor guard stood at attention and a Polish flag was on display. While walking up the small lane from the main road to the clearing where the exhumations were under way, the group was told that the Germans planned to turn the site into a Polish national shrine. Once they reached the clearing, Van Vliet and the others intently observed the procedures being used to identify the dead

Poles. Then they were required to walk down inside the largest grave and randomly select a body for examination. The workers in the pit struggled for a considerable time working to separate the body selected by the British and Americans. After the body was finally removed, it was taken on a homemade stretcher to the examining table for an autopsy. The POWS noticed, nervously, that their movements around the graves were being recorded by still and motion-picture photographers.

During the autopsy, Van Vliet and Stewart reluctantly began gravitating toward an uncomfortable conclusion: This was no German propaganda stunt; it appeared that the Russians had, in fact, murdered the Poles. Too much evidence made it difficult to think otherwise. The Soviet claim that the Germans had planted fake documents on the bodies was absurd. The dead Poles were tightly sealed together. In the largest grave, they were fused into one huge mass. No one could plant documents on a single body under those conditions. Traces of any effort to tamper with the bodies could not be concealed and none were evident. It seemed clear to Van Vliet and Stewart that the bodies had been in their present fused state for a long time. The idea that somehow the Germans had dug up the men only a few weeks earlier to remove incriminating documents seemed preposterous. Both officers also witnessed the painstaking procedures required to remove documents from the Poles' bodies. Each victim's pockets and boots were carefully slit open and searched. The fragile condition of the partially mummified bodies made it impossible to retrieve documents otherwise.

Both Americans felt that the most convincing evidence of Soviet guilt was the condition of the Poles' boots and clothing. The heels of the boots were hardly worn at all. That directly contradicted the Soviet contention that the men had been engaged in road work while in captivity for almost two years. Over that length of time, the boots would have worn out. The fact that most of the victims wore overcoats also contradicted the Soviets' claim that they were captured by the Germans in late summer 1941. Why would they be wearing overcoats in hot weather? It was just too much for Van Vliet and Stewart to swallow.

Later, the POWs were shown a large collection of documents taken from the bodies, none of which were dated after May 1940. Van Vliet and his companions agreed that documents bearing a later date might easily have been destroyed by the Germans. But this was only a possibility. It did not diminish the importance or credibility of the concrete evidence the group had already seen. Furthermore, the Germans had given the visiting POWs complete freedom to roam about the graves and to ask questions of the Polish physicians and the Russian peasants at the scene. All these factors forced Van Vliet, Stewart, and the other POWs to reluctantly modify their views. As they were about to leave, Van Vliet and Stewart were given souvenirs by the Germans—photographs taken earlier in the day as they watched the exhumations and autopsies. They were told that none of the photographs would be used for propaganda purposes, but both doubted the statement.

Their conclusions about what they had seen in Katyń Forest disturbed both men. Later Van Vliet testified that he arrived there wanting "to consider Russia as a friend and an ally." He said he had a "personal grudge" against the Germans and did not want to believe their story. Stewart also testified that "the longer I was a prisoner, the more I hated the Germans; and yet in spite of the animosity I had toward the Germans . . . in this one case the Germans were not responsible; [the Poles] had been executed by the Russians." Recognizing the sensitivity of their conclusions, the two men agreed that when they returned to Rotenburg, they would say nothing to their fellow prisoners. They also agreed that once they were liberated, Van Vliet, as the senior officer, should report what they had seen and learned to the highest authorities possible.

After hearing Van Vliet's story and seeing the photographs of his visit to Katyń Forest, General Collins agreed that the information was sensitive enough that Van Vliet should go to Washington immediately and make a full report. He arranged for Van Vliet to fly immediately to Reims, in France, where the Germans would surrender two days later. From Reims, Van Vliet caught another flight to Paris, where he waited for several days before flying on to Washington. Van Vliet said no more than necessary to any of the personnel he came in contact with between Leipzig and Washington. He arrived in Washington on May 17 and went immediately to the Pentagon, where he explained his story to Lieutenant Colonel William C. Lantaff in the office of the assistant chief of staff, G-2 for the War Department. After hearing it, Lantaff told Van Vliet he should make a report personally to Major General Clayton Bissell, the assistant chief of staff for intelligence under General George C. Marshall. Bissell was out of town and not due back until May 21. Van Vliet agreed to wait, and Bissell saw him on the morning of May 22.

Bissell listened to Van Vliet for about thirty minutes, then told him that a detailed written report should be prepared. Van Vliet was then directed to an empty room across the hall from Bissell's office, where he began dictating his report to a stenographer. The report was finished later that day and presented to Bissell with the photographs Van Vliet brought back from Katyń attached. Bissell then told Van Vliet he was classifying the report top secret and directed him to remain silent on the matter. Bissell also presented the order in writing. In a brief memorandum headed "Special report to War Department," Bissell told Van Vliet:

> 1. You have furnished to the War Department a special report covering a certain part of your experiences. These have been recorded exactly as dictated by you and will be held available for such use as is considered appropriate by United States Government activities. Due to the nature of your report and the possible political implications, it is directed that you neither mention nor discuss this matter with anyone in or out of the service without specific approval in writing from the War Department.
> 2. This confirms verbal orders given to you by the Assistant Chief of Staff, G-2, in Washington, on 22 May, 1945. Your signature on a copy of these instructions left with the Assistant Chief of Staff, G-2, indicates that you understand these instructions.

Although Bissell later claimed that he forwarded the document to the State Department, Van Vliet's report disappeared and was never found. An independent investigation by the Army Inspector General in 1950 concluded that the report had been "compromised" and that there was no evidence to indicate that it ever left army intelligence (G-2).

Seven years later, in heated testimony before the select committee of Congress that investigated the massacre, Bissell admitted that had the Van Vliet report been made public in 1945, its impact would have been explosive. The Soviets were being pressed hard at the time to enter the war against Japan and to participate in the formation of the United Nations in San Francisco. They finally took both steps, but might not have had the report been made public. At first Bissell vehemently denied discussing the report with his superiors. Later, under a barrage of questions from John J. Mitchell, counsel to the committee, Bissell admitted that it was possible he had talked with army chief of staff General George C. Marshall about how to handle the matter.

In its final report, the select committee expressed dismay at Bissell's admission that "I saw in it [the Van Vliet report] great possibilities of embarrassment; so I classified it the way I have told you, and I think I had no alternative." The committee felt that in taking such a position Bissell had strayed into the political province of the State Department, veering far afield from his responsibility to evaluate the report strictly in terms of military intelligence. The committee stressed that Bissell's action was by no means an isolated matter:

> More amazing to this committee is the testimony of three high-ranking American Army officers who were stationed in Army Intelligence (G-2) during General Bissell's command of this agency.
>
> Testifying in executive session, all three agreed there was a pool of "pro-Soviet civilian employees and some military in Army Intelligence (G-2), who found explanations for almost everything that the Soviet Union did."
>
> These same witnesses told of tremendous efforts exerted by this group to suppress anti-Soviet reports. The committee likewise heard testimony that top-ranking Army officers who were too critical of the Soviets were bypassed in Army Intelligence (G-2).

The committee heard from the three high-ranking army officers on February 26, 1952. Looking for the committee's records for this session thirty-nine years later, I found that it remained classified. But these officers and their chief, Bissell, hardly invented the policy of deference toward the Soviet Union. It pervaded the U.S. government from the top down. A few months before the Big Three meeting in Tehran, Harry Hopkins gave Roosevelt and Churchill a document entitled "Russia's Position." This strategic estimate, prepared on "a very high level" at the Pentagon, concluded:

> Russia's post-war position in Europe will be a dominant one. With Germany crushed, there is no power in Europe to oppose her tremendous military forces. It is true that Great Britain is building up a position in the Mediterranean vis-à-vis Russia that she may find useful in balancing power in Europe. However, even here she may not be able to oppose Russia unless she is otherwise supported.
>
> The conclusions from the foregoing are obvious. Since Russia is the decisive factor in the war, she must be given every assistance and every effort must be made to obtain her friendship. Likewise, since without question she will dominate Europe on the defeat of the Axis, it is even more essential to develop and maintain the most friendly relations with Russia.

Such assessments already carried the weight of unspoken policy by the time the Katyń massacre was discovered. On May 3, 1943, Elmer Davis, head of the Office of War Information, an executive agency that reported directly to the president, made a broadcast that accused the Nazis of exploiting their discovery at Katyń for propaganda purposes.

In a statement aired widely abroad, Davis claimed: "The way the Germans did this is a good example of the doctrine Hitler preached in *Mein Kampf*, that it is easier to make most people swallow a big lie than a little one." In 1952 Davis was sharply reprimanded by the congressional investigating committee "for accepting the Soviet propaganda version of the Katyn massacre without full investigation." The committee also sharply rebuked the OWI and the Federal Communications Commission for going "beyond the scope of their responsibilities" in the spring of 1943 in silencing Polish radio commentators in Detroit and Buffalo who, at the height of the controversy, had reported facts indicating that the Soviets might be guilty at Katyń.

This action was carried out through none-too-subtle pressure that succeeded in infringing the commentators' rights of free speech under the First Amendment of the U.S. Constitution. Representatives of the OWI and the FCC arranged a meeting in New York with two station-owner members of the Wartime Foreign Language Radio Control Commission, an industry liaison group that cooperated with the government on war information. One of the owners was in New York at the time to discuss the renewal of his station license with the FCC. As a result of the meeting between the station owners and the OWI and FCC representatives, the owner of the Detroit station that had aired the offending comments was contacted and told to rein in his Polish commentator. The OWI was represented in New York by the chief of its Foreign Language Division, Alan Cranston, who in 1968 was elected as a member of the U.S. Senate from California.

Roosevelt himself was determined that U.S. handling of the Katyń controversy should not offend the Soviets. In 1943 his special emissary to the Balkans, George Howard Earle, gathered considerable intelligence on the massacre through sources in Romania and Bulgaria. Earle was a former minister to Bulgaria and to Austria and an officer in the U.S. Navy. He became convinced of Soviet guilt and in May 1944 brought the material he had collected directly to the attention of the president. After hearing Earle out and seeing a number of photographs of the exhumations, Roosevelt said, "George, this is entirely German propaganda and a German plot. I am absolutely convinced the Russians did not do this."

Earle returned to Turkey but apparently could not put the matter out of his mind. On March 22, 1945, he sent Roosevelt a letter saying he planned to publish a detailed statement on Katyń on March 28, 1945, unless the president instructed him not to. On March 24, Roosevelt replied:

I have noted with concern your plan to publish your unfavorable opinion of one of our allies. . . .

I not only do not wish it, but I specifically forbid you to publish any information or opinion about an ally that you may have acquired while in office or in the service of the United States Navy.

A short time later Earle was abruptly transferred to Samoa, where he remained until Roosevelt's death. Afterward he was recalled to Washington, where the navy's chief of personnel apologized for his transfer and assured him that the decision to send him to Samoa was not the navy's.

To the Poles the Allied handling of Katyń represented a cold-hearted betrayal. But O'Malley's memorandum clearly points up the dilemma that Churchill, Roosevelt, and their top subordinates faced. They could not indulge the dubious luxury of indicting the Soviets for a crime that could not be avenged. And the Poles reacted as would any people who discovered that the murder of their best and brightest was about to go unpunished.

After Tehran, the Allies were determined that nothing should stand in the way of cooperation with Stalin. They had agreed to open a second front in 1944, an offensive that Stalin would support with an attack against the Wehrmacht in the east. Roosevelt and Churchill knew that the Red Army could prevent the transfer of many German divisions to the west, thereby saving the lives of thousands of British and American soldiers. When Churchill's plan to invade Europe through the Balkans, lands he dubbed the "soft underbelly of Europe," was rejected in Tehran, any real hope of "saving" Poland was gone.

CHAPTER 23

Rescue

When the big Russian transport touched down at Warsaw's Okęcie airport on June 27, 1945, thousands of freedom-starved Poles were waiting to cheer the return of Mikołajczyk. Many were gathered at Okęcie, and thousands more lined the route of his motorcade into the city. Before he arrived, a practical question kept rippling through the crowd: What did the former prime minister look like? Mikołajczyk's pro-Western stance was popular and well known. But, after he had spent six years in exile, his face was not familiar to the Poles.

On the plane from Moscow with Mikołajczyk were others who were completely unknown to the Poles they came to govern. The oddly mixed group included twenty-one ministers and a new chief of state, Bolesław Bierut, representing a new Provisional Government of National Unity. Fourteen of the twenty-one ministers were members of the Lublin committee. Bierut was a Moscow-trained Communist and probably a member of the NKVD. Other than the last two years of the war, very little of his career had been spent in Poland.

The decision to set up this government had been made four months earlier at the Big Three conference in Yalta. Responsibility had been delegated there to Molotov, Harriman, and the British ambassador to Moscow, Sir Archibald Clark-Kerr, to draw together a provisional government to run the country until "free and unfettered elections" could be held. Its leaders were to come from within Poland and abroad. The so-called Moscow Commission of Three had invited Mikołajczyk, a few others from London, and representatives of the Lublin committee to the first of several meetings in the Soviet capital on June 17. Over the next few days, a plan for interim rule had been approved. Members of the new provisional government had then left immediately for Warsaw.

For a brief moment, their arrival bathed the burned-out city in euphoria. Release, renewal, even rapture swept aside six long years of

317

agony, years in which one Pole in six—six million overall, of whom half were Jewish and half Christian—had lost their lives. As Mikołajczyk stepped toward the microphone at the airport, a hush fell over the crowd. Bierut stopped him to say that he should use the word *"obywatele,"* "citizens," when addressing the crowd. Mikołajczyk turned toward his countrymen and began:

> My sisters and brothers. It is difficult to speak at this moment, when a long and difficult journey is completed. The path was thorny. It went through Hungary, France, England, Moscow, and now it finishes where it began. Every Pole would like to come home. I hope others will follow me here. We want to be with you—you who underwent so much—and hand in hand with you rebuild . . . heal the wounds . . . and live again in a truly free, independent, and sovereign Polish Republic.

After the speeches, the new ministers rode by motorcade into a moonscape of rubble and ruins still emitting the sickly-sweet smell of decaying bodies. Thousands of Poles all along the route held flowers to throw at Mikołajczyk's car. The flowers were for him and him only. The Poles expected that nothing good could come from the Communists in the new government. Hope for a free and independent Poland rested on Mikołajczyk's shoulders. With Mikołajczyk, they felt, came the support of Churchill and Roosevelt. And with their support, the Communists could be kept at bay.

Ewa Hoffman's husband, Jacek Jędruch, was seated that day on top of a burned-out German tank watching the motorcade come down a long stretch of Marszałkowska Street toward Saxon Gardens. It turned right at the edge of the gardens onto Królewska Street. Behind the tank Jacek sat on, the Saxon Palace lay in ruins. Opposite the palace where the motorcade turned, the Bruhl Palace was also in ruins. Both had been dynamited by the Germans.

"I don't think there was a building left standing anywhere within sight," Jacek told me. "In places the streets were barely cleared of the rubble. As the motorcade got nearer, I could see that several open cars were leading the procession. People were straining to catch sight of Mikołajczyk. But nobody knew what he looked like.

"When they made the turn, I could hear a man who was standing up in the first car shouting 'Second car! Second car!' People immediately began throwing their flowers onto the second car. But when they got closer, I could see that Bierut was riding in the second car, not Mikołajczyk. The flowers were all being thrown to Bierut. Mikołajczyk was several cars back. It was a clever little trick by Bierut's henchmen to make it appear that he was receiving a great welcome from his countrymen."

The cavalcade processed to the Praga section of Warsaw with a huge throng of Poles following. The motorcade stopped where the provisional government would meet. Barbed wire surrounded the building. In his memoirs, Mikołajczyk wrote that

> strange, stone-faced men in Polish Army uniforms guarded the entrance to the buildings. They spoke Russian as I passed them. I walked inside, trying to shake off my depression. . . . I thought of the people outside the building and went to a balcony on the second floor to wave to them across that symbolic chasm of barbed wire.

It was indeed symbolic. Over the next eighteen months, the Communist-dominated provisional government would gradually extinguish every vestige of freedom. Mikołajczyk's Peasant Party was brutally suppressed. The free and unfettered elections called for at Yalta were never held. Nationwide voting took place on Sunday, January 19, 1947, but by then the Communists were able to rig the outcome.

To this day the rescue remains steeped in mystery. Zofia Hoffman died in 1977 having said very little, even to her daughter, about it. Safe assumptions can be made about her reticence in its aftermath and in the years that immediately followed. Zofia was almost certainly determined not to compromise intelligence contacts and information sources that benefited her greatly. Later, the details of her struggle seem to have quietly faded into insignificance. Her years in Russia, the death of her husband, her climb up through the ranks of the Polish Army— all toughened Zofia. She was stoic and strong, disdainful of small talk, devoid of self-importance, contemptuous of boasting. To her, only one thing really mattered: The mission succeeded; after six turbulent years, she and her daughter finally were reunited.

In several conversations with Ewa, supplemented by what her uncle and aunt in Buenos Aires remembered, I have reconstructed as much as possible of Zofia's harrowing journey across a continent in chaos early in 1946. In places her plan and path are unclear, but the main elements of both can be pieced together. A few gaps occur in which it seems reasonable to speculate about what happened and why.

Certainly by the end of 1945, Lieutenant Colonel Zofia Neuhoff Hoffman knew that Poland was lost. Military intelligence reports coming back to London were full of grim reports about the wave of terror spreading across her homeland. At their late-summer conference at

Potsdam, the Big Three had agreed that the Polish government-in-exile "no longer exists." Demobilization of forces fielded by that government under British command was likely to begin at any time. Poland's postwar frontiers were being shifted to the Curzon Line in the east and to the Oder-Neisse Line in the west. Overnight these adjustments caused a chaotic scramble. Millions of Poles in the western Ukraine and western Byelorussia were streaming across the eastern frontier. At the same time, millions of Germans in areas taken from the Reich and given to Poland were pouring across the western frontier into Germany.

The chaos was by no means confined to Poland. Most of Europe was convulsed in economic and political turmoil. Gangs of ex-Nazis, deserters, orphans, and criminals roamed the heart of the Continent, causing a wave of wanton violence. Crime in and near hundreds of camps for displaced persons could not be contained because police often lacked the power to stop it. Starvation was rampant, lodging for strangers in many places nonexistent, and travel of any kind hazardous or even impossible. Germany's transportation system had collapsed. In the British zone of occupation, one in thirteen miles of track was open. Less than half the locomotives in the entire country were operable. A bitter winter left people freezing in their homes because coal could not be delivered. Bottlenecks and breakdowns were everpresent facts of daily life. At the time, these were dangers enough for a man, let alone for a woman.

For Zofia there was one bright side to the chaos. The movement of millions of displaced people provided a degree of cover and protection, a chance to fade into the swirling crowd. It represented a brief moment when sound chances might be taken, when a good plan might succeed. How long that moment might last was unclear. Antagonisms between east and west were growing, becoming hopelessly irreconcilable. That meant the borders might soon be hermetically sealed. The risks involved in a rescue would then be greatly magnified. It was possible that nothing could later be done. Unless quick, decisive action was taken, Zofia faced a growing risk as of late 1945 that she and Ewa might never be rejoined.

At that point, Zofia knew very little about the circumstances in which her brother Zbigniew, his wife, Anna, and Ewa were living. She was aware that they had moved in late August from Jarosław about 160 miles west to the Silesian coal-mining town of Bytom. She knew also that Zbigniew was teaching piano at the Bytom conservatory of music and that the family was living in a small apartment at 8 Fałata Street. These scraps of news had been sent by Zbigniew late in 1945 by acquaintances en route to London. The situation must have been deeply frustrating to Zofia. Half a year after the end of the war, it must have seemed that she was no closer than ever to recovering a child she had not seen since April 13, 1940, the evening of her arrest in Lwów by the NKVD. During her first two years in the Soviet Union, she and Zbigniew had written each other frequently. But all communication had stopped with the Nazi invasion of the U.S.S.R. on June 22, 1941. After that came more than two years of complete silence and wondering how—or whether—her family survived in German-occupied Poland. That mystery had been solved on October 16, 1943, by the short, joyful news cabled back to her through the Red Cross in Lisbon. Then the curtain had closed again. Over the next two years she learned almost nothing about the health, safety, and whereabouts of her family.

Shortly after receiving Zbigniew's message in late 1945, Zofia responded through a woman who was returning to Poland. Her reply came to Zbigniew one day during a meeting with several people at the conservatory. The young woman poked her head through the door and said, "I have a letter for you from your sister in London." He was shocked by her careless statement. Any ties to London, real or suspected, could cause an endless array of problems. With that thought flashing, Zbigniew still summoned a calm reply: "I'm sorry, but there must be some mistake. I don't have a sister in London." The young woman left, saying nothing else. But contact had been established. Other messages from Zofia soon followed and were delivered to the Neuhoff apartment whenever someone had a chance to do so.

In these messages, Zofia strongly encouraged Zbigniew to seize the initiative, to make plans immediately to bring Anna and Ewa out of Poland while there was still time. At the end of January, while Zbigniew was still trying to decide how and when an escape might be attempted, Zofia received an offer of help from two friends who knew how anxious she was to get Ewa out of Poland. An army officer named Adam Dydyński and a woman named Zofia Mścichowska from the Polish Parachute Brigade were going back to Poland together. Dydyński's family apparently had several gold bars, which he hoped to smuggle out of the country. His companion was returning to visit her sick mother. The couple apparently offered to arrange to bring Zbigniew, Anna, and Ewa out at the same time.

Their route took them first from London to Meppen, Germany, headquarters for the Polish First Armored Division in the British zone of occupation. Meppen was a small town, about ten miles from the Dutch border, whose population was swollen by a large influx of Poles after the war. In addition to its military personnel, it had attracted a swarm of former prisoners of war, deportees from forced-labor camps, and many young people who had fled Warsaw when the Germans razed the city. It teemed with DPs and members of the intelligence community going back and forth to Poland. Most used a well-established route that ran south into the American zone, then east for more than 250 miles into Czechoslovakia, which remained free and independent even though Communists controlled key ministries. They crossed into Poland through the mountain corridors near the border town of Cieszyn. From there it was only a short distance to important cities in southern Poland. Dydyński and his companion no doubt followed this route, proceeding from Cieszyn about sixty miles to Kraków and from there another fifty miles to Bytom. The couple expected to follow the same return route to Meppen and intended to arrive there with Ewa, Zbigniew, and Anna sometime in the third week of February. Zofia planned to be waiting in Meppen when her family arrived.

Once the couple reached Poland something must have happened to convince them that it would be unwise to try taking Zbigniew, Anna, and Ewa out at the same time. They arrived without warning at the Neuhoff apartment and had startling instructions for Ewa's aunt and uncle. Zofia, they reported, wanted Ewa out "no matter what!" At first Zbigniew and Anna resisted. Grudgingly, at last, they gave in. "We felt," Zbigniew said, "that we had no choice in the matter."

Preparations for departure were made quickly. Documents identifying Ewa as Dydyński's daughter were secured. Ewa was carefully coached to say that her mother had been killed in the Warsaw Uprising. She was told to call Miss Mścichowska her aunt. Because the weather that February was extremely cold, Anna was anxious to dress Ewa as warmly as possible. To buy anything new was virtually impossible, but somehow, at the last minute, Anna had managed to find a pair of white felt boots with red leather straps—"The most elegant boots I ever had in my life," Ewa told me.

The threesome left Bytom by train for Cieszyn some time during the first week of February. The dividing line between the Polish and Czech parts of the city is the Olza River. At the station on the Polish side, Dydyński, Miss Mścichowska, and Ewa disembarked and walked to the checkpoint at the bridge. Dydyński told the guard they were going to visit a sick relative in the hospital on the Czech side. The guard motioned them through without question.

They then walked straight to the railroad station and left Ewa sitting on a suitcase by the door while they went to buy tickets for the trip on to Germany. "In a few minutes they came back with a man in a brown felt hat," Ewa said, "who herded us off to the police station, where we were promptly locked up. The man in the brown hat was a plainclothes policeman who had followed us all the way in from the checkpoint. I'm sure the couple was inexperienced at this kind of work and we probably stuck out like sore thumbs."

Dydyński was taken to a separate part of the prison, while Ewa and Miss Mśchichowska were put in a cell with another woman and stayed there for three days. At that point, Ewa was moved to a Catholic convent. The nuns gave her a bath and a rosary and then placed her with a nearby farm family. Throughout the detention, Ewa stuck to the identity assigned her. After two weeks, a policeman picked Ewa up and returned her to the station, where Dydyński and his companion were waiting. There was a brief discussion in which Dydyński tried, unsuccessfully, to recover his gold bars. The Czech police refused to return them and there was nothing he could do. A few minutes later, he, Miss Mśchichowska, and Ewa were escorted back to the checkpoint. Three weeks after their departure, they were back in Poland. Ewa was returned to the care of her aunt and uncle without further mishap.

None of these developments were known to Zofia. Following the plan she and her friends agreed to, she left London around the third week of February and went to Meppen to wait for her family at the headquarters of General Stanisław Maczek's First Armored Division. While waiting she renewed acquaintance with a childhood friend, a classmate from the Convent of the Sacred Heart in Lwów, who had married one of the division commanders, General Klemens Rudnicki. After several days, there still was no sign or word of her daughter, brother, and sister-in-law. Finally intelligence sources produced information. By the time it reached her, it was reduced to a few alarming words: "There has been a *wpadunek* [Polish jargon for falling into a trap] at the border."

A hundred questions must have raced through Zofia's mind when she heard it: Had Ewa been hurt? What about Zbigniew and Anna? Where were they—on the Czech or Polish side of the border? Had they all been arrested, or had something worse happened? What should she do?

In her desperation, Zofia turned to General Rudnicki. Through him she learned that a small mission involved in military intelligence would be leaving for Poland almost immediately. He told her that arrangements could be made for her to travel with the group, but warned her about the risks. If she went, she would be strictly on her own, traveling unofficially. If things went wrong, there would be no one to call on. All this went without saying. Zofia was still in uniform and still under British command. As a lieutenant colonel, she was outranked by few women in the Polish army. If she returned to Poland and was caught, she knew what the consequences might be. Obviously her personal safety, Ewa's, and her family's would all be at stake. And because of her rank, Poland's new provisional government would, no doubt, exploit her capture fully. A trial as a British spy might follow. That, of course, could exacerbate the high level of existing tension between the British government and the Polish expatriate community.

Because of the intelligence mission's imminent departure, she had only twenty-four hours to decide about going back. She must have made up her mind on the spot in General Rudnicki's office. There was no time to prepare fake identity documents. Instead she was given an identity card in the name of "Krystyna Kobylecka." There was no time to find civilian attire. The best she could manage was a brown woolen cap and a borrowed civilian overcoat to cover her British-style uniform. To further disguise her identity, she stripped her uniform of its epaulettes and all insignia. She stuffed a few other things into a brown leather travel bag. Her preparations were complete except for one last detail. In her last meeting with General Rudnicki, she was given cyanide and agreed to take the poison to avoid being captured alive. The general stressed that the Communists could be counted on to bring spy charges against anyone of her rank and were likely to use unspeakable tortures to extract a confession. In any event, he told Zofia, her ultimate fate if caught would be death.

Zofia left about the end of the third week in February with the espionage mission, a group of nine or ten people. "They were traveling in the most surreptitious way possible," Ewa told me. "They were staying at hideaways. Some of these people were an unsavory lot." The trip took nine days. They crossed the border near Cieszyn or the Jabłonka Pass, traveling on skis through remote mountain areas.

"I think they made it across the frontier about daybreak on March second or third," Ewa told me. "It was very still and quiet except for the typical sounds of the Polish countryside coming to life, an occasional rooster crowing and dogs barking in the distance. I know that setting foot on Polish soil after six years of exile was a deeply moving experience for my mother."

By mid-afternoon, Zofia reached Kraków, a city she knew well and loved deeply. She and Maks had spoken their wedding vows there in

1930 beneath the towering Gothic spire of St. Mary's parish church. They had stood in front of one of Europe's most exquisite altars, the triptych by Wit Stwosz. Zofia passed the late afternoon making herself as inconspicuous as possible, yet soaking in the familiar sights of the old city. She could not resist a trip to Jama Michalikowa, a famous restaurant at the base of Wawel Castle. There she gulped down a half-dozen cream puffs, her only food that day.

As night fell, she slipped into St. Mary's Church just before it closed for the night. She wedged herself into a confessional booth and slept there through the night. The next day she quickly discovered that the last leg of her journey would be, in many ways, the most difficult. Roads everywhere were choked with people. Jammed buses and trains were running on unpredictable schedules. Long lines of refugees were waiting to take any available space heading west. Agents of the Bezpieka, a Polish equivalent of the NKVD, were everywhere. Hotels were packed and accommodations could not be obtained without a police permit.

The fifty-mile journey from Kraków to Bytom took one and one-half days. The first leg, to the medium-sized industrial city of Katowice, she traveled by a crude new form of public transportation, a tarp-covered truck with benches in the back. Reaching Katowice late in the day, she learned that the truck would go no farther and that other transportation to Bytom was not available. She tried to secure lodging at a small hotel. When the clerk asked for her police permit, she told him that she did not have it with her. He warned her that unless she produced it he had no choice but to call the police. Zofia then told him that she would fetch it from her luggage, which she had left a short distance away. As she left, she warned him that if he failed to hold the room, she would be the one calling the police. Having bluffed her way out of this predicament, she left quickly with no intention of returning. She then walked back in an icy drizzle toward the railroad station where the truck she had arrived in was parked. The driver was sleeping soundly in the front seat. Zofia quietly climbed into the back, where she spent her second night in Poland sleeping under one of the benches.

The next morning she arrived in Bytom. When she found the apartment on Fałata Street, no one was home. Zbigniew had gone to Kraków, where he had been offered the directorship of a much larger music conservatory. Anna was out shopping; she had left Ewa with an elderly woman who lived in an apartment directly across the hall. She and Ewa heard Zofia ring the bell at the Neuhoff apartment.

"The old lady went to look out," Ewa told me. "I was standing behind her and could see this strange woman at our door. The old lady asked her, 'Who are you looking for?' "

"The Neuhoffs," Zofia replied.

"My aunt and uncle are not home. My uncle is away and my aunt has gone shopping," Ewa piped up. The old woman told Zofia that Anna was expected back shortly.

"Could I wait here?" Zofia asked.

The old lady hesitated, but invited Zofia inside. They sat at the dining table and exchanged a few pleasantries. Ewa was absorbed with a rag doll. During a lull in the conversation, Zofia turned to Ewa and said, "You must be Ajka"—Ewa's nonsensical pet name.

The question startled Ewa. "How did you know that?" she asked.

"I am an old friend of your mother's," Zofia replied spontaneously. Then, instantly, she knew her reply, prompted by her first look at her daughter in six years, was a gross indiscretion that could raise the old woman's suspicions.

Almost at that moment, a sound could be heard across the hall as Anna returned from shopping. Ewa jumped up and ran to the door, with Zofia and the old woman following. Anna had just closed her door when Ewa reached the hall. Zofia was standing behind her. The old woman was watching from her door as Ewa knocked and called, "Auntie, Auntie!"

Anna opened the door and was stunned by the sight of her visitor. She lurched back reflexively, gasping as if a ghost had appeared. Ewa bounced by her. Seeing the color drain from Anna's face, Zofia stepped quickly inside the apartment and in one motion slammed the door shut as the old woman watched. She knew that Anna might instinctively call out her name, revealing her true identity.

"My aunt threw her arms around my mother's neck and began to cry almost uncontrollably," Ewa said. "I was surprised that they knew each other so well, because I had never seen the strange lady before." But Ewa's attention soon returned to her rag doll. A few minutes later her aunt called Ewa to the table where she and Zofia were sitting.

"Do you know who this is, Ewa?" she asked, nodding toward the visitor.

"Yes," Ewa replied, "she is a friend of my mother's."

"No, Ewa. She *is* your mother."

Quietly, with intense feeling but little display of emotion, the six-year separation ended.

Zofia quickly began arranging for their departure, making connections almost immediately with a small group that planned to leave Kraków around the middle of March. She then went briefly to Warsaw to visit friends of hers and Mak's, but throughout this time kept in close contact with those organizing the escape. Soon after she returned, their planned date of departure was aborted. She, Ewa, Zbigniew, and Anna finally left on Zbigniew's name day (or saint's day, celebrated by Poles and others in lieu of a birthday). Earlier in the day, Zofia gave Zbigniew a necktie she had bought in Kraków for the occasion.

The return journey began at the courtyard of the Archbishop's Palace in Kraków at eleven P.M. Their small convoy of two tarp-covered military trucks and a jeep carried about thirty people, including Dydyński and Miss Mścichowska. A major concern as they departed was the increased pressures from Western authorities to stop Polish emigration. The guards at the Czech border were bribed. But passing through a checkpoint near Prague, the convoy was shot at by local militia. The next convoy traveling the same route behind them was caught and forced back into Poland.

Just short of Nuremberg one of the trucks broke down on a steep hillside. Someone sped off in the jeep to find a spare part and, without thinking, took the entire group's identity documents along. The longer the jeep was gone, the more nervous passengers of the two trucks became. Finally, the jeep returned with the proper part and the convoy continued its journey west. A short distance down the road they learned that the breakdown had occurred at a propitious time. Shortly before, a motorized patrol had been combing the area. Such patrols carried dogs and moved swiftly from one checkpoint to another trying to intercept refugees. Apparently the patrol had been tipped off that a convoy was coming through. It had been waiting for eight hours when it finally gave up and left. Had the convoy with Zofia and the others arrived any earlier, almost certainly they would have been caught, arrested, and sent back to Poland. There prosecution and a long prison sentence—for Zofia, death—would have awaited them.

The group arrived in Meppen without further mishap. Zofia helped Zbigniew, Anna, and Ewa find a rented room and then went on to London. The final reunion took place in Brussels in June, when Ewa's grandmother, Maria, came from London for a brief visit. With considerable satisfaction, Zbigniew reported to his mother that despite the bombing of the home in Lwów and their other difficulties, all had not been lost. In the dangerous trip west, he had managed to carry all seventy-five pounds of his mother's fine silver tableware.

*   *   *

Police-state terror in its most brutal form was used to intimidate voters in the Polish elections held on January 19, 1947. The Peasant Party nevertheless won a large majority. At thirty-six polling places where its poll watchers were permitted to observe vote counting, the Peasants won with officially recognized majorities of between 65 percent and 85 percent. But these few returns made no difference overall. National returns were falsified completely and a Communist victory declared.

Mikołajczyk gave detailed accounts of the fraud to British and American authorities. But the Poles' Western supporters were again powerless to help them. Mikołajczyk narrowly escaped to the West in October 1947.

The Iron Curtain had finally closed completely on Poland.

The Poles were deeply divided about Mikołajczyk's role in returning to Poland. Sosnkowski, Anders, and other hard-liners held that his acceptance of the Yalta agreement and participation in the provisional government were near treasonous. In 1945 they believed that war between the Western Allies and the Soviet Union was not only inevitable, but imminent. Mikołajczyk believed that a prolonged period of peace lay ahead and that the Western Allies would do little to help the Poles.

Paweł Zaleski, his aide and confidant, returned to Poland with Mikołajczyk and escaped at the same time in 1947. He described for me the atmosphere in which Mikołajczyk made his fateful decision: "Churchill was saying, 'You must go!' Sosnkowski and Anders were saying, 'Don't go.' Stalin did all that he could to keep Mikołajczyk from going back to Poland. Finally Mikołajczyk came to the decision to go back in order 'to save the biological substance of the Polish nation.' "

About two hundred and fifty thousand bitterly anti-Communist partisans remained in the forests. Many were resisting Soviet occupation and expected to continue resisting it at all cost. Forty thousand Poles, mostly from the Home Army, had already been deported since the Red Army's arrival in 1944. Mikołajczyk believed, according to Zaleski, that Stalin was preparing to "drown Poland in a sea of blood." Stalin controlled the country completely and Mikołajczyk expected him "to seal the borders hermetically, then provoke an uprising and crush it mercilessly. After that, Mikołajczyk felt that Stalin would start deporting Poles to Siberia on a scale that would dwarf what he had done between 1939 and 1941. Mikołajczyk also expected another plebiscite after which Poland would be annexed to the Soviet Union as the Seventeenth Republic."

Mikołajczyk's return must have contained an element of déjà vu for Stalin, who could remember all too well how Wincenty Witos rallied the Polish peasants as Tukhachevsky's army approached Warsaw in August 1920. The peasants had played a major role in establishing Polish independence on that occasion. Under Mikołajczyk they still represented a powerful base, which Stalin could not ignore.

For his part Mikołajczyk was determined to provide Stalin no pretext for harsh action. In returning he cast himself in the role of the loyal and open opposition. He held frequent press conferences with foreign journalists and delighted in reminding the Polish public of Stalin's promise of "a free and independent Poland" and "a strong Poland." The deportations stopped almost immediately, according to Zaleski. With Mikołajczyk pressing authorities not to arrest them, the partisans also began to leave the forest. Some were arrested but were later returned to their homes and families.

During this period a pro-Soviet prosecutor approached Mikołajczyk about staging a hearing to acquit the Soviets of the Katyń Forest murders. "Certainly. Let us have a public trial and introduce all the proper documents," Mikołajczyk told him. "A fair trial will unquestionably prove the identity of the murderers." Mikołajczyk told the prosecutor that the documents required for such a trial were in the West. On a subsequent trip to Moscow, the prosecutor reported the conversation and outlined plans to absolve the Soviet Union of responsibility. But Soviet authorities told him to terminate the plan and return to Warsaw.

Members of the Peasant Party were not the only Poles who welcomed the return of Mikołajczyk. On his first visit to Kraków, the Czarneks turned out, as did thousands of others from all the other prewar mainstream parties. Poles from all walks of life turned to Mikołajczyk as an alternative to Bierut and his pro-Moscow claque. His immense following forced several postponements of the so-called "free and unfettered" elections provided for at Yalta. The Communists knew that if they were held, the Peasant Party would score a resounding victory. A campaign of terror then escalated until the Communists finally decided to steal the elections. After that there was no pretext for a provoked uprising, for more mass deportations, or for another phony plebiscite. At that point, Mikołajczyk felt that his return to Poland was a success, according to Zaleski. He knew that sooner or later the Communists would arrest him and that a show trial would follow. Such trials did occur in other Eastern European countries. On October 18, 1947, he learned from reliable sources that a Warsaw court had already been instructed to try him and sentence him to death. Rather than await that fate, Mikołajczyk fled to the West with the ugly truth.

The hard-liners never forgave him for what he did. Fifty years later the name "Mikołajczyk" remained a curse to many émigré Poles. His contribution may be unclear, but the historical importance of his decision to go back is undeniable. War between the East and West was not imminent in 1945; a long, sustained struggle would be required before Poland would regain her freedom. The aspirations of the hundreds of thousands who turned out to see him in 1945 were the same as those of the immense crowds that bowed for the blessing of Pope John Paul II thirty-four years later. In a sense, the experience of Mikołajczyk's return was one link in the long chain that bound both those generations of Poles to their ancestors in the uprisings of 1830, 1863, and 1905.

His contribution also had strategic significance. Poland after all remained, as it has been through the centuries, the bridge between East and West. Her fate had meaning for all of Eastern Europe. Bread riots in Poznań preceded the Hungarian Revolution in 1956. Student protests in Poland preceded the "Prague Spring" of 1968. And it was no accident that the disintegration of the Communist bloc began first in Poland with Solidarity, then spread quickly to the rest of Eastern Europe and the Soviet Union.

After the election had been stolen in 1947, a dispirited Mikołajczyk told the U.S. ambassador to Poland, Arthur Bliss Lane: "I was able to accomplish nothing in effecting free elections in Poland. But I have accomplished one thing: I have shown to the whole world that nobody can believe the promises of the Soviet Government." Privately he told Zaleski on more than one occasion that his decision to return was correct: "Stalin was prevented from exterminating the Polish nation."

CHAPTER 24

Quest for Justice

<del><<<<<<<<<<<<</del>

In 1807 Napoleon created a miniature state from captured territory and called it the Duchy of Warsaw. The gesture fanned the Poles' hopes that, ultimately, the emperor would help them secure national independence. As a result, more than eighty thousand Poles later flocked to Napoleon's banner for the invasion of Russia. Many were with him and fought bravely at Borodino, his great victory at the approaches to Moscow. Many Poles were still at his side three years later at Waterloo. Napoleon's defeat left the Poles without a liberator, but they were no less determined to secure their independence. Rebellion was their only recourse, and in the century that followed "rebellion" and "the Poles" became synonymous. The first great outburst was the November Insurrection of 1830 in Russian-occupied territory. Czar Nicholas I crushed it brutally. The Poles' few remaining constitutional rights were abrogated and thousands of revolutionaries were marched to Siberia in chains. Thousands more escaped to the West in what was known as the Great Emigration. These émigrés played an instrumental role in keeping the Poles' struggle for freedom alive. In the rebellion of Poles at home and abroad, a glint of romantic fatalism was burnished forever into the soul of the stateless nation.

In 1832 Poland's great Romantic poet, Adam Mickiewicz, published what many consider to be the finest work in the Polish language, *Dziady (Forefathers' Eve)*. In the opening scene of the play, an angel looks at a prisoner sleeping in his cell and says:

> Tend him, protect him now, watch every thought,
> 'Twixt good and evil the battle is fought.

A spirit replies:

> Redouble the Guard!
> Whether forces of good or of evil have scored,

331

Tomorrow shall show us in deed and in word.
One moment of battle, the tiniest span,
Determines forever the fate of a man.

The prisoner awakens:

I shall be free—yes, and full well I know
The sort of grace the Muscovite will show,
Striking the fetters from my feet and hands
To rivet on my spirit heavier bands!
An exiled singer, now condemned to go
Where foreign and inimicable throngs
Will take for rude and idle sounds my songs.
Wretches! They leave me with my sword, 'tis true,
But first they break its shining blade in two;
Alive, I shall be dead to these dear lands,
And all I think shall lie within my soul,
A diamond locked within its shell of coal.

For the Poles, history bestowed on these words a ring of eternal truth. Great rebellions came in 1863 and again in 1905, but with no different result than in 1830. Shortly after Stalin's death, the first post-war production of Mickiewicz's play was staged in Warsaw. One critic in the audience on opening night said, "Government ministers were crying, the hands of the technical crew were shaking, the cloakroom attendants were wiping their eyes . . . I know of no other drama in the whole of world literature that could move an audience after 125 years as *Forefathers' Eve* did." During the Prague Spring of 1968, the closing of a production of the play—apparently the Soviet ambassador felt that the production was a device for attacking the Soviet Union—touched off street demonstrations.

Yet another failed resistance prompted a somber Churchill, by then a member of the opposition, to tell the House of Commons on June 5, 1946, that a sham referendum was under way in Poland and that it would deny the country "all free expression of her national will." He then continued with a sad admission:

The fate of Poland seems to be an unending tragedy, and we, who went to war, all ill-prepared, on her behalf, watch with sorrow the strange outcome of our endeavors. I deeply regret that none of the Polish troops, and I must say this, who fought with us on a score of battlefields, who poured out their blood in the common cause, are to be allowed to march in the Victory Parade. They will be in our thoughts on that day. We shall never forget their bravery and martial skill, associated with our own glories at Tobruk, at Cassino and Arnhem.

Three days later, when the victorious Allied forces marched the streets of London, there were no Poles among them. Invitations were extended to twenty-five of the Polish airmen who had played such a large role in the Battle of Britain. They declined, not wishing to participate in a ceremony that excluded the Polish army and navy. Three months later, the provisional government in Warsaw stripped General Anders of his citizenship. The Polish army-in-exile had been demobilized and a big push was on in England and on the Continent to get the Poles to return to their homeland.

Yet another Great Emigration had occurred. It began in late September 1939, when Sosnkowski and his forces slipped through Timoshenko's trap along the Dniester River into Hungary. The tide rose sharply with the wave of deportations to Siberia and elsewhere in the U.S.S.R. in 1940–1941. More than 1.2 million Poles were transported to the East during that period. Only 112,000 escaped with Anders in 1942. An unknown number, probably between 200,000 and 300,000, did return to Poland with Berling and the Red Army in 1944. However, most of these men had been conscripted in Eastern Poland in 1940–1941 and were not among the 1.2 million deportees from that same area. An estimated two million Poles were conscripted by the Nazis as forced labor to work in factories and other parts of the German war economy. In the wave of departures between 1939 and the stolen election of January 19, 1947, those who left to escape political repression represented only a trickle. No one knows how many Poles were taken away against their will during these years. It may have been four million, perhaps more. How many died from starvation, forced labor, and neglect in the Soviet Union and Germany no one knows, but certainly it was a very large number.

Those who remained in or escaped to the West carried with them a litany of injustices almost too terrible to believe. And they, like Mickiewicz and his generation of melancholy Poles, appealed to the West with a messianic fervor. With their homeland trapped under the harsh Stalinist system, their appeals seemed no less hopeless. The West could not help, but the Poles again were impelled to keep the resistance alive.

Shortly after the war, Magda Czarnek, then a medical student at the Jagiellonian University, met on a crowded Kraków streetcar an acquaintance she had not seen for several years. After exchanging a few pleasantries, the woman asked, "And how is your father?"

"Didn't you know?" Magda replied. "We lost him at Katyń."

These words brought a stricken look to the woman's face as she glanced quickly at passengers nearby, worried that some of them might have heard Magda's answer. Turning back to Magda, she whispered, "Don't you know? That is not something to say in public!"

She was right. Discussion of Katyń and other sensitive subjects was an absolute taboo in Soviet-occupied Poland. Among proscribed subjects were the Molotov-Ribbentrop Pact, the Warsaw Uprising, and the deportations of 1940–1941. Strict press controls warned Polish censors to follow the *Great Soviet Encyclopedia* in any references to these subjects. Even so, the Poles all knew about and seethed over these matters. Inside Poland they were kept alive by "flying university" courses patterned after the illegal classes run during the nineteenth-century partitions and during World War II, when Polish universities were shut down. In contrast, German crimes against the Poles could be spoken of openly. Embellishments were even encouraged. But these crimes were in the past; it was Soviet, not German oppression that continued to brutalize the Poles.

Gradually, the litany of Soviet offenses in denying the Poles their freedom, particularly the effort to wipe out the intelligentsia, began to fuse into one symbol: Katyń. With Katyń alone there was no element of expiation for Soviet actions. The Molotov-Ribbentrop Pact *did* buy Stalin precious time before Hitler's onslaught. The annexations that preceded the deportations *did* involve disputed territory that was not, in fairness, Russian or Polish. The Nazis *were* able to mount a success-ful counterattack against the Red Army as it approached the Vistula in August 1944; treachery alone might not explain the Red Army's failure to relieve the beleaguered Polish capital. But with Katyń there could be no doubt: It stood for the ruthless, cold-blooded murder of Poland's "best and brightest," the 4,143 men found by the Germans at Katyń and the eleven thousand others still missing from Starobelsk and Ostashkov. To the Poles, Katyń, the deportations, and the Warsaw Uprising were separate manifestations of Stalin's ruthless plan to exter-minate their intelligentsia.

"Because the people in Poland were forbidden from knowing about these subjects, the memory of them survived to a great degree because of efforts of the émigré community," Ewa told me. "These voices were raised in the West for forty-five years, but after a while the issue became a great bore. People were horrified when the Russian tanks crushed the Hungarians in 1956 and rolled into Czechoslovakia in 1968. There were many demonstrations and it was all heroic, but it soon faded. The West sort of, in a sense, wrote Eastern Europe off. In that situation, you have to learn to tailor protest to the environment you are living in, to keep the embers aglow without becoming a nuisance. We did that pretty well."

In the years immediately following the war, the conscience of the West was pricked deeply by the injustice of Katyń. On the morning of Monday, July 1, 1946, the Nuremberg Tribunal heard its first evidence against the Germans for these murders. The one-sentence indictment read: "In September 1941 11,000 Polish officers, prisoners of war, were killed in the Katyn woods near Smolensk." Supporting detail, labeled USSR-54, had been submitted by the Soviet prosecutor on February 11. It consisted of one document only. The entire case against the Germans had been based on the report prepared by the Soviet "Special Commission for Ascertaining and Investigating the Circumstances of the Shooting of Polish Officer Prisoners by the German-Fascist Invaders in Katyń Forest."

From the outset, despite deep misgivings about the Soviet evidence, British and American prosecutors had little choice but to permit its submission. The four victorious powers, the United States, Great Britain, France, and the Soviet Union, had agreed the previous summer on a division of responsibilities for prosecuting the war crimes to be examined by the tribunal. The United States had taken responsibility for prosecuting crimes relating to Germany's war of aggression. Crimes on the high seas and treaty violations were to be prosecuted by Great Britain. The Soviet Union took responsibility for Wehrmacht crimes in Eastern Europe, and France took those in Western Europe. The chief American prosecutor, Supreme Court Justice Robert Jackson, pointed out years later that if the Soviets thought they could prove their charges on Katyń, "they were entitled to do so under the division of the case." Even so, the British and American prosecutors lodged protests against moving forward with the Soviet indictment.

The German attorneys quickly made clear that they planned to put up a vigorous defense. When he heard about the charge, Hermann Göring scoffed, "I did not think they would be so shameless as to mention Poland." Another of the defendants, Baldur von Schirach, could not contain his amusement: "When they mentioned Poland, I thought I'd die!"

The ineptness and inaccuracies of the report of the Soviet special commission were quickly and painfully apparent when the indictment came before the tribunal on July 1, 1946. It identified Colonel "Arnes" (Ahrens) as the German officer who supervised the massacre. The German defense produced Ahrens's commanding officer, General Eugen Oberhaeuser, in a devastating rebuttal: Ahrens had not yet been assigned to the 537th Signal Regiment quartered at the NKVD dacha in Katyń Forest at the time the Soviet report alleged the murders had occurred.

The following day, the Soviets countered with their best witness, a Dr. Markov, who had served as a member of the international commission organized by the Germans and taken to Kaytń Forest in late April 1943. He had signed that commission's unanimous finding that the murders had taken place approximately three years earlier, in the spring of 1940. Shortly after the Red Army liberated his native Bulgaria, Dr. Markov had been tried as an "enemy of the people" for his participation in the German investigation and had admitted that "I am guilty before the Bulgarian Nation and its Liberator, Russia." He said the Germans had forced him to sign the international commission's report and claimed that all members of the commission knew that its findings were false. With this statement he had been able to secure his release.

Early in 1991, I spoke with Telford Taylor, who replaced Jackson as chief counsel for the prosecution at Nuremberg. At eighty-three, he was still in excellent health, playing squash several times each week. For many years he had been a professor of law at Columbia University. I asked him if the Soviet evidence at Nuremberg was an embarrassment. "Yes, it was," he replied. "We strongly urged Rudenko [the Soviet prosecutor] not to go forward with the case. There was a feeling then that the Russians, not the Germans, were guilty."

Taylor said that the Soviets initially drew an indictment charging the Germans with murdering nine hundred Poles. "Then they suddenly changed the number to ten thousand. It was not the kind of change that sounded genuine." Behind the scenes the American and British prosecutors took the Soviets sharply to task on this matter, according to Taylor. "From that point on everybody said, 'To hell with the Russians. They can stew in their own juice.' "

When the final verdicts were announced on September 30, 1946, nothing at all was said about the Katyń Forest massacre, or about the indictment brought before the tribunal seven months earlier. Had the victims taken their own lives? It was absurd that they could have perished in any way except at the hands of the Germans or the Soviets.

In its obviously awkward position, the tribunal opted for "magnificent silence," according to Taylor.

Expecting that a fiasco was in the works, the Polish government-in-exile had requested early on that the tribunal leave the Katyń issue alone. Its position was that justice could not possibly be rendered under Soviet jurisdiction.

The handling of the indictment revealed an inherent flaw in the entire process. The Soviets approached the proceedings as the international equivalent of the show trials of the late 1930s. There, Vyshinsky's indictments were tantamount to conviction. The Soviet prosecuting team probably expected a rubber-stamp verdict of "guilty" on Katyń. Certainly the Germans were perfectly capable of having committed such a crime. The Soviets knew that Katyń had wounded the Poles so deeply that the issue was unlikely to go away. No doubt to their painful surprise, the Soviets discovered that the rule of law was sovereign in Western jurisprudence and that whatever its limitations, Nuremberg could not be exploited as a show trial.

Once the court decided in private that Katyń was not a German war crime, its responsibilities had been discharged. Only the Germans, not the Soviets, were on trial. Lacking grounds to convict the Germans, the tribunal could go no further with the case and quietly dropped it.

During this period, Poles in London meticulously assembled a complete record on the massacre. In December 1944 the Council of Ministers of the government-in-exile had summoned a special commission to investigate the crime. Its investigators worked for several years to compile a complete record of nearly three hundred pages, which was published in April 1948 under the name *The Crime of Katyn: Facts and Documents*. In its last chapter, that report called for a new international tribunal that would adhere to the Roman-law canon that "nobody can be judge in his own case." Clearly that principle had been violated at Nuremberg. The report also stressed that "only such evidence as is in Polish possession can throw full light on the Katyń crime and clearly reveal its perpetrators."

Demands for such a hearing were voiced by many Poles abroad over the next few years. That cause was aided substantially by Mikołajczyk's presence in the West from late 1947 on. His dramatic escape in October 1947 attracted worldwide attention, fueling dismay for freedom's prospects not just in Poland but in the entire region. In speeches and public appearances throughout the West over the next few years, Mikołajczyk at every turn pressed the Poles' charges against the Soviets for the murders at Katyń. A special committee of prominent Americans that included William (Wild Bill) Donovan, Allen Dulles, James Farley, and Clare Boothe Luce was formed by former ambassador Lane to press for an international investigation. Their efforts resulted in the establishment of a select committee of the U.S. Congress, which on October 1, 1952, began an investigation of the Katyń Forest massacre.

The select committee was the most comprehensive neutral inquiry on the subject ever undertaken. Over the next year, it heard eighty-one witnesses at hearings in Chicago, London, Frankfurt, Berlin, Naples, and Washington. It developed 183 exhibits, took more than two hundred depositions, many from persons with firsthand knowledge of the crime or its victims, and published a detailed record of 2,362 pages. The overall results were comprehensive and accurate, but the committee's deliberations were not without moments of melodrama. One witness who wore a hood to avoid reprisals against relatives in Poland told the committee that he had witnessed the murders. Using a revolver he demonstrated to spellbound committee members how Polish officers were shot. His testimony offered no explanation of how he managed to penetrate the NKVD compound at Katyń, avoid detection by dog-escorted patrols, and escape to the West. Still, newspapers and magazines splashed a picture of the simulated shooting all across the nation. The committee's unanimous conclusion was that the Soviets were guilty. It recommended that Congress request that the United Nations try the case in the International Court of Justice. That proposal died quietly the following year in the House Foreign Affairs Committee after two discussions in executive session at which senior State Department officials advised against its adoption. The records for these meetings remained closed to the public thirty-eight years later.

I asked Roman Pucinski, chief investigator of the select committee, why these recommendations were quietly dropped. "This was part of the whole tragedy of Katyń," he replied. "There were constant efforts at the State Department to downgrade and downplay its significance." The only postwar Republican Congress had just been elected in the Eisenhower landslide. "The Foreign Affairs Committee was dominated by the State Department and the State Department didn't want to make any waves with the Russians just then," Pucinski added.

The congressional hearings on Katyń were one skirmish in the larger battle of the Cold War. In that sense they were anticlimactic—just one more example, albeit a horrible one, of communism's treachery. One of the more sensational aspects of the committee's investigation involved the accusation that some of the brutal methods used by the Soviets against the Poles were being used in the Korean War. The hearings occurred at a time when anti-Communist fervor in America was peaking. The fervor subsided, but Poles never stopped pressing their case.

Half a century after the murders, forty-seven years to the day after the Germans announced the discovery of mass graves in Katyń Forest, the Soviet Union acknowledged responsibility for liquidating fifteen thousand Polish officers and noncoms in the spring of 1940. On April 13, 1990, in a special ceremony at the Kremlin, Soviet president Mikhail Gorbachev gave several cartons of documents concerning the crime to Poland's president, Wojciech Jaruzelski. They contained "indirect but convincing" proof, said Gorbachev, that the murders were the work of the NKVD.

"It is not easy to speak of this tragedy, but it is necessary," Gorbachev told Jaruzelski. A government statement in TASS expressed the U.S.S.R.'s "profound regret over the Katyń tragedy," labeling it "one of the gravest crimes of Stalinism." No answer was given to the question of who, specifically, gave the order to execute the Poles. In his comments at the Kremlin ceremony, Gorbachev said only that the executions were carried out under the direction of Beria and other officials of the NKVD.

Natalya Lebedeva, a historian at the Institute of World History at the Soviet Academy of Sciences, examined the documents, which were found at the Main U.S.S.R. Archives and at the Soviet army's Central State Archives. She said the apparent motive for the crime was Poland's victory in the Russo-Polish War of 1920. When the Red Army marched into Poland on September 17, 1939, war was not declared by either country. Nevertheless, Stalin was still determined, said Lebedeva, to eliminate "those who might in the future enter the struggle for their country's rebirth."

Gorbachev's April 13 acknowledgment shed no light on where the missing men from Ostashkov and Starobelsk were buried. That mystery was further clarified by the KGB sixty days later. The secret police disclosed that the likely burial site for the 6,500 men from Ostashkov was a forest near Miednoye along the Moscow–Leningrad highway, about ninety miles north of the Soviet capital. The likely site for the 3,910 officers of Starobelsk, according to the KGB, was a park north of Kharkov.

Gorbachev's words resolved only one aspect of the question of guilt. His country was guilty as a nation, but what about the individuals responsible for the bloody murders? Zbigniew Brzezinski, a prominent

Polish-American who served as national-security adviser to President Jimmy Carter, observed in December 1990 that

> Hitler's crimes are still being justly punished. But in the Soviet Union there are literally thousands of ex-killers and ex-torturers living on official pensions, attending various revolutionary celebrations decked out in their medals, and perhaps even reminiscing about their struggle against "the enemies of the people."
>
> Recently, several direct participants in the mass murder of the defenseless Polish officers in Katyn and elsewhere—15,000 of them shot one by one in the back of the head—have been identified. If Gorbachev has totally broken with Stalinism, why has not a single one of them been put on trial? The Eichmann of the operation, a former NKVD major by the name of Serepenko who was in charge of the "logistics" of the operation, lives comfortably in Moscow.

Telford Taylor addressed the legal aspects of this question when I spoke with him several weeks later. "A year ago I would have thought it quite possible for Gorbachev to take some effective steps to bring people like this to justice. But now he is going back to military and police methods."

Questions involving national, not individual, guilt come within the jurisdiction of the International Court of Justice. For many years Taylor advocated the establishment of an international court of criminal justice. "The idea died aborning and I doubt that it will come about any time soon," he told me. "That leaves the question of individual guilt squarely on the Russians' shoulders." The movement toward pluralism and democracy "won't go very far there until they face it," he added.

The malefactor finally confessed. History's maxim that murder will out was vindicated at last. But the acknowledgment came only because a system built on lies and deceits, tyranny and murder, began imploding from the accumulated weight of its own grotesqueness. "All hail to the Donets Basin miners. . . . All hail to the heroes of the Revolution. . . ." These were more than empty words. They were outward manifestations of the layers of falsehood and misrepresentations that formed the core experience, the real history, of the bankrupt Stalinist system. Suffused with the cloying, suffocating, mind-numbing rhetoric of the ubiquitous state, such boasting was filled with parody and paradox. To all but a few apparatchiks, the extent of the corruption was clear. To improvise on a phrase from the West, they had "met the degenerates and the degenerates are us." All meaning in life had been squeezed into blandness and boredom, all energy and dynamism were long since dissipated. Reform, renewal, and rejuvenation were impossible without honest reappraisal of the horror-filled past.

And not just in the Soviet Union. The withdrawal of Soviet forces from Eastern Europe meant that to some extent the slate must also be wiped clean with neighbors. Normal relations could not be reestablished otherwise. In that context, nothing more could be gained by withholding the horrible truth about Katyń. Continued Soviet denials could convince no one, nor had they for many decades. Continued silence in the face of the Poles' crescendo of demands for the truth could only damage the credibility of other attempts to confront the record of the Stalinist period openly and squarely. At least a confession might lower the wall of contempt, disgust, and distrust that permeated Polish attitudes toward the Soviet Union.

The acknowledgment came amid the breaking up of the Soviet bloc, a sea change that brought Poland's political odyssey to an end; history in a sense had come full circle.

On November 14, 1990, the Polish and German governments finally signed a treaty establishing the Oder-Neisse line as their permanent border. Stalin's skillful diplomacy at Tehran forty-seven years earlier had resulted, finally, in the compact borders the Poles had fought for for centuries. The population within those borders was fairly homogeneous, resembling the "Poland for the Poles" that Dmowski had called for at Versailles seventy-one years earlier.

On November 9, five days before the signing of the border treaty, the Germans and the Soviets signed a treaty of "good-neighborliness, partnership and cooperation." It contained a nonaggression clause committing the two countries to "never and under no circumstances be the first to employ armed forces against one another or against third states." (Many Poles wondered, understandably, if secret protocols were attached.) The circle was further closed on December 22, 1990, at a special ceremony at the Royal Castle in Warsaw involving Poland's newly elected President Lech Wałęsa and Ryszard Kaczorowski, president of the London government-in-exile. At that time, Kaczorowski turned over the insignia of presidential powers taken abroad during the Nazi invasion fifty-one years earlier. Although it had become an obscure relic, his government had managed to survive the Cold War.

Gorbachev's acknowledgment about Katyń did not close the matter for the Poles. To Maria Pawulska Rasiej, the admission lacked one important element: It contained no contrition. "They owe an expression of profound regret to the entire nation," she told me. "They need to make some commitment that something like this will never be repeated. At least the Germans have attempted an atonement to the Jews. The Soviet crimes against us may not be on the same scale, but there has to be some recognition that so many of our ablest people were taken from us."

She had lived to see the entire story played out. From Digglefold Plantation near Salisbury, Rhodesia, she and her mother had moved to Lusaka and then, in 1948, to England. Shortly after that she met and married Kazimierz Rasiej, who had flown with the RAF during the war. He, too, with his mother and brother, had been deported—to a remote Siberian lumber camp, where they barely survived. They were among the fortunate few who left the U.S.S.R. with the army. Kazimierz's father had been arrested by the Soviets in 1939 and simply vanished. Maria and Kazimierz emigrated to the United States in 1951. Mrs. Pawulska died in London, where she was living with her youngest son, Jerzy, in 1979.

Justice for Poland and the truth about Katyń would remain at the center of Maria's life over the next four decades. The years of near starvation in Kazakhstan, her family's luck in catching the last transport to Krasnovodsk, the screaming families at Dzhambul station who represented tens of thousands of Poles who would never leave the Soviet Union, the memory of her sick mother crawling to the water on the beach at Pahlevi, her own close brush with death in a Tehran hospital—these were more than memories, they were events that cried out for resolution and atonement.

"I grew up with this great tragedy of my mother's," Ewa Hoffman Jędruch told me. "But never once did I hear her say, 'Look what this war has done to me.' In retrospect, I would say that she lost everything. She was a very ambitious woman as far as her profession was concerned. But her legal training meant nothing after she emigrated." In 1948, Zofia married a childhood acquaintance, Karol Angerman. He had fought in Piłsudski's Legions and had graduated as a mechanical engineer from Lwów Polytechnic. He served as a captain in the army-in-exile during World War II. Soon after the conflict ended, he and Zofia met in London. After their demobilization, they emigrated with Ewa to Buenos Aires. Zofia died there in 1977 from complications following routine surgery. Ewa had moved to Boston in 1969 and shortly after that met Jacek Jędruch, who had escaped from Poland shortly after the war ended. They were married a short time later.

The death of her father gave Ewa a strong bond with her generation of Polish émigrés. "We can meet as complete strangers and we establish rapport within a few minutes. . . . It might be a comparable feeling to Americans who lost loved ones in Vietnam. We would have felt differently if these men [the Polish officers] had died on the battlefield. But the brutality of their deaths is difficult to reconcile oneself to. There is an Arlington for people here, but for us there was only oblivion."

Despite Gorbachev's acknowledgment, Maria, Ewa, and Magda were still bitter at the Soviets' long delay. "It was much too late and incomplete," Magda said. "I never felt that there was any remorse or a true apology. Their admission of guilt should be connected with an expression of deep sorrow, of which there was none."

Janina Czarnek died in Kraków in 1980, of old age. She was ninety-one. To the last she was proudest that despite having lost her husband to the Soviets and her son to the Germans the family had held together. "She was always so proud of her arrests," Magda told me. "These were bragging rights, big feathers in her hat. She would tell a perfect stranger, 'Do you know that I was a prisoner of the Gestapo? I was even on the list to be sent to Auschwitz.' She remembered it with such pride."

The Poles as a people remember with pride how they survived. Of all the nations under Hitler's heel, they alone produced no Quisling. After all the terror, brutality, and bloodshed, the Poles were no more Sovietized under Stalin than they had been russified under the czars. Men like Zbigniew Czarnek, Maksymilian Hoffman, and Stanisław Pawulski became idealized in collective memory. They were heroes who triumphed in defeat, and thus they were servants of eternal Poland.

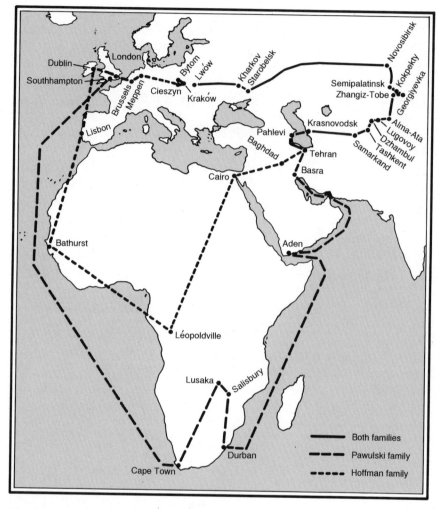

Labels on map:
Dublin, London, Southhampton, Brussels, Meppen, Bytom, Lwów, Cieszyn, Kharkov, Starobelsk, Novosibirsk, Kokpekty, Semipalatinsk, Zhangiz-Tobe, Georgiyevka, Kraków, Lisbon, Krasnovodsk, Alma-Ata, Lugovoy, Dzhambul, Tashkent, Pahlevi, Baghdad, Samarkand, Tehran, Basra, Cairo, Aden, Bathurst, Léopoldville, Lusaka, Salisbury, Durban, Cape Town

Legend:
— Both families
--- Pawulski family
···· Hoffman family

Deportation-Rescue Route of the Poles

This map shows the routes of two Polish families who survived Stalin's mass liquidations. On the night she was deported to Siberia, Zofia Hoffman was separated from her infant daughter, Ewa. Zofia later returned to Poland with an intelligence unit, crossing the Carpathians on skis, and rescued Ewa.

Epilogue

Today, the once-murky truth is indisputably clear: Stalin personally ordered the massacre of officers and other prominent persons in an attempt to render Soviet-occupied Poland leaderless. On October 14, 1992, one year after the original publication of this book, the Russian government made public the Politburo's execution order dated March 5, 1940. It was written by NKVD Chief Lavrenti Beria, signed by Stalin, and applied "the supreme penalty: shooting" without trials. Beria's justification: the captive Poles were "sworn enemies of Soviet authority [and] full of hatred for the Soviet system. . . . Each of them is waiting only for his release in order to enter actively into the struggle against Soviet authority." (The complete text of Beria's order contained in Politburo Minute 13 and a reproduction of the page Stalin signed follow this epilogue.)

To the very end, Soviet authorities refused to admit any guilt on the part of Stalin or other Kremlin leaders. On April 13, 1990, Soviet President Mikhail Gorbachev conceded to the Poles that the Katyń Forest massacre was "one of the gravest crimes of Stalinism." But Gorbachev gave no hint that Stalin and the Politburo were personally responsible. Two years later, the execution order was found in Gorbachev's personal archives.

Russian President Boris Yeltsin released the document and rebuked his predecessor, but the gesture seemed half-hearted to the Poles—especially when Yeltsin snubbed an invitation to lay the cornerstone for a chapel and cemetery at Katyń. Other developments compounded their concern. High-level NKVD officials who helped carry out the executions are still alive. Not one has been brought to justice.

The Russian government also has refused to discuss the highly sensitive issue of reparations for Polish massacre and deportation victims. On this issue, its hands are tied: the costs would be prohibitive, and the Russian public—which feels with considerable justification that it suffered more under Stalin than did the Poles—would never go along.

Despite these sore points, relations between the Poles and Russians are dramatically improved. Half a century ago, Poland was finished, a dismantled state powerless to prevent massive economic destruction and the systematic liquidation of its intelligentsia. When Barbarossa, Hitler's last and greatest blitzkrieg, began on June 22, 1941, the Luftwaffe strafed major rail centers in Soviet-occupied Poland teeming with deportees. The passengers were among 1.2 to 2 million Poles deported from late 1939 to the moment Germany invaded. Most perished due to forced labor, starvation, and neglect.

Ironically, Barbarossa put Poland on the long road back. Had it not occurred, Stalin's deportations would have continued and millions more might have perished. Instead, the German invasion opened the way for an unrelenting search for missing Poles in the Soviet Union—especially the officers murdered in Katyń Forest and those murdered near Kharkov and Kalinin. In that search, Katyń came to symbolize Soviet oppression and Polish resolve to resist.

Today, Poland has been reborn for the second time in this century as a free and independent state. Pluralistic political institutions that first rooted on the European Continent in Poland are thriving. Competitive elections, marked by vigorous debate and surprising results, have been revived. The November 19, 1995, presidential race between incumbent President Lech Wałęsa, one of Solidarity's legendary founders, and Aleksander Kwasniewski, leader of a reconstituted Communist Party, was closely contested. Kwasniewski's narrow victory reflected the Poles' deep disenchantment with Wałęsa's divisive leadership style, the attraction of a fresh face, and a "go slow" attitude toward economic reform. One week after the election, Kwasniewski resigned his party post to signify his commitment to evolutionary change and continued alignment with the West.

Despite recent widespread disenchantment with Wałęsa, the Polish economy has been completely transformed during his tenure. When the Soviet system imploded in 1989, prices were liberalized and hyper-inflation quickly followed. After fifty years of stunted development, shock therapy was needed to revive Poland's economy. The jolt came in the form of a restructuring plan launched in January 1990. Over the next two years, gross domestic product fell by an estimated 5 to 10 percent, real incomes plunged, and unemployment soared to 16.4 percent. But the government stayed the course and recession soon bottomed out. GDP grew 1.5 percent in 1992, 3.8

percent in 1993, and 5 percent in 1995. The totals for 1993 and 1994 were both European highs. They reflected large increases in industrial production, exports, imports, and consumption.

The private sector now accounts for 60 percent of employment and more than half of total output. A staggering 1.3 million new businesses were formed by 1993 alone. Privatization of heavy industry has advanced at a much slower pace, mainly due to a shortage of capital. But long-term investment trends are promising: the Warsaw stock exchange, reopened after fifty-two years in 1991, is one of the world's fastest growing capital markets; and direct foreign investment, which topped $5 billion early in 1995, is expected to continue rising briskly.

The irreversible change goes much deeper than transformation of the old command system. Early in the twenty-first century the Polish economy should be fully integrated with that of Western Europe. Preparations for membership in the European Union will lead to a free trade zone for industrial goods by 2001. Poland also has signed a free trade agreement with EFTA (European Free Trade Association), which includes most of the continent's non-EU countries. Poland and its Central European neighbors have advanced the deadline for liberalizing trade in industrial goods from 2000 to 1998. These agreements, lowering protection for Polish producers, reflect a politically mature willingness to compete.

Security measures desperately sought by Poland's interwar government have been locked into place. The treaty on German unification included a formal guarantee of Poland's western border by the government of Chancellor Helmut Kohl. His and the Weimar Republic are the only German governments since the Partitions began in 1772 to formally recognize their border with Poland. Poland's eastern boundaries with Belarus and Ukraine also have been formally guaranteed. The Poles want to join the North Atlantic Treaty Organization, but German unification, with its gentleman's understanding prohibiting a NATO presence east of the Elbe River, poses a de factor barrier. Seeking a buffer against Russian political instability, Germany quietly favors Poland's admission. But vocal Russian opposition and ambivalent U.S. support make it unlikely that the Poles will be admitted in the foreseeable future. Despite this disappointment, Poland's borders have not been so secure in two centuries.

The Poles are not wasting this historic opportunity. A cultural revival now under way has the country teeming with new monuments, museums, recitals, and exhibitions. An internationally acclaimed film industry has emerged. The nation is preoccupied with the meticulous reconstruction of a half century of lost history. Soviet crimes long hidden, or barely whispered, now are being fully aired. Martyrs, or prominent citizens who died abroad, are often commemorated or reinterred.

The Sejm, or lower House of Parliament, recently voted 356–6 to bring the body of wartime Prime Minister Stanisław Mikołajczyk back to Poland from Mount Olivet Cemetery in Washington, D.C. Many émigré Poles called Mikołajczyk a traitor for returning to Poland from London on June 27, 1945, to participate in a provisional government with the Communists. About 250,000 bitterly anti-Communist partisans were still in the forests, resisting Soviet occupation, when Mikołajczyk went back. Mikołajczyk believed Stalin was preparing to liquidate the partisans, resume massive deportations, and annex Poland as the Seventeenth Republic of the Soviet Union. By stumping the nation, campaigning relentlessly for the "free and unfettered" elections promised at Yalta, Mikołajczyk proved to be a thorn in Stalin's side. The elections were stolen anyway, and the Communists were preparing to execute Mikołajczyk when he escaped to the West late in 1947. Mikołajczyk was living proof of Soviet perfidy that was hard to ignore. He spent the rest of his life appealing to the conscience of the West for a free and independent Poland.

No other Pole more clearly epitomizes victory in defeat. In 1996 the nation will give Mikołajczyk a state funeral with full military honors. He will be buried in Warsaw's St. Johns Cathedral next to the revered Paderewski, who served as the first Prime Minister of the Second Republic after World War One. Mikołajczyk also represents the experience of millions of émigré Poles, mostly from the intelligentsia, who came to the West during and after World War Two. In many ways, they kept the flame of collective memory alive through all the years of Soviet oppression. They pricked constantly at the conscience of the West with a litany of injustices led by the murders at Katyń. In contrast to the less-educated Poles who reached the United States at the turn of the century, these émigrés were quickly assimilated. Many picked up careers cut short by the war, or built new ones. The lives of those who recounted most of the anecdotal detail in this book illustrate this point:

Magdalena ("Magda") Czarnek—Her father, Zbigniew, an Army colonel and physician, was executed at Katyń. She finished medical school in Kraków in 1950, emigrated to the United States in 1957, and pursued a specialization in radiology at Tulane University and the M.D. Anderson Hospital and Tumor Institute in Houston. She is a practicing radiologist in Blacksburg,

Virginia, today. Her husband, Iwo Cyprian Pogonowski, survived internment in a Nazi concentration camp and the Brandenburg Death March in 1945. He finished his education in the U.S. and became a civil engineer. He is the author of several books including *Poland: A Historical Atlas, Jews in Poland,* and a widely used Polish-English dictionary.

Maria Pawulska—Her father, Stanisław, an Army captain, was among the victims from Starobelsk. She met her husband, Kazimierz Rasiej, in London after the war, and they emigrated to the United States on borrowed money. "Kazik" joined a consulting engineering firm as a draftsman and worked his way up to executive vice president. In retirement, he continues to serve as U.S. president of the Polish Air Force Veterans' Association. He makes frequent trips to Poland as president of Polish Assistance Inc., a foundation that operates a retirement home. The mother of five adult children, Maria maintains a keen interest in the history of Lwów, now in the western Ukraine. She is actively involved in the Kościuszko Foundation, the Polish Institute of Arts and Sciences, and Christian-Jewish dialogue.

Tadeusz and Jerzy, Maria's brothers who also barely survived after being deported to Siberia, established successful careers in the West. They both earned engineering degrees at the Polish branch of London University. Today Tadeusz and his wife live in Houston where he works for AirLiquide. Jerzy, now widowed, lives in Wallington, Surrey, near London, where he works for a civil engineering firm.

Paul Zaleski—After escaping from Poland in 1947 with Mikołajczyk, Zaleski emigrated to the United States, where he assisted the former Prime Minister in preparing his widely read memoir, *The Rape of Poland.* Zaleski had barely completed degrees in law and diplomatic sciences at the University of Lwów when the war began. He obtained a second law degree from George Washington University in 1956. Later he was an attorney for the Foreign Claims Settlement Commission, the Office of Foreign Direct Investment, and the Maritime Administration. Today, he is a practicing attorney in Washington, D.C., and suburban Maryland. He will return to Poland for the first time since 1947 to attend Mikołajczyk's funeral.

Zdzisław Peszkowski—A prisoner at Kozelsk, Peszkowski was among the remnant of survivors from all three camps. He lived and served for many years as a priest and history professor at Orchard Lake School in Michigan. After the Communist government fell, he returned to Poland to work with the families of massacre victims and to mobilize public support to commemorate those murdered at Katyń, Ostashkov, and Starobelsk. In 1992 he brought urns with soil from Katyń, Kharkov, and Miednoye, where the victims were buried, to the Polish Air Force Academy at Dęblin, where he held a widely publicized funeral mass.

Ewa Hoffman Jędruch—Her father, Maksymilian, was a prisoner at Starobelsk. After a dramatic reunion with her mother in 1946, she grew up in England and Argentina. She earned a degree in chemical engineering at the University of Buenos Aires and worked in Boston for the multinational food giant CPC International. Today she is a senior manager for the BASF chemical company in New Jersey.

This book is dedicated to Ewa's husband, Jacek Jędruch, who died in a tragic fall while traveling in Greece in 1995. In many ways he typified the tenacity and hard-won success of his generation. Jacek was barely in his teens when he joined the Home Army. He disrupted Wehrmacht lines of communication across Poland during the German occupation. Under the Communists, he was hunted and wounded by security forces.

Jacek went to London in 1946 and emigrated to the United States in 1950. He earned a degree in mechanical engineering from Northeastern University, a master's in nuclear engineering from Massachusetts Institute of Technology, and his Ph.D. in nuclear engineering from Pennsylvania State University. He was a scientist at Westinghouse, Ebasco Services, and Raytheon. He helped design a nuclear engine for space application and the Tokamak Fusion Test Reactor at Princeton. He published more than sixty articles and one book on nuclear engineering.

His avocation was the history of parliamentary institutions. His book *Constitutions, Elections, and Legislatures of Poland*, published in 1982, is probably the best modern source on Polish constitutional and pluralistic development. He was active for many years as a member of the International Commission for the History of Parliamentary and Representative Institutions. In 1990 he translated *Legislatures* by Professor Kenneth Wheare of Oxford into Polish. The book was presented as a gift to each member of Poland's first post-Communist Parliament. Jacek translated the book because, at the time, no such primer was available in Poland. In this and many other ways the struggle for Polish independence defined his life.

History tells us that the West can ill afford to take that struggle lightly. For most of the past two centuries, Poland has been a "no-man's land" where powerful neighbors collided. Today Poland is building a stable future, but it must have strong alliances with the West to succeed. Russian instability remains a daily concern. The Poles know from centuries of experience how fast circumstances change, how quickly the West forgets, and how long it takes to rebuild.

Today, the Poles are rebuilding a parliamentary democracy. It is the one monument that can truly commemorate Stalin's victims at Katyń and countless other places. The survival of parliamentary democracy will mean that they did not lose their lives in vain.

Allen Paul
November 1995

Appendix: Katyń Forest Execution Order

<<<<<<<<

The letter below, written by NKVD Chief Lavrenti Beria, ordered the execution of, among others, Polish officers captured by the Red Army in 1939 and interned at Kozelsk, Ostashkov, and Starobelsk. Beria held that the prisoners should be liquidated because they were "hardened and uncompromising enemies of Soviet authority." Stalin, Klement Voroshilov, Vyacheslav Molotov, and Anastas Mikoyan each signed the letter signifying their approval of Beria's recommendation. The words "Kalinin, in favor," and "Kaganovich, in favor" were written in the margin. This letter proves what most Polish leaders had long suspected: that the order to murder their countrymen had been personally approved by Stalin and the Politburo.

The translation below appeared in RFE/RL *Research Report,* vol. 2, no. 4 (January 22, 1993), p. 22, and is used by permission.

TOP SECRET
5 March 1940

USSR People's Commissariat for Internal Affairs
March 1940
Moscow

To Comrade Stalin:

A large number of former officers of the Polish Army, former employees of the Polish police and intelligence agencies, members of Polish nationalist, counterrevolutionary resistance organizations, escapees, and others, all of them sworn enemies of Soviet authority [and] full of hatred for the Soviet system, are currently being held in prisoner-of-war camps of the USSR NKVD and in prisons in the western oblasts of Ukraine and Belarus [Byelorussia].

The military and police officers in the camps are attempting to continue their counterrevolutionary activities and are carrying out anti-Soviet agitation. Each of them is waiting only for his release in order to enter actively into the struggle against Soviet authority.

The organs of the NKVD in the western oblasts of Ukraine and Belarus have uncovered a number of counterrevolutionary rebel organizations. Former officers of the Polish Army and police as well as gendarmes have played an active, leading role in all of these organizations.

Among the detained escapees and violators of the state border a considerable number of people have been identified as belonging to counterrevolutionary espionage and resistance organizations.

14,736 former officers, government officials, landowners, policemen, gendarmes, prison guards, settlers in the border region [osadniki], and intelligence officers (more than 97 percent of them are Poles) are being kept in prisoner-of-war camps. This number excludes soldiers and junior officers.

They include:

Generals, colonels, and lieutenant colonels—	295
Majors and captains—	2,080
Lieutenants, second lieutenants, and ensigns—	6,049
Officers and junior officers of the police, border troops, and gendarmerie—	1,030
Rank-and-file police officers, gendarmes, prison guards, and intelligence officers—	5,138
Government officials, landowners, priests, and settlers in border regions—	144

18,632 detained people are being kept in prisons in western regions of Ukraine and Belarus (10,685 of them are Poles).

They include:

Former officers—	1,207
Former intelligence officers of the police and gendarmerie—	5,141
Spies and saboteurs—	347
Former landowners, factory owners, and government officials—	465
Members of various counterrevolutionary elements—	5,345
Escapees—	6,127

In view of the fact that all are hardened and uncompromising enemies of Soviet authority, the USSR NKVD considers it necessary:

1. To instruct the USSR NKVD that it should try before special tribunals
   1) the cases of the 14,700 former Polish officers, government officials, landowners, police officers, intelligence officers, gendarmes, settlers in border regions, and prison guards being kept in prisoner-of-war camps.
   2) and also the cases of 11,000 members of various counterrevolutionary organizations of spies and saboteurs, former landowners, factory owners, former Polish officers, government officials, and escapees who have been arrested and are being held in prisons in the western oblasts of Ukraine and Belarus and apply to them the supreme penalty: shooting.
2. Examination of the cases is to be carried out without summoning those detained and without bringing charges; the statements concerning the conclusion of the investigation and the final verdict [should be issued] as follows:

a) for persons being held in prisoner-of-war camps, in the form of certificates issued by the Administration for the Affairs of Prisoners of War of the USSR NKVD;

b) for arrested persons, in the form of certificates issued by the NKVD of the Ukrainian SSR and the NKVD of the Belarussian SSR.

3. The cases should be examined and the verdicts pronounced by a three-person tribunal consisting of Comrades Merkulov, Kobulov, and Bashtakov.

People's Commissar for Internal Affairs of the USSR

L. Beria

Page one of Beria's March 5, 1940, letter to Stalin recommending liquidation of Polish officers and others. The larger underlined signature is Stalin's. Poland lost more than 50 percent of its intelligentsia in World War Two. This order is part of a secret, joint NKVD-Gestapo campaign to liquidate the nation's educated populace. (Reproduced by permission of RFE/RL *Research Report*, vol. 2, no. 4 [January 22, 1993], p. 23.)

Notes

Records of the U.S. House of Representatives Select Committee to Conduct an Investigation of the Facts, Evidence, and Circumstances of the Katyn Forest Massacre are the most frequently cited and most important primary source used in this work. The committee's findings were published in seven volumes at the end of its investigation during the Eighty-second Congress in 1951–1952. In the notes that follow, the committee's record is cited in abbreviated form as "Hearings."

CHAPTER 1: The Interlude

1 Last train to Zakopane: interviews, Jaga, Magda, and Maria Czarnek.

2 In the vacuum caused by the collapse of these empires: Davies, *God's Playground: A History of Poland*, Vol. 2 (New York: Columbia University Press, 1982), p. 394, and Norman Davies, *White Eagle, Red Star: The Polish-Soviet War* (London: McDonald & Co., 1972), pp. 188–220.

2 Piłsudski was a new Sobieski: Jan Karski, *The Great Powers & Poland, 1919–1945* (Lanham, N.J.: University Press of America, 1985), pp. 73, 116.

2 Piłsudski's coup: ibid., p. 94.

2 Authoritarian government in Warsaw: ibid., pp. 186–87.

2 Piłsudski left behind an oligarchy: ibid., pp. 188–94.

2 Hitler's demands to Beck, January 5, 1939: Anna M. Cienciala, *Poland and the Western Powers 1938–1939* (London: Routledge & Kegan Paul, 1968), p. 189.

3 Suddenly German troops rimmed Poland: William L. Shirer, *The Rise and Fall of the Third Reich* (London: Pan Books, 1964), p. 561.

3 German troop movements along the frontier: ibid., p. 566.

3 British and French leaders' decision to draw the line on Poland: Cienciala, op. cit., pp. 207–12.

3 Chamberlain's announcement to Parliament: p. 224.

3 Chamberlain's diplomatic deterrent: ibid., pp. 225–27.

3 April 6, 1939, mutual-assistance pact: ibid., pp. 235–37.

4 Beck's May 5 speech to Sejm: ibid., p. 239.

4 Germany's ninety-eight divisions: B. H. Fiddell Hart, *History of the Second World War* (New York: Putnam, 1970), pp. 17–19.

5 secret signals were flashing: Shirer, *Rise and Fall*, p. 608.

5 "All through the summer": interview, Magda Czarnek.

5 Iwo Pogonowski, a Polish expatriate: interview, Iwo Pogonowski.

6 Czarnek family vacation, August 1939: interviews, Czarnek sisters. The account of the family vacation that follows is also based on these interviews.

9 Germany and the Soviet Union were suddenly partners: See notes for chapter two for references to pact.

10 Anglo-Polish Mutual Assistance Pact becomes formal alliance: Cienciala, op. cit., p. 248.

10 "The French have lied to the Poles": ibid., p. 245.

10 British and French delay war declaration while Mussolini intervenes: Shirer, *Rise and Fall*, pp. 728–51.

11 Poles spurn offer to join Anti-Comintern Pact: Karski, *Great Powers*, pp. 296–97.

11 "With the Germans we risk losing our freedom": John A. Lukacs, *The Great Powers in Eastern Europe* (New York: American Book Co., 1953), p. 241.

11 Thus, false expectations: The author's conclusion here is sharply at variance with those of some authorities on the history of the period. There is considerable merit in their argument that the Poles prepared as well as they could under the circumstances for a German attack, and that European statesmen in general did not believe that Hitler would order an invasion. In that sense, the surreal atmosphere in Poland on the eve of the war permeated Europe as a whole. Moreover, many authorities properly point out that subsequent events clearly suggest that Polish leaders were correct in believing that nothing could be gained by cooperating with the Soviets. The author bases his conclusion on the view that the Poles' untenable position in 1939 was, to some degree, the result of an accumulation of unwise foreign-policy decisions. One crucial result was that the regime in Warsaw was unable to prepare the Polish public adequately for the possibility that an attack might occur. Tens of thousands of reserves were thus left milling about train stations while the Luftwaffe severed transportation arteries during the first few days of the September campaign.

12 "All in all, the Poles are calm": William L. Shirer, *Berlin Diary: The Journal of a Foreign Correspondent 1934–1941* (New York: Popular Library, 1961), p. 135.

CHAPTER 2: Hitler's Command

15 Chamberlain's grueling trip to Obersalzberg: Shirer, *Rise and Fall*, pp. 470–71.

15 Hitler confirms his intention to invade: Galeazzo Ciano, *The Ciano Diaries* (Garden City, N.Y.: Garden City Publishing Co., 1945), pp. 118–19.

15 Stalin's March 10, 1939, radio address: Shirer, p. 581.

15 firing of Litvinov: ibid., p. 585. His association with the concept of collective security, the ease with which he moved in diplomatic circles, and the fact that his wife was British all contributed to Litvinov's immense popularity in the West and made him an object of Stalin's suspicion.

16 "the best file clerk in Russia": Michael T. Florinsky, *Encyclopedia of Russia and the Soviet Union* (New York: McGraw-Hill, 1961), p. 361.

16   "little worms": John Toland, *Adolf Hitler*, Vol. 1 (Garden City, N.Y.: Doubleday & Co., 1976), pp. 433–34.

16   Hitler's deadline for Case White: Shirer, p. 571.

17   Soviets agree to broaden talks with Nazis: James Sontag and James Stuart Beddie, eds., *Nazi-Soviet Relations, 1939–1941* (Westport, Conn.: Greenwood Press, 1976), p. 48.

17   Hitler's August 14, 1939, overture to Soviets: ibid., pp. 50–52.

17   Molotov . . . deftly asked: ibid., pp. 52–53.

17   Hitler's affirmative response on nonaggression pact: ibid., p. 58.

17   Molotov-Schulenburg meeting, August 19, 1939: ibid., pp. 64–65.

17   Molotov's draft nonaggression pact: ibid., pp. 65–66.

17   Hitler's August 20, 1939, telegram to Stalin: ibid., pp. 66–67.

17   Stalin's message agreeing to Ribbentrop's visit: ibid., p. 69.

18   description of Berghof: Albert Speer, *Inside the Third Reich* (New York: Macmillan, 1970), pp. 99–105 and 193.

18   a composite account: Shirer, pp. 641–45. Shirer provides a composite account of Hitler's famous speech based on notes made at the time by Admiral Hermann Boehm, Admiral Erich Rader, and General Franz Halder.

20   provisions of Molotov-Ribbentrop Pact: *Nazi-Soviet Relations*, pp. 70–78.

20   "I know how much the German nation loves its Führer": ibid., p. 75.

CHAPTER 3: A Failed Escape

21   "We have to prepare": interview, Magda Czarnek.

21   "None of us believed that the war was coming": ibid.

21   German use of gas in World War I: *Encyclopaedia Britannica*, vol. 19, p. 952.

21   Hitler blinded by gas: ibid., vol. 8, p. 966

21   after-supper drills: interview, Magda Czarnek.

22   "To us, these moments could be hilarious": ibid.

22   Radio reports . . . described a number of border raids by the Abwehr: Steven Zaloga and Victor Madej, *The Polish Campaign* (New York: Hippocrene Books, 1985), p. 103.

22   British and French object to Polish mobilization: Wacław Jędrzejewicz, ed., *Poland in the British Parliament, 1939–1945* (New York: Piłsudski Institute, 1946, 1959), p. 210.

22   Czarneks on the evening of August 31, 1939: interview, Magda Czarnek.

23   The primary target was Rakowice Airfield: Zaloga and Madej, op. cit., p. 116; and eyewitness accounts in *The German Invasion of Poland* (London and Melbourne: Hutchinson & Co., 1940), p. 33.

23   "Why the black crosses?": interviews, Czarnek sisters. The account in the remainder of this chapter is drawn from these interviews.

24   four panzer divisions had swept east: Zaloga and Madej, op. cit., p. 114.

CHAPTER 4: Case White

27 Ciano's warning to Mussolini of Hitler's reckless gamble: Ciano, op. cit., pp. 119–28.

27 Mussolini's letter to Hitler on the state of Italian war preparations: Shirer, *Rise and Fall*, pp. 671–72.

27 This letter, read over the telephone by Ciano: Ciano, op. cit., pp. 128–29.

27 British upgrading of pact with Poles to formal alliance: Cienciala, *Poland*, p. 248.

28 Poles' failure to recognize border incidents as prelude to invasion: Zaloga and Madej, op. cit., pp. 103–104.

28 Nazi propaganda fanning anti-Polish sentiment: Bernt Engelmann, *In Hitler's Germany* (New York: Pantheon Books, 1986), p. 166.

28 Operation Canned Goods: Shirer, pp. 629–30 and p. 719.

28 Polish troop strength: Zaloga and Madej, op. cit., p. 103–106.

29 Polish general staff's unwise decision: ibid., p. 157.

29 Heinz Guderian as architect of blitzkrieg: David Mason, *Who's Who in World War II* (Boston: Little, Brown, 1978), pp. 113–16.

30 myth of Polish cavalry charging German tanks: Zaloga and Madej, op. cit., pp. 110, 160.

30 Polish counteroffensive at Bzura River: ibid., pp. 131–38.

32 Soviet pretext for invasion: Shirer, p. 754.

32 "The Polish state has ceased to exist": Hearings, part 6, p. 1638.

32 General Timoshenko's appeal to Polish soldiers: *The Crime of Katyń: Facts and Documents*, 5th ed. (London: Polish Cultural Foundation, 1989), p. 12.

33 Polish soldiers' reactions to Soviet intervention: Hearings, part 6, pp. 1639–41.

33 size of Soviet invasion force: *Crime of Katyn*, p. 10.

34 German and Polish casualties: Zaloga and Madej, op. cit., p. 156.

34 Soviet manpower losses: ibid.

34 "Germany having killed the prey": *New York Times*, September 18, 1939.

35 German casualties after joint Wehrmacht–Red Army victory parade: Zaloga and Madaj, op. cit., p. 158.

35 Legal continuity of Polish government: Karski, *Great Powers*, pp. 389–91.

35 Sikorski's coalition government: ibid., p. 389.

36 Saving of Polish government gold reserves: *New York Times*, June 6, 1943. According to this report $80 million in reserves went first to Paris and then, following the fall of France in 1940, to Dakar, in the part of French West Africa that is now Senegal.

CHAPTER 5: Capture

38 Dr. Czarnek's journey east: interview, Staszek Niewiadomski.

40 Soviets were not coming to help the Poles but to capture them: ibid. Accounts similar to that provided by Niewiadomski are common in literature on the subject. See, e.g., *Crime of Katyń*, pp. 7–14.

42 Poles' occupation of Moscow: Bernard Pares, *A History of Russia* (New York: Knopf, 1926), p. 143.

44 The four-hundred-mile journey to the settlement of Kozelshchina: interview, Niewiadomski.
45 "I know why this is taking so long": ibid.
46 "I'll be coming back soon": ibid.

CHAPTER 6: Diabolical Schemes

49 To the Bolsheviks, Dr. Czarnek epitomized the enemy: Hearings, part 6, pp. 1637–38 and p. 1648.
49 "The war of the giants": Davies, *White Eagle, Red Star*, p. 21.
51 "He proposed to the German Command": Davies, *God's Playground*, vol. 2, pp. 391–92.
53 "According to [the Poles] half Europe had been Polish": Neal Ascherson, *The Struggles for Poland* (London: Michael Joseph, 1987), p. 56.
53 It had inherited six currencies: Davies, *God's Playground*, vol. 2, p. 402.
53 Stalin . . . cautioned strongly against any further advance: Adam B. Ulam, *Stalin: The Man and His Era* (Boston: Beacon Press, 1987), p. 186.
53 "It is easier to saddle a cow": Pogonowski, p. 211.
53 "Over the corpse of White Poland": Davies, *God's Playground*, vol. 2, p. 396.
54 Soviet terms for accepting Curzon Line: Karski, *Great Powers*, p. 61; and Ulam, *Stalin*, p. 187.
54 Either through a clerical error . . . or through intentional falsification: Karski, *Great Powers*, p. 59.
54 On July 28, 1920, Białystok became: Mikhail Heller and Aleksandr Nekrich, *Utopia in Power: The History of the Soviet Union from 1917 to the Present* (New York: Summit Books, 1986. Trans. by Phyllis B. Carlos from the Russian language edition of 1982), p. 95.
54 During the advance a dangerous gap opened: Ulam, *Stalin*, p. 188.
55 Yegorov finally agreed to send reinforcements: ibid., p. 188.
55 "Listen, Schaetzl": Jan Novak-Jeziorański, "The Miracle on the Vistula," *Tygodnik Powszechny*, August 19, 1990.
55 "If Charles Martel had not checked the Saracen": Davies, *God's Playground*, Vol. 2, pp. 399–401.
56 The frontier . . . was more than 150 miles east of the Curzon Line: Heller and Nekrich, op. cit., p. 97; and Karski, *Great Powers*, pp. 69–70.
56 An interwar Poland emerged: *Concise Statistical Year-book of Poland, September 1939–June 1941*, 2nd ed. (Glasgow: Polish Ministry of Information, 1944), p. 9.
56 As a result, the leadership of the Polish Communist party was primarily Jewish: Richard Hiscocks, *Poland: Bridge for the Abyss?* (London: Oxford University Press, 1963), pp. 75–77; and Jan T. Gross, *Revolution from Abroad* (Princeton, N.J.: Princeton University Press, 1988), p. 32.
57 "I am not fond of the Germans": Gerald Freund, *Unholy Alliance* (New York: Harcourt Brace, 1959), pp. 82–83.
57 "Only in firm cooperation with a great Russia": Turnbull Higgins, *Hitler and Russia* (New York: Macmillan, 1966), p. 3.

57   "The re-establishment of a broad common frontier": ibid., 4.

57   He organized a secret unit called Special Group R: Freund, op. cit., pp. 203–
     12.

57   During this time, the Germans established a secret air base . . . and tank
     training center at Kazan: ibid., pp. 205–207.

57   The Western Allies were surprised and angered when the Germans used the
     occasion: John Saxon Mills, *The Genoa Conference* (New York: Dutton, 1922),
     pp. 90–95.

58   That policy was an attempt at "beheading" the nation: Władyslaw Anders,
     An Army in Exile: The Story of the Second Polish Corps (London: Macmillan,
     1949), p. 66.

59   "Close your hearts to pity!": See notes for chapter two.

59   Sir Nevile Henderson . . . was "so wrought up he was speechless": *New York
     Times*, August 24, 1939.

59   David Low's cartoon: Anthony Read and David Fisher, *The Deadly Embrace*
     (New York: Norton, 1988), p.341.

60   under which large quantities of Soviet raw materials: *Documents on German
     Foreign Policy*, p. 160.

60   Its secret protocol . . . split the projected spoils: *Nazi-Soviet Relations*, p.
     78. The full text of the protocol appears on pp. 76–78.

61   "as the foundation stone": ibid., p. 101.

62   Stalin put these proposed changes to Ribbentrop: ibid., p. 105.

62   With a few deft strokes of the pen, millions of people were shifted: Karski,
     Great Powers, p. 391; and Anonymous, *The Dark Side of the Moon*, 44.

62   In doing so it scaled new heights of cynicism: *Nazi-Soviet Relations*, p. 105.

63   "Both parties will tolerate in their territories no Polish agitation": ibid., p.
     107.

63   Frank's declaration: Shirer, *Rise and Fall*, p. 795.

63   such units were undertaking a "housecleaning of Jews": ibid., p. 795.

63   The flurry of absurd edicts later even included a ban on dancing: Raphael
     Lemkin, *Axis Rule in Occupied Europe* (Washington, D.C.: Carnegie En-
     dowment for International Peace, Division of International Law, 1944), p. 555.

64   "We have no intention of rebuilding Poland": Shirer, op. cit., p. 793.

64   Molotov gloatingly told that body: *Izvestia*, November 1, 1939.

65   Khrushchev acknowledged that Gestapo representatives came to Lwów: Nik-
     ita Khrushchev, *Khrushchev Remembers* (Boston: Little, Brown and Co.,
     1970), p. 141.

65   "In March, 1940, my staff received information that a NKVD mission had
     come to Krakow": Tadeusz Bór-Komorowski, *The Secret Army* (Nashville:
     The Battery Press, 1984), pp. 46–47.

66   These camps and collectivization may have claimed: Iosif G. Dyadkin,
     Unnatural Deaths in the U.S.S.R., 1928–1954 (New Brunswick: Transaction
     Books, 1983), p. 60.

67   In approach, the Gestapo and the NKVD were fundamentally different: inter-
     view, Paweł Zaleski. Zaleski was assigned by the Polish Intelligence Service
     to Bucharest and Istanbul during 1940–1942. From both those cities, he
     assisted intelligence agents going to and from the Soviet-occupied territories.

CHAPTER 7: Camp Life

70 In contrast, the inmate rosters of Kozelsk and Starobelsk read like a *Who's Who: Crime of Katyn*, pp. 17–20.

70 About 5 percent of the men were Jews: Simon Schochet, "The Polish Officers of Jewish Descent," *Journal of the Józef Piłsudski Institute*, vol. 21 (1988), p. 162.

70 About half the 3,910 men at Starobelsk were captured: ibid., pp. 19–20.

70 "At Kozelsk, I discovered Poland": interview, Father Zdzisław Peszkowski.

71 "You could not help but feel the esprit de corps": interview, Władek Cichy.

73 Janina Muśnicka Lewandowska: *Crime of Katyn*, pp. 33–34.

75 "All sorts of promotions were going on": interview, Peszkowski.

76 Only Father Ziółkowski, who had conducted a secret Mass: *Crime of Katyn*, p. 30.

76 methods and purpose of Soviet interrogations: Hearings, part 6, pp. 1648–50.

77 a small group of prisoners from Kozelsk was transferred to Smolensk: ibid., p. 1659.

77 role of NKVD general Zarubin at Kozelsk: *Crime of Katyn*, pp. 23, 31–32.

78 NKVD commisar Niechorochev's report to Merkulov: *Rzeczpospolita*, no. 186 (2620), August 11–12, 1990.

81 Dr. Czarnek's letter: personal papers of Magda Czarnek. This was the only letter from him that Dr. Czarnek's family received from Kozelsk. His daughters believe that their father attempted to write his family on numerous other occasions and that such letters were destroyed by the NKVD.

CHAPTER 8: House Calls

85 The account of the arrests of the Neuhoff-Hoffman family is taken from interviews, Zbigniew and Anna Neuhoff.

88 "The way it all happened still makes me angry": interview, Ewa Hoffman Jędruch.

89 Thousands of families were being wrenched from their homes: Gross, op. cit., pp. 192–224. *The Dark Side of the Moon* contains an excellent account of the methods used by the Soviets in carrying out four mass deportations in eastern Poland in 1940–1941. See especially "The Occupation," pp. 38–61.

90 Khrushchev took personal responsibility for overseeing the Sovietization process: Khrushchev, op. cit., 146.

91 The plundering . . . began almost immediately: *Dark Side of the Moon*, pp. 46–47.

91 "But while these men [those elected] were well known to us": Khrushchev, op. cit., 146.

92 One man who succeeded in fleeing: interview with Paweł Zaleski. The following account of Zaleski's travels and escape is taken from this interview.

94 The mid-April 1940 roundup . . . involving at least 1.2 million Poles: Gross, op. cit., p. 194. On March 15, 1944, the Polish Foreign Ministry produced a detailed estimate concluding that the deportations totaled at least 1.2 million Poles. The total was based on lists and estimates compiled by Polish

representatives during the twenty-one-month period between the summer of 1941 and the spring of 1943, when the Polish and Soviet governments cooperated with each other. Among those deported were several hundred thousand men who were conscripted into the Red Army, and others who were deported as members of Soviet labor battalions. The Foreign Ministry's estimate is probably quite conservative. A number of reliable sources put the figures considerably higher. The actual number may be closer to 2 million deportees.

95   Maria remembered vividly the atmosphere in Lwów in mid-April: interview, Maria Pawulska Rasiej.

99   Near Lwów Polytechnic Institute the mathematician Stefan Banach . . . scribbled notes: Stanisław Ulam, *Adventures of a Mathematician* (New York: Scribners, 1976), pp. 50–51.

100   Poles were being taken to Siberia and "dumped there": *New York Times*, February 9, 1941.

CHAPTER 9: The Liquidations

103   The conclusion that only one man, Professor Świaniewicz, got to the edge of the forest and lived to tell about it is widely shared by many who have examined the facts closely. However, in February 1952, the select committee heard testimony from an unidentified hooded person who claimed to have witnessed the executions. The anonymity of the witness, the lack of supporting detail—especially any plausible explanation for how the witness penetrated or escaped from the heavily guarded NKVD compound at Katyń—resulted in the author's decision to dismiss this testimony as seriously lacking in credibility.

104   "You know, of course, that I was one of the czar's subjects": interview, Stanisław Świaniewicz.

105   the NKVD decided to spare 448 men: Hearings, part 6, p. 1624.

106   "Something strange was reflected in the eyes of this young man": *Crime of Katyn*, p. 25. Here and elsewhere in this chapter the author has drawn on an English translation of excerpts from Świaniewicz's memoirs, *In the Shadow of Katyn*, provided in *Crime of Katyn*.

106   The curious crowd of onlookers: ibid., p. 50.

106   Further compounding all these surprises were the provisions: ibid., p. 51.

107   "There was not the slightest suspicion": ibid.

107   Each morning about 10:00 A.M. a telephone call came from NKVD headquarters: ibid., pp. 52–54.

107   The festive atmosphere of departure took a sinister turn: interviews, Cichy, Peszkowski, and Świaniewicz. These three men were among the 448 from Kozelsk, Starobelsk, and Ostashkov who survived. All three gave similar accounts of the conditions of transport described in this chapter.

108   Eight miles west of Smolensk the trains stopped for good: *Crime of Katyn*, pp. 57–60.

108   The men left the train in groups of thirty: ibid., p. 59.

108   an autobus commonly known as a black raven: Hearings, part 6, pp. 1657–58.

109 "I saw a fairly large open area with patches of grass": *Crime of Katyn,* pp. 59–60.

110 "April 9: Ever since dawn it has been a peculiar day": Hearings, part 2, p. 184. A complete translation of Major Solski's diary appears in the hearing record. See part 4, p. 926.

110 NKVD use of Walther pistol: interview with Dr. Zdzisław M. Rurarz, former Polish ambassador to Japan.

110 Their hands were lashed tightly behind the back: Hearings, part 6, pp. 1629–30 and 1658–59. The account of the executions that follows was drawn largely from these pages.

110 It is difficult to imagine: Most accounts of the crime suggest, or leave the impression, that the Polish officers knelt at the edge of the graves before being shot, or that they may have been forced to lie on their companions before being shot. Such explanations seem at odds with important facts. Polish fighting men were renowned for their personal bravery, a quality stressed repeatedly in Polish military training and celebrated among the rank and file. In light of this tradition, it seems unlikely that reservist, and certainly not regular army officers, would have meekly submitted. The NKVD used its standard methods in carrying out these liquidations. These methods emphasized considerable care in controlling the victim even to the point of immobilization. Executions often were carried out in basements and cellars where victims were sharply restricted in their ability to move. The black ravens, or special lorries, transported the Polish officers in extreme conditions of confinement. The fact that some of the victims were bound and gagged clearly suggests an unwillingness on the part of these men to submit to their NKVD executioners.

112 The 4,143 victims . . . were buried in eight common graves: Hearings, part 6, p. 1631.

114 Maks Hoffman's possible transfer to Vorkuta: ibid., p. 1712.

114 Soviet President Gorbachev acknowledged on April 13, 1990: *New York Times,* April 14, 1990.

114 Later, one missing man's wife, Catherina Gaszciecka, reported: *Crime of Katyn,* p. 273.

115 Stanisław Mikołajczyk . . . reported that an officer attached to the Soviet embassy in London: Stanisław Mikołajczyk, *The Rape of Poland: Pattern of Soviet Aggression* (Westport, Conn.: Greenwood Press, 1972), p. 38.

CHAPTER 10: Trains to the East

119 In describing the conditions of transport, the author has relied on the personal experiences of a number of deportees interviewed in 1989 and 1990. The experiences reported are quite similar to a number of published accounts of the deportations written at or about the time these events occurred. For a highly detailed and particularly moving account of these conditions, see "The Trains," pp. 62–81, in *Dark Side of the Moon.*

119 Zofia Hoffman and her mother, Maria Neuhoff: interviews, Ewa Hoffman Jędruch and Zbigniew and Anna Neuhoff.

120 Mrs. Pawulska was having second thoughts about taking Amik: interview with Maria Pawulska Rasiej. The following account is based on that interview.

125 Semipalatinsk, Siberia's gateway to Central Asia: See map.

CHAPTER 11: The Remnant

127 For unknown reasons Soviet authorities spared 448: Hearings, part 6, p. 1624.

127 "Maybe the Bolsheviks are human after all": interview, Władek Cichy.

128 Quick on the prisoners' heels came a horde of political agents: Hearings, part 6, pp. 1676–77.

128 The leader of the pro-Soviet faction was Lieutenant Colonel Zygmunt Berling: interviews, Cichy, Peszkowski, Świaniewicz, and Berling's widow, Maria. The literature on Katyń is ambiguous on this point. The interviews cited leave no doubt in the author's mind that Berling led the pro-Soviet faction.

129 A large quantity of planks arrived in early June: Hearings, part 6, p. 1677.

129 Suddenly, in mid-June, the prisoners were further puzzled: ibid., pp. 1677–81.

129 A puzzling and disturbing question began to trouble the men at Gryazovets: ibid., pp. 1679–80, and interview, Cichy.

130 "Everyone who has meat in his soup": interview, Cichy. The following account of Cichy's camp experiences is also based on that interview.

132 On October 10, Berling and six other senior Polish officers: Hearings, part 6, pp. 1681–83.

132 Visit of General Merkulov with Berling's group: ibid., p. 1682. The fact that Beria was personally involved underscores the high level of importance the Soviets attached to the meeting. Beria assumed full command of the NKVD in December 1938 and managed to cling to the post for fifteen years. During Beria's tenure, the Soviet terror apparatus was directed against the twenty to twenty-three million new citizens acquired by the U.S.S.R. in 1939–1940. For a concise overview of Beria's role at the NKVD, see Ronald Hingley, *The Russian Secret Police: Muscovite, Imperial Russian and Soviet Political Security Operations 1565–1970* (London: Hutchinson & Co., 1970), pp. 183–223.

133 "And where will we get the officers?": Hearings, part 6, p. 1682. The sources are unclear as to whether Beria or Merkulov actually replied that a "great mistake" or "blunder" had been made with the men from Kozelsk and Starobelsk. A translation of this exchange, prepared by the Polish government-in-exile, can be found in Hearings, part 4, pp. 563–65. Further light is shed by the testimony of Witness A, part 4, pp. 524, 552, 571.

134 Berling's response: Hearings, part 6, p. 1683.

134 "On so many occasions in which Poles fought the Muscovy clan of robbers": Tadeusz Kościuszko, "The Universal Proclamation of Polaniec," trans. Iwo Pogonowski, in Jan Stanisław Kopczewski, ed., *In History and Tradition* (Warsaw: State Textbook Printing Office, 1957), p. 57.

CHAPTER 12: Life on the Steppes

137 The description of Kazakhstan is taken from the *Encyclopaedia Britannica*, vol. 10, p. 407.

137 Until collectivization, nomadic tribes: ibid., vol. 5, p. 739.

138 Mrs. Pawulska and her three children . . . arrived: interview, Maria Pawulska Rasiej.

138 In theory the members of the kolkhoz: Alec Nove, *The Soviet Economic System*, 2nd ed. (London: Allen & Unwin, 1980), pp. 28–32.

138 the Pawulskis and about ten other Polish families were lodged: interview, Maria Pawulska Rasiej. The following account is taken from that interview.

141 (We now know . . . : "Report of NKVD Burning of Letters," *Rzeczpospolita*, no. 186 (2620), August 11–12, 1990.

146 Nothing in her previous thirty-four years: interviews, Ewa Hoffman Jędruch and Zbigniew and Anna Neuhoff. The following account is taken from those interviews.

CHAPTER 13: Bad-Faith Agreements

151 The account of the blood-red sky is from an interview, Maria Pawulska Rasiej.

151 Władek Cichy and another prisoner were sitting at noontime: interview, Władek Cichy.

152 On the banks of another stream roughly seven hundred miles to the west: interview, Magda Czarnek Pogonowski.

152 Despite staggering evidence to the contrary, he refused to believe: Heller and Nekrich, op. cit., p. 371; and Ulam, *Stalin*, pp. 536–38.

153 Then, on May 12, Soviet superagent Richard Sorge relayed disturbing news from Tokyo: Heller and Nekrich, op. cit., p. 361.

153 "Haven't the German generals sent this defector over": ibid., p. 370.

153 With the invasion, Hitler planned to carve open: Ulam, *Stalin*, p. 550.

154 Relative forces of German and Soviets: Heller and Nekrich, op. cit., pp. 371–72.

154 Stalin was alerted to the disaster in a 4 A.M. phone call: Ulam, *Stalin*, p. 538.

155 At two large prisons, the NKVD began herding prisoners into cellars and shooting them: Gross, op. cit., pp. 178–86.

155 Stalin was not nearly so self-possessed: Ulam, *Stalin*, pp. 540–41.

155 The years of escalating terror, bloodshed, and blundering had caused a deep crisis of leadership: Heller and Nekrich, op. cit., pp. 304–308.

156 Stalin's absence on June 28 at a meeting: Ulam, *Stalin*, pp. 540–41.

156 "It came out badly": ibid., pp. 541–42.

156 Churchill wasted little time: Karski, *Great Powers*, p. 403.

157 One day after the German attack: Hearings, part 6, p. 1685.

157 With Stalin still in seclusion, Moscow did not respond for ten days: Karski, *Great Powers*, p. 404.

158 Sikorski . . . was stunned by Maisky's estimate: Hearings, part 6, p. 1685.

158 Sikorski emphasized that any agreement approved by his government: Karski, *Great Powers*, p. 405.

158 all three parties met face-to-face the next day, July 5: ibid.

158 On October 22, 1939, a few weeks into their military occupation: Gross, op.

cit., p. 71. The decree issued by the Supreme Soviet on November 1 and 2, 1939, appears in Hearings, part 4, p. 973.

159 In their negotiations with the Soviets, Polish authorities proposed: Hearings, part 6, p. 1686.

159 On July 11, Eden snapped at Sikorski: Karski, *Great Powers*, p. 406.

159 Then, on July 17, Maisky added an element of threat: ibid., p. 408.

160 the pact . . . "would be in the interest of Poland": ibid.

160 "As soon as diplomatic relations are re-established": Hearings, part 4, p. 1085. The full text of the agreement appears here.

160 In announcing it by broadcast to Poland, Sikorski emphasized: Hearings, part 6, p. 1686.

161 "You know, Ribbentrop . . .": Joachim von Ribbentrop, *The Ribbentrop Memoirs* (London: Weidenfeld and Nicolson, 1954), pp. 170–71.

162 On August 4, the Soviets released General Władysław Anders: Anders, op. cit., p. 43.

162 On August 12, the Soviet government published the amnesty protocol: Hearings, part 6, p. 1686.

162 The Joint Polish-Soviet Commission to assist deportees: ibid., p. 1690.

163 More complete Soviet figures were presented on October 6: ibid., p. 1692.

163 On August 14 . . . the Poles and the Soviets signed a special military agreement: Anders, op. cit., p. 53.

163 On November 2, 1939, Molotov had said that 300,000 Polish troops: ibid., p. 52, and see *Poland in the British Parliament*, vol., 2, p. 8.

164 Panfilov's manpower estimate: Anders, op. cit., p. 53.

164 Władek Cichy was among those waiting: interview with Cichy. The accounts of Cichy's bulletins and of Anders's address to the men are also taken from this interview.

165 set loose a human tide that neither Polish authorities nor the NKVD were prepared for: Józef Czapski, *The Inhuman Land* (London: Polish Cultural Foundation, 1987), p. 12.

166 Most of the deportees were physically unfit: Anders, op. cit., pp. 63–70.

166 By the end of November, forty-six thousand men had been enrolled: Karski, *Great Powers*, p. 422, and *The Dark Side of the Moon*, p. 226.

166 General Panfilov . . . called for a halt in further enlistments: Karski, *Great Powers*, 422.

167 These men were forced at gunpoint to continue moving south: *The Dark Side of the Moon*, p. 226.

167 Among the lucky few: enlistment documents, in personal papers of Ewa Hoffman Jędruch.

167 There was also a vague, uncooperative, and worrisome aspect in the Soviet response: Hearings, part 6, pp. 1694–97.

CHAPTER 14: Crumbling Hopes

169 General Anders had learned from a cellmate, Captain Kuszel, about the three big camps: Anders, op. cit., pp. 40, 48.

169 the NKVD had arranged for Anders to meet with Colonel Zygmunt Berling: ibid., pp. 48–49.

170 On October 6, he told Vyshinsky: Hearings, part 6, pp. 1692–93.

170 "People . . . are not like steam": ibid., p. 1696.

170 November 14 meeting between Stalin and Molotov, and the account of their conversation: ibid., pp. 1698–99.

171 Was this skillful acting on Stalin's part? . . . Kot thought so: Hearings, part 4, p. 904.

171 "[That] was our weak point": ibid., p. 910.

172 "These men who march past have come out of profound suffering": *The Dark Side of the Moon*, p. 212.

172 Stalin and Molotov received Sikorski, Kot, and Anders: Hearings, part 6, pp. 1702–04; and Kot's testimony at Hearings, part 4, p. 913. Kot wrote detailed minutes of the conversation immediately following the meeting. Important points are corroborated by Anders, op. cit., pp. 83–88.

174 That evening Stalin, who seemed in excellent humor, hosted the Polish delegation: Anders, op. cit., pp. 88–91. This is also the source for the conversation and the description of the agreement that follow.

175 Sikorski wrote Churchill describing his visit as a complete success: Winston Churchill, *The Second World War*. Vol. 3, *The Grand Alliance* (Boston: Houghton Mifflin, 1950), pp. 659–66.

175 On December 23: *Poland in the British Parliament*, p. 157.

175 The delegates covered forty-six administrative districts containing some 2,600 settlements of Poles: ibid., p. 158.

176 Soviet reactions to Polish relief: ibid., p. 159.

176 "It will take us twenty years to efface the impression": Czapski, op. cit., p. 242.

176 "Very often I would place calls to one of our delegates": interview, Paweł Zaleski.

177 In May, the NKVD arrested a number of local representatives of the relief program: *Poland in the British Parliament*, pp. 159–62.

178 General Sikorski wired back an adamant response supporting Anders's position: Anders, op. cit., pp. 96–97.

178 Anders was once again advised that rations for his men would be cut drastically: ibid., p. 98.

178 Efforts to evacuate thirty thousand troops and ten thousand civilians began in late March: ibid., p. 100.

179 Czapski's description of devastating health problems: Czapski, op. cit., pp. 236–39.

179 swarms of disease-carrying insects: interview, Paweł Zaleski, and personal papers of Ewa Hoffman Jędruch.

180 The account of Anders's conversation with Stalin is from Hearings, part 6, p. 1710.

180 1,650 deportees and 110 Soviet guards had frozen to death in a train in February 1941: Czapski, op. cit., p. 34.

180 To the Poles, Kolyma: Anders, op. cit., p. 72.

181 "exclusively by cripples": ibid., p. 74.

181 "ruthless and intentional extermination of human beings": ibid.

182 The account of Staszek Czarnek's work, romance, and arrest comes from interviews, Czarnek sisters.

CHAPTER 15: Exodus

185   when the envoy, a Mr. Heitzman, arrived from Moscow: interview, Zofia
      Kinel Laszewski. The accounts of Mrs. Laszewski's family history, her depor-
      tation, and the reaction to Heitzman's visit also come from this interview.

187   News of the amnesty was slower reaching more remote Kokpekty: interview,
      Maria Pawulska Rasiej. The account in this chapter of the Pawulskis' journey
      to Dzhambul, of their life there, and of their departure is also taken from
      this interview.

191   the family . . . could not stay in Alma-Ata: The city was used as a showcase
      for foreign visitors; special restrictions prescribed who could live there.

194   There were many complaints about the *delegatura*'s operations: See notes for
      pp. 175–77.

199   Czarnek apartment as a safe house: interviews, Czarnek sisters.

CHAPTER 16: Wolf's Find

203   The defeat was a disaster for Germany: Heller and Nekrich, op. cit., 400–401.

203   "a grand style": Joseph Goebbels, *The Goebbels Diaries*, ed. and trans. Louis
      P. Lochner (New York: Award Books, 1983), p. 368.

204   Ahrens testified that attention was first drawn to the graves by a wolf: Hear-
      ings, part 5, pp. 1300–1302.

204   Records of the German field police: Hearings, part 6, pp. 1802–1804.

205   Early in March, the OKW put Gerhard Buhtz . . . in charge: ibid., pp. 1739–
      43.

205   The empty cartridge casings in and near the graves were German made:
      Hearings, part 5, pp. 1577–80.

206   Once a body had been separated from the mass: Hearings, part 6, pp. 1744–
      45.

207   Sloventzik's colleagues described him as gregarious: Hearings, part 5, p.
      1331.

207   tens of thousands of visitors came to the forest between mid-April and June
      1943: ibid.

208   On April 10, 1943, a delegation of prominent Poles . . . was flown to
      Smolensk: Hearings, part 6, p. 1806.

208   The underground also relayed the delegation's assessment: Hearings, part 6,
      p. 1715.

208   role of Polish Red Cross technical commission: Hearings, part 3, pp. 390–
      92.

209   "in the normal course of work done by us the Germans were in general not
      obstructive": ibid., pp. 1807–1808.

209   "When resisting this suggestion, I asked on what basis I could give such an
      untruthful figure": ibid., p. 1816.

210   Just prior to their announcement of the discovery, journalists . . . were taken
      on a tour: ibid., p. 1718.

210   The Germans botched other less significant points as well: ibid.

211   "In launching this monstrous invention": ibid., pp. 1720–21.

212   reactions of Polish press and Gen. Anders: Hearings, part 6, pp. 1719, 1721.

212 "In spite of tremendous efforts on our side we have received absolutely no news": ibid., p. 1719.

212 Defense Minister Marian Kukiel said: ibid., p. 1721.

213 "Public opinion in Poland and throughout the world has rightly been so deeply shocked": ibid., p. 1723.

213 "If they are dead nothing you can do will bring them back": Winston Churchill, *The Second World War,* vol. 4, *The Hinge of Fate* (Boston: Houghton Mifflin, 1950), p. 759.

213 "others were left alive for a special occasion": *Poland in the British Parliament,* vol. 2, p. 169.

213 "The Katyn incident is developing into a gigantic political affair": *Goebbels Diaries,* p. 373.

214 position of the International Red Cross: Hearings, part 6, pp. 1723–24.

214 "Slander spreads rapidly": Hearings, part 6, p. 1725.

215 "PRAVDA SEES POLES AS DUPED BY NAZIS": *New York Times,* April 20, 1943.

CHAPTER 17: The Rupture

217 The relationship worsened as the Soviet military situation improved: Hearings, part 6, p. 1727.

217 December 4, 1941, Sikorski-Stalin declaration: Hearings, part 4, p. 1087.

217 a series of unilateral Soviet actions: ibid.

218 "The fact that the anti-Soviet campaign has been started simultaneously": *Correspondence between the Chairman of the Council of Ministers of the U.S.S.R. and the Presidents of the U.S.A. and the Prime Ministers of Great Britain during the Great Patriotic War of 1941–1945* (Moscow: Foreign Languages Publishing House, 1957), vol. 1, pp. 120–21. Hereinafter referred to as *Correspondence* . . . .

220 "Mr. Eden is seeing Sikorski today": ibid., pp. 121–22.

220 "I fully understand your problem": ibid., vol. 2, pp. 61–62.

220 Romer's summons: Hearings, part 6, pp. 1727–28.

220 Molotov's note: Hearings, part 6, p. 1728.

221 Molotov's note confirmed a premonition Romer had: "Murder or High Strategy?," Admiral William H. Standley, *United States Naval Institute Proceedings,* October 1952, p. 1062.

221 "I am in the same fix": ibid., pp. 1063–64.

221 "In the course of his few months in Moscow": ibid., p. 1065.

222 Standley sent two secret messages to the president: Hearings, part 7, pp. 2067–68.

222 Eden's warning to Sikorski: *Documents on Polish-Soviet Relations, 1939–45,* (London: Heinemann, 1967), vol. 2, pp. 696–702.

222 "Our policy towards the Allies is honest": ibid., p. 700.

223 On April 27 and 28, Sikorski held several meetings with Churchill, Eden, and Drexel Biddle: Hearings, part 6, p. 1731.

223 "so far this business has been Goebbels' triumph": *Correspondence* . . . , vol. 1, pp. 124–25.

223 Stalin replied to this message on May 4: ibid., pp. 127–28.

224   Polish government's decision to withdraw its request: Hearings, part 6, p. 1731–32

224   without question the Soviet Union desired a "strong and independent Poland": Hearings, part 6, pp. 1731–32.

224   "The most important theme of all international discussion . . .": Goebbels Diaries, pp. 389–93.

225   "a very important, one might say, a prime place": Henry C. Cassidy, Moscow Dateline 1941–1943 (Boston: Houghton Mifflin, 1943), pp. 275–76.

226   The year had begun with a chiseled, demigodlike portrait of Stalin: Time, vol. XLI, no. 1 (Jan. 4, 1943), cover.

226   "At banquets . . .": ibid., p. 23.

226   "So far as our intentions are concerned . . .": Life, vol. 14, no. 13 (March 29, 1943), pp. 20–21.

226   "a national police . . .": ibid., p. 29.

226   "If states adjacent to the Soviet Union . . . ": ibid., pp. 52–53.

227   In his April 25 cable to Stalin, Churchill reported: Correspondence . . . , vol. 1, pp. 123–124.

227   "miserable rags": ibid., p. 125.

227   Roosevelt was so concerned about the flap: ibid., pp. 63–64.

228   Twelve of Europe's leading experts . . . were asked to visit the site: Hearings, part 6, p. 1733.

228   The experts quickly determined: ibid., pp. 1734–35.

228   the experts were convinced: ibid., p. 1735.

229   a Nackenschuss, or shot at the top of the neck: Hearings, part 3, pp. 317–19.

229   evidence that the victims had been buried for at least three years: Hearings, part 6, pp. 322–24.

229   He convinced his colleagues: Hearings, part 5, pp. 1468–69.

229   The Soviet accusations . . . were at odds: Hearings, part 6, pp. 1734–35.

230   A detailed account of the visit to Katyń by American officers Van Vliet and Stewart is presented in chapter twenty-two. Van Vliet testified before the Select Committee on the Katyń Forest Massacre on February 4, 1952. The full text of his testimony can be found in Hearings, part 2, pp. 32–74.

CHAPTER 18: Death Knell

233   Strange incantations echoed from the loudspeakers: interview with Magda Czarnek Pogonowski.

233   "Body Number 2129—Aleksander Marek Kowalski . . .": "Materials for the Epitaph of Katyń," Wojskowy Przegląd Historyczny (Military Historical Review), April–June 1989, no. 2, p. 405, and October–December 1989, no. 4, pp. 214, 234. Biographical data for the victims cited in the following text has been drawn from the same two sources.

236   Riding through the center of Kraków on her bicycle: interview with Magda Czarnek Pogonowska.

237   Prisoner number 1193: personal papers of Czarnek family. The order to execute Dr. Czarnek was among the documents transferred by Soviet president

Gorbachev to Polish president Jaruzelski on April 13, 1990. It was obtained by members of his family in Kraków a few months later.

237   The German propaganda service called him "the last victim of Katyń": David Irving, *Accident: The Death of General Sikorski* (New York: Kimberly, 1967), p. 175.

238   a cartoon in . . . *Das Reich:* ibid., p. 176.

238   "I loved that man": Mikołajczyk, op. cit., p. 41.

239   "It has been established however, that this was not an act of sabotage": Irving, op. cit, p. 144.

239   Stalin was disloyal enough to blame his own ally: Irving, op. cit., p. 175.

239   . . . Soviet superspy Kim Philby was in charge of British security for North Africa: Kim Philby, *My Silent War* (New York: Grove Press, 1968), unnumbered page listing career chronology.

239   The Germans . . . could hardly be excluded: Irving, op. cit., p. 177.

240   "I have always believed that there was sabotage": Hearings, part 7, p. 2080.

240   Negative attitude toward Sikorski among Poles: interview, Paweł Zaleski.

241   The pieces had been picked up in France: ibid. See Karski, *Great Powers*, pp. 388–97, for an overview of continuity in the Polish government following the 1939 debacle.

243   A few of the wheelchair patients began arriving: interview with Maria Pawulska Rasiej. The following account of the Pawulskis' life in Iran is also taken from this interview.

243   The July 11, 1943, edition of a weekly: "Funeral Drum," *Polak w Iranie* (The Pole in Iran), vol. 2, no. 52, July 11, 1943, p. 1.

245   Churchill hinted to Stalin that he and Roosevelt were prepared to make major concessions: Herbert Feis, *Churchill Roosevelt Stalin: The War They Waged and the Peace They Sought* (Princeton, N.J.: Princeton University Press, 1957), p. 284; Keith Eubank, *Summit at Teheran: The Untold Story* (New York: William Morrow and Company, 1985), pp. 287–88.

246   Both Churchill and Roosevelt knew: Eubank, op. cit., p. 7.

246   Roosevelt's plan to appeal to Stalin "on grounds of high morality": ibid., p. 362.

246   Roosevelt told Stalin that the upcoming presidential campaign put him in an awkward position: Eubank, op. cit., p. 357.

247   Churchill . . . assured Stalin that his allies were determined "to achieve the security of the Soviet western frontier . . .": ibid., p. 365.

247   "Yesterday there was no mention of negotiations with the Polish government": ibid., pp. 365–66.

248   Stalin had made a clever choice in pushing the Curzon Line. For the Curzon Line, see notes for chapter six.

249   More than eighteen months earlier: interview with Ewa Hoffman Jędruch. The following account is also taken from this interview.

CHAPTER 19: The Whitewash

253   While Stalin was in Tehran: Hearings, part 6, p. 1760.

253   The commission had no members from countries other than the Soviet Union: Hearings, part 3, p. 247.

254 the Soviets claimed that the Germans decided to hide their ugly deed: Hearings, part 3, pp. 239–40.

254 For Alexandra M. Moskovskaya's claim, see Hearings, part 3, pp. 240–41.

254 Only a few paragraphs of medical analysis were presented to support the report's conclusion: Hearings, part 3, pp. 243–46.

254 "there was no complete disintegration of the tissues. . . .": Hearings, part 3, pp. 244–45.

254 . . . the report held that parts of the bodies were of "almost normal color": Hearings, part 3, p. 245.

257 Soviet extravaganza for Western newsmen: Hearings, part 2, pp. 206–19.

257 W. H. Lawrence of the *New York Times* described the trip: *New York Times,* January 27, 1944.

257 a Soviet physician "sliced chunks off the brain . . .": "Day in the Forest," *Time,* February 7, 1944.

258 In her report on the visit, Miss Harriman wrote that the witnesses "were very well rehearsed": Hearings, part 7, pp. 2133–38, includes the full text of her report.

258 "All the statements were glibly given": Hearings, part 7, p. 2150. The full text of Mr. Melby's report may be found at Hearings, part 7, p. 2138–41.

258 "you lose your boots when you lose your life": Hearings, part 2, pp. 211–12.

259 "the testimonial evidence . . .": ibid., p. 2133.

259 "It is apparent . . .": ibid., p. 2141.

259 Harriman's January 25, 1944, cable to the secretary of state: Hearings, part 7, p. 2124.

259 Eight years later, Miss Harriman and Melby both reversed their conclusions: ibid., pp. 2149, 2151.

260 "Katyns existed and are existing and will be existing. . . .": ibid., p. 1941.

260 The document was unanimously approved: Hearings, part 3, p. 247. The full text of the Soviet report appears on pp. 225–47.

260 "Our inexorable foe, the German . . .": Hearings, part 6, p. 1784.

261 In an all-too-familiar pattern, Soviet agents were parachuted: Karski, *Great Powers,* p. 485.

261 Despite these alarming incidents, the London government-in-exile decided to proceed: Ascherson, op. cit., p. 113.

261 On January 20, 1944, Churchill told Mikołajczyk: "If you do not act quickly": Mikołajczyk, op. cit., p. 52.

261 The Pawulskis, minus Tadeusz, were among eight hundred Poles: interview with Maria Pawulska Rasiej. The following account of the *Nevasa's* voyage is also taken from this interview.

265 The raid, on the big Soviet holiday of May 1, 1944: interviews, Ewa Hoffman Jędruch, and Zbigniew and Anna Neuhoff. The following account is also taken from these interviews.

266 The blunder appalled Janina Czarnek: interviews, Agnieszka Czarnek Debarbaro, Magda Czarnek Pogonowska and Maria Czarnek Zaczek. The following account is also taken from these interviews.

CHAPTER 20: Clandestine Designs

269 Each document was issued or processed by Soviet officials: Hearings, part 6, pp. 1781–82.

269 "There were very few [documents]": Hearings, part 2, p. 214.

270 For the Soviet charges quoted here, see notes for chapter sixteen.

271 Those at the scene had no doubt about the absurdity of the Soviet contention: *Crime of Katyn*, pp. 201, 277.

271 Once removed, individual bodies were placed on a stretcher: ibid., pp. 201–202.

271 A metal disk stamped with a number: ibid., pp. 205–206.

271 When these partially reconstructed lists: Hearings, part 6, pp. 1795–96.

272 "In the morning we decided to buy stamps": Hearings, part 4, p. 729.

272 any remaining doubts were removed by the matching of the transport lists: Hearings, part 6, p. 1789.

272 all the envelopes containing the material evidence in Katyń Forest were packed: Hearings, part 5, p. 1513.

273 Dr. Werner Beck: It is unclear from available records whether Dr. Beck was a member of the Nazi party.

273 Beck himself testified at those hearings: ibid., pp. 1511–19.

273 as did Kazimierz Skarzyński: The full text of his testimony appears in Hearings, part 3, pp. 384–415.

273 and Karl Herrmann: The full text of his testimony appears in Hearings, part 5, pp. 1509–11.

274 They might well have been executed: How did members of the Home Army involved in the plot to steal the documents avoid being shot? The author was unable to obtain any answer to this question. Several attempts to locate those involved in this episode, or their descendants, proved fruitless. The fact that the Nazis accelerated the pace of executions as the war reached its conclusion makes the results in this case unusual, to say the least. However, the author believes that there is no reason to doubt the sworn testimony of Kazimierz Skarzyński, the source for this information.

277 Ironically, the spearhead for the liberation of Dresden: interview, Zdzisław Rurarz.

277 Rep. Flood's exchange with Beck: Hearings, part 5, p. 1517.

277 Beck's anonymous informant was his own father, Oscar Beck: unpublished records of the Select Committee on the Katyn Forest Massacre. The author received permission from the clerk of the U.S. House of Representatives to examine these records shortly after they were unsealed in January 1989. The information cited was found in the committee's witness files under "Werner Beck."

278 "the first thing I took care of were the documents . . .": Hearings, part 5, p. 1516.

CHAPTER 21: Moments of Truth

283 Later, Sikorski had heard the murmuring undertone: interview, Paweł Zaleski.

283 Mikołajczyk called a "collaborationist": ibid.

283 Description of Mikołajczyk: ibid.

283 Description of Wincenty Witos and his Peasant Party: ibid.

283 Personal relations between Sikorski and Mikołajczyk: ibid.

285 On January 11, 1944, the Soviets issued a statement saying that their territorial acquisitions: Karski, *Great Powers*, p. 486.

285 "most newspapers and magazines either denied publicity . . .": ibid., p. 489.

286 The next day he and his foreign minister, Tadeusz Romer, told Churchill: ibid., p. 502.

286 For Churchill's speech to the Commons, see Mikołajczyk, op. cit., pp. 53, 54.

287 Stalin's March 3 response to Churchill: *Correspondence* . . . , vol. 1, p. 207. The text of the cable may be found here.

287 Gradually . . . Churchill let the proposed agreement slide: Karski, *Great Powers*, pp. 508–509.

287 Polish-led victory at Monte Cassino: Anders, op. cit., pp. 178, 181.

287 "Stalin wasn't eager to talk about it. . . .": ibid., pp. 59–60. This is the source for the following account of Mikołajczyk's conversation with Roosevelt.

288 For Ciechanowski's description of Roosevelt's June 7 after-dinner speech, see Jan Ciechanowski, *Defeat in Victory* (Garden City, N.Y.: Doubleday & Co., 1947), p. 296.

288 Ciechanowski . . . and Mikołajczyk "left the President at midnight . . .": ibid., p. 300.

288 Mikołajczyk's plane was barely off the ground when Roosevelt cabled Stalin: *Correspondence* . . . , vol. 2, pp. 146–47. The text of the cable may be found here.

289 Soviet radio appeal, "There is not a moment to lose": Karski, *Great Powers*, p. 525.

289 Warsaw's casualties: ibid. p. 530.

289 For Stalin's response to the Warsaw Uprising, see the concise overviews in *The Dark Side of the Moon*, pp. 283–289, and Davies, *God's Playground*, vol. 2, pp. 474–79.

290 "I cannot trust the Poles": Mikołajczyk, op. cit., p. 73.

290 Mikołajczyk left Moscow on August 9: ibid., p. 79.

291 The British and Americans indicated their support: ibid., p. 92.

291 Churchill sent Mikołajczyk a message urging him "to fly at once to join us": ibid., p. 93.

291 The following account of the October 13 meeting at the Kremlin between Stalin, Churchill, Mikołajczyk, Eden, and Molotov, and of the meeting's aftermath, is drawn from ibid., pp. 93–97.

293 "You're no government": ibid., p. 98.

293 Mikołajczyk made one last attempt to compromise with Stalin: ibid., p. 99.

293 Polish cabinet's reactions to Mikołajczyk decision: interview, Paweł Zaleski.

293 Late in 1944, underground authorities in Kraków agreed to send: interviews, Jaga, Magda, and Maria Czarnek. The following account is also drawn from these interviews.

CHAPTER 22: The Allies' Blind Eye

302 "If they are dead . . .": Churchill, *Hinge of Fate*, p. 759.

302 In mid-June 1943, the king and the War Cabinet of Great Britain received a top-secret memorandum: "Disappearance of Polish Officers in the Union of Soviet Socialist Republics," Sir Owen O'Malley, FO 371/34577 and Registry Number C 6160/258/55, Public Records Office, London. Hereinafter referred to as O'Malley memorandum. The complete memorandum and cover notes may be found in Louis FitzGibbon, *The Katyn Cover-Up* (London: Tom Stacey Ltd., 1972), pp. 95–119.

302 "This is very disturbing. . . .": Third cover note attached to O'Malley memorandum.

303 The other cover comments quoted are attached to the O'Malley memorandum: ibid., pp. 1–2 (of cover notes).

306 The account of Churchill's suggestion and the O'Malley memorandum's subsequent path are taken from the file at the London Public Records Office, which contains copies of Eden's note to Churchill as well as Churchill's subsequent exchanges with the White House over the O'Malley memorandum.

307 "contains too much dynamite to be forwarded through regular channels": Hearings, part 3, p. 426.

307 "there are still . . .": ibid., p. 458.

307 The Szymanski reports were filed: Hearings, part 3, p. 477.

308 "After we saw that we were not getting anywhere . . .": ibid., p. 499.

308 an American prisoner of war: Van Vliet's account of his 1943 trip to Katyń Forest, his report of it made to U.S. authorities in May 1945, and the instructions he received forbidding him from making any public statements about the episode are presented in detail in his February 4, 1952, testimony before the Select Committee on the Katyn Forest Massacre. See Hearings, part 2, pp. 32–74, for the complete text of his testimony. Important details of Van Vliet's account of the visit were corroborated in testimony presented on October 11, 1952, by Lieutenant Colonel Donald B. Stewart, who visited the grave site with Van Vliet in 1943. The two men agreed at that time that Van Vliet, as the senior officer, would report these events, as well as their joint observations and opinions, to higher authorities.

308 Van Vliet laid the whole story out for the general: Hearings, part 1, p. 46.

311 For the text of Bissell's letter and instructions to Van Vliet, see ibid., p. 51.

312 An independent investigation by the Army Inspector General: *Final Report of the Select Committee to Conduct an Investigation and Study of the Facts, Evidence, and Circumstances on the Katyn Forest Massacre*, Eighty-second Congress, Second Session (Washington: U.S. Government Printing Office, 1952) (hereinafter *Final Report*), p. 7.

312 Seven years later: ibid., p. 8.

312 At first Bissell vehemently denied: Hearings, part 7, p. 2309.

313 More amazing to this committee: *Final Report*, pp. 8–9.

313 a document entitled "Russia's Position": Robert E. Sherwood, *Roosevelt and Hopkins: An Intimate History* (New York: Harper & Brothers, 1948), p. 748.

314 In a statement aired widely abroad, Davis claimed: Hearings, part 7, p. 1985.

314 In 1952 Davis was sharply reprimanded: *Final Report*, p. 9.

314 OWI and FCC actions in restraining broadcasters: ibid., pp. 9–10. A com-

plete account of these actions is presented in the testimony of Elmer Davis, Alan Cranston, Mrs. Hilda Shea, and Joseph Lang in part 7 of Hearings.

314 Roosevelt's restraints on George Howard Earle: Hearings, part 7, pp. 2196–2215.

CHAPTER 23: Rescue

317 When the big Russian transport touched down: Mikołajczyk, op. cit., p. 130.
317 Bierut's background: interview, Dr. Zdzisław M. Rurarz.
318 "My sisters and brothers. . . .": ibid., p. 131.
318 Ewa Hoffman's husband, Jacek Jędruch, was seated: interview, Jacek Jędruch. The following account of the motorcade is also drawn from this interview.
319 "strange, stone-faced men in Polish Army uniforms . . .": Mikołajczyk, op. cit., p. 131.
319 To this day the rescue remains steeped in mystery: interview with Ewa Hoffman Jędruch. The following account of the rescue is also drawn from this interview.
328 At thirty-six polling places where its poll watchers were permitted to observe: Mikołajczyk, op. cit., p. 200.
328 The Poles were deeply divided: interview, Paweł Zaleski.
328 "Churchill was saying, 'You must go!' ": ibid.
328 Mikołajczyk's reading of Stalin's intentions in Poland: ibid.
329 A pro-Soviet prosecutor approached Mikołajczyk: Mikołajczyk, op. cit., pp. 36–37.
329 Milołajczyk felt that his mission was a success: interview, Paweł Zaleski.
330 "I was able to accomplish nothing in effecting free elections in Poland": Arthur Bliss Lane, I Saw Freedom Betrayed (London: Regency Publications, 1949), p. 7.
330 "Stalin was prevented . . .": interview, Paweł Zaleski.

CHAPTER 24: Quest for Justice

331 "Tend him, protect him now": Adam Mickiewicz, Forefathers' Eve, in Harold B. Segel, ed., Polish Romantic Drama: Three Plays in English Translation (Ithaca, N.Y.: Cornell University Press, 1977), p. 82. See Segel for an excellent overview of the impact of the émigrés on the Poles' continuing struggle for independence.
331 "Redouble the Guard! . . .": ibid., p. 82.
332 "I shall be free . . .": ibid., p 82.
332 "Government ministers were crying . . .": ibid., p. 68.
332 During the Prague Spring in 1968: ibid., p. 71.
332 For the quotations from Churchill's speech, see Anders, op. cit., p. 299.
333 Polish airmen decline; Anders stripped of citizenship: Anders, op cit., p. 299, 301–02.
333 Shortly after the war: This anecdote is from an interview with Magda Czarnek Pogonowska.
334 Discussion of Katyń and other sensitive subjects: Thomas Szayna,

"Addressing 'Blank Spots' in Polish-Soviet Relations," *Problems of Communism,* vol. 37.

334 Strict press controls warned Polish censors: Jane Leftwich Curry, *The Black Book of Polish Censorship* (New York: Random House, 1984), p. 3.

334 "Because the people in Poland were forbidden from knowing about these subjects": interview, Ewa Hoffman Jędruch.

335 "In September 1941 11,000 Polish officers . . . were killed": *The Trial of the Major War Criminals before the International Military Tribunal, Nuremberg* (Nuremberg: International Military Tribunal, 1948), volume XIII, *Proceedings,* p. 274.

335 "they were entitled to do so under the division of the case": Hearings, part 7, p. 1946.

335 The responses of Göring and Schirach are quoted by Janusz K. Zawodny, *Death in the Forest: The Story of the Katyn Forest Massacre* (New York: Hippocrene, 1988), p. 65.

336 It identified Colonel "Arnes": Hearings, part 5, pp. 1252–75.

336 Dr. Markov had been tried as an "enemy of the people": Zawodny, op. cit., p. 68.

336 "We strongly urged Rudenko": interview, Telford Taylor.

337 The tribunal opted for "magnificent silence": ibid.

337 Poles in London meticulously assembled: unpublished document in the files of the Select Committee on the Katyn Forest Massacre, National Archives, No. 581546.

337 "nobody can be judge in his own case": *Crime of Katyn,* p. 278.

337 Mikołajczyk's presence in the West: interview, Paweł Zaleski.

338 Over the next year, it heard eighty-one witnesses: Zawodny, op. cit., p. 187.

338 "This was part of the whole tragedy of Katyń": interview, Roman Pucinski.

339 the Soviet Union acknowledged responsibility for liquidating fifteen thousand Polish officers: *New York Times,* April 14, 1990, p. 5.

339 "It is not easy to speak of this tragedy . . .": ibid.

339 Natalya Lebedeva . . . examined the documents: *Moscow News,* March 25, 1990.

339 "those who might in the future enter the struggle": *Moscow News,* April 8, 1990.

340 "Hitler's crimes are still being justly punished": Zbigniew Brzezinski, letter to the editor, *Commentary,* vol. 90, no. 6, December 1990, p. 2.

340 Telford Taylor's legal assessment: interview, Telford Taylor.

341 The Polish and German governments finally signed a treaty: *New York Times,* November 14, 1990.

341 The Germans and the Soviets signed a treaty: *New York Times,* November 10, 1990.

341 A special ceremony at the Royal Castle in Warsaw: *Zycie Warszawy,* no. 298–299, December 22–26, 1990; and Radio Free Europe/Radio Liberty Daily Report, no. 240, December 19, 1990.

341 "They owe an expression of profound regret . . .": interview with Maria Pawulska Rasiej.

342 "I grew up with this great tragedy of my mother's": interview with Ewa Hoffman Jędruch.

343 "It was much too late . . .": interview, Magda Czarnek Pogonowska.

Bibliography

Documents

Correspondence between the Chairman of the Council of Ministers of the U.S.S.R. and the Presidents of the U.S.A. and the Prime Ministers of Great Britain during the Great Patriotic War of 1941–1945, 2 vols. Moscow: Foreign Languages Publishing House, 1957.

"Disappearance of Polish Officers in the Union of Soviet Socialist Republics," memorandum from Sir Owen O'Malley to Sir Anthony Eden, FO 371/34577 and Registry Number C 6160/258/55, Public Records Office, London.

Documents on Polish-Soviet Relations, 1939–45, edited by the General Sikorski Historical Institute, 2 vols. London: Heinemann, 1961–1967.

Final Report of the Select Committee to Conduct an Investigation and Study of the Facts, Evidence, and Circumstances on the Katyn Forest Massacre. Washington, D.C.: U.S. Government Printing Office, 1952.

The German Invasion of Poland: Polish Black Book. London/Melbourne: Hutchinson & Co., by authority of the Centre for Information and Documentation of the Polish Government, 1941.

The Katyn Forest Massacre. Hearings before the Select Committee to Conduct an Investigation of the Facts, Evidence and Circumstances of the Katyn Forest Massacre, Eighty-second Congress, Second Session. Part 1 (Washington, D.C.), October 11, 1951; part 2, February 4, 5, 6, and 7, 1952; part 3 (Chicago, Illinois), March 13 and 14, 1952; part 4 (London, England), April 16, 17, 18, and 19, 1952; Part 5 (Frankfurt, West Germany), April 21, 22, 23, 24, 25, and 26, 1952; Part 6, exhibits 32 and 33, presented to the committee, in London, by the Polish government-in-exile; Part 7, June 3 and 4 and November 11, 12, 13, and 14, 1952. Washington, D.C.: United States Government Printing Office, 1952.

Kościuszko, Tadeusz. "The Universal Proclamation of Polaniec," trans. Iwo Pogonowski, in Jan Stanisław Kopczewski, ed., *In History and Tradition*. Warsaw: State Textbook Printing Office, 1957.

Sontag, James, and James Stuart Beddie, eds. *Nazi-Soviet Relations, 1939–1941: Documents from the Archives of the German Foreign Office.* Westport, Conn.: Greenwood Press, 1976.

Wacław Jędrzejewicz, ed. *Poland in the British Parliament 1939–1945: Documentary Material Relating to the Cause of Poland in World War Two*, 3 vols. New

York: Józef Piłsudski Institute of America for Research in Modern History of Poland, 1946, 1959.

The Trial of the Major War Criminals before the International Military Tribunal, Nuremberg, 42 vols. Nuremberg: International Military Tribunal, 1948.

Interviews

Each person listed below was interviewed by the author at least once between the beginning of 1989 and the end of 1990. Most of these interviews were taped and transcribed. More than fifty interviews were conducted with members of the families of Lieutenant Colonel Zbigniew Czarnek, Captain Maksymilian Hoffman and Captain Stanisław Pawulski during that period.   ·

Maria Berling, widow of the late General Zygmunt Berling
Władek Cichy, former Soviet prisoner, Kozelsk
Agnieszka Czarnek Debarbaro, daughter of Lieutenant Colonel Zbigniew Czarnek
Dr. Zbyszek Debarbaro, grandson of Lieutenant Colonel Zbigniew Czarnek
Kazimierz Dziewanowski, Polish ambassador to the United States
Zdzisław Jagodziński, librarian, The Polish Library, London
Ewa Hoffman Jędruch, daughter of Captain Maksymilian Hoffman
Jacek Jędruch, husband of Ewa Hoffman Jędruch, historian and former member of the Polish underground
Władysław Klimczak, director, Kraków Museum of History and Photography
Colonel Wojciech Kołaczkowski (ret.), former wing commander, Kościuszko Squadron (303), Royal Air Force
Zofia Kinel Łaszewski, former deportee to Siberia
Anna Neuhoff, sister-in-law of Zofia Hoffman and aunt of Ewa Hoffman Jędruch
Zbigniew Neuhoff, brother of Zofia Hoffman and uncle of Ewa Hoffman Jędruch
Dr. Stanisław Niewiadomski, former Soviet prisoner at Kozelshchina
Jolanta Osmańczyk, widow of the late Edmund Osmańczyk, senator, the Polish Sejm
Father Zdzisław Peszkowski, former Soviet prisoner, Kozelsk
Magda Czarnek Pogonowska, daughter of Lieutenant Colonel Zbigniew Czarnek
Iwo Cyprian Pogonowski, husband of Magda Czarnek Pogonowska, author and former prisoner of war of the Nazis
Andrzej Pomian, historian
Roman Pucinski, former special investigator, Select Committee to Investigate the Katyn Forest Massacre, United States House of Representatives
Kazimierz Rasiej, husband of Maria Pawulska Rasiej and former deportee to Siberia
Maria Pawulska Rasiej, daughter of Captain Stanisław Pawulski and former deportee to Siberia
Dr. Zdzisław M. Rurarz, former Polish ambassador to Japan
Maciej Siekierski, curator, Anders Archives, Hoover Institution, Stanford University
Wojciech Stasiak, mathematics professor, University of Warsaw
Dr. Stanisław Świaniewicz, former Soviet prisoner at Kozelsk
Paweł Zaleski, former aide to Stanisław Mikołajczyk
Maria Czarnek Zaczek, daughter of Lieutenant Colonel Zbigniew Czarnek
Martin Zaczek, grandson of Lieutenant Colonel Zbigniew Czarnek

Memoirs and Other Primary Sources

Anders, Władysław. *An Army in Exile: The Story of the Second Polish Corps*. London: Macmillan, 1949.

Anonymous. *The Dark Side of the Moon*. New York: Charles Scribner's Sons, 1947.

Bór-Komorowski, Tadeusz. *The Secret Army*. Nashville, Tenn.: The Battery Press, 1984.

Cassidy, Henry C. *Moscow Dateline 1941–1943*. Boston: Houghton Mifflin, 1943.

Churchill, Winston S. *The Second World War*. Vol. 3: *The Grand Alliance*. Boston: Houghton Mifflin, 1950.

Churchill, Winston S. *The Second World War*. Vol. 4: *The Hinge of Fate*. Boston: Houghton Mifflin, 1950.

Ciano, Galeazzo. *The Ciano Diaries*. Garden City, N.Y.: Garden City Publishing Co., 1945.

Ciechanowski, Jan. *Defeat in Victory*. Garden City, N.Y.: Doubleday & Company, 1947.

The Crime of Katyn: Facts and Documents, 5th ed. London: Polish Cultural Foundation, 1989.

Czapski, Józef. *The Inhuman Land*. London: Chatto & Windus, 1951; reprinted, London: Polish Cultural Foundation, 1987.

Davies, Joseph E. *Mission to Moscow*. London: Victor Gollancz, 1942.

Goebbels, Joseph. *The Goebbels Diaries*, ed. and trans. Louis P. Lochner. New York: Award Books, 1983.

Herling, Gustav. *A World Apart*. Oxford: Oxford University Press, 1987.

Karski, Jan. *Story of a Secret State*. Boston: Houghton Mifflin, 1944.

Khrushchev, Nikita. *Khrushchev Remembers*. Trans. and ed. Strobe Talbott. Boston: Little, Brown and Co., 1970.

Lane, Arthur Bliss. *I Saw Freedom Betrayed*. London: Regency Publications, 1949.

Lesueur, Larry. *Twelve Months That Changed the World*. New York: Alfred A. Knopf, 1943.

Maisky, Ivan. *New World*. Moscow: [No publisher given] 1964.

"Materials for the Epitaph of Katyń." *Wojskowy Przegląd Historyczny* (Military Historical Review), no. 2 (128), April–June 1989; no. 4 (130), October–November 1989.

Mikołajczyk, Stanisław. *The Rape of Poland: Pattern of Soviet Aggression*. Originally published 1948; reprinted, Westport, Conn.: Greenwood Press, 1972.

Miłosz, Czesław. *The Captive Mind*. Trans. Jane Zielonko. New York: Vintage Books, 1990.

Ribbentrop, Joachim von. *The Ribbentrop Memoirs*. London: Weidenfeld and Nicolson, 1954.

Shirer, William L. *Berlin Diary: The Journal of a Foreign Correspondent 1934–1941*. New York, Alfred A. Knopf, 1941; New York: Popular Library, 1961.

Speer, Albert. *Inside The Third Reich*. New York: Macmillan, 1970.

General Sources

Ascherson, Neal. *The Struggles for Poland*. London: Michael Joseph, 1987.

Bullock, Alan. *Hitler: A Study in Tyranny*. Revised ed. New York: Bantam Books, 1961.

Cienciala, Anna M. *Poland and the Western Powers 1938–1939*. London: Routledge & Kegan Paul; Toronto: University of Toronto Press, 1968.

Concise Statistical Year-book of Poland, September 1939–June 1941. 2nd ed. Glasgow: Polish Ministry of Information, 1944.

Conot, Robert E. *Justice at Nuremberg*. New York: Harper & Row, 1983.

Curry, Jane Leftwich. *The Black Book of Polish Censorship*. New York: Random House, 1984.

Daniels, Robert V. *Russia: The Roots of Confrontation*. Cambridge, Mass.: Harvard University Press, 1985.

Davies, Norman. *God's Playground: A History of Poland*. Vol. 1: *The Origins to 1795*; Vol. 2. *1795 to the Present*. New York: Columbia University Press, 1982.

Davies, Norman. *White Eagle, Red Star: The Polish-Soviet War, 1919–20*. London: Orbis Books, 1983.

Deighton, Len. *Blitzkrieg: From the Rise of Hitler to the Fall of Dunkirk*. New York: Alfred A. Knopf, 1980.

Dyadkin, Iosif G. *Unnatural Deaths in the U.S.S.R., 1928–1954*. New Brunswick, N.J.: Transaction Books, 1983.

Engelmann, Bernt. *In Hitler's Germany*. New York: Pantheon, 1986.

Eubank, Keith. *Summit at Teheran: The Untold Story*. New York: William Morrow and Company, 1985.

Feis, Herbert. *Churchill Roosevelt Stalin: The War They Waged and the Peace They Sought*. Princeton, N.J.: Princeton University Press, 1957.

FitzGibbon, Louis. *The Katyn Cover-Up*. London: Tom Stacey Ltd., 1972.

Florinsky, Michael T., ed. *Encyclopedia of Russia and the Soviet Union*. New York: McGraw-Hill, 1961.

Freund, Gerald. *Unholy Alliance*. New York: Harcourt, Brace, 1959.

Gerhart, Eugene C. *America's Advocate: Robert H. Jackson*. Indianapolis: Bobbs-Merrill Company, 1958.

Gross, Jan T. *Revolution from Abroad: The Soviet Conquest of Poland's Western Ukraine and Western Belorussia*. Princeton, N.J.: Princeton University Press, 1988.

Grudzinska-Gross, Irena, and Jan Tomasz Gross, eds. *War through Children's Eyes: The Soviet Occupation of Poland and the Deportations, 1939–1941*. Stanford, Cal.: Hoover Institution Press, 1981.

Halle, Louis J. *The Cold War as History*. New York: Harper & Row, 1975.

Heller, Mikhail, and Aleksandr Nekrich. *Utopia in Power: The History of the Soviet Union from 1917 to the Present*. New York: Summit Books, 1986. Trans. by Phyllis B. Carlos from the Russian-language edition of 1982.

Higgins, Turnbull. *Hitler and Russia*. New York: Macmillan, 1966.

Hilger, Gustav, and Alfred Meyer. *The Incompatible Allies: A Memoir of German-Soviet Relations, 1918–1941*. New York: Macmillan, 1953.

Hingley, Ronald. *The Russian Secret Police: Muscovite, Imperial Russian and Soviet Political Security Operations 1565–1970*. London: Hutchinson & Co., 1970.

Hiscocks, Richard. *Poland: Bridge for the Abyss?* London: Oxford University Press, 1963.

Irving, David. *Accident: The Death of General Sikorski*. New York: Kimberly, 1967.

Jędruch, Jacek. *Constitutions, Elections and Legislatures of Poland, 1493–1977: A Guide to Their History*. Washington, D.C.: University Press of America, 1982.

Jędrzejewicz, Wacław. *Piłsudski: A Life for Poland*. New York: Hippocrene, 1982.

Karski, Jan. *The Great Powers & Poland, 1919–1945*. Lanham, N.J.: University Press of America, 1985.

Kaufman, Michael T. *Mad Dreams, Saving Graces: Poland, a Nation in Conspiracy*. New York: Random House, 1989.

Krolikowski, Lucjan, O.F.M. *Stolen Childhood: A Saga of Polish War Children*. Buffalo, N.Y.: Father Justin Rosary Hour, 1983.

Lebedeva, Nataliya. "The Katyn Tragedy." *International Affairs*, June 1990.

Lemkin, Raphael. *Axis Rule in Occupied Europe*. Washington, D.C.: Carnegie Endowment for International Peace, Division of International Law, 1944.

Liddell Hart, B. H. *History of the Second World War*. New York: Putnam, 1970.

Lukacs, John A. *The Great Powers in Eastern Europe*. New York: American Book Co., 1953.

Mackiewicz, Joseph. *The Katyn Wood Murders*. London: Hollis & Carter, 1951.

Mason, David. *Who's Who in World War II*. Boston: Little, Brown and Co., 1978.

McSherry, James E. *Stalin, Hitler, and Europe 1939–1941: The Imbalance of Power*. Cleveland and New York: World Publishing Co., 1970.

Mee, Charles L., Jr. *Meeting at Potsdam*. New York: M. Evans & Co., 1975.

Mills, John Saxon. *The Genoa Conference*. New York: Dutton, 1922.

Natkiel, Richard. *Atlas of World War II*. New York: The Military Press, 1985.

Nove, Alec. *The Soviet Economic System*, 2nd ed. London: Allen & Unwin, 1980.

Pares, Bernard. *A History of Russia*. New York: Alfred A. Knopf, 1926.

Philby, Kim. *My Silent War*. New York: Grove Press, 1968.

Pogonowski, Iwo Cyprian. *Poland: A Historical Atlas*. New York: Hippocrene Books, 1987.

Read, Anthony, and David Fisher. *The Deadly Embrace: Hitler, Stalin and the Nazi-Soviet Pact, 1939–1941*. New York: Norton, 1988.

Schachet, Simon. "The Polish Officers of Jewish Descent." *Niepodległość* (Independence), *Journal of the Józef Piłsudski Institute*, vol. 21 (1988).

Segel, Harold B., ed. *Polish Romantic Drama: Three Plays in English Translation*. Ithaca, N.Y.: Cornell University Press, 1977.

Sherwood, Robert E. *Roosevelt and Hopkins: An Intimate History*. New York: Harper & Brothers, 1948.

Shirer, W. L. *The Rise and Fall of the Third Reich*. London: Pan Books, 1964.

Standley, William H., with Arthur A. Ageton. "Murder or High Strategy? The U.S. Embassy, the Kremlin, and the Katyn Forest Massacre." *United States Naval Institute Proceedings*, vol. 78, no. 10 (October 1952).

Steven, Stewart. *The Poles*. New York: Macmillan, 1982.

Szayna, Thomas. "Addressing 'Blank Spots' in Polish Soviet Relations." *Problems of Communism*, vol. 37 (November–December 1988).

Taylor, A.J.P. *The Origins of the Second World War*, 2nd ed. Greenwich, Conn.: Fawcett Publications, 1968.

Toland, John. *Adolf Hitler*, two vols. Garden City, N.Y.: Doubleday & Company, 1976.

Ulam, Adam B. *Stalin: The Man and His Era*. Boston: Beacon Press, 1987.

Ulam, Stanisław. *Adventures of a Mathematician*. New York: Scribners, 1976.

Wandycz, Piotr S. *Soviet-Polish Relations, 1917–1921*. Cambridge, Mass.: Harvard University Press, 1969.

Zaloga, Steven, and Victor Madej. *The Polish Campaign*. New York: Hippocrene Books, 1985.

Zamoyski, Adam. *The Polish Way: A Thousand-Year History of the Poles and Their Culture*. New York: Franklin Watts, 1988.

Zawodny, Janusz K. *Death in the Forest: The Story of the Katyn Forest Massacre*. New York: Hippocrene, 1988.

Periodicals

Izvestia
London Observer
Naval Institute Proceedings
New York Times
Newsweek
Problems of Communism
Rzeczpospolita
Time
Tygodnik Powszechny
Wojskowy Przegląd Historyczny (Military Historical Review)

Chronology

1772

Aug. 5   Austria, Russia, and Prussia undertake first partition of Poland.

1791

May 3   Polish Sejm adopts Europe's first written constitution.

1793

Jan. 23   Russia and Prussia undertake second partition of Poland.

1795

Austria, Russia, and Prussia undertake third partition of Poland.

1918

Jan. 8   President Wilson calls for an independent Polish state in his "Fourteen Points" speech.

Nov. 11   Second Polish Republic is established; begins questionable occupation of eastern territories almost immediately.

Nov. 1918–
April 1919   Ukrainians form Republic of Western Ukraine, which precipitates lengthy Battle of Lwów, won by Poles.

Dec. 8   Allied Supreme Council proposes temporary eastern boundary of Poland.

1919

Jan. 12   Soviets launch Operation Target Vistula hoping that Red Army can capture Warsaw and ignite a proletarian uprising in Germany; Soviets had occupied Wilno and Minsk, cities with large Polish populations, in the wake of German retreat two months earlier.

Feb. 9   Piłsudski orders Polish Army to advance against Soviets; forces engagement on Feb. 14 resulting in small-scale Polish victory.

March–Aug.   Poles capture Wilno, Minsk, Lwów; Piłsudski rejects march on Moscow, accepting armistice talks with Soviets.

Aug.   German army withdraws from Białystok region of Poland.

1920

Jan. 20	Piłsudski's plan for federation of border states presented to other Baltic states, but most fear to join without Allied support.
May	Poles launch offensive on Kiev aimed at establishment of independent Ukrainian state; Western Allies recoil in anger at actions of upstart Polish state. Soviets complete buildup of huge strike force to oppose the Poles.
July	Soviet army under Tukhachevsky breaks through against Poles in Byelorussia, drives Poles back toward Warsaw.
July 11	Lord Curzon proposes eastern-boundary settlement; neither party accepts.
Aug. 18	Poles defeat the Soviets at the Battle of Warsaw, also known as the Miracle on the Vistula. Red Army is chased far to the east; front finally stabilizes approximately 150 miles east of the Curzon Line.

1921

March 18	Treaty of Riga defines Poland's eastern frontiers—a step recognized by the Allies as implementing the Treaty of Versailles.

1932

July 25	Nonaggression Pact between Poland and U.S.S.R.

1939

Mar. 31	Britain and France guarantee Poland's defense.
April 6	Britain and Poland sign mutual-assistance pact.
Aug. 23	Nazi-Soviet/Nonaggression Pact.
Aug. 25	Anglo-Polish Mutual Assistance Pact is upgraded to formal alliance.
Aug. 31	Germans stage Operation Canned Goods.
Sept. 1	Germans invade Poland.
Sept. 3	Britain and France declare war on Germany.
Sept. 17	U.S.S.R. invades Poland.
Sept. 28	U.S.S.R. and Germany sign formal partition of Poland.
Sept. 17–30	U.S.S.R. captures 250,000 Polish POWs, including 15,400 officers and noncoms; these men are detained in more than 100 transition camps in the eastern third of the U.S.S.R.
Sept.–Nov.	NKVD segregates 15,400 officers and noncoms and interns these men at Kozelsk, Ostashkov, and Starobelsk.
Oct.	NKVD begins interviewing men to establish in-depth background files. Great emphasis on social origin, political views, etc.—especially whether they participated in Poland's 1920 defeat of the Bolsheviks. Focus was conversion but apparently only six did.
Nov. 30	U.S.S.R. attacks Finland.

1940

Feb.	Red Army asks Stalin at about this time what to do with Poles at Kozelsk, Starobelsk, and Ostashkov.
Feb. 8	First of four mass deportations of Poles to U.S.S.R.; last comes only days before Hitler's invasion; total of 1.2 million Poles taken into exile.
Mar.	NKVD sets up Camp Pawlishtchev Bor as transfer camp for 448 prisoners of Kozelsk, Starobelsk and Ostashkov; some later are taken to Gryazovets and liberated in 1941.
Mar.	Gen. Zarubin (probably fourth-ranking in NKVD) suddenly leaves Kozelsk for good; returns to Moscow, probably to plan details of the executions.
Apr. 3	62 men from Kozelsk taken to Katyń.
Apr.–May	Poles at Starobelsk and Ostashkov disappear, except for 203 men. Trail of men from Starobelsk ends at Kharkov railroad station, that of men from Ostashkov at Vyazma station.
May 11	Last 50 men taken from Kozelsk to Katyń.
May 12	Last 90 of Kozelsk's 245 survivors sent to Pawlishtchev Bor, later to Gryazovets.
May	Letters from all but 448 survivors stop.
Oct.	NKVD heads Beria and Merkulov admit to a small group of pro-Soviet Polish officers that a "great blunder" has been made with their fellow officers from Kozelsk and Starobelsk.

1941

June 22	German armies attack Soviet Union; last of four mass deportations from eastern Poland is under way when invasion begins.
July 16	Smolensk and Katyń Forest area fall to Germans.
July 30	Gen. Władysław Sikorski, president of the London Poles, signs formal diplomatic agreement on behalf of the Polish government-in-exile with the U.S.S.R. and Great Britain.
Aug.	Efforts to form Polish army-in-exile center on setting up a point of concentration at Buzuluk.
Aug. 4	Gen. Anders released from Lubyanka prison; assumes command of army to be formed.
Aug.	Anders misses his own chief of staff; the influx of Polish army to Buzuluk reflects the fact that 15,000 men are missing; a handful of prisoners from Camp Gryazovets report their prior removal from camps at Kozelsk, Ostashkov, and Starobelsk.
Aug.–Sept.	Cross-checks of reports by men of Gryazovets reveal that the missing men were held until spring 1940.
Aug.	Germans, according to Soviets, murder the Polish officers and bury them at Katyń.
Aug. 14	Britain and U.S. issue Atlantic Charter, rejecting territorial changes without free assent of those concerned.
Fall	Gen. Anders establishes a "search office" to find the missing men, under captains Jan Kaczkowski and Józef Czapski, a former

Starobelsk prisoner, who knows many of the missing men personally.

Nov. 14   Stalin evades Polish ambassador Kot's questions on missing prisoners; calls the NKVD personally in Kot's presence, but reports nothing.

Dec. 3   Sikorski flies from London, meets Stalin, who says the Polish officers may have escaped to Manchuria; Stalin orders that prisoners be located and freed.

1942

Mar.   Lt. Col. Henry I. Szymanski, assistant U.S. military attaché at Cairo, is named U.S. liaison officer to Polish army-in-exile

Mar. 18   Gen. Anders meets Stalin on Katyń issue; personally hands two prisoner lists to Molotov. Stalin shrugs the matter off.

May 27   U.S. Ambassador Standley complains to Vyshinsky about failure to release Polish prisoners; later has run-in with Molotov on the matter [Note: The Soviets took at least 1.2 million Poles into exile. List of those taken were never produced. Individual files, including photographs, were developed on each of the 15,000 officers and noncoms at Kozelsk, Starobelsk, and Ostashkov. None of these records has ever been produced.]

Nov. 23   Lt. Col. Henry I. Szymanski reports to U.S. superiors on the devasting results that exile has had on the Poles; Gen. Strong of army G-2 warns him to "avoid political involvement"; Szymanski's report is suppressed.

1943

Jan. or Feb.   Wolf digs bones from mound where Polish officers are buried in Katyń Forest.

Feb. 4   Germans are defeated at Stalingrad.

April 13   Goebbels announces finding of mass graves at Katyń.

April 15   Soviet Information Bureau says Poles were engaged in construction work west of Smolensk and fell into the hands of the Germans, who executed them.

April 15   Polish government-in-exile approves Red Cross appeal.

April 16   Hitler and Goebbels decide to time their Red Cross appeal to give an appearance of cooperation with the Poles.

April 17   Formal requests from Germans and Poles arrive in Geneva less than an hour apart.

April 19   *Pravda* accuses Poles of "collaboration," citing the timing of the Red Cross requests.

April 19   Warsaw Ghetto uprising.

April 21   Stalin sends secret messages to Churchill and FDR accusing Sikorski of collusion with Hitler; claims the Polish government-in-exile has forced a break.

April 26   U.S.S.R. makes formal break with Poles, openly begins grooming the Union of Polish Patriots, a group of pro-Soviet Poles formed weeks earlier.

April 28–30   International commission of 12 medical experts visits Katyń at invitation of Germans; in its report it unanimously agrees that the men were shot three years earlier.

April 30   Churchill writes Stalin that recognition of a new Polish government in U.S.S.R. would not be possible.

May 3   Elmer Davis of U.S. Office of War Information calls German story "very fishy"; Allies try to patch up Soviet-Polish relations; U.S. government tells Polish radio stations at home to "pipe down"; Katyń story hits at a time when Soviet leaders are being glorified by the U.S. media.

May 13   Lt. Col. Van Vliet and Capt. Stewart examine graves.

June 3   Germans complete their exhumations.

June 7   Germans rebury the last victims and close the last of seven graves at Katyń.

July 4–10   Battle of Kursk; Germans retreat after this defeat.

Sept. 26   Smolensk falls to the Soviets; a special Soviet commission prepares to conduct its investigation of Katyń murders..

Fall   Soviet commission interviews local citizens and collects statements alleging German guilt at Katyń.

Nov. 28–   Allies meet at Tehran; at Stalin's insistence, secretly agree on Curzon
Dec. 1   Line as postwar eastern boundary of Poland; Polish government-in-exile is unaware of the decision.

1944

Jan. 24   Soviet Special Commission to Investigate the Katyń Massacre issues its own report stating that the Nazis were guilty.

May   FDR recalls George Howard Earle for consultation; is given evidence of Soviet guilt, but tells Earle he is "absolutely convinced" the Nazis are guilty.

1945

Feb. 4–11   Allies meet at Yalta; Stalin's position on Eastern Europe is strengthened.

Mar. 24   George Howard Earle, FDR's secret emissary to the Balkans, gets letter from FDR forbidding him to say anything negative about Soviet responsibility at Katyń; Earle is soon transferred to American Samoa.

May 22   Lt. Col. Van Vliet and Gen. Bissell, head of G-2, meet alone about Van Vliet's 1943 visit to Katyń; Bissell orders Van Vliet to write a report, then classifies it top secret; all traces of the original of this report disappear. During this period the U.S. is pushing hard for Soviet participation in a United Nations that will help establish a new world order.

July 17–   Allies hold Potsdam Conference—issue statement that Polish govern-
Aug. 2   ment-in-exile no longer exists.

Aug. 16   Soviets and new provisional government of Poland agree on Curzon Line. as mutual frontier.

1946

July 1–2   International Military Tribunal at Nuremberg heard testimony from both German and Soviet witnesses on Katyń; no decision on guilt announced; the charges are finally dropped because the Soviets have such a weak case.

(n.d.)   Soviet diplomat in London tells leaders of the Polish government-in-exile that Katyń murders were due to a bureacratic blunder, that is, confusion about Stalin's order to "liquidate."

1950

April 26   Van Vliet is told to reconstruct his report, which has been "lost" by the Defense Department.

May 11   Van Vliet complies with this order.

1951

Oct. 11   Select committee on Katyń holds first hearing.

1952

Feb. 4–7   Select committee holds more hearings in Washington, D.C.

March 13–14 Select committee hearings in Chicago.

April 16–27   Select committee hearings in London, Frankfurt, Berlin, and Naples.

June 3–4   Select committee hearings in Washington.

Dec. 22   Select committee issues a unanimous final report; it blames the Soviets for the Katyń murders and calls for a trial in the World Court.

1981

Solidarity erects memorial to victims of Katyń; date of massacre is listed as 1940; Polish government removes this memorial.

1985

March   Jaruzelski government erects monument, on same site as the former Solidarity monument, inscribed: "To the Polish soldiers—victims of the Hitlerite fascism that arose on the soil of Katyń"; this inscription is undated.

1988

March 8   Appeal by 59 Warsaw intellectuals to Russian intellectuals to speak up about Katyń, describing it as one of the most sensitive issues in Polish-Soviet relations. Wałęsa and others sign and release the appeal following a new session in Warsaw of an official Polish-Soviet commission charged with clearing up "blank spots" in the two countries' relations.

July 10   Polish dissidents speculate that Gorbachev will make an official admission of Katyń during his impending six-day state visit; no revelations are made, however, during this visit.

1989

Feb. 17   Polish government permits first publication of evidence of Soviet guilt at Katyń; the issue becomes a major test of glasnost in Poland and the rest of Eastern Europe.

Mar. 7   Polish government publicly concludes for the first time that "everything indicates" that the Soviets were responsible for the Katyń massacre.

1990

April 13   Soviet president Gorbachev acknowledges his country's responsibility for the murder of the 15,000 Polish officers and noncoms who disappeared in the spring of 1940. He turns over documents about the case to Poland's President Jaruzelski.

1992

Oct. 14   Russian government makes public Minutes 13 from the Politburo's March 5, 1940, meeting at which Stalin personally ordered the execution of 20,000 Polish prisoners at Katyń, Ostashkov and Starobelsk, and other sites.

Index

About the Author

<<<<<<<<<<

Allen Paul became profoundly interested in the Katyń massacre while study-ing at the Johns Hopkins University School of Advanced International Stud-ies, where he earned a Masters of International Public Policy. He has an A.B. in English from Guilford College. Mr. Paul began his career with the Asso-ciated Press and later managed two successful congressional campaigns. He is currently President of Unisphere Institute in Washington, D.C., which helps small to mid-sized high-tech firms find overseas partners.

The **Naval Institute Press** is the book-publishing arm of the U.S. Naval Institute, a private, nonprofit, membership society for sea service professionals and others who share an interest in naval and maritime affairs. Established in 1873 at the U.S. Naval Academy in Annapolis, Maryland, where its offices remain today, the Naval Institute has almost 85,000 members worldwide.

Members of the Naval Institute support the education programs of the society and receive the influential monthly magazine *Proceedings* and discounts on fine nautical prints and on ship and aircraft photos. They also have access to the transcripts of the Institute's Oral History Program and get discounted admission to any of the Institute-sponsored seminars offered around the country.

The Naval Institute also publishes *Naval History* magazine. This colorful bimonthly is filled with entertaining and thought-provoking articles, first-person reminiscences, and dramatic art and photography. Members receive a discount on *Naval History* subscriptions.

The Naval Institute's book-publishing program, begun in 1898 with basic guides to naval practices, has broadened its scope in recent years to include books of more general interest. Now the Naval Institute Press publishes about 100 titles each year, ranging from how-to books on boating and navigation to battle histories, biographies, ship and aircraft guides, and novels. Institute members receive discounts of 20 to 50 percent on the Press's nearly 600 books in print.

Full-time students are eligible for special half-price membership rates. Life memberships are also available.

For a free catalog describing Naval Institute Press books currently available, and for further information about subscribing to *Naval History* magazine or about joining the U.S. Naval Institute, please write to:

Membership Department
U.S. Naval Institute
118 Maryland Avenue
Annapolis, Maryland 21402-5035

Telephone: (800) 233-8764
Fax: (410) 269-7940